Africa and the Africans in the Nineteenth Century

Africa *and the* Africans *in the* Nineteenth Century

A TURBULENT HISTORY

CATHERINE COQUERY-VIDROVITCH

Translated from the French by Mary Baker

M.E.Sharpe
Armonk, New York
London, England

Library of Congress Cataloging-in-Publication Data

Coquery-Vidrovitch, Catherine.
  [Afrique et les Africains au XIXe siècle. English]
  Africa and the Africans in the nineteenth century : a turbulent history / by Catherine
Coquery-Vidrovitch; translated from the French by Mary Baker.
      p. cm.
  Includes bibliographical references and index.
  ISBN: 978-0-7656-1696-8 (cloth : alk. paper)—ISBN: 978-0-7656-1697-5 (pbk. : alk. paper)
  1. Africa—History—19th century. I. Title.

DT28.C6713 2009
960′.23—dc22   2008033387

Printed in the United States of America

The paper used in this publication meets the minimum requirements of
American National Standard for Information Sciences
Permanence of Paper for Printed Library Materials,
ANSI Z 39.48-1984.

∞

| MV (c) | 10 | 9 | 8 | 7 | 6 | 5 | 4 | 3 | 2 | 1 |
| MV (p) | 10 | 9 | 8 | 7 | 6 | 5 | 4 | 3 | 2 | 1 |

Contents

List of Tables, Figures, and Maps

Figures

Tables

Maps

Preface to the American Edition

The goal of this book is to show how important the nineteenth century was in the history of the African continent as a whole. My priority has been to try to render this history as it was experienced by Africans, rather than as it has been described by Western observers.

Naturally, Western historians tend to focus on European colonial control, but how was that occupation experienced by Africans at the time? When we look at it more closely, we find that, for most Africans, the colonial intrusion, which was to have huge consequences, was not seen as the major issue in most of the continent during this period. Of course, in North Africa, Napoléon Bonaparte landed in Egypt in 1799 and the French in Algiers in 1830, and, in southern Africa, the British were in the Cape in 1795. However, elsewhere, across the vast majority of the continent, the new European presence became crucial only in the last third of the century. Before then, many Africans were not even aware of it. This is the reason why the European conquest enters the picture only toward the end of this book.

At the time, what was felt to be most important were the political and religious processes that were *internal* to African societies. Most of them were still independent. It is only in hindsight that it becomes apparent that some of these changes were at least partly in reaction to outside economic influences: for example, the gradual end of the slave trades, both across the Atlantic and, half a century later, across the Indian Ocean, was more or less related to the early impact of the British Industrial Revolution.

Nevertheless, the most important issues in the nineteenth century were the ideological and cultural changes that resulted, in many areas, in mass conversions to Islam. Christianity, by contrast, did not become popular until the end of the century. Other crucial factors were the social and political transformations caused by changes in the motivations behind and organization of African slavery and the internal slave trade. The increase in internal slavery was inseparable from world history, but, except in Portuguese areas, it had little to do with colonization, even though its growth was used as a justification for European colonialism at the end of the century.

These factors were common to all areas of the continent, which is why I have presented the analysis thematically. The broad outlines are clear in the table of contents. Naturally, I had to make choices, and the study is not exhaustive. It focuses on the internal aspects of the era's major historical changes, and is intended for readers (especially but not only university students) who seek to understand the history of Africa as seen from the inside.

This book contains no earth-shattering "revelations" flowing from new research. It contains no new discoveries. Most of it is based on the work of innumerable researchers who have devoted themselves to describing the history of Africa. It is primarily a work that adopts a different point of view and tries to be as "Afrocentered" as possible, though the author is of course conscious of not being an African. In short, it is a concrete attempt at African history situated from a postcolonial perspective. The goal may not be to write history "from below," but it is at least to write history from Africa, with an African viewpoint. Whatever our nationality, as historians it is our duty and desire to try to see things from multiple points of view.

Here, I can only express my warm gratitude to the earlier authors who made it possible for me to write this book. Many of them have written in English. There is an incomplete list of their works in the bibliography, which includes mainly the works that I used directly. But my research has been informed by many, many others, and I am only too aware that they have not all been acknowledged here by name.

I would also like to give special thanks to the readers of the French edition, whose comments allowed me to amend and complete some of my arguments. I am especially grateful to Roland Oliver and Jean-Louis Triaud, but of course there were many others. I was also greatly aided by the questions my students asked at Diderot-Paris 7 University, and at Binghamton University, SUNY, where I had the opportunity to teach part-time from 1981 to 2005. In fact, this book results from years of teaching the topic, and I hope that this record will be useful for the next generation.

Finally I thank my translator, Mary Baker, for her efficiency and kindness, and also my production editor, Angela Piliouras, for skillfully and attentively guiding the English-language edition to publication. I take complete responsibility for any remaining errors and omissions. I have probably been too ambitious, and it was perhaps unrealistic to try to make such a vast quantity of knowledge on such a huge topic available to the greatest possible number in so few pages.

Introduction

When the sun rose on the nineteenth century, Africans already had a very long history behind them. Not only had Africa been the cradle of humanity several million years before, but, with records from ancient Egypt and archeological and linguistic research, we know that its history, properly speaking, dates back seven millennia before the Common Era. From around 7000 B.C.E., peoples speaking so-called "Nilo-Saharan" languages (such as Songhai) and "Afro-Asiatic" languages (such as Berber and Hausa) began flowing to the edges of the Sahara. Creeping desertification led them to move both into the Maghreb and also into the Chad basin and western Sudan. In the millennia that followed, with the progression of the Congo-Kordofanians (better known under the reductionist appellation "Bantu-speakers"), there were many developments, including the gradual spread of iron smelting and agriculture, which were among the primary engines of change. The first wave of transformations continued into the tenth century of our era, though earlier technology dating back to the Stone Age continued to be used, even in the nineteenth century. Both kinds of technology were often used in the same period by the same people. This made it possible for farming and foraging societies to coexist. The best known of these hunter-gatherers are the forest Pygmies, whose name varies depending on the location. They have recently been discovered to have been part of the Bantu-speaking people's expansion, who probably adapted genetically to the forest milieu. Another example of adaptation is the foraging culture of the Khoisan-speakers, who were pushed toward and into the Kalahari Desert.

The reason for evoking the faraway past is to point out that since that time people have been able to adapt, surmount obstacles, and pass through stages, from the ancient Iron Age to complex societies. Thus, in Africa, demographic changes; long-term environmental transformations caused by human activity; contact with Islamized Arabs starting in the seventh and eighth centuries; interactions with East Indians, a few Chinese traders in the fifteenth century, and finally Europeans; religious and cultural syncretism among animist and monotheist religions; and the development of political systems have differed over time and space. These are among the many factors that have set off a wide range of long-term adaptation and transformation processes.

Continuities and Ruptures

It is difficult to paint a picture of the whole continent at the beginning of the nineteenth century because the period was such a pivotal point. It was a time of flux; everything was changing and blending together, old with new. At the time, people's experiences in Africa were part of a shifting whole in which continuities were at least as powerful as ruptures, since the continent was under pressure from potent mixed currents from both inside and out. Thus, in the seventeenth century in West Africa, there began a wave of jihad, religious wars undertaken by holy men. In the nineteenth century the clashes intensified, and the groups began to take permanent shape in the form of empires (such as Uthman dan Fodio's sultanate in the north of present-day Nigeria). Similarly, when the sultan of Oman transferred his capital to Zanzibar, one result was the expansion of colonization on the eastern coast of Africa. This was a natural sequel to over one hundred years of domination by the sultanate. Likewise, the military and cultural upheavals that followed from the Nguni rise to power in southern Africa (including Shaka's ascendancy) resulted from the formation of small political bodies in the eighteenth century. Many similar examples can be given of changes that may have seemed sudden at first, but were in fact produced by an underlying past history that had to deal with new events.

At the end of the eighteenth century, people's lives were changing radically. While it is obvious that developments in the world outside of Africa were catalysts that accelerated the transformations owing to a very rapid integration of the continent into the global system of the time, it would be reductionist (and a repetition of an only too common approach) to situate the changes in Africa only in relation to events and periods in the rest of the world, such as the periods before and after the Western Industrial Revolution. Of course such events did play roles and explain some of the more or less brutal ruptures that changed the courses of many people's lives. The official end of the Atlantic slave trade; the beginning of international markets for raw materials sought by European industries; Napoleon Bonaparte's expedition to Egypt in the first years of the century; and the official creation of the very first colonies, namely, Sierra Leone in 1807, the Cape in 1815, and Algeria in 1830, all had major impact. Generally, Africans found themselves required to react to outside imperatives that they had not solicited. The French arrived uninvited in Egypt and Algeria, and the British in South Africa and Egypt. The Western Industrial Revolution and political rebalancing in the Indian Ocean were also beyond African control, not to mention the changes in the slave trade (that is, its abolition by the Europeans in the Atlantic but intensification by the Arabs in the Indian Ocean). However, the integration processes were not new, though they had taken the predatory form of the slave trade for several centuries.

Indeed, they were also consistent with a form of continuity in the history of the peoples, their leaders, and, more generally, their culture. Africans were required to find responses to new demands. Their inherited culture provided them with a remarkable gift for innovation, which is also explained by a long experience with cultural assimilation. This shows the power of the syncretism that was at work, and in some cases had been for centuries. The nineteenth century is when African societies underwent the greatest cultural mixing at a time when they, as many civilizations have in history, hung on to the illusion that they themselves would be able to harvest the fruit of their transformations in the near future.

In fact, historians have been wrong to write the precolonial history of Africa *a posteriori.* "Precolonial" usually implies certain concepts that are obvious today but were unimaginable for contemporaries at the time except, to a certain degree, around 1800 near Cape Town or Loanda and in the tiny village of Freetown in West Africa. We have to reconstitute the history of the peoples as they experienced it and not as it has been rewritten for at least a century by so many Western historians.

If we have to focus on the impact of new influences in the first half of the nineteenth century, the avatars of Islam in North Africa and Islam's spread south of the Sahara have been far more powerful in Africa than Western penetration. Islam has been both a political and a religious phenomenon from the western tip of the continent, across the great central Saharan landscape, along the eastern coast, and all the way to the Horn of Africa. Aside from in Algeria (but beginning in 1830 only), the north of Egypt, around Luanda and the island of Mozambique, and around the Cape Colony, which was still very small at the time, Western presence amounted to only a few individuals who were apparently inoffensive and could even be seen as bearing good news. The British abolition of the slave trade in 1807 was barely felt until at least two decades after the fact, except in the peninsula of Sierra Leone.

Christian missionaries were not new either, though there were virtually none north of the Sahara, despite a weak intrusion on the Egyptian coast following Napoleon's expedition and Lavigerie's limited attempt in the Maghreb. There were also a few traces in the north of present-day Angola, in the ancient kingdom of Kongo, the king of which had, under the influence of missionaries, commanded that Kimba Vita, known to the Portuguese as Beatrice of the Congo, be burned at the stake as a heretic at the beginning of the eighteenth century. Conversion efforts never flagged in the port of Luanda, which had been held firmly by the Portuguese since the sixteenth century. There were trading forts run by European entrepreneurs nearly everywhere along the coasts, and around them a flourishing Creole society with roots that dated back to the first contact during the Age of European Discovery. Christianity became more of a force once the end of the slave trade made it possible to have direct contact with the people in the backcountry. Work on changing mentalities began earliest in the heart of southern Africa, in Tswana country close to the Kalahari Desert.

We now know that powerful, more or less centralized political groups had been emerging and living out their histories in Africa for at least a thousand years. The groups ranged in size from extended families linked by the chief of the line to long-distance trading empires. Nations clearly began appearing in the eighteenth century, but the phenomenon was not new. Besides ancient Egypt and Ethiopia, groups had been forming before any contact with Europeans. For example, there was the kingdom of Kongo and that of Benin City (in present-day southern Yorubaland). The states and even "nation-states" that were at the peak of their power in the first half of the nineteenth century, such as the modernist attempt by Mehemet Ali in Egypt, the slave-trading state in Zanzibar, the small interlacustrine kingdoms, Shaka's Zulu empire and his less well-known neighbors, and the slave-trading kingdoms of Abomey and the Asante, all had their beginnings in the seventeenth century.

In short, as John Iliffe notes in his book *Africans: The History of a Continent,*[1] the people of Africa, in the nineteenth century as in the rest of their history, had to deal with two major challenges: survival despite an overall difficult environment that was gradually becoming drier, and effective resistance against aggressors from less underprivileged places in the world.

At the turn of the eighteenth century, the crisis was at its height. To the north the Muslim world had plunged into a depression, to the west the Atlantic slave trade had weakened the peoples, the east coast of continental Africa was in the process of being colonized by the sultanate of Oman, and to the south the Khoi had already been pushed across the "border" by Dutch settlers.

Yet the people's vitality was undeniable. Against all odds, the population grew throughout most of the nineteenth century, despite illegal slave trading, which continued until the mid-century at the same rate as when it was legal in the worst of the preceding years. It was not until the crises at the end of the century that the population dropped. Religious ideologies gave rise to political reactions, and the Western slave market made the fortunes of strong, ruthless chiefs. The mixing of ideas and peoples increased. This was both the strength and the weakness of the nineteenth century. In the last third of the century, the clash proved too great, and this facilitated colonial conquest. Hope for renewal would be dashed for many years.

This Book

Since Africa is such a huge continent, with many different histories and subject to major traumas throughout the century, it is impossible to be exhaustive. We have tried to focus on what has been less discussed in other recent (and mostly French) works.[2] Our goal here is to write, as much as possible, the history of the interior, seen from "below" and with special attention to the obvious relationships between history and environment, since physical, climatic, and demographic factors are so powerful in Africa, though technology and Western aggression (in particular the spread of epidemics) had major consequences.

What is important is the way that Africans experienced and dealt with the outside aggressions that increased throughout the century (the slave trade, international markets, exploration promoted by Europeans, Zanzibar-Arab ambitions, prodromes of colonization, conquests). Since these aggressions have been studied in depth elsewhere, we have not paid special attention to them. The reader will find little if anything on the rise of the antislavery movement in Europe, on the African diaspora, on the general conditions of Atlantic trade as it shifted from slaves to "legitimate" products, or on the details of exploratory expeditions and military campaigns and conquests. From our point of view, these topics belong more to European and American history than to African history. The idea of the book is to suggest how people saw things in the nineteenth century when the signs of globalization were much less clear than they are today. Of course, we have not ignored these issues, but have only mentioned them rather than discussing them directly.

In contrast, we have focussed on issues related to internal changes in African societies, which have, in general, received less attention. For example, we have carefully analyzed the social and political changes resulting from the unchallengeable increase in the slave trade within the continent and the growing use of slavery by African societies.

This approach has proven difficult. Indeed, the *chronology* of the events is so different from one place to the next in Africa that we have chosen to track the changes and highlight factors in relation to *regional differentiation* and *themes* that recur across the whole continent. The features discussed include cities, gender relations, trade methods, and Christian influence.

Among the processes at work across the whole continent, *religious factors* emerge as primordial and as necessary reference points. In the nineteenth century, aside from in North Africa where there was an ancient Muslim past, Islam conquered much new ground, triumphing in the Sahel and western Sudan, where it had hitherto taken an aristocratic, urban form. It became popular and political in West Africa, quasicolonial and merchant in East Africa, involved in the slave trade in both cases, and a factor in definitive change. Christian missionary intervention, which was more or less prohibited in Muslim lands in the throes of jihad, proved powerful elsewhere, despite the apparent lack of results in terms of conversions at the end of the century. Its ideological and intellectual impact was strong and lasting along the west coast of Africa, and especially in southern Africa. In contrast, central Africa, which was in a way protected by the prolonged anarchy of the slave trade to the Atlantic and hostile to the predatory Muslim inroads from the east, remained until the end of the century a bastion of resistant "conservatism"; in other words, there was a clear will to remain impervious to the nonetheless major upheavals that managed to reach the area.

This explains why the usual regional differentiation (West Africa, central Africa, eastern Africa, southern Africa) is in some ways disconnected from the ideological contrasts existing in various parts of Africa: for example, in the northern and western areas, a religious and popular form of Islam dominated, but in the east it was merchant and colonial, though in neither case was the situation exclusive. We will discuss these different points in detail because Islamization was the dominant factor of the nineteenth century (much more so than Christianization, which was a twentieth-century phenomenon). This is probably why Islamization has been one of the best-studied episodes. There is also a large part of Africa that was out of the reach of Islam. In addition to the many varied Christian attempts, which were, during this period, unsuccessful except in a few cases, there were many ancient societies that did their best to resist both major currents. Unfortunately, these societies are the least well known, for believers in the two great monotheisms have written little about them, and local oral traditions have been gathered and preserved very unequally. In our necessarily arbitrary sectioning of the continent, we have also reserved space specifically for nontropical areas: for the very different yet in some ways similar cases of Algeria and South Africa, where colonies of settlers arrived relatively early, owing, among other things, to similar ecological and demographic conditions; for Egypt, where there was an exceptional attempt at domestic development; and finally for Ethiopia, a mountainous region with an unclassifiable history because it was so strongly influenced by the diverse factors that we have just mentioned.

Finally, looking back in part at two synthetic works on the major themes of *cities* and *women* or rather gender relations,[3] it becomes clear that there is a need to discuss aspects that have received little or no specific attention, such as *cultural history*. Such history is difficult to write since the data are hard to date and also because it is not easy to understand from the outside. A few stimulating works from the so-called "afrocentrist" school remind us of this, if only by pointing out how closely culture is related to language, and language to concepts that are often poorly understood by both Western and

African observers if they content themselves with approximate translations into the languages inherited from colonization.[4] How is the history of the nineteenth century translated into artistic creation? There is literature in Swahili, Arabic, and Pular, as well as in created languages such as Bamum, in English, and in other Western languages, though more rarely. We also need to study changes in songs, dances, and religious art, which, despite being at the heart of very vibrant societies, have been little discussed as they are poorly known, and which should not be reduced to "traditional art." This requires an incursion into an area that is as yet less explored, except by a few historical anthropologists. Here we can do little more than evoke the research possibilities, for the topic remains neglected, unlike political, religious, and economic history, where works are abundant, especially in English, as can be seen in the revised bibliography, of which nearly two-thirds covers titles published after the 1980s.

Note on the Transcription
of Proper Nouns

Linguistic harmonization is a sensitive issue, and all the more problematic since there is no consensus among historians and different countries that use different systems. For lack of a better solution, we have opted for very simple spelling generally based on pronunciation rules in English. Most often the names of geographical locations and historical personalities have colonial origins, though they have sometimes been corrected by contemporary historiography (e.g., "Tukuloor" instead of "Toucouleur"). We have tried to adopt a neutral spelling for the names of peoples that are supposed to have been transcribed from African languages (e.g., "Yoruba" and "Wolof"), and Anglicized words created through colonization (e.g., "Tuareg"). After much hesitation, we have nonetheless sometimes kept spellings that have been imposed by usage. Finally, we have minimized transcriptions from Arabic and Pular; indeed, the plural of "Fulani" should be "Fulbe" in simplified international transcription: we adopted a common word, Fulani, although these people are known by various names according to the language and area. It would be impossible to require the reader (and the author!) to be competent in all of Africa's languages.

Africa  and the Africans
in the
Nineteenth Century

1

People and Their Environment

Africa's Climate and Demography

Contemporary research showing renewed demographic growth supports the fact that despite strong regional variations, the nineteenth century was a relatively prosperous period for Africa. Specialists disagree about whether the upswing began in the period between 1760 and 1840 when the slave trade was at its height. The debate is likely the result of differing reference points, given the vastness of the continent.[1] West Africa flourished earlier because it was the first to be absorbed into modern capitalism. In contrast, slave trading remained a scourge in East Africa into the nineteenth century. Nonetheless, general population growth occurred before the last third of the century owing to relative economic prosperity, at least among members of the ruling class. The increase in wealth was a result of more active, broader markets (including the slave market) and a more favorable ecological environment marked by better rainfall toward the middle of the century. This was a change from the series of droughts that began at the turn of the eighteenth century and included several of severe intensity in the final third of the nineteenth century. By the mid-century, demographic pressure had become obvious, including an unprecedented increase in population movement related to the Fulani jihad in West Africa and the Nguni migrations, formerly known as the Zulu *mfecane*, in southern and eastern Africa.

The Perils of Rainfall Variations

Fluctuations in population and migratory movement were largely the result of the continent's climatic history, which is why it is so important to identify alternating periods of rain and drought. Seen from a distance of a few hundred years, the period from 1500 to 1630 was probably a more humid phase during which the desert retreated. The period from 1630 to 1890, on the other hand, was a long, relatively dry period during which desertification of the Sahel increased. Relatively dense forests that were home to tsetse flies could still be found in the Senegal Valley circa 1750.[2] Corn was still cultivated there, but gradually gave way to sorghum and millet. As a comparison, in Saint-Louis 20.3 inches of rain fell in 1754 and only 15.6 inches in 1755. Between 1860 and 1899, the annual average barely reached 15.9 inches and dropped under 15.6 inches in the second half of the twentieth century. Around the year 1600, camels, cattle, and agriculture were 100 to 200 miles farther to the south than they were 250 years later. This is consistent with indicators that desertification occurred at the same time in eastern Africa. Thus, after the decline of Axum, the Ethiopian political center inexorably moved southward, from Gondar to Addis Ababa, as the highlands of Eritrea and the Tigris River dried up and people migrated. Nonetheless, this trend sometimes paused, as it did in the mid-nineteenth century.

Today, researchers agree that, despite a strong tendency toward drought, there was sufficient rain in sub-Saharan Africa during these decades. Of course, there were many exceptions, particularly at the beginning of the century. A severe drought hit all of southern Africa between 1800 and 1803. There was drought followed by an epidemic in Walata in 1804–5, and again in the same area in 1812–13. Finally, poor harvests caused the price of food to shoot up in 1821–22. The 1820s were extremely parched in southern Africa. However, from the 1830s to the 1870s, periods of dryness were far enough apart to allow people to recover. No matter how bad they were, droughts occurred on average only every ten years (for example, in Lesotho droughts occurred in the following years: 1800–1803, 1812, 1816–18, 1826–28, 1834, 1841–43, and 1851–52).

Major difficulties returned toward the end of the century. Lake Victoria's water level began to drop in 1880. The recrudescence of epidemics was probably related to repeated climatic calamities that led to population movement and concentration, but was due mainly to foreign penetration into the region. By the middle of the century, epidemics were a major issue. It is not known whether they resulted from changes in rainfall, but it is very likely. In West Africa, 1830–31 was called the "year of disease" in the *Walata Chronicle* and corresponds to the beginning of a period of drought identified by geographer J. Gallais.[3] Drought returned between 1833 and 1843, causing famine in Takrur, Walata, and villages across the west Sudanese area and leading to the deaths of many children. This indicates that drought went hand in hand with an increase in epidemics, perhaps exacerbated by malnutrition. There was a lull between 1827 and 1864, and then things took a serious turn for the worse. Too many drought years occurred too closely together for water resources and populations to recoup between calamities. In 1861–62 the people in Walata were reduced to eating saplings; in 1865–66 a severe epidemic struck livestock; and in 1869–70 a new epidemic spread through Takrur, Walata, and the rest of the western Sudan. It struck again even more forcefully the following year in Walata, when nomads took refuge in the city. Smallpox resurged in Walata in 1879–80, and an unidentified eruptive illness (the "spotted disease"), which was probably smallpox or measles, was brought back from Mecca in 1880–81.

Figure 1.1 **Rainfall Fluctuations in the Sahel**

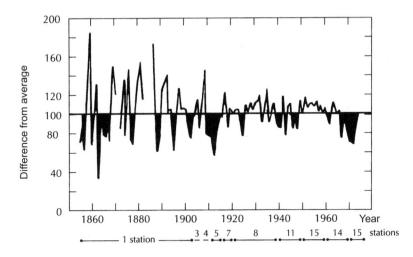

Source: Mason, B.J., *Quarterly Journal of the Royal Meteorological Society*, 1976.

Smallpox devastated nomads in 1884–85, and the scourge culminated in Walata in 1888–89 with a great famine. Another famine occurred in the same area in 1893–94, followed by a particularly severe year of epidemic that continued into 1896–97 and resulted in the deaths of many women and children from fever and dysentery.[4] Beginning in the 1860s, droughts occurred in southern Africa on average at less than five-year intervals. For example, in Matabeland there were droughts in 1867, 1872, 1882, 1884, 1887, and 1889.[5]

The Mediterranean climate of North Africa did not undergo the same fluctuations as the other parts of the continent. After the hard years of drought that peaked in Algeria in 1848–49 and 1865–67 and in Morocco in 1878–79, from the Maghreb to the Egyptian coast there was relatively abundant rain between 1884 and 1892. However, as in the rest of Africa, difficult times returned regularly through the end of the century as droughts, locusts, storms, and hail combined to destroy crops and livestock.[6]

Everywhere on the continent, the climate was similar to what has been described; increasingly frequent changes in rainfall resulted in more droughts in the last third of the century throughout the continent south of the Sahara. This is corroborated by an analogical chronology from Ethiopia. In 1800 there was a famine that killed people and horses; in 1811–12 there was an invasion of locusts, and smallpox was already flourishing in the highlands; in 1826–27 the grain and cotton harvests were insufficient; and in 1835 people died from drought in Shoa.

Table 1.1

Comparative Data on Famine and Epidemic Years in Sahel Locations

		Location	
Decade	Kano	Walata	Tichitt
1800	1807 (E)	1804–5 (E)	
1810		1812–13 (E)	1810–11 (F)
1820		1821–22 (F)	
		1822–23 (E) Khartoum	1822–23 (E)
		1823–26 (F) Hafsa	
1830	1830 (F)	1830–31 (E)	
		1833–34 (F) Cherouag	
1840	1847 (F) Dawara		
1850	1855 (F) Banga-Banga	1854–55 (F)	
1860		1861–62 (E)	1861–62 (F+E)
	1863–68	1864–65	1865–66 (F)
		1865–66 (E)	1866–67 (E)
		1869–70 (E)	1869–70 (E)
1870		1870–71 (E)	
	1872–73 (F) Daura (Malali)		1872–73 (F) Limkabul
		1879–80 (E)	
1880		1880–81 (E)	
	1884 (F)	1884–85 (E)	
	1888–89	1888–89 (F)	1888–89 (E)
1890	1890 Ci-Koriya		1889–90 (F)
	1899 (Katsina)		1890–91 (F)
	= Tashi-Namaka*	1893–94 (F)	1892–93 (F)
	(Daura)	1894–95 (E)	Arandanet
	= El-Komanda*	1896–97 (E)	1896–97 (E)
		1898–99 (E)	1900–1901 (E)

Source: Gado, 1993, p. 33.
Note: E = epidemic; F = famine.
* Indicates local name for the catastrophe.

In Ethiopia the situation became especially critical after the 1860s. The crisis began with a severe famine in Tigray in 1865. One village saw its population, weakened by hunger, drop from 280 to 60. However, during the crucial 1888–92 years there was an unprecedented famine known as the *yakefu qan* (cruel days), which was described by many witnesses and remains in oral memory. It devastated almost all of Ethiopia. One hot, dry year followed another, which led to a catastrophic spread of cattle plague that killed 90 percent of the livestock. The situation was made even worse by an invasion of locusts and rats. These dramatic circumstances had extreme results: the suicide rate went up, cannibalism occurred, and wild animals, which were also starving, attacked people. It is estimated that a third of the population perished. Drought occurred again only two years later, in 1895–96, and again people and livestock died. Finally, in 1899–1900, a drought of unprecedented proportions caused the level of Lake Rudolf (now Lake Turkana in southern Ethiopia) to drop distressingly.

The frequency of drought was similar in the southern hemisphere, with catastrophic events occurring in 1851–52, 1858–59, 1860–63, and especially 1865. Then, toward the end of the century, dry conditions returned with a vengeance in 1877–80, 1883–85, 1887, 1890, and 1894–98. Each time, the drought was accompanied by serious epidemics (smallpox in 1861 and again in 1883–85, typhus and typhoid in 1866–68, yellow fever, smallpox, and measles in 1888, and whooping cough and typhoid again in 1889–90) and, as in eastern Africa, by dramatic epizootics. Missionaries in Lesotho reported that harvests were destroyed by drought or locusts almost every year from 1860 to 1864; herds were decimated by pleuropneumonia in 1852 and 1855–57; over half the sheep and horses died in 1865, and tens of thousands of cattle in 1864–66. Livestock was again devastated by famine in 1877, and cattle plague made a lethal appearance in 1896. By the end of the century, the Sotho had lost half their livestock.[7]

Records from Angola, based essentially on the succession of epidemics, show similar trends: prior to 1863–69, hardly any difficult periods were noted aside from events such as the return of locusts nearly every five years from 1830 to 1869. However, after 1869, epidemics occurred one after the other: between 1870 and 1880 in Kasanje, Golongo, Malange, and Kwanza, again in 1879–84 in southern Angola and Congo, and especially between 1894 and 1898–1900 with locusts and famine, which reappeared in 1930–33.[8]

These hard times continued intermittently into the first third of the twentieth century, with increased drought in 1901–2 and 1913–14 in the western Sahel, a resurgence of cattle plague in eastern Africa in 1905–6, a complete absence of rain between October 1920 and May 1921 (a year of cattle plague in Sudan-Mali), and again a drop in the level of Lake Rudolf in 1932–34 (while at the same time a drought in West Africa tragically followed the "year of the locust").[9]

Population Growth and Decline

Compared with the accumulation of misfortunes in the late nineteenth century, conditions in earlier years appear to have been relatively good. As a result of this positive environment, the people of Africa were able to react effectively to human aggression. Indeed, they had been faced with obstacles of all kinds for thousands of years and had generally been able to deploy efficient compensatory strategies. For example, Portuguese censuses in 1777–78 suggest that in Luanda the massive departure of men connected with the Atlantic slave trade was compensated by an increase in female fertility. The latter was probably helped by systematic polygamy; the man-to-woman ratio was more or less alanced among free people but fell to 43 men to 100 women among slaves. This pattern was probably found in all regions where population density and resilience permitted. Elsewhere, social organization was based on extended family, which encouraged collective granaries and periodic crop diversification. These strategies could attenuate the severity of famine.[10]

Was demographic growth stronger in southern Africa at the very beginning of the nineteenth century because the slave trade was less developed there? Could an increase in population, rather than pervasive drought, have led to the so-called Zulu revolution?[11] This is a controversial idea (see Chapter 5). In fact, the slave trade and demographics may not be related. Records from circa 1840 show that in Igboland (present-day southern Nigeria), an area where the slave trade was intense, there was a net increase in the population. Agricultural colonization was in full expansion, and large tracts of land were being cleared for cassava farms, to the point that a land shortage was beginning to be felt.

In the backcountry (or hinterland), internal trade structures did not change with the times. Slave "production" continued long after Atlantic demand had dropped as a result of the risks involved in illegal trade. From the 1820s on, a large portion of the slaves that were "produced" remained on site and were employed in local occupations, such as palm nuts harvesting in the coastal groves of Dahomey and Nigeria, elephant hunting for ivory in the Congolese basin, urban cotton cloth industries in the western Sudan, and war. Their profitability contributed to, for example, the Igbo expansion, even though slave fertility rates remained generally very low. The hinterland areas that were previously raided, such as the Nigerian plateau between the Niger and Benue rivers and the Angolan and Congolese backcountries, were able to recover before the resurgence of the deadly epidemics in the last third of the century and the heated competition in central and eastern Africa among new slave traders from the Indian Ocean.

Population growth, which was always threatened by war and a high death rate, was consistent with preindustrial rates, along the lines of 0.1 and 0.5 percent per year (a rate of 1 percent has to be considered utterly exceptional compared with 3 to 4 percent today in underdeveloped countries). The population is estimated to have been about 90 to 100 million at the beginning of the seventeenth century. This level was reached again only toward the end of the nineteenth century, despite the fact that North and South Africa's population was in full expansion at the time. It can be supposed that the population grew to some 120 or even 150 million in 1860–80 before droughts, epidemics, and colonial conquest ravaged the continent. Indeed, it is sometimes estimated that between one-third and one-half of the population died (for example, in the Congolese basin and along the Rift in the sleeping-sickness belt), but this will never be known for sure. The demographic growth before the 1880s would explain both the relative prosperity in Africa at the time and the increase in the number of state structures, which became necessary when a growing number of people and communities were competing for the same land.

These trends did not occur at the same time in the north and south as they did in the central areas of Africa. The difference was most marked with respect to North Africa, but southern Africa, where colonization began earlier, was also out of step with the rest of the continent. Destruction occurred earlier in South Africa, where the Xhosa were decimated between 1853 and 1862 following their desperate messianic revolt. Beginning in the last third of the century, however, improvements in public health and penetration of the market economy restarted population growth. Even in Zimbabwe, after the ravages of the Nguni invasions during the great droughts (1827–29 and 1833–36), climate changes at the end of the century caused severe food shortages rather than famine, according to missionaries who were there at the time (and who had introduced major local progress in agriculture). Then the shock of the huge revolt in 1896–97 caused the population to drop again.[12] Xavier Yacono has shown that Algeria's demographics declined during the conquest of 1830–70,[13] and Lucette Valensi suggests a downslide in Tunisia's population in the 1860s. In other words, the population dropped every time European pressure was felt. In contrast, it was not until the end of the century that societies in sub-Saharan Africa crumbled from the increase in ecological shock and human aggression. The spread of disease by the first colonizers in Africa was apparently the major cause.

Local data is available on only a few countries. The population of Egypt increased from 2.5 (or 4.5?) million in 1800 to nearly 10 million in 1897. Algeria, which had at least 3 million inhabitants at the time of the French conquest in 1830, had apparently dropped to 2.5 million by 1856. In 1866–70, drought, poverty, cholera, and famine combined forces, and the population figures did not rise again until 1886. Growth began again in the last decades of the century, enabling the population to reach 4.7 million in 1900 with an annual rate of growth of 1 percent, which was remarkable for the time. The population of

Figure 1.2 **Demographic Changes in Algeria**

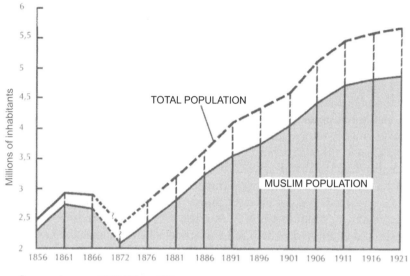

Source: Ageron, 1968, T.I., p. 550.

Tunisia followed a similar route, stagnating at 1 million from the beginning of the century to 1.1 million in 1860, and then doubling by 1914. In Morocco an estimated 3 million in 1800 increased to 4 million in 1914, though the growth occurred after clear drops during the 1878–81 famines.[14]

In contrast, in sub-Saharan Africa, except for southern Africa where growth returned earlier, a severe drop in population was probably seen at the time of the conquest at the end of the century, between 1880 and 1920. Between one-third and one-half of the population died at that time (depending on the case and study) with major losses especially in central and eastern Africa. The causes were the same as those that had depopulated the Americas four centuries earlier: diseases against which the population had no immunity. The European conquest of Africa, which peaked in the last quarter of the century, produced its most violent effects at that time, such as in the future Belgian Congo where war, disease, and hunger killed half of the population between 1876 and 1920.[15] Elsewhere, about a third of the population died, partly as a result of the dramatic spread of sleeping sickness.[16] The great epidemics, one of the major causes of death, did not abate until after the Spanish flu epidemics in 1918–19 and 1921–22.

The overall growth speculated to have occurred between 1880 and 1900, which would have placed the number of Africa's inhabitants at approximately 120 million, was probably due to the increase in population in the northern and southern tips of the continent.

The Ecology of Health

The situation in North Africa and, to a lesser degree, West Africa was different from the rest of the continent. Eastern and western central Africa suffered most from the epidemics of the nineteenth century. Some diseases, such as malaria and sleeping sickness, and even the plague in North Africa, have a long history on the continent, and their centers of infection spread during this period. The plague, which had been present for many years, recurred in Egypt[17] and Tunisia[18] in the first half of the nineteenth century. Cholera was also present in 1836, 1849–50, 1856, and especially 1867 (in Algeria). Sleeping sickness spread over all of eastern Africa in the second half of the nineteenth century as a result of an increase in slave raids[19] and later in the path of deforestation. It expanded through Sierra Leone after 1865 and central and West Africa in the beginning of the twentieth century. The maximal spread of other diseases, such as smallpox imported from India and, locally, venereal diseases, probably introduced by Arabs, coincided with the beginnings of colonial penetration. Smallpox flourished in southern and northern Africa in the eighteenth century, in Zanzibar in 1809, and in the rest of eastern Africa, particularly in the second half of the century. It caused the most damage in 1885, 1891, 1895, 1898, and 1900.

In addition to human epidemics, sickness in animals also impacted famine on the continent. Bovine pneumonia was introduced into South Africa in 1853, and by 1870 it had reached Chad. A cattle plague that originated in the Russian steppes in the early 1860s caused the worst damage. It struck Egypt first, and reached the western Sudan in 1865. Then, beginning in the 1880s, infected livestock was imported from both Russia and India, and this had severe consequences. From 1889 on, the epidemic periodically decimated eastern and southern Africa's livestock. Cattle crises strongly influenced subsistence and survival and so political history in the area has to be closely connected to cattle epidemics.

Greater Demographic Disparities

At the latest by the beginning of the nineteenth century, population distribution in Africa had settled into a pattern of alternation between virtually deserted areas and centers of relatively high density. In the middle of the desert, there was a ribbon of population along the Nile. There were also many people along the shores of the Mediterranean; in the Bight of Benin from the coast of Ghana to Nigeria, and in the refuge area of the great lakes around politically defined areas such as the Buganda, Ankole, and Rwanda kingdoms. In the immediate vicinity of these populated zones, there were areas that were almost completely devoid of inhabitants, including true desert lands, such as along the edges of the Sahara and Kalahari, and the broad grasslands. The latter included the high Maghrebian plateaus separated from the sea by the Middle Atlas mountain range, and the Niger-Benue plateau, which had been the cradle of the proto-Bantu language in the distant past. Along the "frontier" behind the Cape, the first Dutch settlers (slave-owning, gun-carrying petty planters who shot Xhosas on sight since they were easy targets and could retaliate only with bows and arrows) had been ingeniously pushing the indigenous people back since the mid-seventeenth century. The east side of the Cape was more highly populated (since the west bordered the desert), and the small Salt and Liesbeek rivers near the Cape were used as temporary boundaries separating the Dutch East India Company's area from that of the Aboriginal people. The introduction of imported diseases, especially a severe smallpox epidemic in 1713, quickly pushed the border back farther. From an original line located about 30 miles from Cape Town, the borderline had moved 150 miles away by 1700, and 500 miles away by 1800.

The major difference between early patterns of population density and those of today lies in the distribution between coastal and interior areas. The evolution is clear in West Africa, which is divided into two main regions—the coastal forest and the interior savanna. In medieval times, the savanna was the location of high civilization. The golden empires of western Sudan, and the Shona cultural area in southern Africa, which peaked at Great Zimbabwe between the eleventh and fifteenth centuries, were major focal points for the relatively sparsely populated surrounding areas. The rain forest was a rather unattractive area; the region's ancient activities of hunting, fishing, and gathering could sustain ten times fewer people per square mile than farming, yet agriculture required major effort to clear land because technology was limited. The climate was insalubrious, and natural dangers such as snakes, mygalomorphea (poisonous spiders with often deadly venom), and proliferating microorganisms thrived in the heat and humidity. Inhabitants of such areas were gathered into relatively crowded hamlets that surrounded a village square or marketplace. Enclosures protected by fences in more or less concentric rings branched into paths that snaked out to fields that were painstakingly carved out of the forest. These trails were immediately reconquered by nature during very long fallow periods. Beyond this was the great forest, a frightening place of spirits, evil, and herbalists, and even witches and secret societies.

The Atlantic slave trade probably changed this structure, particularly in West Africa. The more open interior areas became dangerous and vulnerable to raids by neighboring slavers. This was certainly the case in the Fante backcountry of the Gold Coast, which was an active, populated region of a relatively dense, modern, urban, and commercial network in the sixteenth and seventeenth centuries.[20] The towns and villages built on trade in gold dust and grain were open and accessible and, in particular, had no surrounding walls. They were located 35 to 60 miles into the interior, which was a reasonable distance conducive to regional trade, given the means of transportation at the time. However, these villages were also prime targets of raids by slave traders from the coast and elsewhere, and they disappeared one after another, beginning in the second half of the seventeenth century. Most of them were gone a century later, while in a less vulnerable area, a more consolidated military power arose: the Asante Empire.

This general process occurred elsewhere, depending on regional conditions. For example, in Angola, Portuguese colonization attracted a large population of middlemen around the port of Luanda. This helped to depopulate the interior and probably more or less destroyed older political structures, such as the Lunda Empire, in favor of more "modern" entities—those better adapted to the new market, such as the Bakuba people.[21] In southern Africa, it was precisely at the turn of the nineteenth century that a similar process began: it emptied the Rand and made the land more vulnerable to European greed.

Two centuries of intense slave trade on the Atlantic also attracted intermediaries and traders to the coastal forts. Thus, earlier networks were changed. To the west, there was reconfiguration of the population between the forest and the Sahel. International trade no longer focused only on the northern Sahara, but extended toward the ocean. Between the two centers, the land was emptied of people who had once been prosperous but had been raided to excess.

A similar process occurred in eastern Africa, where Swahili ports had been drawing in neighboring people for centuries. In contrast, the interior plateaus were raided by slavers, activity that increased in the nineteenth century. This hinderland emptied as people took refuge in areas that were still more protected by distance or altitude; sometimes in the shelter of volcanic mountain ranges, particularly in northern Rwanda and the Ganda Kingdom. This was probably when the population in those areas became denser.

In the Maghreb, particularly in Tunisia,[22] a similar contrast existed between coastal areas populated by migrants and the southern semidesert steppes from which they originated. Western modernity drew people to the lively ports on the Mediterranean Sea, which connected with the caravan routes to the south. Tripoli and Tunis in particular became the primary storehouses of European manufactured goods.

Greater Mobility

The fact that populated areas were scattered was both an advantage and an obstacle. While it often hindered regular exchanges between some groups, it gave others the opportunity to strengthen their autonomy. Except in the special case of Egypt, where the people remained attached to their narrow band of exceptionally fertile land, the sparse population of vast areas aided population movement. This has always been a special feature of Africa's demographic structure, and in the context of change in the nineteenth century it became very significant. In the first half of the century demographic expansion probably occurred, clearly manifested by the jihads in West Africa and *mfecane* (scattering of the Nguni) in southern and eastern Africa. The shift toward zones of contact and markets also occurred elsewhere, such as among the Fang in Gabon, who descended toward the southwest Atlantic coast at the end of the century, and the Zande of eastern central Africa, who began slave trading with Khartoum.

In addition to these population movements, which had for long existed in Africa, there were migrations of workers attracted by the labor markets created through entry into the Western system. Migrant workers included *navetanes,* the seasonal workers who traveled from the interior of the Sahel to the peanut-growing areas of Senegambia, and contract workers recruited for the diamond and gold mines in the Rand at the turn of the century. Europeans also began to move into the interior, such as the Boers in South Africa in 1836.

The Inflow of Foreigners

The greatest change in the nineteenth century was the arrival of droves of European settlers, in particular, in two areas that were considered to have a favorable climate. First, in the coastal cities and grain fields of Algeria, the number of French increased from 8,000 in 1833 to over 500,000 in 1901. Subsequently, from 1896 on there were more Europeans born in Algeria each year than there were new immigrants. Other North African countries did not experience such a drastic influx. Napoleon Bonaparte's arrival in Egypt was accompanied by a small wave of European immigration, with only 40,000 in 1840 and barely 100,000 at the end of the century; Europeans made up only slightly more than 1 percent of the total Egyptian population. The white population of the Cape Colony increased from about 20,000 in 1798 (approximately one-third of the total) to 74,000 in 1840 (closer to one-half of the total population). In addition to the well-established Dutch settlers, and to a lesser degree Germans and French Huguenots, an estimated 20,000 British settlers arrived in the 1820s. The inflow increased at the end of the century with the discovery of diamonds (1867) and gold (1886). By 1890, about 24,000 people were arriving each year so that in the last decade of the century there were an estimated 750,000 Europeans in South Africa, and about the same number in North Africa.

Elsewhere, the number of Europeans could be counted in the hundreds at most, with a maximum of an estimated 5,000 attracted by the gold rush in southern Rhodesia in the 1890s. In the Portuguese possessions, which had been continuously occupied since the sixteenth century, particularly Luanda and the island of Mozambique, mixed marriage was very common; as a result, Europeans merged into the local population. In all, the number of Europeans in Africa exceeded 1.5 million in 1900. Other emigrants included a few thousand Indians, who were brought to Africa in the 1860s to work on sugar plantations in Natal and to build the first railroads in Kenya and Uganda. In Africa in 1900, there were about 200,000 Indians and Arabs from Asia. In the end, a total of 2 million foreigners came to Africa over the course of the century, and most arrived in the final two decades.

A Harsh Environment

At the end of the nineteenth century, Africa was still on the fringes of the European technological revolution. African societies experienced the effects, but within the context of an environment that continued to be strongly affected by natural conditions. There is an extraordinary range of such conditions in Africa—from desert to dense forest on a continent three times larger than the United States—but people traveled great distances in spite of this.

Except in a few cases, Africans did not use a solar calendar. In general, their lives were organized by lunar months and the major climate alternation between the dry and rainy seasons. The alternation is characteristic of almost the whole continent, though it takes a Mediterranean form in the extreme north (the Maghreb) and extreme south (the Cape). Lifestyles were closely linked to local ecological conditions. In the desert, there were foragers (in the Kalahari), camels, long-range trade caravans, and nomadic shepherds (in the Sahara). The Sahel, the semidesert band along the south of the Sahara, gets 7.5 to 15 inches of precipitation per year, and all the rain falls over a period of a few days. The only people living in the Sahel were transhumant shepherds looking for greener pastures during the long dry season, which lasts from at least October to June in the northern hemisphere. The increase in population very likely exerted great pressure southward, and when people found areas with more water and better land, they did more farming. Thus, the Kikuyu, who had originally been shepherds, began to enter the Kenyan highlands in the second half of the seventeenth century. Their migration into the region continued throughout the nineteenth century until Whites, Arabs, and Swahili came inland from the coast, and the British arrived. At the same time, demographic development in southern Africa and the Nguni expansion into the interior also helped to change earlier movements. Moreover, the

Map 1.1 **Major Zones of Natural Vegetation**

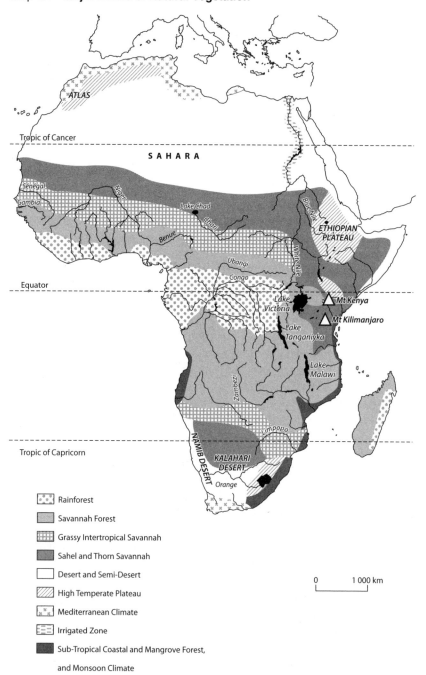

Rainforest

Savannah Forest

Grassy Intertropical Savannah

Sahel and Thorn Savannah

Desert and Semi-Desert

High Temperate Plateau

Mediterranean Climate

Irrigated Zone

Sub-Tropical Coastal and Mangrove Forest,

and Monsoon Climate

spread of Tswana shepherds contributed to the displacement of the Khoi into the desert after a long period of retreat that had begun with the Bantu expansion centuries beforehand.

The geographical zones are less clearly demarcated in East Africa owing to high plateaus where the relative coolness of altitude helps compensate for proximity to the equator. This explains why the intertropical savanna, which is favorable to mixed farming, is much more widespread there than in West Africa. Grassland covers about three-quarters of the continent. In parallel with demographic growth, a variety of plants were introduced by the Portuguese beginning in the sixteenth century; but these were not necessarily adopted immediately. In the nineteenth century, corn, which had been abandoned in West Africa owing to desertification, became the major grain grown on the high plateaus, while in the forest, manioc continued to spread and replace the yam. Note that it was not until World War I that *gari* (manioc flour) was adopted in southern Nigeria. These changes in diet reflect Africans' ability to adapt to new conditions. One of the most remarkable examples is that of the Yoruba-speaking people. (The term *Yoruba* was invented by the British to "create" the corresponding ethnic group; it had previously designated only inhabitants around the city of Oyo.) In the nineteenth century, the Yoruba descended southward. Although they originated from the savanna, they were able to adapt to the forest environment and consolidate their cultural and social solidarity in a remarkable way.

2

Political and Warlike Islam

The Maghreb and West Africa Before the Colonial Conquest

Unlike Egypt, North Africa remained relatively unknown to Europeans until the conquest of Algiers. The only sources of information were freed slaves and consuls confined to the cities in which they were living, such as Tunis, Algiers, and Tangier. Yet contact with Christianity dated back to ancient times: the Spanish Catholic nobles conquered Melilla on the north coast of Morocco in 1497, and King Charles V passed through Oran. European powers persistently attempted to gain a foothold in Algeria under the banner of crusades, attempts to free slaves, and defense of their national and commercial interests. However, while contact was particularly frequent between Algerians, French, and English, there were almost no Christians living in Morocco. (Though there were in Ceuta and Melilla, which the Spanish had retained.)

Maghrebians wrote little during this period and did not yet use the printing press. Thus, North Africa was known only through the spread of Sufi ideas from Egypt (see Chapter 3). Even though their borders were first mapped by the colonizers, the three kingdoms—Tunisia, Algeria, Morocco—had been formed in the thirteenth century after the dissolution of the Almohad Empire. Their relations were sometimes difficult: Tunisia began paying tribute to Algiers in 1756, but broke free in the early nineteenth century, rebuilt fortifications at border locations, and launched a victorious campaign in 1807. The Ottoman Porte was unable to impose peace until 1821. The Algerians had supported the revolts of Moroccan warlords and religious leaders (marabouts) against Moulay Ismail, founder of the Alawite Dynasty. His successors in turn supported the revolt of the Derkawa sects in Oran province in the early 1800s. The borders were gradually drawn until the three political entities were quite distinct and were perceived as such by the people.

The Maghreb Before the Conquest

Tripolitania

Reinforced by the pilgrimage route, a clear continuity existed between the three Maghrebian entities and Egypt, especially in the case of Tripolitania where there was a more marked Turkish influence. From 1711 to 1835, a Greco-Turkish dynasty, the Karamanli, reigned there, which the Ottomans eventually expelled in order to reestablish their direct authority. This expulsion caused a revolt by tribes that were furious about losing their independence; one of the leaders of the rebellion, Ben Khelifa, took refuge in Tunisia. The region of Cyrenaica became the fief of a Berber-Saharan brotherhood that expanded across the great oases and southward into the Saharan areas around Lake Chad. Its founder, Es Sanusi (1787–1859), was born in southern Algeria. After studying in Morocco and spending time in Cairo and in the Middle East during a pilgrimage to Mecca, Sanusi established control on the basis of strict doctrine and an authoritarian conception of power. The brotherhood was rather conservative and respectful of local powers, given the fact that its members were free to pray and trade. In spite of that, the Sanusiyya, as the brotherhood is known, was to resist for nearly a century against varied invaders, from Muslim slave trader Rabīh az-Zubayr to the Italian, British, and French colonizers.

Morocco, a Protected Area

Only Morocco, which had remained sheltered from Turkish occupation, claimed to date back to the Prophet and steadfastly refused to acknowledge the Ottoman Porte. The monarchy was both inherited and elected. The sovereign was chosen from within the royal line but also through a complex agreement among major cities, tribes, and army corps. As in areas south of the Sahara, succession often gave rise to much competition: it took Moulay Slimane, who reigned until 1822, almost four years at the end of the eighteenth century to gain recognition from the south. Similarly, in the provinces, tribal chiefs had to gain recognition from their communities, and local and regional conflicts were common. The primary instruments of the central government (*makhzen*) were the armed forces and repression of insurgents. Moulay Slimane ended his long reign with constant campaigns (1811–22), which finally gave rise to general rebellion. His successor, Abderrahmane, who reigned 1822 to 1859, used diplomacy as a remedy by rallying loyal tribes and employing both the authority of local chiefs and that of officers of the central government.

Algeria and Tunisia, Turkish Provinces

Algeria and Tunisia were more directly under Ottoman control. Both were in the hands of a Turkish military aristocracy, and recognized the emperor of Constantinople as caliph. In Algiers, the dey was a soldier chosen by the divan. The superior council of the Turkish militia (*odjaq*) was made up of senior officers and officials, janissaries recruited in the Levant that were constantly renewed from outside sources. The dey succeeded in breaking away from janissary control to some degree after 1816 by moving to the Casbah in Algiers and became the elected representative of Algeria's governing castes. Most deys that came later died violent deaths by strangling or decapitation while competing for power.

The rest of the country was governed by provincial beys: Titteri in the center, Oran to the west, and Constantine to the east. The right to rule went to the highest bidder, who had only to pay taxes twice a year. He relied on caids, who were generally Turkish, and local sheiks chosen by villages and tribes. Each bey maintained a small court in the capital: in Medea, Constantine, and Oran. In order to ensure that their authority was respected, caids and beys requisitioned the help of tribes of nomadic horsemen and camel riders, *deira* or *ahl el-Makhzen*. They also won recognition from the leaders of large tribute-paying communities and religious federations, including some that refused to acknowledge the authority of Algiers, such as the Tijaniyya brotherhood, which was founded in 1798. The result was that the beys' revenue tended to be greater than that of the dey, who compensated for the imbalance by controlling commerce and privateering in the Mediterranean; he monopolized the reciprocal slave trade and banditry between Christians and Muslims. In Tunis, in the eighteenth century, the bey had broken away from Algiers and managed to create a dynasty. Following a revolt in 1811, Hamuda Pasha, who was then bey of Tunis, finally dissolved the Turkish militia in Tunisia.

Muslims were in the majority by far. Most of the population was made up of fellahs (peasants), who were grouped by language: the Berbers of ancient times (those whom the Romans called "barbarians," which explains the current rejection of that appellation and today's preference for the name *Kabyle*) belonged to the Afro-Asian language group and lived mainly in the highlands of Kabylia and the Aurès Mountains, in Morocco and Algeria, but also in Tunisia and Tripolitania.[1] Arabs who had arrived since the conquest could be found everywhere. At the pinnacle of society, there were only a few thousand individuals of varying status. There were fewer than 10,000 Turkish soldiers (Janissaries) in Algeria and Tunisia in the early nineteenth century. Their descendants, resulting from unions with local women, became *kouroughli*, who could inherit their father's property but not his rights. In principle, this prevented the establishment of a hereditary aristocracy. Members of this class were found in cities where there was a garrison: Algiers, Oran, Blida, Tlemcen, Medea, and Constantine. The Andalusians, descendants of Moors who had been forced out of Spain, considered themselves to be an aristocracy; renowned artisans, they were numerous mainly in Morocco, though some were scattered across a dozen villages in Algeria and Tunisia.

Among the despised minorities, there were several thousand Jews, particularly at Tunis, where there were probably 15,000 (out of the 20,000 in the Regency of Tunis). Most of them were of the working class, but there were some very wealthy families, in particular Livornians with ties to Mediterranean ports. Elsewhere, they were more scattered across rural areas. They were allowed to practice their religion, but were subject to ignominious regulations: they had to live in reserved districts, wear special clothes, and could not ride horses. They were also not allowed to use Arabic writing, which was reserved for believers. (They thus wrote the Arabic language using Hebrew letters.)

Black Africans purchased from the south were used (like Christian captives) as women in harems, servants, and soldiers, particularly in Morocco where, in 1808, 18,000 Black African men loyal to the dynasty intervened in the power struggles. In 1856, there were between 6,000 and 7,000 scattered across Tunisia, most of whom were descendants of freed slaves. Finally, there were a few hundred infidels, such as Christians, renegades, slaves, traders, and consuls, whose numbers had grown since there were fewer corsairs plying the Mediterranean Sea.

In rural areas, both Berbers and Arabs had social structures similar to those of Africans south of the Sahara. Their structures and oral traditions were always built on the idea of a founder of a lineage who came from abroad and whose settlement in an area gave rise to a right to occupy it. Only marabout lines based their land rights not on occupation but on gift. The basis of social organization was the extended family, which formed larger social groups, hamlets, villages, and tribes united in the tension and precariousness of power relations. The family lived in a *douar*, in other words, a camp with the chief (*sheik*) in the middle, surrounded by his children, parents, servants, and slaves. In principle, the tribe was defined, and in any case justified, by kinship ties; it was an "ideological product [. . .] of political, religious and matrimonial practices."[2] It should be noted that the word *tribe*, which has become pejorative in francophone Africa south of the Sahara (*tribu*), has been retained in French in North Africa, particularly among nomads. It refers to a political unit governed by a council of notables and linked with other tribes in the area through a complex system of alliances (*soff*) and oppositions that operate mainly in case of conflict. The tribal system's power was felt throughout the century, and the same alliances operated during the great tax revolt against the bey of Tunis in 1864 as in the 1729–40 civil war.[3]

The primary resources were grain and livestock; the rare travelers in preceding centuries had noted the wealth of the great coastal flatlands, such as the Mitidja and Arzew plains. Sophisticated irrigation systems remained as extensive as they had been in the Middle Ages. In 1830, vast farms managed by intendants and worked by *khammès* used local salaried workers lodged in tents, and immigrants from the mountains housed in *gourbis*. The high plateaus of the interior were left to nomads: "a great deserted countryside [where] there are many wandering and vagabond Arabs . . ."[4] Most people lived in rural areas, though sometimes in agglomerations: large towns had several thousand inhabitants, both along the coast and around oases. Sedentary lifestyles had gained ground; unlike in Africa south of the Sahara, in the nineteenth century there was neither a spread of nomads nor village migrations. Yet people did gravitate to some areas; for example, people from Djerba and the Kerkenna Islands tended to move to the mainland, either to the north, to places on the Mediterranean coast, or to the south, toward the Sahel, a constantly moving area characterized by ethnic mixing. Kabylia was also a source of emigrant workers.

The principal cities were ports and hubs for international trade, both with the Mediterranean to the north, and with caravans traveling south. The consumer market and most re-exporting were concentrated in Tripoli, Tunis, and Algiers. Trade with the Saharan interior and between southern Algeria and its neighbors was intensifying, and relied largely on Mozabite and Biskra caravan guides. In 1830, approximately 30,000 people were living in Algiers, as many as were in Constantine. Tlemcen had about 15,000 and Oran 10,000. In all, the urban population of Algeria on the eve of the conquest was about 150,000, just 5 to 6 percent of the total population. In the interior, cities were rare, and were located in scattered pockets of sedentary life. In general, they were very small, with only 2,000–3,000 inhabitants. They were characterized by their Friday mosque, *souk* (market), and *medersa* (schools). Tunis had perhaps 160,000 inhabitants (15 percent of the country's total population) and boasted a university.

Islam and Politics

More than politics, religion was the social glue; the feeling of belonging to the *umma* (community of Muslim believers) united Arabs with the Berbers, whom they had converted long before. The unity of interest and culture spread all the way into Egypt, where Cairo was a compulsory step on the way to Mecca. Locally, people gathered around marabouts, particularly those who were deceased, making pilgrimages to and worshiping at their tombs as was done in Egypt. These burial places were centers of *zaouia*, which were large villages occupied by members of the tribe. Among the Ouartan in

Tunisia, for example, nearly 5,000 people (a fifth of the normally nomadic tribe) lived near marabouts. Tombs were also destinations for pilgrimages and brotherhood gatherings that transcended *douar* and tribal borders, and sometimes resulted in clear syncretism of ancient agrarian religions and Islamic practices.

In the nineteenth century, the brotherhoods, which had existed for generations, were portrayed by the French as subversive, political-religious, secret societies. One example was the "black legend" of the Sanusi order (Sanusiyya), a brotherhood created in Cyrenaica toward the end of the 1830s.[5]

Whatever their official political organization, the regimes of the three countries barely differed; the central government manifested itself essentially through taxes transmitted to the provinces by the caid, an officer of the bey. This system was inseparable from the tribes' real autonomy. In the patrilineal Muslim system, elder notables wielded authority over young people, and women were completely absent from public affairs. Lucette Valensi[6] has shown how difficult it is to describe the land regime. In Muslim law, land is taxed differently depending on whether it is subject to *kharadj* (taxes on conquered land), in which case all land would have been the bey's inalienable possession, or to Muslim taxes (in particular the dîme or *ashur*). Later colonizers preferred the former interpretation, which was more convenient to them since it set out that the colonial state would inherit the land from the bey. Yet, the situation was more complex than this. There was a dîme on grain, and some private property (*melk* land) could be transmitted, even to women in some cases. There are notarized documents attesting to land sales in Tunisia that date from the end of the eighteenth century. (Some such sales were made to freed slaves.) In Algeria, as in the area south of the Sahara, absolute private property hardly existed, and there was a complicated hierarchy of use rights. The bey owned extensive lands, but there were also cases of undivided ownership of lands that belonged to a group. In the oases, such as at Gabès in southern Tunisia, all inhabitants who did not earn their living through the army, trade, or crafts were peasants who owned land. Such *melk* lands fell under the bey's authority only figuratively. Even former slaves could own land, though very little, and they could not leave except by hiring themselves out to others as farm workers or *khammès*; they were responsible for about a hundred date palm trees, from which they were permitted to keep one-fifth of the harvest. Year after year of debt tied them to the land. The kind of contract most advantageous to poor peasants was that for *habou* (marabout) land, for which they could pay a fee for a perpetual use right, which made the sacred land inalienable. Before the conquest, the *khammès* system was widely used by the bey and major land owners in the grain lands of the north. Elsewhere it was employed only moderately.

Financial Crisis, Agricultural Crisis, and Slave Trade Economy

In the nineteenth century, a great rupture occurred as a result of increased international trade. Since antiquity, Tunisia had supplied grain to southern Europe. In the nineteenth century, Tunisia and Tripoli both received more and more European textiles in exchange for grain. Some of the fabric was then traded in sub-Saharan Africa. However, very little foodstuff was imported from Europe into the area, aside from luxury goods reserved for the upper classes and city dwellers. In most of Africa, sugar, coffee, and tea were still quite unusual, if not unknown: they would be colonial imports.

Following the Napoleonic wars and the ecological disaster in the first third of the century, the European market began looking to the first settlers in Algeria, the Ukraine, and the vast grain plains in Eastern Europe for supplies. In Tunisia and the Algeria of the fellahs, meanwhile, the grain market collapsed. In Tunisia, grain farming was replaced by olive oil production, which had already begun in the eighteenth century. Bey Hamuda Pasha had an intelligent policy. He used the European wars to strengthen his army and fleet without raising the dey's suspicions, and then became independent from Algiers. He restructured the customs service in his favor and commissioned works in the port of Tunis. Finally, he encouraged local manufacturing, in particular weaving fabric in Djerba and producing oil for export. In 1834, Tunisian exports on French ships were worth over 17.5 million francs, including over 10 million francs of oil destined for the soap industry in Marseille.

In Algeria, however, the crisis proved irreversible. At the end of the seventeenth century, privileges were granted to the Compagnie d'Afrique in the Constantinois region. A French consul was established in Algiers, soon to be followed by representatives of other powers. This began the deadly process of concessions, which filled the government's coffers. Privateering had been prohibited since 1780, and profits from piracy were gradually eliminated through international agreements. The end of slavery ruined most merchants and craftspeople, except for those who dealt with the bey, in particular a few French, Livornian, and Andalusian Jewish families. Since he completely controlled money circulation, the dey prevented the development of a business bourgeoisie, for which he substituted foreign, in particular French, traders. At the same time, he increased taxes on those who lived in the countryside. The return to nomadic and pastoral life in the plains of Bone at the beginning of the century reveals the poverty of peasants seeking to escape taxation at any price.

Though they were under very different regimes, North Africa and French West Africa happened to be subject to the same trading economy at almost the same time. It was based on raw materials in the form of vegetable oils: palm and peanut oil in French West Africa, and olive oil in Tunisia. Initially, the bey of Tunis, who had appropriated the trade monopoly, charged customs on exports, but at the price of his independence with respect to European demand. When that demand dropped (in 1826 and especially when tropical oils took over the market), he began selling harvests against advance payment, fell into debt, and sought to remedy this by pressuring his subjects. When the French took Algiers, they were able to impose an advantageous treaty in 1830, which eliminated the bey's monopoly. This resulted in the bey's loss of most of his tax revenue, while private producers succumbed to the suicidal process of advance payment sales. European trading houses with headquarters in Tunis sent agents into interior towns and recruited "indigenous traders" and "oil brokers." The trading houses' new recruits negotiated prices with producers eight to ten months before the harvest. Competition between the bey's requirements and those of the trading houses were devastating to the local peasantry, especially after foreigners gained the right to acquire land locally through the so-called *Pacte Fondamental* of 1857.

From that time, one bey after another used ingenious means to reform the tax laws and expand the tax base in order to replenish the coffers. In 1819, the bey added a dîme on oil, and all agricultural products were taxed, including olives, dates, and grain. In 1856, a new monetary tax was added: the *mejba*. This was despite the fact that Muslims were not in principle subject to a head tax, though there had been one in Algeria before the conquest.[7]

The public financial crisis in Tunisia alienated peasants, who were subject to taxes and usury, which was aggravated by a reform at the beginning of the century that had changed the way beys were appointed. Initially chosen on the basis of merit, individuals were eventually able to buy the position. This all resulted in a series of major revolts that weakened the government. Every new tax increase was met with resistance: in the Kef in 1831, at Kairouan in 1834–35, and at Bizerte in 1837. Social unrest translated into raids, and individual banditry increased. When the head tax was doubled, the revolt spread in 1864 around two focal points: the tribes in the center and west, and those in the Sahel. Both the notables and common people of every community organized their defenses. The leader of the revolt, Ali ben Gdahem, was called the "bey of the Arabs." The government was shaken.

Therefore, it was not so much the bey's extravagance, but trade in rural products that led the way to European control.

In Algeria, there was also heavy dependency on foreign trade. It would be a mistake to think that the affair of the dey of Algiers was the first crisis: the "Fan Affair" was used as a pretext by the government of King Charles X to invade Algeria, but the ties were ancient. It largely explains why the July Monarchy, as the reign of King Louis-Philippe was known, continued in the same vein after the revolution of 1830.

As in Tunisia, the agricultural crisis was deep. However, although it was facing competition from Ukrainian wheat, the export economy did not convert to trading olive oil. The overall volume of trade, in particular with France, dropped steeply in the 1820s since Algeria was able to offer only raw materials that were undervalued at the time, such as wool, skins, and wax. Faced with a weakened government, foreign intervention increased.[8] As early as 1808, Napoleon was preparing an attack on Algeria. As for the United States, after a war that lasted four years (1812–16), it stopped its previously agreed-upon annual payments. The same year, since the lease on its concessions had not been renewed, Great Britain sent its fleet to recover a debt for naval armaments. This was the beginning of a "cannon policy" that led in 1819 to the formation of a French-British fleet to enforce definitive compliance with the prohibition on piracy. Despite a reaction from the dey, who expelled the British Consul, retorted with economic sanctions, and had French establishments searched (this would later be used against him to justify the conquest), his power was decreasing. Colonization plans were emerging in both Britain and France by the 1820s. In any case, the Algiers fleet was not able to recover from this series of events. Partly rebuilt in about 1826, it was again destroyed the next year when it attempted to support the Turkish fleet against the British, French, and Russian forces.

In the interior, the dey was also weakened. The Kabyle tribes of mountain-dwelling fruit farmers rose up a number of times, and even accepted illicit help from the French in 1824. Above all, Algerians began to unite against the Turkish regime, which they accused of collusion with Christian powers and Jewish financiers. The Derkawa sect, supported by Morocco, called for unity in the name of Islam. At the center of the emancipation movement was the Hachem tribe, from which Abd el-Kader came. Abd el-Kader was strongly influenced by his father Mahi Eddin, a marabout in the Qadiriyya brotherhood who was hostile to the Tijaniyya order that the French were to favor.

The Western Sudan at the Turn of the Nineteenth Century

In the early nineteenth century, the Niger River Bend was a busy area full of travelers and traders, despite the fact that it had been governed in a diffuse manner for a number of centuries. The river remained an incomparable communications route, making it possible for interregional trade networks to expand, even though the Sudan was no longer the "dazzling country" of which Al-Mansur had spoken in 1591. Farming had suffered from three long droughts in the second half of the eighteenth century and into the beginning of the nineteenth century (1786–1806). The Gao area was where the countryside had changed greatly since Songhai times. Under military pressure from the Arma and owing to gradual deterioration of the environment, the area had gone from having the best rice and millet farms to being a land of nomads cut off from trade networks. In contrast, the Bambara had increased agricultural colonization, which fostered the beginnings of Fulani sedentarization in Masina and the establishment of Tuareg groups around Timbuktu.

Timbuktu, a Venerable Crossroads

Timbuktu continued to be a primary crossroads. In 1798, it was "nearly the size of Tetouan," with about 10,000 inhabitants.[9] It was an unfortified market town where people worked cotton and were involved in the salt trade. Aside from a few details, it was much the same as it was when René Caillié described it thirty years later:

> The city of Timbuktu is perhaps three miles in circumference. It forms a kind of triangle: the houses are large, not very tall, and have only one floor. Some of them have a small room over the entranceway. They are built of round bricks, rolled by hand and dried in the sun. The walls resemble and are about the height of those of Jenne.
>
> The streets of Timbuktu are clean and wide enough for horsemen to ride three abreast. Inside and out, there are many almost circular straw huts like those of Fulani herders. They are used to house the poor and slaves, who sell wares for their masters.
>
> Timbuktu has seven mosques, including two large ones, each topped by a brick tower with an interior staircase.[10]

The area dependent on the city apparently covered "fifteen days" (by foot). The region had virtually forgotten that it was under Moroccan control. It was still governed by a caste made up of descendants of soldiers who had come from the north long before to conquer the Songhai Empire of Gao. The caste was known as the Arma (from the Arabic al-Ruma, tirailleurs). Its members chose from among themselves the local pasha, or military leader, who acted as a kind of governor for the region. In 1828, the explorer René Caillié met the last pasha of Timbuktu, Uthman b. Abu Bakr, five years before he was expelled by the Fulani conqueror Seku Ahmadou. Over time, an Arma "governing class" had been formed out of a dozen leading Arab-Berber families. This ethnic allegiance had been imported from Morocco but had lost all real meaning and could be detected in just a few customs and prohibitions. The Arma divided themselves into marrakshi (those from Marrakech) and Fasi (those from Fez). Marrakshi could not wear indigo cloth, and Fasi were not allowed to eat certain fruit. This mixed social and political group had melted into the rest of the population both culturally and physically.

Map 2.1   **Principal African Peoples and States at the Dawn of the Nineteenth Century** (just before the Great Jihads)

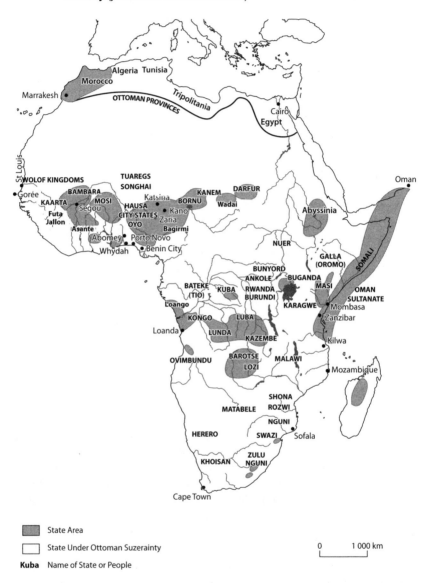

State Area

State Under Ottoman Suzerainty

Kuba   Name of State or People

0   1 000 km

The great lineages were identified by their political power and the economic control guaranteed by repeated access to power. Some Arma leaders accumulated great wealth: a clear example of this was when, in 1800, Caid Abu-Bakr b. Mubarak al-Dari gave a friendly chief "one hundred bars of salt, ten *rial* (*douros*) of silver, eleven caftans of fine fabric with matching accessories and bonnets."[11] In addition to their military earnings, most took part in commercial activities for income, acting as *diatigi* offering hospitality and protection to rich merchants from the north. Their tribal groups included, in the same area of the city, people who shared an ancestor, their slaves, their freed slaves, and their *haratin* (black slaves). From the seventeenth century on, they had to cope both with the Saharan Tuareg nomads who came from the Adrar to establish semisedentary camps in the Niger Valley, and with the Bambara (or Bamana) in the Segu area, who were flourishing thanks to the farming hinterland of the Muslim principalities between the two rivers.

The Arma resisted the Tuaregs only through hasty raids. Their small military scope was equal to their political insignificance. They had been avoiding Bambara villages since a catastrophic expedition at the beginning of the seventeenth century. However, they needed them to supply Jenne and Timbuktu with grain.

The Pachalik no longer had any control over the outlying areas. It was reduced to four settlements along the river that were virtually independent from one another: the Jenne enclave, and the Timbuktu, Bamba, and Gao areas. In the Gao region, the Arma accounted for nearly a quarter of the total population, and the caid's power still appeared strong at the end of the nineteenth century. However, regardless of their decline, the Arma in both Timbuktu and Jenne still considered themselves to be superior to the Tuaregs, as well as to the Songhai and Bambara, despite the formidable Segu Kingdom nearby.

At the beginning of the nineteenth century, the most powerful group in Timbuktu was the Kunta, a large family of Saharan Arab origin. Kunta members formed a network of priests and merchants who had been playing an important role linking the desert and Sahel, and Tuaregs, Moors, Jula, and Bambara for a century. Their essential function as intermediaries for long-distance trade made it easy for them to practice a flexible form of Sufism. Ahmad al-Bakkay quickly became the most eminent representative of the group. Around 1832, he was warmly received at Sokoto by Uthman dan Fodio. He was also able to oppose the rising ambitions of Al Hajj Umar Tall, partly because he had close ties to the new Muslim leader of Masina, Seku Ahmadu.

The Pagan Dynamism of the Bambara Kingdoms

Bambara peoples, who spoke a Mande language close to that of the Malinke, lived to the southeast and southwest of Timbuktu. They held power in the 1800s. The rise of the Segu Kingdom had increased conflicts between the impoverished Bambara farmers (from whom came the first king, Mamri Koulibali) and the Marka, Islamized Soninke who had become rich through trade in the area. The Bambara of Segu (who are now known as the Bamana) were conquerors and had even occupied Timbuktu in about 1670, an embarrassing episode that the writer of the *Tarikh* agreed to omit.

Downstream from Sansanding, the Fulani blocked Bambara progress to the south of Masina. They had also resisted the Jula of Kong. In contrast, to the east of the Niger River, their expansion was facilitated by the rulers of Jenne, who had built fortified villages more or less everywhere to protect themselves from Fulani, Songai, and Arma raids. Their lands screened Timbuktu from the nomads of Masina and Gourma, and also from the Tuaregs, against whom they sometimes helped the Arma.

The heart of the Segu Kingdom was situated in the middle valley of the river, between Bamako to the west and the Masina delta to the northeast. Owing to its geography, population density, and strategic position, Segu was known even to Whites on the coast in the nineteenth century. The river provided water in all seasons, making irrigated farming possible, and the rainfall was appropriate for both grain and cotton. Above all, Segu had come to control trade between the desert and Sahel to the north, which provided salt, horses, and livestock, and the savanna bordering the forests to the south, which provided gold, slaves, and kola nuts. The area attracted camel caravans from the north, donkey trains from the south, and fleets of pirogues on the river, which provided abundant fish. The regime was a combination of Bambara warriors and industrious farmers who provided Marka merchants with grain and slaves. The Marka produced cotton and indigo, ran the textile industry, and controlled the caravans that carried everything. Warriors were all the more devoted to the king because they were former slaves and prisoners of war. They made up the *tonjon* and held strategic positions with respect to power and trade. In the second half of the eighteenth century, one of these individuals became so strong that he usurped power, and created the Jarra Dynasty, of which three kings in a row reigned from 1750 to 1827. Under their reign the government became more structured: a series of subordinate but relatively independent provinces were acknowledged in exchange for tribute. Outside of the provinces, to the south and west, the country was open to raids on livestock, grain, and slaves.[12]

To the southwest there was the Bambara state of Kaarta, which was well situated for contact with the Senegambian trade network. Evidence of this connection is in the Bambara use of cotton cloth as a monetary equivalent (which it had adopted). They were also connected with the upper Niger, where cowries were preferred.[13] From the mid-eighteenth century, Kaarta had been dominated by a group of Bambara who had fled the civil wars in Segu. Within the group, known as the Masasi, the primary Coulibaly lineages vied for power. Kaarta was a vast Sahelian land that covered approximately

200 square miles and had some 250,000 inhabitants. Most were Soninke, and the various groups shared the diversity characteristic of the area. This was a zone of transition where Soninke, Malinke, and Bambara sedentary farmers as well as Fulani shepherds generally got along well, except during the frequent droughts, which gave rise to quarrels. A varied and more or less syncretic set of polytheist religious practices corresponded to the mosaic of peoples. The Malinke were rather open, while the Bambara had a centralized ritual in which priests belonging to the primary royal courts practiced fertility rites using altars and sacred objects (*bori*). The Soninke were Muslim, at least in principle. The Islam of the Fulani was acknowledged but not especially respected. This eclecticism mirrored the structure of a contact economy based on a combination of regional and international trade. The area, which produced meat, milk, and leather, also supplied beasts of burden and horses for cavalry; horses were exported to both Senegambia and the Upper Niger. Farther away, Kaarta was a crossroads for Moorish caravans that came to trade salt, gum arabic, and livestock for slaves, kola nuts, gold, and fabric from the south and Senegambia. To the west, along the Kolombine River, which is a tributary of the Senegal, the population density was eighty inhabitants per square mile, which was considerable for an area where the "famine season" could last from April to the October harvests. The dense population resulted from the flood zone used for growing millet, which made two harvests possible—the main one in the fall and the other one in February. A slave system as hierarchical as that of the Moors provided the mainly Soninke population with many hands for working the land. A long tradition of cottage industry and trade also gave rise to quite a few towns of several thousand inhabitants.

Toward the less prosperous south, the villages of the Malinke who, like the Bambara, practiced a minimum of domestic slavery, rarely exceeded 500 inhabitants and subsisted on small-scale agriculture, raising livestock, and hunting. Only the center, which was inhabited mainly by the Soninke, had a well-established political tradition with, as in Senegambia, a clear dichotomy between political and military lineages, and commercial and religious lineages. Because they lacked strong kinship ties owing to their recent migration, the Masasi Bambara maintained control largely through the *tonjon*, a body of warriors and bureaucrats attached to the court, which differed from the system used at Segu. In peacetime, the *tonjon* military combat units acted as garrison forces for the princely cities. When the king died, they played a major role in the wars of succession. The pretenders from various lineages each lived in different fortified towns, and were protected by their own *tonjons*, surrounded by blacksmiths, leatherworkers, griots, and bodyguards armed with old guns in poor condition that "were dangerous only to those who used them."[14] They had no land claims, but also did not seek to integrate the traditional chiefs.

They lived as parasites and predators, requiring their subjects to pay tribute and taxes and enjoying the spoils of war: male prisoners were enrolled in the army or sold as slaves, while female prisoners were distributed among the royal princes to fortify the propagation of dynasty. In the 1820s, the Masasi succeeded in expanding to the east at the expense of the Segu Kingdom. They later had to yield to the Fulani Empire of Masina, and were never able to subjugate the Moors, whose horse- and camel-riding warriors were too fast for them.

While it was unpopular, the system, relatively well known thanks to French explorer Jean-Baptiste Raffenel's forced stay in 1847, was maintained until the Fulani conquest toward the middle of the century.

The Bornu Kingdom and Malinke and Soninke Chiefdoms

To the east, beyond Hausaland, which the Fulani began occupying in the early nineteenth century, were the desert steppes of the central Sudan. Since the mid-sixteenth century, the land had been drying out; problems were accentuated by the major famines in the eighteenth century. The drought increased pressure from the Tuaregs on the area formerly dominated by the Songai of Gao. The Tuaregs had come down from the Aïr Mountains, and destabilized the Bornu Kingdom. The traditional Bornu king, the *mai*, exercised flexible power that was attentive to Muslim influences conveyed by trade with the north, but also faithful to customary animist practices. The mai, who had tried to support the Hausa against the advancing Fulani of Uthman dan Fodio, was unable to hold off the fanatical troops of Sokoto. Routed in 1809 and dispossessed of half the country, he transferred his capital to Kurnawa and, discredited, abdicated in favor of his son. The latter had no choice but to seek the support of a leading local religious authority: Malam Muhammad El-Amin el-Kanemi, whom he offered to reward with half of the revenue from the freed provinces.[15] From then on, the mai's power was nothing more than a sham behind which Sheikh El-Kanemi operated as the real leader of the country thanks to his charisma and a strong army of Kanembu warriors. A modern thinker, he took advantage of the area's livestock resources and the farms around Lake Chad, and especially of its role as a hub for the trans-Saharan slave trade. Yet, he was careful to entertain cordial relations with the English, who were putting growing pressure on the desert and from whom he hoped to obtain weapons and cannons. (In 1825, Sheikh El-Kanemi received the English explorers Dixon Denham and Hugh Clapperton.)

To the west, the upper valley of the Senegal River was populated by Mande-speaking peoples, who acted as links between the Niger River Valley and Senegambia. They formed a mosaic of small peoples torn apart by struggles for succession among weak chiefs: the Soninke of Gadaja and Gi-dimaka to the north and upstream of Futa Toro, and the Malinke of Khasso and Bambuk between the Senegal and Faleme rivers. No group had more than 50,000 members. They were settled in villages without any centralized organization, which made them vulnerable to Moorish raids from the right bank and subject to Bambara demands. Like the Bambara, the Soninke had a social hierarchy that distinguished not only among free people, people belonging to castes and slaves, but also between warrior and merchant lineages. The traders, who were more likely to say they were Muslim, maintained constant contact with other places, including some that were very far away, such as Saint-Louis at the mouth of the river and sites along caravan roads in the Sahel and Sahara. Warriors lived in smaller, less prosperous villages, and created conflicts that often went against commercial interests. They recognized the leadership of the Bathily lineage, which broke in two toward the middle of the nineteenth century. Villages upstream grouped together under the name of Makhana and allied themselves with the Bambara of Kaarta. Downstream, they took the name of Goy and instead took the side of the Fulani of Futa Toro.

François Manchuelle[16] has shown how the alluring possibility of making money attracted migrant Soninke workers. The trend began as soon as the French returned at the beginning of the nineteenth century and increased as the century progressed. Soninke peasants put their slaves to work produc-ing grain (millet and rice) destined to feed slaves held on the coast. Starting in the 1830s, peanut farming changed the course of migration; the Soninke were among the first *navetanes*, migrants used by Senegambian farmers. In 1848, they were growing over half of the peanuts produced in Gambia. (The word *navetane*, derived from the Wolof *nawet*, which means "rainy season," appeared in the 1920s.[17]) Very early, opportunities offered in ports attracted even Soninke princes to the coast, either to trade or to hire them-selves out to Whites as "laptots" (servants, militiamen, or sailors). Service proved profitable. Throughout the entire nineteenth century, the French allowed their African soldiers to have booty, including slaves. As a result of the fight against the Moors and jihad leaders, engaging as a mercenary became rather prestigious, and above all, lucrative; soldiering was more profitable than farming in the interior. In 1791, the leading example was the father of a Makhana chief, who had been a laptot in Saint-Louis in his youth. Like the Krou, who had long been doing the same on the Slave Coast, the Soninke made great profits through working for Whites. When they returned home, this enabled them to acquire wives and slaves, and to gather around themselves the dependents, judges, and hangers-on necessary to have their status acknowledged in the clan. This trend began as early as 1885 since it is estimated that at that date between 11 and 14 percent of adult men in the Bakel area had worked for Whites.[18]

Upstream, the Khasso Kingdom was in decline on both sides of the Upper Senegal River. A dynasty of Fulani origin had established a relatively large state there in the seventeenth century. Struggles over succession divided the country in the following century. At the beginning of the nineteenth century, the lands of the former royal family were limited to a few villages around Medina. Finally, Bambuk continued to attract people thanks to the gold produced there on a small scale by hand: men brought the ore up from depths of thirty to forty feet, and women panned the riverbeds and separated the gold from the gangue. Gold dust and jewelry were sold to the caravans that crossed the land. The ground was stony and poor. Mountain villages, some of which had 2,000 inhabitants, were protected by natural ramparts and strong walls. They were used as places of refuge for a disparate population that had been chased from Senegambia and included dispossessed dynasties, escaped slaves, and victims of raids. The most famous of these centers was Farbanna, where captives were set free after five years and fugitive slaves were never turned over. Bambuk attracted the greed of both the Africans and the French, while defying the governing classes of Khasso and Bundu.[19]

Senegambia, a Syncretic Space

To the west, beyond Futa Toro, home of a well-rooted, ancient form of Islam, there was Senegambia. It was the only area in Africa where European trade had spread inland by grafting onto native trade networks, aside from the backcountry of Loanda and Zambesian Mozambique. British ships traveled 300 miles up the Gambia River, and the French went twice as far up the Senegal River during the high-water season from August to December though there was a hiatus during the Napoleonic wars. They maintained active trade relations with Soninke and Malinke merchants, and attracted Moorish caravans that brought gum arabic into the river area. Since neither the English (who occupied Saint-Louis at the mouth of the Senegal River and Goree across from Cape Vert until 1816) nor the French had the means to invest in the backcountry directly, they maintained good relations with the region's merchants, at least in the first half of the century. The merchants acknowledged them as "masters of the water" on the condition that they were acknowledged as "masters of the land." Senegambians became used to seeing a few Whites, accompanied by many Africans, traveling into the backcountry every year. The local name of Saint-Louis was Ndar, and many of its inhabitants, who were Muslim, were familiar with villages along the river as well as in Futa Toro. The Futanke organized markets to supply Saint-

Louis with grain, and levied a trading tax on the river. Contact was structured and beneficial to both parties.

The small Wolof kingdoms were distinguished by their degree of Islamization, which varied. The coastal kingdoms, such as that of the Serere, were the least inclined to convert. All of the groups lived according to a similar social structure, which was all the more hierarchical because it was based on a multilayered history. At the top of the social scale, the nobility was composed of old families that held the political power. Their warrior class had allowed them to fight for power and win it from marabouts in earlier periods. These warriors, called the *tyeddo*, were originally slaves owned by the king. However, free peasants, *jambur*, demanded a say in political decisions as free people, superior in status to the *tyeddo*. Peasants were superior in number but not in power. Below these classes were the castes of artisans and griots who, as in the rest of western Africa, played major roles as dependents of great families. Finally, there were the slaves who performed most tasks and had been well integrated into the social system ever since the Atlantic slave trade had been sharply reduced. Naturally, there were many tensions among the groups, between chiefs and marabouts, peasants and warriors, and slaves and the others. There was great internal political insecurity, but everyone found it profitable to trade with the coast.[20]

Southern Jula: Gonja and Salaga, the Kong Kingdom

Southward down to the woodlands, Muslim Jula merchants to the west and Hausa merchants to the east had already appeared in the forest states on the Atlantic coast and inland. The Jula had come into contact with the Portuguese in the sixteenth century. There is mention of Muslim and *Malaye* (probably in reference to ancient Mali) merchants in the Dahomey Kingdom in the eighteenth century. However, Muslims did not descend en masse toward the forest because, for them as for Europeans, it was less dangerous and more profitable to use people from the coast as intermediaries for trade. Penetration followed the course of the Volta Valley, as Mandinke-speaking horsemen had come down from Mali. With the help of Muslim traders of Jula origin, known locally as Wangarawa, they created a small state known as the Gonja Kingdom to the north of the Black Volta River. The cultural mixture was similar to that of the Hausa. Converted chiefs maintained many native rituals through the device of "priests of the land" and by transforming objects of Muslim origin, such as fragments of manuscripts, into amulets and medicine. The common people generally remained animist. Islam was also known in the three primary Moagi (Mosi) kingdoms that ran north-south. Among the Mosi of the north, in Ouagadougou and Yatenga, Islam was feared as the religion of invaders.

In the south, which was protected by its relative distance, the king was just as likely to consult local priests as the Jula *yarna* or Hausa imam. Farther away, in the small state of Wa, Islam was also gaining ground: in the first half of the nineteenth century, the local Muslims sent their *imam* to study at Kong (to the north of present-day Ivory Coast), which, under Jula control, became a center for Islamic studies.

Salaga in Gonja played an intermediary role. This market town had been established by Jula merchants around 1775, but quickly came under the control of the Asante of Kumasi. Salaga was the supply center for kola nuts produced in the southern forests, which were carried by Mosi donkeys and sold as far away as Jenne by Jula merchants and to the Hausa throughout Yoruba lands. Contact with the north was so great that Hausa became the most widely spoken language in Salaga. At the end of the eighteenth century, the Asante Kingdom began to use Muslim scholars to structure its government. It also used them as astrologists and doctors. The great reformer, Osei Bonsu (1800–1823), continued this policy. In the 1820s, when the Asante began negotiations with the British, Muslim scholars acted as intermediaries. Cordial relations were even established with Seku Ahmadu of Masina. However, the relationship gradually deteriorated. In the second half of the century, the Asante kings, concerned by rising Muslim power, finally established tight control over Islamic presence in the country by assigning the merchants to a specific quarter. They loosened their control only after the sack of Kumasi (1874), when they asked for Muslim help against the British. By then, the jihad had completely shaken the established structures.

However, coastal agglomerations did not need Muslim merchants to prosper. At the dawn of the nineteenth century, they were in full expansion, no matter what their politics or status (centralized state, city-state, kinship-based society, or even British colony, such as Freetown in Sierra Leone).

A Major Focus: Trans-Saharan Trade

In the Niger River Belt, the weakening of central power did not necessarily lead to the country's ruin because the foundations of interregional trade were not threatened. At both Timbuktu and Jenne, livestock was produced locally, and in the backcountry many other things were found. People ate well; the basic diet consisted of rice or millet couscous mixed with fresh meat provided by the Fulani, or dried or fresh fish, of which there was also an abundant supply. Wheat and bread, which Moroccans had introduced, were reserved for the highest classes. The cloth industry was based on cotton and wool, indigo and *da*, a kind of linen used for making fishing nets. Wax for candles was produced, along with the iron of Bandugu, and kola nuts and gold were imported from the forests. In contrast to the Atlantic slave trade, the trans-Saharan slave trade did not simply plunder societies. It certainly carried as many if not more slaves, but also goods and ideas. A whole array of items ranging from food, salt in particular, to manufactured products continued to make their way from the Maghreb to the savanna, and vice versa, following routes that had barely changed since the Middle Ages. What had changed was not the amount of trade, which, as we will see, had the same tendency to grow in the nineteenth century, but its overall economic and political impact.

The Trans-Saharan Routes

The western route was unfailingly maintained by the rulers of Morocco, who wanted gold and slaves. Starting in 1765, the new port of Mogador became the primary gateway to the sea for caravans from the south. In the eighteenth century, Goulimine became the relay station from Morocco, replacing Taghawust, which had played that role in the preceding centuries. Caravans were guided by "good Muslims" to Shinguetti and Wadan. At the end of the eighteenth century, these cities were inhabited by approximately 2,000 Udaya, who watched over the rock salt storehouses. From there, caravans went to Saint-Louis in Senegal by way of Trarza lands, or to Galam or Hodh by way of Brakna country. From Hodh, a number of routes went to the Bambara kingdoms of Kaarta and Segu, where salt and horses were traded for slaves and gold.

Similar trade was carried out more to the center, between Segu and Gumbu in the Sahel. A route also linked Walata to Sansanding and the interior delta. Pirogues traveling up the Niger from Segu did not break bulk; Sansanding gradually stopped depending on Jenne for its supply of products from the Maghreb, and became a hub between the Jula to the south and Moors and even Moroccans to the north. To the east, the city of Agades at the southern foot of the Aïr Mountains became the crossroad for trade between Hausaland, and Bornu, and also from Gao, Tripoli, and Egypt.

Trade and meetings between Berbers and Arabs from the north, and the Soninke, Futanke and Wolof from the south were not new. On both edges of the desert, mixing had been growing since the Moroccan incursions on the Niger. In 1670, a jihad of Berber origin had affected not only the desert area, but also the Black African states of Waalo, Kajoor, Wolof, and Futa. In the nineteenth century, owing to the growing clash between expanding desertification and increasing demographic pressure, there were more opportunities for conflict in every direction: between people from the north ("Whites"), between people from the south ("Blacks"), and between "Whites" and "Blacks." Indeed, these terms tended to be used by the people themselves, who were very often of similar skin color but had cultural and historical differences. On the

Map 2.2   **The Maghreb and West Africa in the Nineteenth Century:
Trans-Saharan Routes**

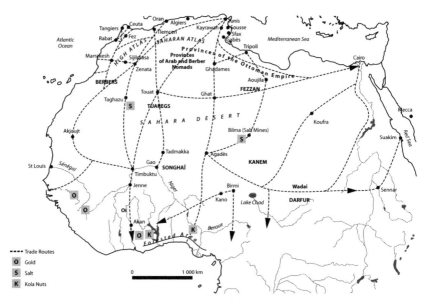

fringes of the desert, both were mixed, but elsewhere political choices and
economic strategies differentiated those who could be considered dominant
(the "Whites") from those who were dominated (the "Blacks").

Warriors and Merchants

Especially toward the west in the first half of the nineteenth century, two parallel hierarchies were formed within the two groups: on one hand there were
warriors, and on the other merchants and clerics. On the side of the "Whites"
(whom the French called Moors), the division was between Hassani warriors,
who were often of Arab origin, and Zwaya merchants, who were instead of
Berber ancestry. Both categories acknowledged the territorial authority of the
same emir, and the emirian families were divided into two great tribes: the
Trarza to the extreme west, and the Brakna, who lived at the latitude of the
middle Senegal River and began trading with the French as the latter traveled
up the river. The Hassani were great nomads who used camels and horses to
ensure their mobility and usually lived in small groups. Their highly structured system included dependent tribes of herdsmen, known as the Znaga.
The Zwaya instead engaged in transhumant livestock raising. They were
organized into larger camps and used more slaves. Through war and slave
raids, the Hassani scoured the south of the Senegal River and shores of the

Niger for Black peasants. They often raided fields for women and children, and held them for tribute or took them to oases to labor on farms and maintain date palm plantations. In such cases, the "White" policy was based on terror spread by incursions on the left bank of the river. The "Blacks" had even more trouble defending themselves because they did not have the means to take revenge by raids in the desert. The primary Black Senegambian, Wolof, and Tukuloor leaders on both sides of the river, as well as the Soninke and Bambara chiefs, finally had to acknowledge the supremacy of the Moors. They paid them tribute when they made their annual expeditions. The Trarza warriors, who were more centralized, were the most terrible: they came down into Waalo and Kajoor lands, even all the way to Bawol. The Brakna targeted the Futa instead, and went as far as Wolof country. The French put an end to these practices in the second half of the century, and forced the Moors to stay on the right bank of the river.

The Zwaya also managed to achieve the same end, but did so by placing the emphasis on the spread of religion and trade, which also required slaves, as long as they were infidels. The most influential group south of the Senegal was the Idaw al-Hajj, who spread Islam in Waalo and Kajoor, which became their home in the seventeenth century. They played an important role in the marabouts' wars in the area from that time forward.

Toward the Niger Bend, the distinctions between warriors and holy men, and between Berbers and Arab bedouins were less clear. All of these groups supplied salt, as well as horses and weapons to the great leaders of the Fulani jihads. The Fulani paid them in raided grain and slaves captured when their cavalry charged. At the edges of the desert and in oases, male slaves were used in the fields, and female slaves as domestic servants. The system culminated mid-century with the formidable rise of Al Hajj Umar, which brought the demand for horses and supply of slaves to a paroxysm.

At the time, contact between the people living in the desert and their neighbors to the south was very intense because desertification in preceding centuries had made nomads dependent on the grain supplied by or stolen from Black peasants. At the beginning of the century, desert demand for supplies was much higher than that of the Whites and their allies on the coast, who remained few in number; there were between 10,000 and 13,000 inhabitants at Saint-Louis between 1800 and 1840, in comparison with about 55,000 Trarza and 60,000 Brakna at about the same time.[21]

This is why, when the French returned in 1817, they considered Waalo to be a breadbasket. They tried to establish plantations in the flood plain of the lower river, and negotiated with the Idaw al-Hajj for workers (who were probably slaves) in 1819. The plan was poorly conceived and stalled in 1831. However, faced with the French threat, Trarza Emir Muhammad al-

Habib nonetheless tried to guarantee his formal supremacy by marrying the daughter of the *brak* (king) of Waalo in the early 1830s. This union resulted into the first direct conflict between the French and the Trarza, in 1833–35. A second conflict occurred in 1854–58, during which the French blocked the river and the Trarzas' grain supply. In response, the Trarza refused to sell gum arabic, which was a product in growing demand in Europe in the first part of the century. The Trarza lost 1,000 men, 30,000 head of livestock, and 200 horses. Businessmen from Saint-Louis and Zwaya merchants intervened to reestablish trade routes. In 1858, the French governor of Senegal, Louis Faidherbe, prohibited the Trarza from crossing the river. At the same time he offered to act as an intermediary to eradicate the tribute that the Black states had to pay to the Moors. This prefigured the Senegal-Mauritania border and the beginnings of French imperialism. It was received in different ways by the Trarza themselves: warriors were eliminated but Zwaya merchants rejoiced over the newfound commercial peace.

Until the middle of the eighteenth century, Moroccans had conducted quasi-annual slave raids on the Niger. However, in the nineteenth century, primary trade was not in gold, slaves, or cloth from the savanna. Cotton was in competition with blue cotton cloth from India. The leading commerce was in grain for salt. The Soninke, who were in constant contact with the Berbers, gradually formed a mixed population along caravan routes on the fringes of the desert. By the beginning of the nineteenth century, given the degree to which the desert had advanced, the formerly Soninke capital of the Jarra Kingdom was incorporated into the Saharan world. As early as 1796, Mungo Park described it as a major settlement, the inhabitants of which were almost all Black and paid heavy tribute to Moorish imperial protectors. From that point on, Soninke interest in trade never flagged. They had major dealings with both the Muslims to the north and the French in Saint-Louis. The Soninke peasants-warriors-marabouts used the lengthy dry season, which is the off-season for farming in such latitudes, to travel all around West Africa, acquiring kola nuts and slaves in exchange for cotton cloth and horses. The nuts and slaves were brought home, where they were sold. Soninke lands also exported grain to the Sahara and even the Maghreb. Therefore the Soninke migratory tradition long preceded the labor market migrations that were so powerful in the twentieth century.[22]

Salt and Grain

The people of the desert ate mainly *aysh,* a porridge of sorghum and milk, which was the basis for their only meal of the day, taken in the evening. The environment forced them to seek the grain further and further to the south, where they also had to pasture their flocks in the dry season. For the Bambara, salt was so important that the word they used to designate the Sahara was *kokhodugu*, which means "land of salt." In the western Sudan, caravans carrying salt mainly from Ijil to the northwest were based in the Adrar Mountains, by that time located in the middle of the desert. The route from Ijil was less dry than the one more to the east, which led to the main deposits of Taghaza and Taoudeni. From the Adrar Mountains, caravans could reach Timbuktu by passing through the Tichit oasis, a great crossroads for caravans then inhabited by some 10,000 people. Before the French intervention, huge rest stations there could accommodate caravans of 200 or more camels, and were places of remarkable cultural diversity. From the Adrar to the savanna, the sorghum route took a month to travel. However, if the same caravan also carried salt, it took most of the year, especially if it had already delivered the grain on the north shore of the Sahara along the fringes of the Maghreb.[23] For the people of the desert, trade was profitable because a bar of salt was worth twenty to twenty-five measures of sorghum, except if there was a famine, as in 1833 when there was parity between salt and grain. In the first half of the nineteenth century, the operations were largely controlled by the Kunta; the influence of that large group, which had until then dominated the corridor between the Touat and Timbuktu, increased under the sway of a few Qadiri mystics, the most famous of whom was Sidi al-Mokhtar al Kunti (d. 1811). The Kunta's rivals included the Idaw Ali tribe, which was won over by the Tijaniyya between 1780 and 1830. The problem for Zwaya groups was thus to protect themselves against pillaging, and their storage techniques were varied. Grain was rarely buried by nomads, as it was in the north of the Sahara, but was instead kept in large leather bags in the middle of the camp or, as in Walata, stored in fortified buildings. Salt was buried in the sand, where it would keep for several years.

Horses and Gum Arabic

In addition to salt, desert peoples traded horses. There has been a tendency to focus on the horse trade prior to the sixteenth century. There is every reason to believe that the desertification that followed was rather favorable to horses in the northern savanna because it broke the hold of trypanosomiasis. In the nineteenth century, both the coastal Wolof and peoples of the Niger River Basin acquired horses in exchange for a considerable number of slaves. The number of slaves offered was significantly higher because the Atlantic slave trade was coming to an end. To the west, the little Senegambian pony was ineffective as a war horse. In order to obtain horses for cavalry, Arab or Maghrebian horses had to be crossed with the local pony to create *mbars* or *mbayars,* which were more resistant to disease than imported horses. Toward the end of the century, a "river horse" developed, which was less fragile than those imported from the north. Generally, they were raised in the Tagant in the northern Sahel because bringing them from the Maghreb was too perilous. The few existing estimates indicate that there were between 5,000 and 10,000 horsemen in Kajoor at the beginning of the nineteenth century, which was more than twice the number thirty years earlier. It placed Kajoor well above Waalo, which had only 2,000. Apparently, the Kajoor *damel* even had horses brought from the Marrakech area. In 1789, he was ready to buy a desert horse for the fabulous price of 100 slaves, 100 cows, and twenty camels![24]

Cavalry developed even more on the Niger. The demand for horses gave rise to an increase in the slave trade. In the first decades of the century, a good horse was worth ten to thirty slaves. Horses died quickly because the climate did not suit them. In the second half of the century, a horse cost only one to three slaves. The drop in price is less indicative of an increase in the price of slaves than of the horse's decline. In Senegambia, Europeans had virtually eliminated opportunities for raids. Above all, local horse breeding had developed, aided by desertification. The Fulani raised hybrid horses as well as cattle; Al Hajj Umar bought horses at Segu, and Samori procured them in Soninke country. Horses from the north, which the French were acquiring at the turn of the twentieth century at a rate of fifteen per year, arrived in too poor a state to be very useful.

In the meantime, gum arabic had replaced horses as the leading item of trade. Gum arabic was produced by several varieties of acacia trees, which were grown on plantations that moved southward as desertification progressed. Toward the end of the seventeenth century, acacia plantations stopped 120 miles north of Portendick; a century later, they had moved 200 miles south. The shift can be seen in the descent of trading points along the Atlantic coast. By the beginning of the nineteenth century, gum arabic trade had virtually disappeared from the ports of Arguin and Portendick where sources of drinking water were no longer found; virtually all had been moved to along the Senegal River. In the two preceding centuries, massive imports of indigo-dyed Indian cotton fabric and *guinées* (a guinée was a piece of cotton cloth measuring approximately eighteen yards by one yard) were traded for gum arabic. The Indian cloth and guinées had gradually replaced local cotton cloth in Moor lands. In addition, desert people had to travel ever farther south to obtain grain. One of the reasons for the increased demand for gum arabic was that more uses were being found for it. Local people had long used it as a remedy for diarrhea, a thickener for drinks, an ingredient in cosmetics, and to make glue and ink. Europeans did likewise, and soon they used it for preparing dyes. Demand increased rapidly with the growth of the textile industry and

Table 2.1

Trading Terms (1776–1849): Value of a Ton of Gum Expressed in Guinées
(Pieces of Cotton Cloth)

Year(s)	Guinées	Index
1776	14.3	54
1788	31.9	121
1823–27	51.5	196
1830	41.1	156
1833	63.1	240
1838	70.6	268
1849	50.2	191

Sources: Curtin, 1975; Webb, 1995.

popularity of printed cotton cloth. Demand was also created by the use of gum arabic in copper etching. Exports from the western Sahara doubled over the course of the eighteenth century, and toward the end they reached a thousand tons. Production doubled again in the 1830s (2,000 tons). In the nineteenth century, gum arabic was the only product that could be exported from Saint-Louis by people who were not French. It became a form of currency for paying for merchandise imported from both London and France. From 1790 to 1870, when the Atlantic slave trade became increasingly impossible in the area, it was almost Senegal's only product. This continued until, at the end of the century, eastern Africa, particularly the Sudan, took over. It remained Senegal's top export until peanut production finally surpassed it. Exports of gum arabic increased quickly in part because Europeans made a handsome profit on it: bought at the beginning of the century from Saint-Louis traders for between £60 and £90 (at a price 25 percent higher than in the interior), it was resold in London and Paris for at least twice that much, between £160 and £180.[25] Therefore there were frequent "gum wars" among competing groups of European traders in the first half of the century. This was one of the major reasons that the French gradually took control of the river.[26]

The Moors were also interested in the trade because they made large profits on it in the first half of the century. Between 1788 and 1838, the worth of a ton of gum arabic went from 32 to 70 *guinées*.

In the area, the gum harvest carried out by slaves was convenient because it occurred in the dry season. It was well adapted to the work cycle of shepherds. At a rate of 3.5 ounces of gum per tree per year, and a production of 6.5 pounds for two and a half acres, a slave could harvest up to nine pounds of gum a day so that, in three months, the average length of the harvest, two workers could make up to a ton. This means that in the eighteenth century, 2,000 slaves, which was only a small percentage of those in the area, would have sufficed to produce all the gum exported. Even at the height of the gum trade in the first half of the nineteenth century, production was easily ensured by a slave population made up of people taken in raids in Black countries. The emir of the Trarza, assisted by the *shamsh* or the political and commercial leader of the Trarza Idaw al-Hadj, negotiated closely with traders in Saint-Louis, but other Zwaya groups also participated in the transactions.

The *grande traite* (big business) took place from February, when the waters receded, to July: the Zwaya harvested the gum in the dry season and carried it to the river on the backs of beasts of burden (donkeys and camels). Traders came up the river to the first ports, which were busiest during the rainy season, beginning in June–July. Two ports were in Trarza country: Darmankour, which was sixty miles from Saint-Louis, and the Desert, 2.5 miles farther. The third, the *Escale du Coq,* was 120 miles from Saint Louis in Brakna country, where the emir had an arrangement with his Tukuloor ally in Futa. Traders could spend long weeks there waiting for the caravans and delivering gifts, blankets, cloth, grain, and tea. They entrusted their items to intermediaries, *maîtres de langue* ("language masters"), responsible for intercepting caravan leaders to arrange transportation for goods. For boats larger than pirogues, the upper river was navigable only from July to December. Until the beginning of the nineteenth century, before the slave trade was prohibited by the British occupying Saint-Louis in the Napoleonic era, trade on the upper river had been very busy. Most slaves and gold came from that area. It had been the monopoly of the Galam Company, in the hands of Saint-Louis merchants, who had the exclusive right to navigate it during the rainy season. Until the 1820s, a few backwater merchants continued to trade grain, dried fish, and local crafts out of season, but the activity had greatly decreased. From 1824 on, after a few false starts, the colonial government liberalized trade on the upper Senegal River in the rainy season. Traders and river merchants took over the grain business in the relatively fertile area of Gajaaga. When the demand for gum arabic doubled in the 1830s, the season became longer, stretching from three months to six, from January to July. Competition increased in the ports between traders linked with Saint-Louis and Moorish gum producers, who continued to exact high fees and duties.[27]

Traders who had bought *guinées* at high prices at the beginning of the season, later risked finding themselves seriously in debt: gum producers could try to break their commercial agreements by threatening to bury their gum until the next season or simply offer it to the English in Gambia or at Portendick. It happened more than once in 1819. The same year, the emir of the Trarza sent a representative to Bathurst, which began doing business with him again. In 1825, a group of merchants established the British Portendick Company, which diverted up to 10 percent of the gum from the river, and even more during the French-Trarza war of 1834–36.

In 1837–42, strong competition combined with the effects of the economic crisis in Europe ruined many traders: the massive import of *guinées*, which had gone from about 50,000 to nearly 200,000 a year, and the collapse of industrial prices led to a major crisis on the river. Paris reacted by taking control in an authoritarian manner (the Royal Order of 1842): the river became once again the exclusive domain of a limited number of independent traders, namely those who had been involved in major trade since at least 1836 (before the crisis). European merchants and traders in Saint-Louis had to focus on the import-export business. Trade in the river ports was carefully regulated.

This measure, and especially the very poor years for gum arabic (1842–44), which pushed up the price, enabled traders to recover temporarily. However, the regulations went against the irrepressible free trade movement: the Second Republic began by opening the river to the entire indigenous population of "Saint Louis and dependencies." The military campaigns of Louis Faidherbe in 1854–58 completed the triumph of free commerce. This was the end of the traders' reign: firms were able to return to the river, and set purchase prices that became definitively very low. Whether they liked it or not, the Moorish emirs would be forced to accept that the duties they had levied since ancient times would be reduced to a standard rate of 3 percent. Senegambian peasants turned away from such trade in favor of peanut farming. The economy was becoming colonial.

The growing numbers of slaves sold to the north and trade of horses and grain for gum and *guinées*, which increased and became better defined in the nineteenth century, had the same result in the Sahel and in the desert. Both economic developments helped to reinforce and internalize the differentiation that had certainly existed for a long time, but had never had the same rigidity: that between the Whites from the north and the Blacks from the south. In the first half of the nineteenth century, trade and wars between the two groups had a greater impact than the problems caused by the Atlantic influence. Europeans remained a tiny minority since only in exceptional, relatively limited cases had they marked out a political territory. While their economic intervention may not have been limited, it was indirect: the partners in contact with one another were the Moors and Senegambians, and soldiers of the jihad and conquered peoples. The demand for grain, horses, and slaves was at the time greater toward the north than on the Atlantic coast; its major effect was an increase in conflict, violence, and slavery. The nomads of the desert, who in reality had long been a blend of Arabs, Berbers, Wolof, Soninke, and Futanke, developed a kind of identity based on a shared opinion of being superior, because White, in relation to the growing slave population along the fringes of the desert.

Whites no longer enslaved their brethren, unlike the Blacks of the savanna, and thus their internal wars no longer produced slaves. Colonial intervention occurred in Senegal at the middle of the century, which was relatively early, and fostered the exploitation and exacerbation of these contrasts by making the Senegal and Niger rivers the borders between White and Black lands.

The Sanusiyya and Slavery in the Central Sudan

In the central Sudan at the time, the frontier was more difficult to identify. The trade crossing the Sahara was inseparable from a group of Arab-Berber origin that was to settle very far to the south. This was the Sanusi brotherhood that, beginning in the mid-nineteenth century, spread from Cyrenaica to the shores of Lake Chad.

In the mid-nineteenth century, the brotherhood was both a link and a break between North Africa and Africa south of the Sahara owing to its astonishingly hybrid nature. Like the jihads, the movement was simultaneously religious, political, and economic. It was based on intense trade, which was only partly in slaves (as opposed to that of Rabīh a few years later), dominated by Arabic speakers and led by a Sufi reformer from North Africa. The founder of the brotherhood, Es Sanusi (also known as Muhammad, b. Ali Al-Sanusi), was of Berber-Saharan origin, born in southern Algeria (1787–1859). In 1837, after studying in Morocco and visiting the Middle East on the occasion of a pilgrimage to Mecca, he began to establish his power based on structures that were more organizational than intellectual. He decided to settle on the edges of the desert.[28] Al-Sanusi's doctrine centered on work and strict piety; fasting and prayer played major roles. The Sanusiyya brotherhood, like others of Maghrebian origin, began in Cyrenaica, between Egypt and Tripolitania. Al-Sanusi initially settled in the Djebel. From there the movement spread southward from the large oases to the heart of the Sahara. In 1847, Heinrich Barth passed through the area and probably met the first Sanusi without knowing who they were. Around 1854, the founder was living near Ghadames, between present-day Algeria, Tunisia, and Libya. At the time, Ghadames was one of the major crossroads for trans-Saharan trade. The Tuaregs controlled the area and protected the routes, while the people of Ghadames dominated trade. Three years later, Al-Sanusi was living in Jaghbud, in the middle of the desert, and then moved to Ghat, 400 miles south of Ghadames. The brotherhood also controlled the route to Wadai. The French presence in Algeria (the founder's disciple, Muhammad ben Abd Allah, was imprisoned in Bone) and the abolition of slavery in the Maghreb condemned the Sanusi followers to finding their fortune ever farther southward. They settled in oases that took the form of small independent principalities based on palm tree plantations, gardens, and commercial exchanges. While they called themselves "whites" and Arabs, most of the population was Black or very mixed, often descending from new slaves from south of the Sahara. Berber languages predominated. Social and political life was the result of opposition between and alliances among factions, clans, and tribes, and rivalries between neighboring groups made the overall system appear fluid. The south became a missionary goal: Touat, to the south of the Sahara, was reached in 1855–60. Muhammad al-Mahdi, the son and successor of Al-Sanusi, left Jaghbud in 1895 for Kufra. The brotherhood, which despite French myths never became hegemonic except in Cyrenaica, was expelled southward by the Italian conquest and fled into the African continent toward Borku. At its height, it covered the central and eastern Sahara from near the Nile to the Ajjer Mountains, and from southern Tunisia to Lake Chad.[29] The brotherhood became known to the French when they first attempted to penetrate the area in the mid-nineteenth century. After the 1870s, the French became as obsessed with trying to eliminate the brotherhood as they were with Rabīh. Yet, rooted deep in the desert, the brotherhood was declining. It did not resurface again until the early twentieth century, organizing a desperate resistance against European ambitions.

Jihad and the Religious Islam of Conquest

Islam was not new in Africa. In Senegambia, it began to spread out of the cities and into the countryside in the seventeenth century. However, it was at the end of the eighteenth century that an irrepressible movement began, which was to cause violent upheavals throughout the century. Islam was not the source of all the excesses, in particular the enslavement of people from virtually every ethnic group. Indeed, it was no more responsible for that than for the Nguni (including the Zulu) explosion at the beginning of the century or for the political creations of African slavers at the end of the century. Such internal inventions, which were often inspired by brilliant thinkers, cannot be dissociated from the overall history. The growth of slave trading in southern and eastern Africa by Boers, Arabs, and Indians partly explains the changes in the context, just as the prodromes of the Industrial Revolution played a role in West Africa. The closure of the Atlantic slave market left hordes of slaves on the internal market. Owing to their great number, they became a major source of internal labor. These complex interactions cannot be reduced to a simple relation of cause and effect.

Mysticism and Brotherhoods

All of Muslim Africa was affected by a mystical trend, called Sufism, which spread from Egypt. A number of factors contributed to the explosion: the decline of the Ottoman Empire unbalanced the Muslim world, the European intrusion was becoming threatening, and Wahhabite puritanism was influential. Wahhabitism was a fundamentalist movement that advocated a return to the strict Islam of the time of the Prophet and his immediate successors, the Patriarchs. It rejected practices that it considered unorthodox, but that were frequent in Africa, such as the worship of saints and pilgrimages to their tombs. The Fulani were not Wahhabites, but they were influenced by them.

Sufism spread toward the Maghreb and West Africa. Africa's great reformers, such as Ahmad b. Idris (Al-Sanusi's teacher in Mecca), Al-Tijani, and Al-Sanusi were all marked by the Moroccan intellectual milieu, which was encouraged in the mid-eighteenth century by the reforming Sultan Sidi Muhammad b. 'Abd Allah.[30] In West Africa, a parallel popular conversion was in progress, unlike in the Maghreb, which had long been Islamized. Sufist influence caused major political upheaval. It was based on the primacy of mystical knowledge, *faná* (absorption into God), through the special intermediary of the Prophet. The most ancient form was the Qadiriyya, which began in Baghdad in the twelfth century and was well represented in the North African tradition. From there, it entered the Niger Valley and then spread into Senegambia to the southwest from Kankan, and into Hausaland to the southeast through Takedda and Agades. In about 1850, it dominated the Fulani of the Sokoto caliphate. At the turn of the nineteenth century, one of the Qadiriyya's main teachers was the great Saharan Arab mystic Sidi al-Moukhtar al-Kabir (1729–1811), whose extreme piety was believed to give him the power to perform miracles. From southern Morocco, his reputation crossed the Sahel to Bornu and Hausaland. It made many converts among the Soninke, Jula, and Hausa, who were merchants used to adapting to unconverted trading partners.

Beginning at the end of the eighteenth century, the Qadiriyya, an elitist movement that had become a bastion of religious conservatism, was overtaken by another that was also born in Egypt. It was called the Tijaniyya, after its propagator, Sheik Ahmad al-Tijani (1737–1815). He came from Algeria and spread his teaching from Cairo to Fez, where he was buried. From there, his ideas diffused toward Mauritania and Senegal. In reaction to the aristocratic strictness of the Qadiriyya, the Tijaniyya was a populist movement. Though its proponents were highly educated, they willingly taught in Berber, Pular, Hausa, and other local languages, as well as in Arabic. Faith did not require erudition. The common people were in that respect the equals of the educated, as long as they all worked toward converting infidels. The movement suited common folk, young people, warriors; in short, all those who believed in action as much as in scholarship. They were fond of worshipping saints. They believed they needed a *wali* (holy man) to unite with the Prophet, and the best holy man was considered to be Tijani, because he had had a vision of the Prophet. Like Timbuktu, Agades remained not only a crossroads for trade, but also a center of Islamic learning. The city became the conduit for Sufi ideas. The doctrine spread quickly among the Tukuloor, the people of Kanem and Bagirmi, and the inhabitants of northern Nigeria; the Fulani, however, remained linked with the Qadiriyya.

These innovative movements spread rapidly because the *wali* who taught and those who sought their teaching led intrinsically itinerant lives.

The Tijaniyya Trigger

From 1825 on, the primary vector of the Tijaniyya in West Africa was Al hajj Umar, who brought the movement from Cairo after his pilgrimage. He began sowing its seeds along his route home through Sokoto and Hausaland, where he wrote some of his most important works.

Islam had begun expanding across the land before this period: in the Niger Valley, from Futa Toro in upper Senegal to Hausaland and beyond, all the way to Kanem and Bornu near Lake Chad. Spreading from Jenne, the diaspora of Jula merchants of Mande origin who controlled the caravan routes from the Mali Empire to the southern area of the Volta played a major role. After the decline of the medieval empires, the Mahdist ideal popularized the notion that the end of the world was near. It would be announced by the coming of a Mahdi, a savior, who would ensure the rule of universal justice. Here and there, this gave rise to jihads or holy wars. In the sixteenth and seventeenth centuries, it resulted in an explosion of "marabout revolutions," led in Senegambia by local learned saints against animist chiefs. In the seventeenth century, there was a religious renaissance of the Tuareg Ineslemen at Agades. In the eighteenth century, there was an attempt by the neighboring Fulani in Gobir against the royal authority, which was criticized for religious laxity.

In the second half of the eighteenth century, a series of holy wars erupted that were political as well as religious. In every case the sheikh succeeded in establishing a theocracy that completely revamped the existing order. The common denominator of the jihads was that they corresponded to a wave of Fulani demographic developments. There was a migratory expansion from west to east of a population that had until then kept a rather low profile. There, specific linguistic and physical features were resulting from a prehistoric flow of people toward the Senegal Valley as the desert advanced, which caused early blending (*metissage*) with local people. The demographic growth was related to the massive conversion of Fulani herdsmen who had until then been considered pagans living mainly from banditry in the margins of political structures and on the fringes of urban trading crossroads.

This demographic growth was probably connected to the increase in cattle. Usually, the focus is put on religious factors, but the pastoral dimension of the

Map 2.3   **West Africa: Primary Political Formations in the Nineteenth Century**

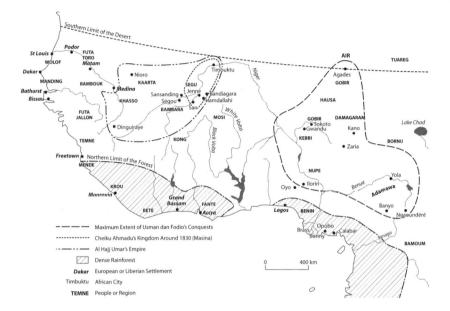

Fulbe lifestyle was a major impulse for their expansion. It has to be compared with what we know, for example, about the nineteenth-century enlargement of the Tutsi kingdoms of Rwanda and Burundi, which was motivated more by the expansion of the bovine population than by that of the human one. The same would be true of the Masai expansion down the line of the eastern Rift. Again, in southeastern Africa, the rapid spread of Nguni-ruled kingdoms from Zululand northward to Tanzania represented primarily the search of pastoral minorities for new grazing territory for their expanding herds. This point of view must to be added to the traditional view based solely on religious impact. It fits with recent research focusing on the interrelationship between political and ecological factors.

The Fulani jihads that succeeded in setting up Islamic states were initially domestic, as in Futa Toro, Futa Jallon, and Masina, and then involved conquest, as in Hausaland under the leadership of Uthman dan Fodio and in western Sudan under Al Hajj Umar. The mixture of Fulani and Muslim identities helped to create a formidable cultural unity, which was encouraged by circulation of traveling thinkers throughout the land. Al Hajj Umar, who came from Futa Toro, began his training in Futa Jallon. He taught the Pular in Hausaland, where he became friends with the sultan of Sokoto, Muhammad Bello. Muhammad Bello was the son and successor of Uthman dan Fodio, and remained a member of the Qadiriyya despite his friendship with Al Hajj Umar. Throughout their conquests, the Fulani considered themselves to be the elected people invested with a divine mission to make all of the west African savanna a Muslim land (*dar al-islam*).

The traditions describing the origins of the great leaders employ inventive means to underpin genealogies leading back to the founders of Islam: in 1812, Muhammad Bello of Sokoto penned the first written version of the tradition: according to his writings the Fulani would be descended, via the Torodbe of Futa Toro, from one of the first Arab conquerors of the Maghreb. Another tradition invoked by Al Hajj Umar refers to the word *Tur*, which designates both the Sinai and the Toro people of Futa. Biological links with the most ancient Muslim saints were invented. The narratives, which were spread by scholars, helped to legitimate the idea of a Fulani community. In the nineteenth century, a belief even arose that the Prophet himself had blessed the western Sudan: around 1820 in Khasso and 1840 in Kano, there was a story of Muhammad praying and leaving a knee print on a stone. Paradoxically, around 1910–20, a century later, Europeans gathered such reports, which were consistent with their own tendency to ascribe all facts pertaining to civilization to extra-African origins. This gave rise to theories that the Fulani had eastern, Persian, Yemenese, Phoenician, or even Jewish origins. Thus, in a hundred years a unique ethnic group was constructed politically and ideologically, and assigned the duty of converting West Africa to Islam.[31]

In 1785 there was an upsurge in Sufist and Mahist belief, which was exacerbated by the beginning of a new Muslim era: year 1200 of the Hegira. Those waiting for the Mahdi became increasingly anxious. Muslims saw the emergence of Christian pressure from the West as a sign of the end of the world. Demographic pressure, European threats, and the aristocratic conservatism of the ancient Qadiriyya elites combined to create a climate of insecurity conducive to the growth of the ideological populism of the Tijaniyya.

The first two Fulani jihads, at Futa Jallon and Futa Toro, date back to the eighteenth century. They were regional and concerned only a relatively limited number of people.

Futa Jallon, Cradle of Culture

In the rainy mountains of Futa Jallon, where the sources of the Niger, Senegal, and Gambia rivers are found, there had been a century of intense rivalry over control of trade with the coast in slaves, arms, livestock, and grain. The Fulani herdsmen, farmers, and scholars, some of whom owned considerable head of livestock and many slaves, finally triumphed over the Mande-speaking Jalonke farmers who had been dominant until then. Around 1770, they had set up a confederation of nine provinces controlling the north-south and east-west routes along 200 miles. In principle, the system was balanced, marrying the autonomy of the provinces with recognition of the almamy's (chief's) central power in Timbo. The almamy was controlled alternately by representatives of two competing royal lineages: the Alfayas, successors of the learned ancestral founder, and the Soriyas, who came from a military and merchant tradition inherited from an ancestor who had restored the family to power in the mid-eighteenth century. The history of the dual almamat is that of the two great families' implacable struggle for the throne. From the beginning, each family had a solid clan of relatives and allies in every province. This gave rise to serious political and military competition. In the first half of the nineteenth century, the struggle for leadership of the almamy became violent. Civil wars, which were often harsh, resulted in fights and deaths in the capital, and massacre or exile of part of the royal family, which then in turn plotted to regain power. For example, in 1824–25, a bloody confrontation occurred between Abdul Gadiri, an elderly Soriya almamy, and Bakar, a younger rival from the Alfaya family. In 1841, when he became the leader, Umar Tall (Al Hajj Umar) seems to have succeeded in getting the two sides to agree to a more regular alternation.

These problems led to decadence and corruption, even though Futa remained prosperous until the French conquest, which was facilitated as a result. The prosperity was based on a combination of a hierarchical internal system that employed many slaves, and relatively abundant production of rice and meat. This was aided by the high altitude, which protected the herds from tsetse flies, and relative proximity to the coast, which Futa supplied without being directly exposed to European rapacity. Trade was particularly active toward the southwest via the lagoons of the river country. The Rio Pongo and Rio Nuñez made it feasible to circumvent control by the British fleet based in Freetown. Throughout the nineteenth century, they made it possible to increase the slave population through jihads, since all non-Muslims could be made into slaves (whereas Fulani Muslims were not supposed to be). War provided slaves needed for both trade and farming, in an increasingly authoritarian system that was becoming more and more dependent on slave labor.

At the time of its maximum expansion, Futa Jallon dominated the backcountry all the way to the Gambia, but it did not manage to control the Bure gold mines directly to the east, which were jealously guarded by the little Malinke kingdom of Tamba. A crossroads of far-reaching routes, Futa favored trade along the caravan routes, which attracted not only Fulani but also Islamized Soninke and Malinke merchants and teachers.

Futa Toro and the Tukuloor

An analogous phenomenon developed at the end of the eighteenth century in Futa Toro on the left bank of the Middle Senegal River. About 300,000 inhabitants, and some Muslim lineages, or *torodbe*, had settled there because the threat of Moorish incursions had forced them away from the right bank. They refused to pay tribute to the Moors, rejected domination by the earlier Denyanke Dynasty even though it was Muslim, and seized power in the 1770s. However, the area was less hospitable than Futa Jallon. Certainly, the floodable valley made a second harvest possible in a rather dry area, thus allowing surrounding areas to be supplied with food. However, it was narrow (fifteen to twenty miles wide) and difficult to protect against Moorish and even Moroccan incursions. It was also too far from both slave-producing areas and French posts on the river. Nevertheless, a 1785 trade agreement with the French gave the chiefs living along the river the right to charge tolls. The almamy succession was a problem. Between 1797 and 1807, the old Almamy Abdul attempted a number of unsuccessful jihads, in particular against the Kajoor Kingdom. Faced with his adversary's scorched-earth tactic, he finally lost lamentably at the Battle of Bunguy and spent several months imprisoned in Kajoor. He nonetheless undertook an equally unsuccessful campaign on the other side against the Bundu. He also failed to renew the trade agreement with the French. In 1807, he was assassinated in a revolt of discontented *torodbe* in the central area, who controlled the rest of the country. Afterward they spent their time electing and removing powerless almanies, who were in principle chosen from among the leading families in accordance with their Islamic scholarship.

From the nineteenth century on, the *torodbe*, aware of their political and intellectual superiority owing to the fact that Takrur had been Islamized for a very long time, took the name of Tukuloor (Toucouleur in French colonial texts). Their Muslim education was strict, and they felt they were invested with a special mission that made them look upon other ethnic groups with disdain and Christian invaders with hostility.

Yet, of all Fulani undertakings, that of Futa Toro was the least successful; even though the teaching there was modeled after that of Futa Toro, it did not have its intellectual reputation. This is one of the reasons why Umar Tall, who came from Toro, chose to exile himself to continue his studies, and eventually to launch a religious and political renewal, which was nonetheless well received in his area of origin.

In the meantime, a third hegemonic Fulani group appeared in Masina, in the interior Niger delta, between Timbuktu and Segu, where Fulani herdsmen accounted for about a third of the mixed population (of around 370,000). While they acknowledged a shared culture based on language, their nomadic lifestyle, devotion to their herds, and tradition of pre-Islamic migrations entailed that they did not yet have a political organization that could oppose their powerful neighbors in the Segu Kingdom. Adding the Muslim god to their pantheon did not pose a problem for the Bambara, who were animists. They had a flaw-less military organization that enabled them to station their *tonjon* (soldiers) at strategic points and organize many raids on their neighbors. This ensured a regular supply of slaves to be sent to the north and to Senegambia. Their Muslim Marka partners were spared for economic reasons, and had only to pay heavy tribute and provide services on the slave markets. The Fulani, who were also exploited by the rich merchant families of Jenne and whose pastures were hemmed in between the Tuaregs to the north and the Bambara to the south, were severely harassed. Theoretically, there was an implicit division among the Bambara, masters of the land, the Sorogo, masters of the water, and the Fulani, masters of the grass. However, since for everyone the best lands were those that could be flooded, conflicts frequently erupted.

Ahmadu of Masina, an Original Political System

More clearly defined political formations were emerging virtually everywhere. The competing Kingdom of Kaarta arose to the west, and the Senufo King-dom of Kenedugu appeared to the south, not far from Sikasso. The Fulani of Masina were more affected by the emergence, at the same time, of the state of Futa Jallon and especially by the victorious jihad in Hausaland of Uthman dan Fodio and his son Muhammad Bello, who were both faithful to the Qadiriyya. This event was a trigger: a lowly educated man from the countryside, Ahmadu Lobbo-Bari, whose social origin and culture did not predispose to such a great adventure, took the jihad as an inspiration for the Masina Empire.

He was soon known as Seku Ahmadu (*seku* means sheikh in Pular, and the title was probably conferred by Muhammad Bello). He began by preaching against the taxes imposed by the great chiefs of Fulani lineage from among whom the local chief (the *Ar'do*) had been recruited until that time. He de-manded a form of Islam stricter than the flexible version that had scandalized him during his studies in Jenne. The city was still controlled at the time by the *arma* of Moroccan origin, who were less concerned with religious purity than with business. They would have been quick to drive the uncooperative peasant away, but he gained the support of the scholars of Jenne, who were excluded from major trade and power. He was also able to speak with the herdsmen in the Sahel. He had the skill to ask for the endorsement of Uthman dan Fodio, to whom he sent a delegation in Sokoto. In 1818, buoyed by the growing number of disciples and against all expectations, he defeated a Bambara army expedition that the *Ar'do* had called in to help. This was less a military exploit than a psychological victory, because the number of combatants in-volved was derisory on both sides. At most a few thousand were involved, but perhaps only a few hundred soldiers and even fewer horsemen. However, the repercussions were enormous. The battle rallied a massive number of people to Ahmadu's cause. He put the support to good use by organizing a Muslim state in the center and to the south of the delta. It was called the *diina*, in other words, Islamic state (the word comes from the Arabic *din*, religion). It was a theocracy officially governed by the sharia. Modest scholars saw it as a means of escaping anonymity. The sedentary non-Fulani farmers and fishermen had been living for so long in an economy completely interwoven into that of the Fulani that they fell into step with no resistance.

Ahmadu proclaimed himself Commander of the Believers. He sacralized his legitimacy by falsifying, with the help of his first councillor Alfa Nuh Tayru and a few scholars from Timbuktu, the *Tari'kh-al-Fettash*. The text was enriched with apocryphal passages based on a fifteenth-century prediction that a khalif named Ahmadu would come to the interior delta. To give it more weight, the prophecy was placed in the mouth of a famous scholar from Cairo, Al-Suyuti, at the time of the pilgrimage of the Askya Muhammad of Songai. In the hierarchical system that Seku Ahmadu set up, that tradition also guaranteed him ownership of "24 castes of slaves." It was quickly adopted. However, his centralized, authoritarian, caste-ridden, and slaving regime was far from the social revolution promoted at the beginning of the movement.[32]

Surrounded by a council of forty scholars led by his first companions, Seku Ahmadu established forts and a series of civil and military institutions in the provinces. Above all, he imposed a new lifestyle on the Fulani by regulating the movements of herds and forcing nomads to become sedentary. His reign began with major population transfers. Islam desacralized the relations between the Fulani and their cattle. The herd, which was subdivided into groups of 100 to 300 head, could have numerous owners and was guarded by only a few youths when it left on major transhumance. From then on, adult men remained in the village, or *wuro*, where they used slaves to work their land.

In 1821, Seku Ahmadu established a new capital city, Hamdullahi ("Praise God"), to the east of the floodplain. The location was a well-settled, protected site on the trade route from Jenne. The city had perhaps 40,000 inhabitants. Little is known about it because no explorer visited it. It was destroyed in 1864 by the fire that protected the flight of Al Hajj Umar. The city's inhabitants were kept on a war footing (all men aged eighteen to sixty could be conscripted). They were required to perform many public works. The army, of which the cavalry was the essential component, was expensive even though, unlike in the Bambara military, firearms were rarely used. Military expenses motivated in part the centralization of the state and nationalization of the economy, since all land in escheat became Ahmadu's property, as did slaves captured in war, who were settled into hamlets of workers. The state's money came from booty, of which a fifth was retained before the sharing provided for under Islamic law. Taxes were heavy and varied, and paid in kind or cowries. The *jakka* that was supposed to apply only to subsistence was extended to all grain. The conquered also had to pay taxes on subsistence crops.

To the north, Ahmadu conquered Jenne after a nine-month siege and confiscated the wealth of the ancient arma, a third of which went into state coffers. This was the end of the remnants of Moroccan domination. From 1825 on, he extended his influence to Timbuktu so as to control the Tuaregs between that city and Hamdullahi. However, the Tuaregs, who were most threatened by the sedentarization policy, repelled him in 1840. Through Sheik Al-Bakkay (from the Kunta family, a Qadiriyya religious congregation rather than a political body), the clerics of Timbuktu then negotiated a compromise to maintain the independence of their city in exchange for tribute. To some extent, they disdained the new fanatics, whom they considered provincial. They feared puritanism would not be good for business.

The whole thing was inseparable from an Islamization program directed from the capital toward every village. Austere Islam included prohibition of tobacco, seclusion of women, and simple habits. Schools spread popular Islamic knowledge, without affecting the custom that clerics had to complete their religious training by leaving the area and studying under new masters. Yet Seku Ahmadu, who consolidated the strict cohesion of the whole until around 1840 when his lands were conquered by Al Hajj Umar, hardly ever wrote. There is no account in Pular similar to that produced in Futa Jallon.

A long reign of twenty-eight years marked the *diina*'s apogee. Seku Ahmadu's succession was difficult because there was a contradiction between the Fulani customs of the Bari clan, according to which power should be transferred to the oldest brother, and patrilineal Muslim law. The latter won out in 1845, and power went to Seku Ahmadu's son, Ahmadu Seku, who reigned for only eight years. At Ahmadu Seku's death in 1853, the problem was even thornier because his son, who was barely twenty, was not yet a scholar as required by the sharia. He was elected by the council with difficulty and received the name Ahmadu Ahmadu. His authoritarianism and also his modernism were poorly received by the old companions, whose advice was ignored. The diina isolated itself from the rest of the Muslim world. Al-Bakkay of Timbuktu considered Ahmadu to be an ignorant tenderfoot. He did not move closer to him until threatened by Umar. In 1862, Al Hajj Umar's inexorable progress eastward reached Hamdullahi, which he conquered. He had Ahmadu executed, and that was the end of the diina.

In the nineteenth century, the two greatest Fulani leaders, in terms of both religion and politics, were unquestionably Uthman dan Fodio and Al Hajj

Umar. This takes us from "revolutionary" Islam[33] to conquering Islam, since those two leaders alone controlled nearly all of West Africa for a time.

Uthman dan Fodio: Scholar and Prince

Chronologically, the first of the conquest empires was established by Uthman dan Fodio around Sokoto and Gwandu, stretching from Gobir to Hausaland. Uthman dan Fodio was a great Fulani scholar born in Gobir in 1754. He claimed that his group had Toro origins dating back to the fifteenth century, from before the Tuaregs and even the Hausa. He spent the first part of his life preparing the intellectual foundations of his mission. He was the son of an imam and, surrounded by books and precious manuscripts, including some brought from North Africa and Arabia, he learned to read and write Arabic at a young age. He grew up in a large polygamous household with many slaves and where Fulani, Hausa, and Tuaregs rubbed shoulders. Many Tuareg women were married to Fulani men, which resulted in a degree of syncretism among nomads and sedentary people. Uthman dan Fodio also engaged in meditation and was well-versed in Sufi mysticism. He continued his studies at Agades. The regret of his life was to have to renounce a pilgrimage to Mecca after a failed attempt in his youth. The basis of his beliefs, which were transmitted to him by a Tuareg teacher influenced by Wahhabi fundamentalism, was the need to eradicate the animist practices that polluted Muslim orthodoxy. Not only was it necessary to fight against idolatry and signs of decadence, but a stop also had to be put to unfair taxes not prescribed by the sharia. This required seizing the political power held by a rapacious Hausa aristocracy. From the time he was twenty, assisted by his younger brother Abdullah (also known as Abd Allah, born in 1766), he began trying to restore Islam to Kebbi and then to Gobir, the easternmost of the small Hausa states. Gobir's frequent attacks on the Hausa cities of Kebbi and Katsina irritated the Fulani. Uthman dan Fodio's piety, exceptional intelligence, and charismatic personality began attracting many disciples. From 1789 to 1804, he had a number of visions of the Prophet and of the founder of the Qadiriyya, which shows his degree of mystical excitement and that of his entourage. The foundations of his teaching were both political and religious: his claims concerned not only believers' practices, but also the desire to see the state governed by the laws of Islam, in particular the sharia. He wanted to block any attempt to create syncretism with animist tradition. Uthman criticized the abuses of the Hausa authorities, confiscation of land, widespread corruption of the courts, and exercise of the lord's right over the daughters of his subjects (probably linked to the Bori religion and fertility rites). He also opposed the practice, frequent at the time, of enslaving Muslim Fulani. This was probably increasing in the eighteenth century, as the Hausa acquired guns. Finally, at the same time, under the impact of a growing population and unpredictable rains, there was increasing rivalry between Fulani herders and Hausa farmers.

While he himself never made the pilgrimage, he had a vision of the Muslim community gathered in Mecca as a thing of beauty, pure of any mixing. His vision owed much to the mystical Qadiriyya that had been brought from Egypt by the Tuaregs of Agades. His followers were made up of Fulani who had come to study under him. They had the perfect solution to the problem common to all Fulani theocracies: How could they transform their religion from one that chiefs tolerated and adopted only when it seemed useful to them into a state religion and imperial ideology? How could they take a small fundamentalist Muslim group that was geographically isolated and had begun long after the original religious orthodoxy, and turn it into an engine for winning recognition that the western Sudan was the *dar al-islam* (land of Islam)?

He was faced with the reticence of the old chief of Gobir, Bawa Jan Gwarzo, and then the chief's son, who wanted to reduce the reformers' impact by prohibiting them from wearing the turban and tunic that they used as signs of membership. Uthman called for a jihad in 1797. The "civil" power of the ruler of Gobir was associated with the pagan religion, but the real power had to be in the hands of the religious leader, in other words, the imam. The jihad began openly in 1804, when Uthman was fifty years old. On both sides, the armies were composed first of cavalry wearing leather and even Maghreb-style chain mail armor, and second of Hausa archers and infantry armed with lances, swords, and clubs. The army was supported by slave porters and camels. The Gobir army was even provided with concubines and luxury products, for Gobir had faith in its superior numbers. The important point was the acquisition and establishment of fortified cities. Both armies had the same kinds of fighters: Fulani, Tuareg, and Hausa soldiers. On the Fulani side, most of the leaders were great scholars.

The most difficult feat was taking Gobir's fortified capital, Alkalawa, after a number of unfortunate sieges. In the meantime, more than 1,000 Muslims perished in conquering Gwandu, which was accomplished only in 1808. From then on, the sheik used both diplomacy and threats. The Hausa communities of Katsina, Kano, Daura, and later Zaria joined relatively easily, but he had to give up advancing on Bornu, which was ferociously defended by El-Kanemi. After a few years, he established the capital city of Sokoto to the east in Adamawa country. The empire covered the greatest territory between 1809 and 1812. Tactical superiority as well as ideological strength and motivation were keys to victory. However, from 1810 on (he died in 1817), Uthman retained the title of caliph, but withdrew from public life and devoted himself to his studies. He once again followed the example of the Prophet, whose hegira, or migration away from infidels, he had imitated several times before.

He gave the reins of political and military affairs to his brother Abdullah and his second son, Muhammad Bello (born in 1781). Abdullah, who was succeeded by Bello, continued to govern Gwandu, the capital of the southwest, until 1829. Bello reigned in the northeast, at Sokoto, until 1837, when his companion the wazir (prime minister) took over until 1842. The actual conquest was relatively quick: on one hand, the Hausa were not able to unite their various competing city-states and, on the other hand, many of them took the Fulani side. Except at Gobir and Katsina, the symbiosis between the Hausa, who were already Muslim (though the form of Islam in question was still steeped in animism), and the Fulani was ancient. Proof of this lies in the conquering Fulani's rapid adoption of the language of the land, Hausa. Moreover, the Fulani quickly realized that it would be impossible to eradicate ancestral customs. They proved more tolerant than expected. For example, at Kano, the faithful continued to honor their ancestors with sacrifices on their graves. Neither "unfair taxes" nor slavery were eliminated. Since the provinces were organized in a very loose manner, people suffered little from the jihad, at first.

What is striking is the unequalled alliance between, on one hand, the learning and philosophical and literary talents of the Fulani leaders, and, on the other hand, political will. Within a few years, the area controlled was 800 miles from east to west, and 400 miles from north to south, in other words, three or four times larger than the conquests of other jihads. The heart of the confederation was Uthman and his associates in Gobir, Zanfara, and Kebbi, where the two capitals of Gwandu and Sokoto were established. In turn, the Fulani in the rest of Hausaland used this success to legitimize their victorious revolt between 1806 and 1812. Even the Fulani of Bornu revolted against their mai. To the south, the Fulani gained ground on the Yoruba by creating the Ilorin Emirate and forcing them into the southern forest. The jihad was stopped less by men than by the tsetse fly, which attacked the horses.

The wide expanse of the savanna was perfect for cavalry, as long as they were able to also take over cities, all of which were walled, for use as bases for expeditions and control. According to Muslim tradition, fortresses (*ribat*) then had to be built along the borders with infidels. The cavalry was an elite unit made up of *ulama* Fulani, who were both scholars and warriors, and their Tuareg allies. The main body of the troops was composed of Fulani archers and Hausa soldiers who had been won over to the cause of the jihad. It has been claimed that the tactics used were those taught in classical military manuals in the Arab world. The Fulani also improvised and used guerrilla tactics whenever necessary.

To the east, throughout the nineteenth century, the Fulani continued to colonize states until the British conquest of 1903. Throughout the entire nineteenth century war was waged (*dar al-harb*) in the lands of infidels (*dar al-kufr*) beyond Hausaland, in addition to the wars of succession and rivalries between leading vassals of Sokoto. This explains why slave raids were devastating to the region.

It was in Hausaland that the foundations of the political and social revolution in the nineteenth century sprang up. The various states resulting from Uthman dan Fodio's jihad were led by sultans and emirs. In principle, they acknowledged the superior power, in short, the divine right, of the central caliphate in Sokoto. The educated *ulamas* asserted themselves over the illiterate former elites, whose practices still included traces of animism. They claimed to be the only ones able to guarantee real political power because they could read and write and thus had access to the words of the Koran. The new distribution of power also made it possible to take action with respect to the trade networks, which linked the various cities that had been created or rejuvenated by the Fulani. Western Hausaland, which was conveniently located at the crossroads of the north-south and east-west routes, prevailed over Gobir, which was crushed under the weight of the jihad. It had been proven that, thanks to weapons, Fulani reformers could assert their authority over broad expanses controlled through conquest. The lesson was not to be forgotten: the example was immediately imitated in a more "national" manner at Masina. Above all, it was followed by Al Hajj Umar a few decades later: through violence and war, he was able to achieve in a few years what preaching had been unable to accomplish in several centuries.

Al Hajj Umar, the Conquering Believer

The passage from political to military Islam was even clearer in Al Hajj Umar's case than for Uthman dan Fodio. Before European colonization, which they involuntarily facilitated, these exceptional people imposed religious colonization, which was also military and political. After the manner of the sultan of Zanzibar and as would soon be the case in the Samori episode, Umar's undertaking was essentially colonial: its purpose was to assert his domination over conquered peoples whose prior political and ideological systems were in opposition to those promoted by the new power. This power was in the hands of an aristocracy that had settled by force; they were authoritarian slave owners who were deeply convinced of their civilization's superiority. In this colonial context, there was cultural syncretism and mixing, but also violent resistance and opposition, which generated popular regional and national revolts. These uprisings have yet to be studied in depth. The little we know about them comes from local manuscripts in Arabic, travel journals, and oral traditions. This suggests that we should reassess the idyllic vision of mass conversion to Islam. For example, at Kaarta, the Futanke settlers had great difficulty imposing control.[34]

Al Hajj Umar's enterprise can be broken into two distinct phases. In the first, until the middle of the century, in the tradition of his great predecessors he developed and refined his religious knowledge and learning. He gradually became known throughout West Africa, where he traveled frequently, as one of the leading scholars of the century. In the second phase, he became a formidable military leader in the name of religion. Within fifteen years, from 1852 until after his death in 1864, the jihads he initiated ravaged a large part of the region and changed the economic and political stakes throughout. However, his transformation into a war leader did not quench his passion for teaching. He wrote voluminous memoirs, which even today are useful sources for historians, in which he justified his actions in the name of the true religion. With Samori, who was to succeed him with comparable hegemonic goals, he covered the land with fire and blood. By doing so, he joined the ranks of those who unintentionally laid the groundwork for colonial domination.

Al Hajj Umar was born in the small village of Halwar in Futa Toro. He spent the first part of his life studying in Futa Jallon, where he was initiated into the Tijaniyya by a local scholar, Abdoul Karim, who had studied in Mauritania. Umar then spent many long years traveling and teaching, first visiting the tomb of Tijani at Fez and then going on to Hamdullahi in Masina, at the invitation of Seku Ahmadu, who was curious to know how Islam was evolving in Futa Jallon. He probably issued an open invitation for the foundation of his capital, built "to the glory of God." Umar then decided to make the pilgrimage to Mecca, which at the time was a long and arduous undertaking requiring several years. He went back through Toro to gather the money necessary for his trip, to which some merchants and scholars of Saint-Louis seem to have contributed. Umar left with his younger brother and a few companions. He went through Masina again, skirted Bornu, which was at war with Sokoto, by traveling around it to the north through the Aïr Mountains, and then joined the caravan of pilgrims coming from the Touat oases. From there they went on to the Fezzan and Cairo. Between 1828 and 1830, he traveled in the Middle East, and even visited Jerusalem. He did the pilgrimage three times, and began to write his first work. It was there, under Muhammad El-Ghalo, that he received the secrets and final revelation of the Tijaniyya, which made him a *khalifa* of Sheik Al-Tijani. This authorized him to perform all rites, direct spiritual retreats, and name his own lieutenants, which was essential to justify his mission to convert the western Sudan.

The voyage back took ten years, which he put to good use preaching and increasing his renown. The legend about him began at the Al-Azhar University in Cairo, where it was reported that a Black Muslim had triumphed over the most learned Egyptian scholars in a theological contest.[35] In 1831, he went through Bornu again, where he initially had difficult relations with the sovereign, the religious Sheikh El-Kanemi. El-Kanemi had risen up against the mai and had made Kukuwa the de facto state capital. Kukuwa became the hub for trade with the north, from which it bought weapons and to which it sold slaves. Al Hajj Umar then spent six years at Sokoto, from 1831 to 1837.[36] After a difficult beginning, he won acceptance by Muhammad Bello, though the latter remained faithful to the Qadiriyya and some Sanusiyya ideas. His success was clear from his marriages to a noble woman from Bornu, a Sokoto cleric's daughter (who gave him his future successor, Ahmadu), and Bello's own daughter. Then he returned to Futa Jallon, though not without having accumulated the wealth that would enable him to pursue his religious ambitions. It should not be forgotten that throughout the period, he and his disciples were earning their living through teaching, naturally, but also through major trade.

At this point, Al Hajj Umar's career was recast. He went from being a scholar to leading a jihad. Indeed, as early as the 1820s, Al Hajj Umar had, by affiliating himself with the young Tijaniyya, shown his desire to break away from the established order. He felt he was invested with an unusual task: to spread the good word throughout West Africa. For him, asceticism did not mean renunciation, but action. The struggle was always the same: was not the greatest jihad the one conducted against oneself and one's passions? He very often repeated to his disciples that, as heir of Tijani, he had received special grace from the Prophet Muhammad. In particular, he had the gift of being able to read the hearts of men, had received a direct vision of the Prophet, and knew God's great name. Since the latter two gifts were questioned, he wrote abundantly to justify them. No less important, he explained that there was no contradiction, on the contrary, in devoting oneself to God and seeking the wealth needed to accomplish this mission. Indeed, he became very wealthy during his travels. He actively engaged in slave trading all the way to the coast, in particular toward the Pongo and Nuñez rios, which made it possible for him to acquire the weapons needed. Finally, his privileges required complete submission from those faithful to him. He did not have the right to abandon his divine mission. This made his struggle implacable: since he was God's soldier, his work would be done only when his mission was achieved. As Madina Ly notes, what is important is not whether he was right but that he was convinced that he was right, and so were thousands of his disciples.

Umar's genius was to begin his conquests by attacking infidels, particularly the Malinke and Bambara. At least until he attacked the Sheikh of Masina, this permitted him to deliver a social message. This message was well received by those who had until then been subject to many abuses of power: Muslims had the right to be subject to only the obligations set out by religion, particularly with respect to taxes. The call for social justice did not address Muslims alone, for it was pagans' lot to be enslaved. Thus, he undertook to move his community into pagan lands, to the northeast of Futa.

A small Malinke kingdom had been created in the 1820s around Tamba, between Futa Jallon, Kaarta, and Segu. The kingdom was formidable because it controlled the interfluvial area between the Upper Niger and the sources of the Gambia, Faleme, and Bafing tributaries of the Senegal River: the gold-producing area. Despite all efforts, Futa Jallon had never managed to conquer the region. Accepted by the local chief, in the late 1840s Umar discreetly moved to a site that was fertile enough to create the town of Dinguiray, which remained the capital of his possessions until Nioro was taken in 1855. The threatening growth of the town, which quickly reached 2,000 inhabitants, its surrounding ramparts, which enclosed a strong citadel, and its dominance over a series of villages began to worry Malinke authorities. The conditions for a jihad were met, and one began in 1852. The siege of Tamba, the capital of the small pagan kingdom, lasted from November 1852 to March 1853. After that, Umar took over Bure to the east, which had gold that would be useful in his plans. The initial successes attracted many Fulani, who were excited by the huge, profitable slave raids.

Al Hajj Umar's policies in the Tamba Kingdom can be seen as a model for the rest of his enterprise. From then on, half of the approximately 25,000 inhabitants were Fulani. The war had been profitable for them because the Koran requires that the spoils be divided among all participants, and this was a source of wealth. The other half of the inhabitants included subjugated Malinke peasants and the many slaves who had been brought by their new masters. The settlers, who had the largest herds, took local women as wives and concubines. Their children were assimilated into the governing class. Aside from some exceptions, Umar's conquests, though soon blocked to the west by the French, took the same form elsewhere: troops were recruited among militants in the west, especially in the two Futas, and they were armed with guns, powder, and even cannons provided by the French of Saint-Louis along the ports of the Senegal River, until the embargo that began in 1854. The British also provided arms via the Upper Gambia or from Freetown via the Futa Jallon and Pongo rios. Umar's soldiers numbered about 10,000 at the time. They were more efficient than their enemies in the interior, who were barely equipped with poor muskets, and sometimes only lances, and bows and arrows.[37]

Initially, Umar's adversaries were the infidels of Tamba, Kaarta, and Khasso, the terrible Bambara who were still terrorizing Fulani shepherds at the beginning of the century. Thus, the jihad could only be popular among neighboring Muslims. However, in the next stage, forced by French advances to operate ever farther eastward, Umar attacked not only the Bambara of Segu but also other Muslims, and even Fulani like himself, namely those of Masina. This was his downfall.

In Senegambia, the French took advantage of the Umarian threat to get small chiefs along the river, who were divided by internal rivalries, to agree to the creation of forts upstream. After Bakel in 1818, there was Podor in 1854 in western Toro, and then Senubedu in Bunde on the Faleme to open the way to the gold of Bambuk, and finally, in 1855, Medina in Khasso, which was then occupied by Umar. For a time, the French and Umarians both strove to control the area. The only direct confrontation chosen by Umar taught him a lesson: the siege of Medina lasted from April to July 1857, and cost him 2,000 of his best soldiers. It soon resulted in the desertion of many of those who had survived. While both sides fought heroically, the confrontation nonetheless demonstrated the crushing technological superiority of the westerners under siege. The French garrison was saved from famine *in extremis* by a gunboat that managed to travel upstream at the beginning of the rainy season. Al-Hajj Umar saw that it was pointless to confront the Whites and, in 1860, having decided to return toward the east for good, he signed a status quo agreement with the French, who were happy to have the truce since they had few means in the backcountry.

Unlike that of some of his generals, Umar's faith was so strong that it was not shaken. However, having lost most of his army, he had to recruit more than ever. Drawing the conclusion of his inferiority in the face of the Europeans, this time he argued that there was a religious duty of hegira. In other words, believers had a duty to flee when they found themselves dominated in infidel lands in order to avoid becoming soiled, as Muhammad had done when he left Mecca for Medina in 622. Umar traveled for two years, 1858 and 1859, in Bundu and especially Futa Toro, his homeland, calling on good Muslims to migrate to the east with their families and possessions, and requiring, or imposing on recalcitrant families, the scorched-earth tactic. He put all of his moral and political prestige on the line. Ten thousand inhabitants of Bundu and possibly a quarter of the inhabitants of Futa Toro came together in what was perhaps the largest migration ever seen in Senegambia. Approximately 40,000 people moved toward the east, requisitioning millet and livestock along the way. They swelled the ranks of Umar's faithful, settlers, and troops. In 1859–60, they left behind them a devastated land plunged into famine. Faidherbe had no trouble taking it over when he launched an offensive to set up a protectorate with the Toro and to acquire the upstream Umarian fort of Genu, once again at the cost of heavy combat.

The *fergo* (Pular for hegira) was a turning point in the nineteenth century in West Africa. The French agreed to the 1860 agreement. Indeed, Umar left them free rein in western Senegambia, where the newest and most hostile threats to the French had been eliminated. This is to be compared to the *mfecane,* which left to the South African Boers a backcountry emptied of inhabitants by the columns of the Nguni chiefs who had preceded them.

In 1860, after having led some 25,000 soldiers and perhaps 10,000 women and children hundreds of miles from their homes, Al Hajj Umar launched an offensive against Segu. His superiority was guaranteed by better weapons, including multiple-shot muskets, four small cannons, and munitions carried by teams of camels. He also trained carpenters and blacksmiths to repair the weapons and forge bullets. The equipment defeated the Bambara ramparts. Umar gained a definitive victory in September 1860 at the battle of Woitala, echoes of which traveled throughout the western Sudan. This was the culminating point of the jihad against the infidels. He then designated his son Ahmadu as his successor and moved to Segu, which was to become the capital of his empire. The episode gave birth, a few dozen years ago, to a brilliant historical novel by Maryse Condé.

However, Al Hajj Umar's undertaking took a fateful turn. Faced with the catastrophe, the Bambara *fama* (king) Bina Ali had no choice but to beg for the aid of his traditional enemy, the caliph of Masina, whose cavalry was reputed to be invincible and who was also worried by the advances of the Umarian Empire. Bina Ali paid tribute to the caliph and accepted the introduction of Islam into his state. The coalition extended to Ahmad al-Bakkay of Timbuktu, who was also hostile to the advances of Umar's aggressive Muslims. Umar's action could only cause problems for the region's economy, since trade was based on reciprocal tolerance among Muslims and animists. Umar was thus forced to fight the state that was in principle closest to his own: a Fulani Muslim state that had engaged in its own jihad barely forty years earlier. He did so with the support of many arguments designed to justify the ideological legitimacy of his undertaking in relation to the infidelity of his adversary, accused to be the primary protector of unbelievers. The confrontation was huge: 30,000 Umarian soldiers faced 50,000 Fulani from Masina. At the terrible Battle of Caayawal in May 1862, probably 30,000 Malinkes and 10,000 Futanke died. Umar entered the capital city of Abdullahi, but both sides were left drained.

From then on Umar's undertakings became erratic. The sheikh had religious and military objectives, but neither he nor his associates had a talent for business or politics. In every case, they left behind a country that was conquered, but had little government. The Fulani conquered by force, demanded tribute that was made higher since Muslims were exempt, and gathered slaves. They began to give the impression that their only goal was armed religious conquest. They consistently sought new lands and sent emissaries in all directions, to Timbuktu to the north, from Mosi country to Saint-Louis in the west, toward

Kong lands in the south, and even all the way to Sierra Leone. At the same time, under Ahmadu's rule, Segu was abandoned as a crossroads for trade, and this cut off its sources of wealth.

Neither the princes nor the people of Masina accepted the conquest. A general uprising was brewing. Paradoxically, Umar's only allies were people from eastern Masina, Hausa Muslims, but also Dogon and Tombo animists who had never really accepted Fulani domination: he found himself forced to do what he had reproached his adversary in Masina for doing. The insurgents allied with the Kunta of Timbuktu, and laid siege to Hamdullahi in June 1863. In February 1864, Umar succeeded in fleeing from the burning city in extremis with a few loyal followers. However, he was blocked by the highlands and cliffs. Pursued by the Bambara and hiding in a cave, the little troop perished, asphyxiated by the explosion of their last stores of ammunition. The hypothesis of a suicide pact cannot be excluded, though it was in theory prohibited by Islam.

Yet the battle continued. Control was taken over by Tijani, the nephew of Al Hajj Umar, whose reinforcements had almost arrived in time to save his uncle. Tidjani established his capital at Bandiagara, in the heart of the allied countries not far from sacred cliffs. Taking advantage of the dissension that quickly erupted among his Fulani and Bambara adversaries, he spent twenty years continuing the jihad and imposing his power on the interior delta, including on Timbuktu in the 1880s. As Ahmadu's rival, he took the title "Commander of the Believers," but he died four years before his cousin. Ahmadu, Umar Tall's son, whom the French forced toward the east in 1891, took refuge in turn in Bandiagara, where he finally succeeded in ousting Tidjani's son. Nevertheless Ahmadu was again forced to flee from the French, who finally caught him in 1893.

In the end, the policy of perpetual raids spelled the end for the Sahel. A battlefield for all conflicts, Masina became a devastated land open to pillage. The colonizers simply took advantage of the situation. The French set up, under close watch in Bandiagara, another son of Al Hajj Umar, Agibu, the "friend of the French."

Senegambian Attempts

In Senegambia, Islamization followed a more complex path, owing to older contacts with European traders and stronger competition among local chiefs and proselytizing marabouts. The most tenacious stumbling block remained the more or less extensive Islamization of the people. Those who lived closest to the coast, the Serere, along with the Sine, resisted the longest. However, as elsewhere, reformers were in style. There were many jihads, which often fizzled out, as in the case of Al-Kari of Bysse, which lasted only two years.[38]

Ma Ba was a Denianke preacher originally from Futa who studied in Kayoor and Wolof and had once met Umar Tall. He began preaching jihad in Rip, on the right bank of the Gambia. The novelty was that in the area marabouts had until then coexisted with pagans. Ma Ba proclaimed himself almamy and, in the name of an intransigent religious puritanism, accepted no compromise with infidels. In only two years of campaign, 1862–63, he covered all of Wolof country and converted the chiefs, who saw him as the ultimate recourse against the French. He was endorsed by Lat Dior of Kayoor, who opposed the construction of a telegraph line by the French, as he would that of a railroad in the 1880s. There was a provisional treaty in 1864, which allowed both parties to gain time and gave Ma Ba control of Saloum, though he agreed to recognize the French right to trade. Nevertheless he was finally beaten and killed in 1867 by the Bur of Sine, who continued to refuse conversion. Ma Ba failed at what Umar Tall, who was more realistic, had not even tried: combating the French with an empire unified by Islam. From then on the divisions among the chiefs were accentuated by their maneuvers. Most chiefs tried to get the French to take their side against their adversaries of the moment. For example, Lat Dior helped the French against the Tukuloor marabout Ahmadu Cheikhu in 1875; Abdul Boubakar, Tukuloor chief, cooperated in 1887 with the French against the Sarakolle marabout Mamadou Lamine. The dispersion facilitated the colonial conquest, which became inevitable;[39] it was completed in Senegal in 1887. The borders were subsequently under negotiation from 1890 until World War I.

Surprisingly, the French conquest defeated the most stubborn opponents of Islam, the Serere of Saloum. The final conversion of the Bur of Saloum, Guédel Mbodj, in about 1891, can be interpreted as the ultimate manifestation of ideological resistance to the West.

Adrift Under Western Pressure: Samori

So, should Samori's undertaking be counted as a jihad? That would be a mistake. Despite the delayed reactions in Senegambia, it took place in a different time. Initially, in the early 1860s and especially after 1865, Samori (born around 1830) tried to create an empire on a limited political and social basis. Islam played little role except as an efficient passport for trade. Samori was Jula, in other words, from a southern Malinke group, the product of long-term intermixing between local animist peoples and Malinke from the north. He was part of an active, affluent minority group of Islamized merchants who had been spreading from Jenne since the twelfth century along the trade routes crisscrossing all of West Africa, in a manner similar to that of their Hausa competitors to the east. From the Niger River to the fringes of the Guinean forest and the "southern rivers" linking to Sierra Leone and the Atlantic Ocean, the Jula carried slaves, gold, and kola nuts. They sought sea salt and European manufactured goods, cloth, guns, gunpowder. From the north, they received Saharan salt and livestock. A little like the busy Nyamwezi traders, and the Swahili and Arab-influenced slave traders in East Africa around the same time, Samori was led to create a centralized structure in his economic territory. By doing so, he was a political innovator in an area that had until then known little state structure since it was on the border of the Sahel, traversed by jihads to the north and slave-trading kingdoms to the south. Until then the only centralized structures had been the small state of marabout Sise and the Kankan Kingdom.

In 1861, after training as a soldier with local chiefs, Samori began establishing his power on an efficient organization of space. He reworked to his advantage and ultimately transformed into administrative circumscriptions the ancient local communal entities known as *kafu*. These communities had previously encompassed at most a few villages of 100 to 15,000 inhabitants.[40] His political and economic objective initially received the support of the Malinke to the south, which assured him of relative cultural unity. He expanded, on a new scale, control of the country. The land was gradually brought under territorial governments administered by chiefs who had both economic and military goals. They were assisted by many slaves, for whom there was no longer a market on the Atlantic coast. He proclaimed himself *faama* (king) in 1867. With a well-equipped army, and supported by his commercial activities, he proceeded to engage in a series of conquests, especially around 1875. Increasingly, he expanded his army by forcibly enrolling all of his new subjects. Samori's goal became to replace Sikasso, the capital of his rival the faama of Kenedugu (in present-day Mali and Burkina-Faso), whose military strength was comparable.

It was only then that Samori, crossing over his original cultural borders, needed a unifying principle. In 1884, twenty years after he had begun, he claimed the authority of Islam by proclaiming himself almamy. He asserted, like his great ancestors, a theocratic power demanding the compulsory conversion of his subjects. However, it was too late; his interests were coming into conflict with those of Westerners. He was not against trading with Europeans; he had long been doing so whenever his business dealings brought him into contact with them. This led to an initial compromise with General Joseph Gallieni, who wished to gain time owing to his entanglements with the jihadists. Samori signed a series of treaties with the French between 1886 and 1889. As their presence became stronger, he sought, like others, to play on Western rivalries and gain time, even negotiating a protectorate treaty with the British (1890).

Samori found himself facing the colonial advance. He had to strengthen his military force and improve his weaponry workshops. However, he was constantly forced to retreat eastward, beyond, he hoped, the reach of the Whites. Therefore, he had to transform himself into a pure conqueror, and he did not shrink from systematic use of the scorched-earth tactic. Finally, he was opposed by the "war of refusal," a broad insurrection of animist peoples exasperated by the regime of incessant war (1888–89). He had no choice but to radically change the borders of his lands, and in 1892 he engaged in a desperate attempt to found a new empire in the north of present-day Ivory Coast. It is clear why Samori's memory now divides Africans today: he is considered a heroic reformer in Guinea, but an oppressor in Burkina-Faso and the Ivory Coast. In 1898, he had to surrender to the French; he was deported to Gabon, where he died in 1900. He was buried on a small island in the Ogooue River.

3

Political and Merchant Islam

East Africa

Modernity as an Option: Egypt

In the first half of the nineteenth century, Egypt was a special case, a precocious attempt to establish a modern state. The case is all the more intriguing because at first sight the revolution did not occur in an independent nation but in a colonial province of the Ottoman Empire, which Egypt had been since the Mamelukes were conquered in the sixteenth century. The Mamelukes, who were originally converted Caucasian slaves, had been transformed into a corps of approximately 12,000 privileged soldiers and bureaucrats who continued to maintain their numbers through the purchase of boys. They formed an "order" bound together by a community of status and function. Nonetheless, beginning in the eighteenth century, merchant, agrarian, and urban capitalism had been growing, and it was relatively widespread when Napoleon Bonaparte led the French expedition in 1797.

Bonaparte's Legacy

It is well known that Napoleon Bonaparte saw his expedition as an interlude in the pursuit of his ambitions in France. What was special about his undertaking was that Bonaparte, a son of the Enlightenment, brought with him a remarkable team of researchers and scientists, some of whom remained in Egypt as advisors to the future Muhammad-Ali. Thirty-five thousand men, including 2,000 officers, landed simultaneously in Egypt's three main ports, Alexandria, Damietta, and Rosetta, on June 27, 1798. The Mamelukes had never faced a modern army, and it took the French only three weeks to conquer Cairo. Bonaparte skillfully made alliances with Egyptian notables against the existing regime, and solemnly founded the Institute of Egypt to "spread the Enlightenment in Egypt, and study Egypt's land, industry and history."[1] It was through his impetus that the first newspaper was published: *Le Courrier de l'Egypte.* However, Bonaparte soon found himself trapped in Egypt when British Admiral Nelson destroyed his fleet in Aboukir Harbor (July 1898).

The people began to rise up, unhappy with the review of land titles that was being done to spread property taxes in a more equitable manner. Bonaparte left Egypt in June 1799, and his successor, Jean-Baptiste Kléber, was murdered in 1800. Finally, an English-Ottoman expedition forced the French, who had retreated to Alexandria, to leave the country at the end of August 1801.

The psychological and economic shock caused by this short episode was analogous to what later occurred throughout Europe when it was occupied by Napoleon. Egyptian notables, who had until then been kept down by the Turks, became aware of some of the ideas of the French Revolution. They became accustomed to being consulted on policies, and no longer accepted the authoritarian regime of the past. A major public works program was begun, which was continued by Muhammad-Ali. Ironically, Ali, an exceptional man of Albanian origin, was responsible for awakening Egyptian national awareness.

Muhammad-Ali's Rise to Power

The Ottoman regime (the Porte) had never had direct contact with the Egyptians. Two million Egyptians, most of whom were of Arab and Muslim origin, were settled in villages in the Nile Valley or were nomadic Bedouin livestock herders or caravan operators. In Upper Egypt there were some 150,000 Copts, who were descendants of the original population and remained Christian. Egyptian notables were responsible for their extended families, and had to pay taxes and tribute in accordance with the Muslim law applying to conquered lands (*kharaj*). Aside from a few village sheiks, the Porte could rely on only a few prominent traders and a number of *ulama,* or religious scholars who received income, which was sometimes a significant amount, from managing *mainmorte* property (land that passed to the lord on the death of the owner). Power was shared among the Ottoman military corps (*askar*), which was relatively small and stationed at Cairo; the pasha (*wali*) appointed by Istanbul; and the military judge (*qadi askar*), who was also appointed by the Porte and was assisted in the provinces by a corps of Ottoman *qadi.* The Pasha's primary function was to raise tribute for the central government. He was at the head of a number of tax circumscriptions under military power and gathered into districts (*willayah*), each of which was composed of five administrative divisions. In each village or group of villages, there was a public servant appointed and paid by the military, who was assisted by the village chief.[2] The former Mamelukes continued to be used as heads of *willayahs,* owing to their financial skills. They eventually ended up supplanting the Ottoman military while increasing their control of the land, which they put in their wives' names despite the fact that doing so was contrary to Muslim law.

On the eve of Bonaparte's arrival, they owned more than half the land (59 percent), compared with the Arabs (19 percent), women (13 percent), *ulama* (7 percent), and merchants (1.5 percent).

At the same time, just before the French arrived, Europe's demand for grain (wheat, rice) had led the Mamelukes in the Nile Delta to recruit paid farm workers and to import laborers from Upper Egypt. For the army, they also needed money, which they borrowed from merchants acting as lenders. These partners in a nascent capitalism began to collude against the Ottoman regime. This resulted in an ideology that reconciled contradictory components: the vectors were cenacles in the form of religious brotherhoods where prophetic traditions that could justify trade were discussed. This led to new interest in the social sciences, history, philology, natural sciences, etc.

The military situation was complex. The Ottoman army was composed of rival Turkish and Albanian corps, each of which had between 5,000 and 6,000 men. The Turks were divided into two Mameluke factions that wanted to control the country. Tension increased with the arrival in 1804 of a new Ottoman *wali* who was accompanied by a corps of *dehli* ("madmen") who had been recruited in Syria among the Druze, Kurds, and Shiites. Particularly rapacious and extortionist, they made themselves intolerable to the people. Indeed, since people were already accustomed to resistance thanks to the struggle against the French, they united with the notables against the old order. The Albanians were especially concerned: their home province had been undergoing major change since the mid-eighteenth century, especially in the south, where the pasha of Janina had been the leader since 1785. They had converted to Islam but, owing to their location in the Balkans, they were open to Christian influences. For them, it was a question of survival: in 1803 they had briefly tried to impose their pasha as leader of Egypt, but he was assassinated three weeks later. Then Muhammad-Ali took over. His family's activities allied land and trade. He made both the *ulama* and the notables of Cairo his friends, prohibited pillaging, and brought grain from Upper Egypt to feed city dwellers. In May 1805, the Ottoman *wali* was under siege in his citadel, and an assembly of notables appointed Ali as his successor on the condition that they could oversee his government. The assembly asked the Porte to ratify its decision, which it did a month later. The very idea of demanding a form of control over the future governor was a major innovation.

State Modernization

Initially, Muhammad-Ali's objective was to get the maximum resources out of the country. His plans developed empirically, and took form only gradually, at least until the 1840s. (His son Ibrahim succeeded him briefly in 1847.)

Egyptianization was undertaken through progress in education, the creation of specialized upper-level schools beginning in the 1820s, and educational missions abroad. Ali learned to read, and his sons became engineers. The printing industry was developed, followed by newspapers. Government reform began in 1814 and improved between 1825 and 1830; it targeted not only tribute, but also agricultural productivity. Egyptian village chiefs became the core of public service. In 1829, there was a consultative committee of 157 members, which included about a hundred Egyptian nationals, as well as thirty-three senior public servants and religious dignitaries, and twenty-four Mameluke district heads.

The goal was to tame the capriciousness of the Nile. Muhammad-Ali had thirty canals dug, forty dams built, ten dikes constructed, and millions of trees planted. He introduced nearly 200 new species of plants, including cotton in 1817, and the long-fiber variety the year following its discovery. In short, he changed Egypt's landscape. The new plants affected the peasants' corvées: the *fellahs* had to work for two months, but from then on they were in principle paid and fed during that period, though there were some infractions. A second harvest became possible in the delta; grain production increased fourfold, and exports to Europe went up sevenfold.

Placed under the government's direct control, land was registered in each peasant's name in accordance with his right of use. Beginning in 1826, those who had the means were encouraged through tax rebates to clear and plant crops on fallow land. However, in Egypt, private property emerged only around 1858, and it was adopted definitively only between 1871 and 1874.

In the 1830s, seven *diwans* (government departments) were established. The primary department was the treasury, but there were also departments of education and industry. Each department was composed of a network of offices, workshops, and archives. Today, 36,000 files remain that are available to researchers. While Turkish remained the official language until the end of the century, documents were systematically translated into Arabic.

Muhammad-Ali can be described as a capitalist government entrepreneur who adapted the techniques of his time to the Egyptian context. The members of government were primarily Ali and his family, who worked within the framework of widespread mercantile capitalism.[3] He was a man of transition: while his past involved the conquest of power by the sword, and he desired to ensure that his family, the military elite, and his supporters became wealthy, he was modern in his practice of rewarding merit regardless of a man's origin and in his economic innovations. He had to deal with many threats: on the domestic front there were the Mamelukes, and internationally there were the Ottoman and British empires. He therefore opted for a centralized state, a strong army and navy, and safe domestic financial resources in the form of precious metal reserves. His goal was not only to monopolize land and raise tribute, but also to invest in export crops and control foreign trade.

Finally, he wanted to industrialize the country to ensure a positive balance of payments. This involved expanding the market by controlling neighboring areas and exploiting their natural resources. His first objective was military. The war industry was a state monopoly, governed by an inspector general. In 1805, a cannon foundry and river barge construction workshops were set up to wage war in Upper Egypt, where he launched many expeditions. However, the barges were also used to transport grain on their way back. Alexandria's shipyards provided Egypt with a navy, and the city boomed, going from 12,000 to 164,000 inhabitants from 1812 to 1846. Initially, Muhammad-Ali used foreign specialists, who were often former soldiers of the Napoleon expedition. Later, engineers, in particular Saint Simonians, were involved. He made full use of them as salaried employees. The first steam engines were introduced in 1830, and the textile industry began growing in 1834 (some thirty factories) with the introduction of private enterprise to replace corvées levied on corporations. By mid-century, there were over 200,000 urban workers (out of 5 million inhabitants and about 600,000 city dwellers), a quarter of whom worked for the government. The result was that Egypt's balance of trade quickly showed a comfortable surplus and, despite the huge investment, the budget increased 113 percent over thirty years.

Yet, power remained fundamentally military. In 1820, the conquest of the Sudan began. The Sudan was seen as a storehouse of food supplies, raw materials, and slaves. The army had been restructured under the French administration. To the rallied Mamelukes, who were still viewed poorly by the people and whose system was dismantled in 1811, 100,000 men were added after the introduction of three-year conscription in Egypt. While Egyptians were "subjects," they could become junior officers, and Muhammad-Ali's control extended from Syria to Bahr al-Ghazal, encroaching on Cyrenaica and Ethiopia. In Syria in 1839, the Ottoman fleet was forced to surrender to Egypt.

Western Revenge

The decision for Europe to react was made by a coalition of Prussia, Austria, Great Britain, and Russia. The Europeans forced Muhammad-Ali to withdraw from Syria in 1840, and compelled a return to what Egypt had never ceased to be in law: a province of the Ottoman Empire. In 1841, Westerners obliged the Porte to impose free trade on its Egyptian province and dismantle its war industry. The army was reduced to a maximum of 18,000 men. Egypt was brought back into Africa. In particular, foreigners took back key positions and the growing Egyptian bourgeoisie had no recourse but to refocus on land. The government nonetheless remained the largest contractor, and the country's finances stayed more or less healthy.

Abbas, the grandson of Muhammad-Ali, was worried about Western control but was also in favor of a conservative Muslim point of view. He led a reactionary, and expensive, policy. He pitted the Saint Simonian–French plan to dig the Suez Canal against the Alexandria-Cairo-Suez railroad concession granted to the British. He eliminated schools and invested in sumptuous buildings. He was assassinated in 1854, which enabled his successor, Said, who was a fervent pro-Westerner educated by the Saint Simonian diplomat Ferdinand de Lesseps, to authorize the creation of the Suez Canal Company that same year.

Things began to go seriously downhill in 1860, owing to the unfair terms imposed by the Western powers to lend the money needed to dig the canal, and to the excessive tribute demanded by the indebted Ottoman Empire. In line with the diplomats of the time, Western historians have charged Sultan Ismail with every sin. Yet, he was a visionary and a cautious leader who brought about a series of fundamental reforms of schools and the legal system, as well as colonization of the Sudan. He even experimented with an advisory committee. However, such domestic modernization was no longer appropriate in the face of colonial imperialism. The 1880 bankruptcy led to the loss of independence two years later. The British took financial and military control while maintaining the fiction of the Ottoman Empire, a paradox that was not replaced by a proper protectorate until 1914.[4]

Until then, the ambiguity of Egyptian modernization had resulted from state authoritarianism. The brutal intervention at the end of the century by colonial authorities put an end to a fascinating experiment, which was, in its own way, comparable to the Meiji period in Japan.

At the Crossroads of Worlds: Ethiopia

The people of Ethiopia evolved in the isolated mountainous bastion among the influences of North Africa, the Middle East, and sub-Saharan Africa. While Ethiopia was mostly Christian, it was encircled by Muslim peoples to both the north and west, where Egypt was predominant, and to the south and east of the Horn of Africa. Ethiopia has a special place in history because of its relationship to the Maghreb, owing to a religion linked to a scholarly written culture (in the Ge'ez language), and its relationship to sub-Saharan Africa, owing to the form of writing and an economic organization based on farming using the plow and animal traction.

Upheaval in the North

At the beginning of the nineteenth century, the Ethiopian Empire was facing a major crisis. We try below to summarize as clearly as possible the complexity of rivalries between provincial chiefs, which resulted in multiple and rapid change of dynasties. The emperor, who was chosen from among the descendants of King Solomon by a college of priests and nobles, had lost all real power. From the end of the seventeenth century, power had in principle been exercised by the *ras,* the general-in-chief, who had precedence over all other nobles and had established a kind of dynasty. The Church was divided between the Unionists, who followed the Alexandrian orthodoxy according to which Christ was both god and man, and the Unctionists, according to whom the unction of the Holy Spirit had made Jesus a divine entity inseparable from the Holy Trinity. As soon as the emperor expressed a preference for the latter, the Ethiopian Coptic Church, led by the *etchege*, the highest ecclesiastic dignitary, became isolated. Despite the nobility's reticence, for most nobles were Unionists, unionism was no longer represented locally by a metropolitan bishop appointed by the Orthodox Church.

The emperor's control was diminished. He received 300 Maria Theresa silver thalers annually from the Muslim merchants of Gondar,[5] which permitted him to subsist. The ras did not have much more authority. For at least half a century, there had been numerous eliminations owing to disputes over succession. Constant civil war resulted from the fact that the power was in the hands of the most enterprising and best-armed provincial leaders. In the first half of the nineteenth century, the formerly prosperous north experienced a growth in deadly conflicts between factions with allegiances that changed according to interests.

The leaders of the Yeju province south of Tigray were vying for power. Until 1788, the position of ras had been held by Ali I of Yeju, a converted ex-Muslim whose Christian allegiance was challenged by his peers. At his death, it was approximately fifteen years before Ras Gugsa of Yeju managed to impose his authority. He finally succeeded in 1803, and held the position until 1825, though not without difficulty. He had to deal with the opposition of a conservative Christian chief, Wolde Selassie (d. 1817). Selassie had taken control of the primary passes from Gondar (the official capital) to Tigray at the turn of the century. He tried to impose his suzerainty over the Muslims on the coast, and succeeded in taxing their trade with the interior. At the beginning of the nineteenth century, he was undoubtedly the most famous Abyssinian and the primary champion of Solomon's imperial tradition.

In 1825, the death of Ras Gugsa weakened the Yeju Dynasty for a time, to the benefit of the conservative coalition of the traditional aristocracy of Gondar

Map 3.1 **Ethiopia in the Nineteenth Century**

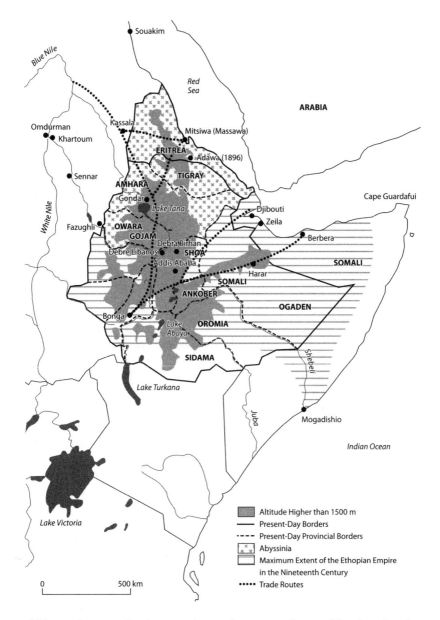

and Tigray. It was only six years later, after many plots and battles, that the new ras came to power. Ras Ali was a grand-nephew of Gugsa, and at the time was still a minor. His mother, Menen, a skillful politician, had converted to Christianity to enter the family. Moreover, in 1840, she married the last emperor of the dynasty, Yohannes III, in order to gain a degree of legitimacy, which explains her title of empress from that date. Wube of Semien, one of the chiefs of Tigray, rapidly became the head of the conservative coalition. Though he was one of Gugsa's grandsons, he accused Menen and her son of apostasy for seeking the support of their Muslim kin.

Wube played the Unionist religious card and, as the leader of Tigray, officially requested Cairo to send a metropolitan bishop as a last resort to counteract Unctionism. As soon as Bishop Abuna Salama arrived, he excommunicated Ras Ali. In 1847, he excommunicated tens of thousands of Unctionists, beginning with the *etchege,* who was the head of the Ethiopian Church. In the midst of the chaos arose the Egyptian threat: Muhammad-Ali was moving southward, and that year he occupied the port of Mitsiwa (Massawa) and the surrounding countryside in the northeast of Ethiopia. The danger led Ali, Wube, and the bishop to agree to a truce, especially since there was a new threat from the west, namely, Ras Ali's own son-in-law, Kassa Hailu, the future Emperor Theodorus II (1855–68).

Kassa Hailu came from an area near the Sudan, to the west of Lake Tana. It was a poor, low-lying area where people eked out a living from contraband between Abyssinia and the Sudan. Banditry was the primary means of social mobility. Born in 1818 to a minor local chief (who was later given an apocryphal Solomonian genealogy), Kassa Hailu was raised in the court, where he learned the arts of politics and war. He was also a keen reader, especially of ancient and modern European history. However, he was impeded by the death of his father and became the leader of a band and a slave raider. He soon led 300 men. His expeditions cut into Empress Menen's revenues, which led her to try to win him over by giving him one of her granddaughters in marriage. However, it turned out that her granddaughter was just as ambitious as Kassa Hailu, and the spouses worked together to win power. Kassa Hailu took over Gondar and, at one point, even held the royal couple (Yohannes III and Menen) hostage.

Rather than continuing to fight, Ras Ali preferred to secure Kassa Hailu's services against the Tigray coalition. In the meantime, Kassa Hailu had discovered modern weapons. In 1848 he ordered 16,000 men to attack the small garrison that Muhammad-Ali kept at Sennar on the Upper Nile, but found his forces brutally repelled by only 800 soldiers armed with muskets and two cannons. Having equipped himself in turn with modern artillery, he returned against Ali. The latter had become closer to Goshu, Chief of Tigray, and deployed his new ally against Kassa Hailu. A series of battles in 1852 and 1853 enabled Kassa Hailu to crush his enemies, take over Gondar once more, and rise to power. Initially proclaimed ras, he finally declared himself *negus negast* (king of kings or emperor) under the name of Theodorus II. He tried to win

Tigray by giving its chief the enviable title of ras. To his political and military power, which was rapidly recognized by almost all, he added religious power. Aware of the need to rebuild Orthodox unity, he firmly supported Bishop Aluna Salama, who received control of the Ethiopian Church and management of its property. In 1854, the new Emperor Theodorus presided over the Council of Amba Chara, which officially condemned the Unctionist doctrine.[6]

The troubles did not result only from a rocky history of competition among war chiefs in the context of weak central power threatened by advancing foreign states, such as Egypt and Western countries. From the mid-sixteenth century, unrest was also related to a number of converging negative factors: the ecological crisis in northern Ethiopia was exacerbated by demographic pressure, which was in turn a source of cultural and social problems. Turmoil also resulted from the northward movement of the Oromo, a people who spoke the Kush language and originated in the Horn of Africa. Their migration was the result of a powerful jihad in the sixteenth century, as well as the aridity of the area. The Oromo (also known as the Galla), whose semidesert homeland had made them herders, generally adopted the Amharic language and practices. The degree to which they merged was uneven. It was only after the Amhara took power in the late nineteenth century that oppression by the dominant group began, resulting in pan-Oromo claims in the twentieth century.[7] However, at the time, the new arrivals merged with the local population to such a degree that they could hold the highest positions, including that of ras, despite the imperial aristocracy. Some became Christians, most were Muslim, others kept their ancient beliefs, but all adopted the plow and became farmers to some extent. This is evidence that African adoption of technology was determined by environmental and social conditions.

The Oromo made a solid contribution to the spread into southern Ethiopia of what had until then been specific to the north, namely, use of the ancient plow, made of eight relatively simple bits of wood that could be adjusted to adapt to virtually any soil condition, crop, and slope. It is so efficient that it is still in use today.[8]

Growth of the Central Province of Shewa

Many Oromo settled in the center of Ethiopia, in the province of Shewa (the region of the future capital Addis Ababa). From the eighteenth to the nineteenth centuries, they became farmers like their Amhara neighbors, and helped spread use of the plow in the area. The leader of Shewa, Sahle Selassie, willingly welcomed the new labor force, which also provided a strong additional source of horsemen in case of conflict.

Focusing on domestic development, Shewa had not been involved in the north's struggles for imperial power, especially since most Amharas were Unctionists while the Tigrayans were Unionists. Sahle Selassie quickly distanced himself and, from 1813 to 1847, concentrated on consolidating local power. Thus, in the first half of the nineteenth century, Shewa became the primary economic and trading center of the empire. In the second half of the century, it reaped the political and cultural benefits of its growth.

Rather than getting involved in the north's internecine conflicts, Sahle Selassie chose to pursue more profitable objectives, such as increased domestic productivity and expansion to the south. Annexation of new lands in the name of the supposed rebuilding of the Solomon Empire was seen as a means of gaining resources for slave raids and trade. Selassie gained popularity by building roads and bridges, as well as churches, and by encouraging handicrafts and the arts. Compared with the harshness of the north, his realm appeared as a haven of prosperity and peace; he gradually furthered a movement promoting an imperial renaissance in his favor. Before his death, he was able to ensure that his son, Haile Malakot, was recognized as his heir. In the early 1850s, Haile Malakot began challenging the emperor directly, but the encounter worked against him. After his death in 1856, Haile Malakot's brother surrendered on behalf of the young Menelik II, his nephew and heir. Emperor Theodorus once again ruled over the empire.

Western Intervention

The new emperor was open to innovative ideas, but his methods remained brutal and clumsy. Unable to convince the princes to submit through negotiation, he exhausted his resources in wars of repression. Finally, in 1861, he had no choice but to seek outside support to fortify his domestic authority. In defiance of Islam, he looked first to the West. It was a risky course to take. He began by soliciting technological assistance from Protestant missionaries, namely, the brothers of the Basel Mission because he preferred the Protestants over the Catholics, whose influence was feared by Orthodox Christians. He took a step further by negotiating with European states: in 1843, he signed a friendship and trade treaty with the British and, soon after, a military accord with the French, who supplied him with arms from Obok on the Red Sea. Naively optimistic, he wrote to Queen Victoria proposing an alliance against the Turks. However, since there was no answer, he decided to provoke her by arresting several diplomats and missionaries. The British response was immediate: either release its nationals or face a punitive expedition. British forces landed in Mitsiwa in January 1868, and secured the support of Kassa, Protector of Tigray (not to be confused with Emperor Theodorus [Kassa Hailu], who died the same year). Kassa provided supplies for the troops during their advance to the capital of the time, Maqdala

(Mekdela). In the end, 4,000 demoralized imperial soldiers fled before a solid Indian-British contingent of 32,000 men, who sacked the city. They made off with 350 rare religious books (now in the British Museum), among other things. Theodorus committed suicide, and the English rewarded their allies from Tigray with large supplies of weapons and ammunition.

Kassa finally proclaimed himself Emperor in 1872, and was crowned Yohannes IV at Axum, the most ancient capital. He reigned until 1889. In addition to trying to keep the peace as well as possible in the north, from that date on, his major task was to force Menelik to surrender. However, even more than before, the empire's ever fragile internal politics were affected by complex, changeable foreign policy. There was strong pressure from Egypt: its forces landed in Mitsiwa and gradually took over the ports to the south. Beginning in 1875, Khedive Ismail ordered four expeditions to take over the Horn of Africa. Two of them were successful, and the Egyptians occupied Harar's great market square and consolidated their positions on the Somalian coast. War then raged between the Ethiopians and Egyptians. In November 1876, despite the excellence of their artillery, 25,000 Egyptians were defeated by 70,000 Ethiopians. Emperor Yohannes was free to portray the war as a conflict between two major religions: Christianity and Islam.

Menelik, who had refrained from intervening, drew the conclusion that his army had to be modernized. He increased contact with French and Italian merchants, who were given access to the Shewa route and could thereby avoid the northern territories controlled by the emperor and the Egyptians. He also sent an Ethiopian priest to Europe to make contact with local geographical societies.

However, Menelik was not yet strong enough to challenge the emperor directly. The conflicts turned to his disadvantage. In 1876, he was forced to officially agree to become a vassal of the emperor, though he negotiated his submission in exchange for official acknowledgment that he was the king (*Negus*) of Shewa. Political submission went along with religious submission: two years later, an agreement between churches (Debra Libanos in Shewa and Garra Haymanot in Tigray) confirmed Unionist supremacy. The agreement decreed that pagans would be converted immediately, and Muslims over time, which contradicted Shewa's tolerant tradition. Menelik also had to expel the Catholic missionaries that he had begun allowing into Shewa.

Menelik: Advancing Toward an Empire

Despite these measures, Menelik maintained a form of regional autonomy. More than ever, he made his province the center of expansion toward the south, particularly in the year of the victory at Embobo (1882) in the southwest. Since he had to pay tribute to the emperor twice annually, Menelik was led to engage in raids (for gold, honey, coffee, gum arabic, and slaves) ever farther away in order to avoid despoiling his own lands. More daring than the emperor with respect to Westerners, he revived Theodorus's modernizing plans. He hired a young Swiss man, Alfred Ilg (1854–1916), who stayed in his service until 1908 and acted as an engineer, doctor, builder, and political advisor. He brought foreigners of all kinds to his court, including Asians, Arabs, and Europeans, as long as they favored business. Interested in obtaining access to the sea where it was not controlled by the emperor, he negotiated with the French and Italians to gain access to the Obok route, which had been opened through his conquests. At the turn of the twentieth century, it was he who authorized the French to build the railroad that penetrated all the way to his capital city. Until the railroad was completed, the alternating dry and wet seasons meant that major caravans could travel only during two periods: October–November and March–April. Military and commercial success continued with the support of the Oromo, while attempts to recuperate trade from the north also resulted in military advances for Menelik to the northwest. The emperor's attempt to control his awkward vassal by imposing on him marriage with a princess from the northern province of Yeju backfired because Taytu Betul was as brilliant as she was ambitious. She and her husband worked together to ensure his supremacy.

Over those years, Western pressure increased. The Egyptians were forced to retreat owing to the Mahdist revolt, and they accepted the British suggestion to withdraw. This resulted in a treaty among Ethiopia, Great Britain, and Egypt, in which Yohannes agreed to allow Egyptian troops to travel across the empire. The following year, the Italians, who had been interested in the Horn of Africa since the early 1870s, entered the "scramble for Africa." They landed in Mitsiwa with the intention of gaining a foothold on the Red Sea. From then on Menelik's political maneuvering became more subtle. He understood that war between Italy and Ethiopia was probable, which did not displease him since such a turn of events would weaken the north. While the ras was annihilating an Italian column of 500 men in Tigray, an attempt at reconciliation with the British was proving hopeless, and the emperor was facing Mahdist forces that were attacking and burning the former capital of Gondar. Menelik moved south to take over Harar in 1887, which the Egyptians had evacuated two years earlier. Though he tolerated Islam there, he argued in favor of "reconquest" of an area that was claimed to have belonged to Shewa in the sixteenth century.

His alliance with the Italians was satisfactory, owing in part to the actions of Count Pietro Antonelli, head of the Italian Geographical Society. He acted as an intermediary so that Italy provided Menelik with commercial assistance and the promise of Remington guns in exchange for, at least, his neutrality in the conflict with the emperor. The draft of the Italian-Ethiopian treaty dates from 1879 and, in a secret clause from 1887, the Italians already recognized Menelik as a potential emperor, long before the issue was resolved domestically. Nonetheless, he did not sign the treaty until 1889 (Treaty of Wichale), after the emperor had been killed in a clash with the Mahdists without ever having penetrated into Shewa. Things continued to go badly: Menelik had just unilaterally proclaimed himself *Negust Negast*, in other words, king of kings. He thought he was signing a friendship treaty, which suggested that Italian assistance was possible with respect to foreign affairs. However, the Italian version of the treaty made Italian control compulsory. Italy claimed Menelik's lands as a protectorate, and the assertion was supported for a time by the British. Menelik nonetheless had the Bishop of Shewa (who was the metropolitan bishop from 1889 to 1927) crown him Emperor of Ethiopia on November 3, 1889. The event took place in Entotto, which he had chosen as capital city in reference to a supposed tradition of the sixteenth century. In the wake of these developments, he received the support of the Ras of Tigray who, finding himself between a rock and a hard place, preferred to belong to an independent empire rather than to have his lands colonized by the Italians.

Pursuing their advantage, the Italians occupied Adwa in January 1890. In September 1895, Menelik declared mass conscription and thereby increased his forces to over 100,000. He led them northward against some 8,000 Italians and 10,000 Eritreans. Crushed at Adwa in February 1896, the Italians lost 70 percent of their troops, an enormous disaster for a modern army. Despite some 7,000 dead, the Ethiopian army fared much better under the leadership of Ras Makonen, Prince of Harar (whose glory was useful to his son, the future Emperor Haile Selassie, who was overthrown in 1974, almost a century later).

At that point, Menelik prudently decided not to push into Eritrea. When the peace agreement was signed, he was the first Ethiopian sovereign to deal a blow to the country's integrity by ceding the province to Italian colonization. He lost all hope of direct access to the sea, but he had a secure outlet to the southeast. Moreover, simultaneously weakening his traditional rival, Tigray, could not displease him. He probably also believed he had to salvage whatever he could in order to erase the protectorate debacle, in which he had been forced to grant control to Italy. He probably feared that the Italians intended to reactivate the protectorate, and wanted to avoid the predictable retaliation of an offended Western power.

At the same time, Menelik took the precaution of ensuring international recognition by negotiating with the Mahdists (whom he recognized in the Sudan), the French, and the British (whom he simultaneously promised that he would not support the Mahdists). The British-Ethiopian treaty of 1897, renewed in 1902, guaranteed the borders of the country and signified the end of European threats. Through complex and skillful foreign policy, Menelik thus finessed long-lasting independence from the rest of the empire, and, in the ten years that followed, spread his control far into the south. Of course, in 1904–6, France, Great Britain, and Italy took advantage of the first bout of illness that would be his end, and they signed a tripartite agreement that defined their interests as if Ethiopia did not exist, including the area of French influence around the Aden-Addis Ababa railroad, British rights over the Nile Basin, and Italy's coastal possessions.

However, the West's attitude changed overnight: from a country of bandits ravaged by a murderous slave trade, Ethiopia had become the vessel of the most ancient Christian civilization. Europeans suddenly discovered that Ethiopians were like them: Whites who were simply tanned by the strong tropical sun. Menelik used the lull to build national unity. In order to show his desire for general reconciliation, he symbolically married his daughter to a prince of a northern province (Wolo) who was also a former Muslim who had converted. His diplomatic work was combined with legal and land title systems designed to integrate northern Ethiopia (traditional Abyssinia) with southern Ethiopia. He consolidated his lands through a series of fortified villages peopled by settler-soldiers, who were assisted by farmers responsible for supplying them and local administrators. The settlers were chosen from the traditional elites. Thus, alongside the clergy, soldiers and public servants became the twin keys to the regime. They based their power on property rights, which had grown in importance owing to the promotion of private property that could be inherited. Menelik imposed this innovation on the north, and the system of tribute maintained in the southern provinces was sufficient to ensure economic independence. In parallel, he neutralized Islam by placing Christian princes from the north in control of local southern authorities and by encouraging the southward migration of people from the north. These migrants were from then on known as the Galla, in contrast with the Amhara of central Shewa.

Yet, while Emperor Menelik had grasped the usefulness of modernization, he did not see any point in changing the autocratic nature of his own power since he considered his victory over the West as confirmation that his approach was correct. He thus fostered imports of manufactured goods, but not changes to the mode of production or social system, though he gave the country its own currency in 1894. For his people, the great innovation was limited to construction of the railroad, which began in 1902. It stimulated investment by Indian capitalists and brought the country into the world economy. Only the new capital city, Addis-Ababa, which had become the focus of the link between the north and south, reflected the new political and economic order. It was soon provided with a modern school, hospital, telephone and telegraph services, and even heating and running water in the palace. As a result, the city became stable instead of shifting, like most earlier seats of imperial power. The turning point was in 1890–91, when a lack of firewood seemed to make it once again necessary to move the royal residence, which was then home to nearly 50,000 people. However, the construction boom occurred soon after the battle of Adwa, which had the effect of increasing urban migration: Ethiopians from all regions flocked to the city and began to spread a new, mixed urban culture. There was nothing yet to indicate that the emperor had the intention of breaking with custom. In 1901 he seemed to have his eye on a new site about twenty-five miles away. However, the move never occurred. In the meantime, the palace had become an enormous center of production and consumption with many different structures. The move became less certain. Each day, the palace provided for the needs of at least 3,000 people, though the number could reach 45,000 during major government celebrations. In 1897, Menelik replaced the traditional ceremonial tent by a huge permanent reception hall. Deforestation was made up for by eucalyptus plantations. In 1905, a British banker wrote, "In view of the buildings, roads, bridges, etc. currently under construction, it is clear that the choice of Addis Ababa as capital city has become irrevocable."[9]

Old-Style Colonization: Zanzibar

Toward the end of the eighteenth century, a British traveler described the port of Zanzibar as "a city [. . .] composed of a few houses and straw huts."[10] However, the apparent simplicity of the architecture masked the growth of the island's commercial power. Around 1800, Zanzibar had become the primary center for trade along the east coast of Africa. It was where Arabs, Indians, and, increasingly, Europeans interested in African products met. Gradually, Zanzibar left the orbit of Indian mercantile capitalism, which dominated in the first half of the century, and entered Western industrial capitalism.

The Indians' Piloting Role

The Indians considered that Zanzibar had the best ivory in the world, and they had had a busy slave trade there for two centuries.[11] The monsoon winds helped the enterprise because from November to March they blew from the northeast and allowed Indian and Arab sailboats to reach East Africa, while from April to October the dry winds from the southwest carried them back to their home ports. Moreover, the September–October return sailings were synchronized with the arrival in Swahili ports of caravans from the interior, since caravans took advantage of the dry season to cross and raid the hinterland. Dynamic trade between Zanzibar and Bombay contributed to the growth of Swahili cities. While they used to spend more time in the southern ports held by the Portuguese, particularly Mozambique, from the 1780s on the Indians turned to the areas dominated by Zanzibar. Producers followed the movement: the Yao and the Makua reoriented their travel toward the northern route leading to Kilwa. The primary beneficiaries were the Indians, whose numbers increased. At the end of the eighteenth century, there were around 1,200 at Muscat, seat of the sultanate of Oman in southern Arabia; they had increased to 4,000 by the beginning of the nineteenth century. In 1811, they dominated trade in Zanzibar, where at least two Indian traders had their permanent residences in 1819. From 1841 on, it became easier for them to settle there owing to the appointment of a British Consul funded by the government of Bombay. In 1844, there were 800 (compared with eighteen Europeans) and nearly 4,000 around 1870, most of whom were Muslim and had come with their families. Their presence was vital because they introduced the people of Zanzibar to the complexity of trade around the Indian Ocean. They traded cotton cloth and beads for slaves and ivory, which was in great demand in India, especially for wedding jewelry. In 1859, Indians were still trading for 310,000 thalers of ivory and 100,000 thalers of cloves annually, almost as much as the Westerners ($350,000 and $250,000, respectively). At the time, the Americans were responsible for three-quarters of the West's ivory trade.

The Omani and the Shirazi: Armed Peace

The Arabs of Oman had long claimed control over the area, and had solid trade relations with it, despite the fact that their capital city of Muscat was 2,000 miles away from the coast of Africa. Muscat was at the time the best port in the whole area, and the city had at least 10,000 inhabitants. It had secured its position by maintaining prudent neutrality toward the French as well as the English during the Napoleonic Wars and by acknowledging British supremacy in the Indian Ocean. Omani Sultan bin Ahmad (r. 1796–1804) obtained two treaties in exchange: one in 1798 and the other in 1800. They permitted him to continue his activities as long as they were not contrary to British economic or strategic interests along the route to India, which he controlled at the tip of the Persian Gulf.

Like his predecessors, the sultan claimed rights along the coast of Africa, from Cape Delgado in southern Somalia to and including some vague stakes in the Comoro Islands and even Madagascar. In fact, his real authority was limited to Kilwa (Kisiwani), an old Swahili port that was rather dilapidated, and the Island of Zanzibar *stricto sensu*. The French had been present since the second half of the eighteenth century in settlements along the Indian Ocean, such as Isle de France (Mauritius) and Isle Bourbon (Reunion). On the formerly uninhabited islands, they had established plantation economies for which they needed slave labor. Madagascar and the coast of Mozambique did not provide them with enough, so they went looking for more in the sultan's lands. In particular, they went to Kilwa, which in the 1770s became one of their primary sources as a result of the Yao caravans from the interior, which were interested in acquiring guns for hunting.

The period was dominated by the refusal of the Swahili city of Mombasa, controlled by the powerful Mazrui family, to bend before the Omani sultan. In 1814, the new Mazrui dignitary refused to acknowledge the sultan's authority. The Mazrui's antagonism was a main reason for the Omani intervention, though the problematic succession of Sultan bin Ahmad, who died in 1804, weakened the dynasty for a number of years: his two sons vied for the throne until one of them expired in 1812. The survivor, Said bin Sultan, finally consolidated his power in 1820.

The Omani and Mazrui disputed the Lamu Archipelago for ten years. There, as elsewhere, the local Swahili, the Shirazi, who later claimed distant Persian roots, had an excellent relationship with the Arabs. The cities of Mombasa and Pate had launched a failed expedition against Lamu, in which the inhabitants of the archipelago had reacted by calling on the sultan's forces for aid. Finally, the sultan's power was recognized in 1822, and two years later the Omani also occupied Pate on the coast. Two Shirazi chiefs of the Isle of Pemba seized the opportunity to seek the sultan's support against the Mazrui, who occupied their island. The agreement, which was signed in writing and blood, stipulated that if the sultan expelled the Mazrui, the people of Pemba would show allegiance by paying tribute. So, when Pemba was taken in 1823 by the Omani governor of Zanzibar, it was a major blow to the Mazrui, for the island had long been the breadbasket and source of wood for the area. From then on it played that role for Zanzibar, which was given over to producing cloves for export.

In the midst of the confusion, the sultan of Oman decided to travel to Africa in person to protect his interests. He arrived at Mombasa in 1828. Already weakened, the Mazrui had no choice but to accept the Omani garrison. Struck by the obvious activity in Zanzibar, which was the primary transit point between Asia and the backcountry of continental Africa, the sultan immediately appointed his own son Khalid as resident. Khalid was thirteen years old, and was assisted by the Vizir Suleyman bin Hamid. The latter remained second in command until his death in 1873.

The sultan returned in 1833 and in 1836, and finally decided to move his

Map 3.2 **Central-Equatorial Africa in the Nineteenth Century**

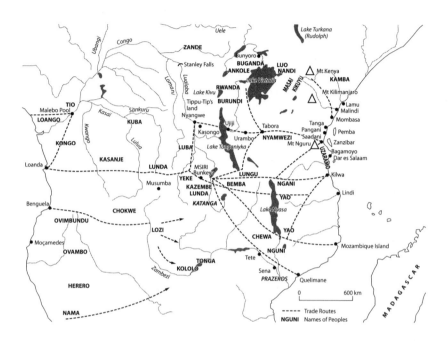

capital to Zanzibar in 1840, as soon as he had reduced his last serious opponents on the coast, the Mazrui of Mombasa. During that period, there were
repeated skirmishes in Mombasa until, in 1836, the Mazrui agreed to become
governors under the sultan's authority. However, since he had little trust in the
family, the sultan gained the support of dissident factions and succeeded in
eliminating almost the whole clan the following year. He had some of them
executed, and the rest deported to Oman. The other major families of Mombasa (known as the twelve families) accepted the measure on the condition
of being given a large degree of internal autonomy. The sultan agreed to give
them a regular indemnity in compensation for the lost revenue owing to the
city's inclusion in the Zanzibar customs system. While some Mazrui leaders
caused problems in surrounding cities in following years, the greatest obstacle
to Omani hegemony was thus removed.

Zanzibar's Growth: Production, Trade, and Slavery

Said bin had used the years to familiarize himself with the economic and
political potential of his island. He began a series of actions that, in a few
decades, would confirm Zanzibar as the major crossroads for trade among

Asia, Europe, and even the United States, and define it as a land of planta-tions. Until then, the aristocracy had been formed mainly of Shirazi and Indian merchants, some of whom had become landowners. The Omani were also major landowners. There were approximately 1,000 plantation owners in 1819, and 5,000 by the 1840s. From that time on they began building their typical two-story homes with large sculpted wooden doors, as well as most of the fifty-odd mosques around the city.

The sultan's most crucial decision was to encourage clove growing on the islands of Zanzibar and Pemba. The highly sought-after spice, which comes from the tree's unopened buds, grows in very few places. The Dutch had brought it from the Moluccas, and, at the end of the eighteenth century, a Frenchman, Pierre Poivre, succeeded in introducing it to Ile Bourbon. Around 1800, both Ile Bourbon and Ile de France were producing it. In the 1820s, an Arab named Saleh bin Haramil al-Abry probably introduced it to Zanzibar with the help of a Frenchman named Sausse. It turned out that Zanzibar and Pemba had ideal ecological conditions for growing the difficult spice.

The enterprise was courageous because it takes a tree six to seven years before becoming productive, and it becomes truly profitable only after ten years. The undertaking has been explained by both increasing problems in the international slave trade and the need to find a dynamic response to stiffer competition from Indians.[12] In contrast, the crop provided relative security. Trade in the region had not previously focused much on produc-tion, and the hazards of such commerce were unfamiliar to the people; but they were already acquainted with the style of farming, which was similar to date farming in Oman.[13] The trees planted in the 1830s began producing 9,000 frasila (thirty-five pounds) in 1839–40, reached 97,000 in 1846–47, and 143,000 in 1856, the year Sultan Said died. The rapid expansion led to a drastic drop in the price of cloves, which were exported mainly to India and Arabia. A frasila, which cost forty thalers in the 1830s, was worth only two in 1856. This is why the plantations stopped spreading. Yet, all the Ar-abs in Zanzibar had by then acquired a lifestyle entirely organized around plantation property, farming, and harvesting. This was the determining economic and cultural focus of the people of both islands, both before and after the abolition of slavery.

Naturally, clove farming required a large labor force of both Omanis and slaves, and considerable land had to be cleared at first. The work established two forms of organization. At Zanzibar itself, where there was strong dual pressure from the sultan's orders and expansion of his capital city, a two-tiered society prevailed: masters, who were mostly Omani, and slaves. The new farming required fertile virgin soil, which could be found around the city and in forested areas where there was enough rain, such as along the fault line that runs north-south a few miles from the western coast. Until then, the area had been inhabited by hunter-gatherers. The Shirazi people living there prior to the Omani had been content with the less fertile land in the north and east since it was easier to cultivate. There is not much information available about how the land rights were transferred for the areas that had not yet been farmed. Arab private law certainly won over the concessions that had probably been granted according to custom by the Shirazi. The Shirazi were confined to the less profitable part of the island, while the more fertile areas went to a rich Arab aristocracy of plantation owners. The result was a society broken into two distinct, antagonistic classes, to which a third was added when the slave population began to grow. It was estimated that about two-thirds of the inhabitants of the two islands, some 300,000 people, were slaves in 1860. Work on the plantations was intense, particularly when the buds were harvested between August and December. Every tree had to be visited at least three times. Especially initially, the local people were little inclined to abandon their former agricultural practices, and plantation owners had to rely on a huge slave labor force imported from the neighboring coasts. The slave trade flourished because the annual death rate was estimated to be between 22 and 40 percent on the two islands, which meant the entire slave population had to be renewed every three years. This also meant that between 10,000 and 15,000 people arrived on the islands every year, with a marked spike in the trade in 1840–50, when perhaps half the slaves were re-exported from Zanzibar toward the north and from the Arabian Peninsula all the way to India.

At Pemba, in contrast, the arrival of Arabs was more spread out over time, and all of the land on the island had long been fertile and cultivated. A rich class of plantation owners established homes there. Syncretism with the local inhabitants, largely through intermarriage, was more complex. A class of midsized and small plantation owners developed in parallel, and the process accelerated when Pemba became the primary producer after a catastrophic cyclone in 1872.

Controlling coastal trade in gum copal, cowries, and skins; long-distance trade in ivory and slaves; worldwide exports of cloves from its islands; and Pemba, the breadbasket (rice and manioc), the sultan of Zanzibar was the great power of East Africa in the nineteenth century. Around 1850, his income, estimated at his death at about 500,000 thalers a year, flowed in more or less equal proportions from the slave trade and other exports, particularly cloves. The trade required a form of authority that was both flexible and unyielding. This established a kind of colonial power in East Africa: formal on the coast, informal toward the interior.

A Differentiated Aristocratic Society

The sultan's domestic policy resulted from subtle interplay among the Arab clans of Oman. Indeed, that was how the Busaidi Dynasty, from which he came, had taken power. From the beginning of the century, he had carefully filled the government of Zanzibar with men who were devoted to him either because they had risen from slavery or because they belonged to his clan. He openly protected the families of Arab notables and clergy who were already established in Zanzibar, and he was attentive to meet with and consult them often.

The sultan dealt with the preexisting local Shirazi people, who wanted to differentiate themselves from non-Muslim African immigrants and especially slaves, by interfering as little as possible in their affairs. At Zanzibar, even the largest group, the Hadimu, was led by a dynasty of chiefs whose ancestor had recognized Arab domination as early as 1728. Said was careful to meet the reigning chief, Ahmad bin Hassan al-Alawi, whose capital city was located some ten miles from the city of Zanzibar. Hassan al-Alawi agreed to pay an annual tax of two thalers per married man and to fulfill requisitions for laborers to carry out local works. In exchange, the Shirazi would remain free to govern themselves as in the past, in villages generally managed by a committee of four elders and grouped into districts under the control of a *sheha* (sheik). However, over the course of the century, the chief's power declined and troubles increased as the best land was cleared by plantation owners. Nonetheless, since the island was not really penetrated by practicable roads before the twentieth century, everyday life did not change very much. On Pemba, the local people prolonged their relatively decentralized ancestral political practices under the control of an Arab governor whose power remained limited until the last third of the century.

The sultan avoided intervening in the everyday lives of those he governed. His major concern was collection of the customs tariffs on which his income depended. In 1820, he had the cunning to contract the collection to the traders themselves, represented by an Indian Bhatia, Sewji Topan, so that the responsibility was shifted to that milieu. The role of the customs master became crucial. The sultan left him free to collect duties as he wished, since abuses of power were virtually impossible owing to international treaties. In 1841, Jairam, the son of Sewji, told a French officer that the position was not so profitable in itself, but gave the holder a de facto monopoly over the state's commercial affairs. The sultan simply asked for advances on customs duties, and the accounts were balanced every six months. The amount of customs duties increased from 84,000 Maria Theresa thalers in 1819 to 310,000 in the 1860s. The advantage for the Indians in charge was that they became their master's creditors. That ensured they would keep their position, which involved maintaining the difficult diplomatic balance necessary for the sultan's predominance in the Indian Ocean.

This explains why a considerable share of the sultan's income went toward the maintenance of a merchant and military fleet, which in the 1820s included seventy to eighty sailboats armed with as many as seventy-four cannons. According to the British consul, in 1834 it was more impressive than all of those in the seas between the Cape of Good Hope and Japan combined. Between 1830 and 1850, the sultan's ships could be seen at New York, London, and Marseille. However, the fleet was not sufficiently maintained, and over time it declined. While it continued to impress the people living on the coast, it was impotent against the British fleet. Owing to his naval superiority, the sultan did not have to deal personally with the coastal cities, especially since he was careful to pay subsidies to the most important local chiefs, such as those of Mombasa. Another consequence was that, unlike his navy, the sultan's army was minimal. The Arab tradition was to raise troops in one's own tribe as required. While the practice was necessary in Arabia, it was not really required on the coast of Africa, where the sultan preferred to use negotiation. His soldiers generally came from Baluchistan and Hadhramaut, and were limited to his personal guard and the police of the city of Zanzibar, as well as a few men responsible for protecting the Indians appointed to the customs posts scattered along the coast.[14]

International Ambitions

Parallel to this development, international interests rapidly became interwoven into local affairs. As soon as they were defeated by Pemba, the Mazrui had sought support from abroad, initially from the Indians and then from the English. The latter were beginning to get seriously involved in the struggle against the slave trade, and therefore feared Said's expansion in East Africa. After the Napoleonic Wars, the British had taken over Mauritius (1810), which they made the center of their antislave trade crusade in East Africa. In 1821, a delegation visited Zanzibar and submitted a request to the sultan to cooperate in abolition of the slave trade. The sultan apparently acquiesced in 1822, signed a treaty at Oman and, in 1826, agreed to appoint one of his subjects as a British agent in Zanzibar. However, it is dubious that he ever took any action. Likewise, in Mombasa the Mazrui agreed to the presence of a British resident in exchange for the promise that they would be helped to recover their former possessions. However, there was no further action, for the Mazrui manifestly did not intend to keep their side of the deal.

Clove plantations and the corollary growth of slavery increased opportunities as well as frictions. Surprisingly, the first Westerners to participate directly in the market were Americans from the (non-slave-owning) north of the United States. Faced with the relative indifference of the Europeans, New England traders wishing to open new markets to their nascent maritime operations prospected "legitimate" trade opportunities in the Indian Ocean. Cloves appeared in Zanzibar at that time. The boat of a New England merchant who visited the coast regularly in 1820–30 first stopped over in Zanzibar in 1817. An American trader was present when the sultan visited Zanzibar in 1828. He took advantage of the opportunity to complain about extortion by public servants. He established the initial terms of a trade agreement that was reworked by a representative of the federal government in 1833 and ratified in 1835. The treaty established very equal terms, according to which the Americans were assured that they had to pay the sultan only a maximum customs duty of 5 percent on their imports, while Zanzibar would in return receive most favored nation status in American ports. In 1837, Richard Waters of Salem was assigned to Zanzibar. He was the first Western consul in the country, and helped to promote inexpensive American cotton cloth, known as *amerikani*, on the Zanzibar market.

This initiative led to a change in the British attitude: they revised the 1822 accord and signed a new trade agreement in 1838–39. However, they sent hardly any representatives until 1841, and their antislavery attitude was an impediment to business relations. They paralyzed the sultan's first attempt to extend to sugar cane the success achieved with cloves. To do so, he needed the knowledge and technical skills of English plantation owners. However, he met with the British consul's refusal to agree to have English experts use the slaves he provided. The sultan nonetheless proceeded: in 1847, 250,000 tons of sugar were produced. Toward the end of the century, the number of plantations employing slave labor shot up on the east coast of Africa. A concrete French attempt met with failure (some thirty settlers from Reunion did not survive the climate), but a treaty was signed in 1844, and a consul was also sent. German traders began arriving in the area in about 1850. Their interest grew with the expansion of steamboat navigation and the 1869 opening of the Suez Canal. That enabled them to trade directly with the Tanzanian coast and the coast of West Africa, which they flooded with low-quality cowries gathered in large quantities on the beaches of Zanzibar.[15] Around 1850, there were in fact people of a dozen different nationalities trading in Zanzibar. There were at least nine large American, French, and German companies, as well as many Indian traders, most of whom were from Bombay: there were 2,000 at Muscat in 1840.

In the first half of the century, the British were in an ambiguous position: officially against the slave trade, they pretended to believe Sultan Said's promises because they needed a stable power along the route to their Indian and Asian interests. However, in 1832, when the sultan decided to make Zanzibar his main residence, the British consul at Muscat was obliged to follow him, especially since the central government was transplanted there in 1840. The sultan, who could have found support from other foreign powers, knew very well that there would be a price to pay if he ignored the British. They would stop at nothing to protect their dominant position in the Indian Ocean. Though he did everything he could, his power gradually diminished. After Said's death in 1856, one of his successors, Bargash, even considered leaving Zanzibar and creating a port on the coast of Africa to escape British control. Indeed, the site he had in view was where the Germans later established Dar es Salaam. However, when he died in 1888, the plans were abandoned, and Bargash's son, Sultan Ali bin Said, had to resign himself to agreeing to the creation of the British protectorate in 1891. The British decided who would become the next sultan: in 1896, following a forty-five-minute battle that destroyed the palace and killed some fifty Zanzibarites, they imposed their choice, namely, Hamoud bin Muhammad Al-Said. The fiction of the sultanate was maintained until 1964.

By 1897, the British had abolished slavery (though concubines were permitted until 1911). They tried to solve the labor shortage by creating a labor office, but the ruined Arab aristocracy did not recover from the shock, and former slaves, who numbered 40,000 in 1897, swelled the masses of the poor. Agricultural production collapsed, and the colonial government did nothing to bring the island out of its lethargy. On Pemba, though it provided three-quarters of the country's exports, no serious effort was made until 1972.

Societies in the Interior and Acculturation

Until the nineteenth century, while Swahili ports had long been integrated into trade in the Indian Ocean, African societies in the interior had been relatively out of reach. Slave trading had a long history, but in a diffuse form. In the nineteenth century in Zanzibar, the plantation economy increased the demand, as it had in the Americas in the seventeenth century. Prior to that time, Indian demand for ivory and slaves had been far from negligible, especially in the eighteenth century. In the south, Yao caravans from Mozambique crisscrossed the countryside, from west of Lake Malawi, where the Nkhotakota market was located, to the coastal ports, of which the main one was Kilwa. Demand generated by French settlers on the islands and the tolerated continuation of the Portuguese slave trade helped to open up the backcountry, essentially to slave trading. Zanzibar drew its supplies mainly from the center: the Nyamwezi became the primary suppliers of both ivory and slaves. At the time, there were more than 100,000 Nyamwezi. (In 1957, the Nyamwezi population was estimated at 365,000; if the closely related Sukuma to the north are included there could be over a million.) The Nyamwezi were organized into tiny chiefdoms, each of which was under the orders of a chief, the *ntemi*, whose authority was more religious than political. They cultivated mixed farming in the rainy season with a harvest around September, but also participated actively in interregional trade thanks to their complementary activity of elephant hunting. Around 1800, they reached Katanga in central Africa, and, at the end of the century, Msiri, a Nyamwezi, became a warlord and slave trader controlling a large part of Katanga. The Nyamwezi also appeared on the coast around 1800. A route was opened in (present-day) Tanzania, from Ujiji on Lake Tanganyika to Bagamoyo on the coast. Throughout the nineteenth century, Indian, American, and European demand for ivory grew consistently.

The routes also followed the Upper Congo River and its tributary the Lualaba, with its ports of Nyagwe and Kassango. Smaller groups of traders began to move from the coast into the heart of central Africa, into the kingdoms of Buganda and even into Rwanda, Burundi, and Kasembe, to the east of the Lunda Kingdom. More to the north, the Kamba of Kenya began to travel across the land, from the Ethiopian border and Lake Victoria, around Mount Kilimanjaro to the port of Mombasa.

These three main routes took definitive form in the first half of the nineteenth century. Small colonies of Arabs and Swahilis scattered into the backcountry to escape the sultan's direct control, though they acknowledged the consistency of his system and his regulatory role. Some merchants kept their rainy-season lodgings in Zanzibar, where they had houses in the city and even plantations. This was the case of Tippu-Tip, a businessman who met the explorer Stanley in the Upper Congo.[16] In the second half of the century, the Arab and Swahili notables' desire for supremacy began to cause direct conflicts with the people of the interior.

Mirambo, an Enlightened Minor Despot

This was the case with Mirambo, originally a minor Nyamwezi *ntemi*. Born around 1840, he probably cut his teeth as a fighter while working as a caravaner when he was a young man. He also adopted the military techniques of a dynamic group that had recently entered the area: the Nguni. They had arrived at the beginning of the century under their leader Zwangendaba, a Zulu chief who had broken away from Shaka. Mirambo spoke Nguni as well as Nyamwezi, and also understood Swahili and the rudiments of Arabic. He established an army employing Shaka's military practices, such as the use of young unmarried soldiers who had to consecrate themselves to warfare until they were authorized to marry. Mirambo became *ntemi* around 1857, and by the early 1860s he was a well-organized chief leading some 6,000 people. He began engaging in conquests around his new capital city, Urambo, which was about sixty miles to the west of Unyanyembe (Tabora). Despite five years of war (1871–75) he did not manage to take Tabora, but the troops sent by the sultan of Zanzibar did not manage to reduce him either. The political rivalry led to de facto recognition, which was advantageous for the commercial interests of both adversaries.

Mirambo obviously needed to procure many weapons and much ammunition, but he also wanted to understand what made the Europeans superior, as he said to the missionaries. He had the political wisdom to take care in his relations with Westerners, especially the British, through the intermediary of the all-powerful Consul John Kirk of Zanzibar. He received the explorer Stanley twice, and Stanley's praise made him popular among Europeans. In 1879, he received a mission from the London Missionary Society in the person of Dr. Southon. The doctor was more interested in setting up a hospital than in converting people, and was Mirambo's best advisor until his accidental death in 1882. Mirambo always reserved an excellent welcome for foreign visitors, whether they were traders or missionaries; he also maintained friendly relations with the powerful Arab merchant Tippu-Tip. Both had interest in amicable dealings: Mirambo needed an advocate with respect to Sultan Bargash, and Tippu-Tip wanted his caravans to travel in peace through Nyamwezi country: his business center was in the Upper Congo, especially rich in ivory and slaves. Tippu-Tip therefore refused to get involved in the quarrel led by his fellow Taborans, and visited Mirambo in 1883.[17]

Mirambo was unquestionably a great politician in his time. He succeeded in establishing absolute authoritarian order in his centralized state. He even avoided the worst when in 1880, in one of his military campaigns toward the south, his troops inadvertently killed two Scottish explorers who were traveling under the auspices of the king of Belgium. Here we can see the difference in the way Western historiography treats him: it is relatively indulgent with respect to his activities as a leading slave trader, though it denies the possession of any good qualities in the case of Rabīh, to whom the same sort of misfortune occurred; namely, one of his allies assassinated the members of the little Crampel Mission. Nonetheless, the incident only facilitated a rupture that rapidly became predictable with the advance of Western ambitions toward the interior. Mirambo's death in 1884 left only weak successors. In 1885, the White Fathers, who had recently moved to Urambo despite the Protestants' hostility, left their weakened missionary post. The kingdom was unable to stand in the way of the German advances, which began the same year.

In the Margins between Worlds: Rabīh

In the Sudan area, the beginning of the nineteenth century was a time of withdrawal and transition. At the other side of the Sudan, in Hausa country, the Muslim renewal was flourishing under Uthman dan Fodio. In the eastern Sudan, in contrast, the ancient dynasties had broken down long before. The Nilotic dynasty of the Funj had disintegrated into a multitude of tiny tribal groups. The area was open to all ambitions, namely those of the new Viceroy of Cairo, Pasha Muhammad-Ali. The Sudan was overlooked by the Egyptians until 1820. The fertile basin of Bahr al-Ghazal contained wealth in the form of ivory and ore to replenish the Egyptian treasury, finance conquests, and, since the area was relatively well populated, provide the slaves Muhammad-Ali needed as soldiers for his army. He began by conquering Dongola and then, the next year, Sennar and Kordofan.

Egypt and the Conquest of the Sudan

Where the two Niles meet, Khartoum, principal garrison of the army, became the capital city in 1830. It was the center of a vast ivory-, weapon-, and slave-trading network led by people from Khartoum, as well as Egyptians, Syrians, and the first Europeans (there is a record of the presence of a Frenchman in 1844). Muhammad-Ali himself came to Khartoum in 1838, and launched three expeditions toward the Upper Nile, along the White Nile toward Darfur, where his men found large stocks of ivory. At the death of Muhammad-Ali in 1849, Egypt's power extended all the way to Abyssinia, at least nominally. The instruments of conquest were former Nubian slaves from Upper Egypt and Sudanese irregulars, known as *bazinqirs*, who were known for their fierceness in combat. They were under Mameluke command. A group of 500 of them was even recruited in 1863 by Napoleon III for his Mexico campaign. Survivors of that disastrous expedition formed the core of the army of conquest in the Sudan.[18] However, after a revolt in 1864, the pasha decided to replace them with Egyptians and cavalry of Turkish origin.

Darfur resisted until 1869. Abbas Pasha, Muhammad-Ali's successor, sought to make the area profitable by closing it to free trade and giving a monopoly to a few wealthy people. They paid substantial tribute to the government in order to have control over the ivory market. His successor Ismail was, despite what the Europeans may have said, probably the most modernizing of Egypt's sovereigns. He was against the slave trade, but what could he do given the interests operating in the area?

During wars that inflicted long-lasting damage on the country, a rich slave trader, Zubair Pasha, was called upon to play a decisive role between 1858

Map 3.3   **Central-Eastern Africa in the Nineteenth Century**

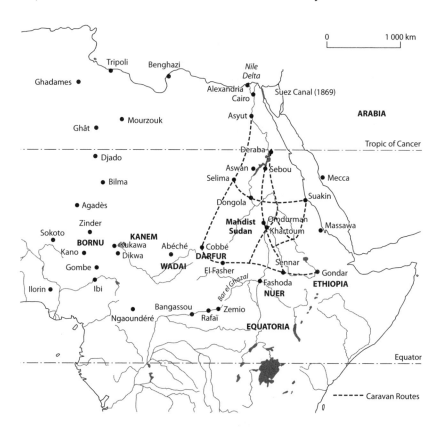

and 1876. However, in 1876 he was placed under house arrest in Cairo after having been, paradoxically, appointed viceroy of Bahr al-Ghazal for a time in order to suppress the slave trade there. This shows the lamentable state of the area, which was subject to constant raids. The son of Zubair Pasha, Sulaiman, tried for a time to rule the Sudan with the help of a faithful officer of his father, Rabīh, who had entered his service around 1860 at the age of about twenty. Rabīh was probably of slave origin and born in the Sudan. Sulaiman and Rabīh opposed the forces of the Khedive Ismail. To reestablish order and put an end to the slave trade, Ismail had recruited a brilliant British officer named Charles Gordon, who first replaced Sir Samuel Baker as governor of the province of Equatoria in 1874, and then was appointed governor-general of the Sudan in 1877. In 1879, Gordon succeeded in obtaining the capitulation of Sulaiman and his primary chiefs with the promise (which was reneged on) that they would not be executed. Only Rabīh, who had refused to surrender, was able to escape the massacre with a few men who had accompanied him.[19] Note that some fifteen years later, when he had become one of the great slave-raiding chiefs of the central Sudan, Rabīh had epistolary contact with his former master Zubair, who in the meantime had become an agent of the British secret service in Cairo.

The Rise of Rabīh, the Warlord

Rabīh thus began his career as an independent warlord followed by a band of some 2,000 bazinqirs. Wishing to put himself out of the grasp of the Egyptian authorities, he traveled to the south of Darfur to the edges of Bahr al-Ghazal and the Azande sultanates in Nzakara country (East Central Africa), where he waged war in the subsequent years. His success in the area was facilitated by the relative weakness of Nzakara social organization in which Islamized local sultans (including Rabīh's ally Rafai) dominated animist peoples with little political structure. His slave raids integrated into the area's slave trade, which was in full renewal since Gordon had left the country a second time following the overthrow of khedive Ismail. In the 1880s, Rabīh's troops probably numbered 15,000. From then until the end of the century, he made the Chad basin the base of his operations. He was therefore a wholly remarkable link between Muslim powers that were apparently very distant from one another, but were in reality linked through real diplomatic relations: the Sokoto Sultanate to the west, the Sanusiyya Empire in the center, Tippu-Tip's areas to the south, and the Mahdist Sudan in the east.

However, the wave of holy wars that originated in West Africa finally flowed into the center and east in the form of the powerful Sanusiyya brotherhood and the Sudanese Mahdiyya movement.[20] Rabīh, who crisscrossed the area for some twenty years, played the part of an intermediary between the Sanusi Mahdi and the Sudanese Mahdi.

The latter, Muhammad Abd Allah, was a pious Muslim born at Dongola on the Nile in 1843. His influence extended mainly to Kordofan (to the northeast of Bahr al-Ghazal). In 1881 he declared holy war against the corrupt Turkish-Europeans who controlled the Sudan. He gradually extended uncompromising control, based on strict respect for Islam, over a number of kingdoms that had until then been independent.[21] The strictness of the doctrine went hand in hand with the anticolonial revolt. One of the movement's mobilizing slogans was unequivocal: "Kill the Turks and refuse to pay taxes!"[22]

The situation became such that the Egyptians sent Gordon to the Sudan for the third time, on this occasion to liquidate their claims in the area. This was accomplished all the more easily when Gordon was killed trying to prevent the taking of Khartoum. Indeed, the Mahdi had victoriously resisted a number of attacks from Bar al-Ghazal. He had established his capital city at Omdurman, facing Khartoum where the two Niles meet. In 1883, he decided to follow the prophet Muhammad's example by appointing four caliphs. He offered one of the positions to Al-Sanusi, namely, the Al-Mahdi himself and leader of the Sanusiyya brotherhood that had been gaining ground in the heart of the continent since the mid-century. This was haughtily rejected. Rabīh had on several occasions unsuccessfully attacked the powerful Wadai (to the west of Darfur), which was controlled from the capital city Abeche by Sultan Yusuf (1878–1898) of Sanusi obedience. Rabīh kept up apparently cordial relations with Muhammad Abd Allah, the declared enemy of Yusuf. Indeed, Rabīh had everything to gain from maintaining his access to the eastern Sudan where he could get supplies of weapons and ammunition, and there was a better outlet for slaves. It is probable that Rabīh never met Abd Allah. He nonetheless proclaimed himself and his soldiers Abd Allah's representatives. Later, when he controlled Bornu, he did so in the name of the Mahdi, who was Abd Allah's successor after his death in 1885. This led the sultan of Sokoto, who was hostile to the Mahdi, to believe they were related.

Toward the West

Rabīh seems to have been the last and only Khartoumian to have traveled so far into the interior of the continent. In 1886, he crossed the Chari and the following year he began slave raiding in southern Bagirmi. He protected his Sudanese flanks by ensuring the docility of Dar Kuti through its leader, Al-Sanusi (who was unrelated, despite his name, to the head of the Sanusiyya). He gradually moved toward central Sudan, where the opulent markets, large herds, and relatively fertile riparian plains whet his appetite for conquest. At the time, Bagirmi was a sultanate in full decline, sometimes under Wadai control, sometimes under Bornu control, and sometimes even paying tribute (mainly in slaves) to both at once.

In 1891 Rabīh became aware of the first French colonial push into the country: the exploratory mission led by Major Paul Crampel from Brazzaville. Almost everyone in Crampel's small group, including Crampel, was murdered in an ambush set up by Al-Sanusi. While he requisitioned for his own use the weapons and personnel of the French expedition, Rabīh had not been involved in planning the massacre. He was not ignorant of other Western advances. Indeed, noticing that he was getting farther away from his Sudanese bases, he considered procuring weapons from the West through the Royal Niger Company, members of which had traveled to Yola on the Benue River, where a *lamido* reporting to the Sokoto Sultanate reigned.[23] Nonetheless, in 1892, after a four-month siege, Rabīh took Manjafa, the fortified town in which the

Bagirmian forces had taken refuge. Sultan Gaorang of Bagirmi had unsuccessfully sought help against Rabīh from the sheikh of Bornu, which was in full decadence. Rabīh then moved toward the western Sahel, where Bornu, compared with the dry and desolate Sahelian steppes of Bagirmi, looked like a vast fertile oasis. This was his last conquest. Rabīh was at this point a neighbor of the Sokoto Sultanate, and, for a short time, the east and west of the Sudanese Sahel were joined.

Bornu, located to the west and southwest of Lake Chad, had been a prosperous empire for nearly 500 years. It was well situated at the crossroads of trans-Saharan trade routes between Tripoli, Timbuktu, and Kano. At the beginning of the century it had nearly fallen to Uthman dan Fodio, but a brilliant military leader, Al-Kanemi, had taken control of the real power from the capital city of Kukawa. (He became the official chief after the death of the last king of the preceding dynasty in 1846.) In Rabīh's time, the Bornu Empire was again in decline. Kanem beyond the lake had fallen to Wadai control. Bornu's primary vassal, Bagirmi, was then paying tribute of only 100 slaves a year, as were the kingdoms on the border of Sokoto. To the north, the Damagaran region had broken away, and the eastern area near Lake Chad had become impracticable owing to constant raids by Toubou nomads from the oases of Fezzan in the north.

It was easy for Rabīh to present himself as the representative of the Mahdi, of whom the Sheikh of Bornu was aware despite the distance. In 1893, Rabīh decided to take over the empire. He began by moving to Karnak-Logone on the eponymous river. Karnak-Logone was the capital city of a vassal state; in 1852, Heinrich Barth had described the city's wide streets and two-story homes. Through a series of victorious sieges, Rabīh occupied a line of fortresses along the Chari River. From there, he allied himself with other leaders, such as Hayatu, a great grandson of Uthman dan Fodio on a dissident side of the family. Disinherited, Hayatu had allied himself with the Sudanese Mahdi (which shows the extent of contact across the continent), who had appointed him as his representative in the Sokoto Empire. Hayatu was living in the city of Yola in Adamawa. Rabīh prepared the attack against the capital of Bornu, Kukwa, a city famous for a large weekly market, known as the "Monday market." Kukwa was encircled by a solid earth wall, but the sheikh had only between 5,000 and 7,000 men to fend off Rabīh. He escaped northward to Damagaran, abandoning the city to complete pillage by Rabīh's troops. Over 3,000 inhabitants were executed, 4,000 others were taken into slavery, and at least 1,000 horses, 1,000 ivory tusks, 1,000 oxen, and 30,000 heads of small livestock were raided. In short, the city was completely destroyed and never recovered. Rabīh set up his capital at Dikwa in the south, where he kept a number of princes from the former dynasty as hostages, though he did not mistreat them. By early 1896, Rabīh, who spoke only Arabic and was almost never without his Kanuri interpreter and a bodyguard of some forty men, could consider his conquests to be complete. His principal officers (standard bearers) were from the Upper Nile, and, like Rabīh, who was nearly fifty, they were aging. The time for conquests had past.

The Master of Bornu

Once established at Bornu, where he experienced a few years of peace before the French intervention, was Rabīh a wise politician? It seems that good governance did not extend outside of the borders of his new capital city, Dikwa. It was similar to the situation in the many other city-states in the area. The countryside's organization remained rudimentary. In short, Bornu was used to provide Rabīh and his army with an opulent life at Dikwa and in the surrounding area: it was a kind of fortified city-state in the middle of the country. Dikwa was located to the south of the former capital, Kukuwa, and closer to the Chari River, Bagirmi, and Wadai, which always had to be monitored. In 1851, Heinrich Barth described the city as having 25,000 inhabitants. It was already surrounded by a fortified wall, and was the empire's second-largest agglomeration. The palace enclosure was in the Turkish style that Rabīh had known in the Sudan. The regime was a military, slave-trading, commercial dictatorship. All of the tribute willingly or forcibly paid by vassals and all the booty from raids was brought to Dikwa, where the grand chief had complete control over the treasury and public works. With the exception of beautifying the city and especially the palace, which it is said had 100 bedrooms and where the armory and ammunition stores were under his direct control, the only public works that Rabīh ordered were the construction of fortified towns and fortresses, notably along the Chari.

Outside the city, he had a country home built, wells dug, and orchards planted. He even had his own farm. Naturally, this was in addition to the construction of lodgings for his harem (some 300 women) and slaves, and those of his principal military commanders and standard bearers. He placed the city's justice in the hands of an *alkali* (from the Arabic word *al-qadi*, judge), had a mosque built, and prohibited alcohol production in the city. This was probably intended to maintain his reputation as a Muslim. He appointed Hayatu as iman (until his son assassinated him in 1897). However, his fits of anger and expeditious justice were well known, and he did not hesitate to cut the throats of adversaries and clumsy servants.

Outside the city, the country was more or less distributed among Rabīh's standard bearers, and remained in the hand of elite bazinqir troops. The rest of the country mainly suffered horrifying raids, which imposed obedience through terror. The provinces paid heavy tribute in the form of hundreds and even thousands of slaves, Maria Theresa thalers, and corn. In exchange, Rabīh let local governors, who were often former generals who had received the title as a reward, do whatever they wanted. Peasants were constantly in danger of being abducted, and their fields, herds, and villages raided. The regime thus helped to impoverish and empty the land, which had previously been described as relatively fertile and well-populated. This was similar to what Nguni raids had done to south-central Africa at the beginning of the century. Many people fled to the Fulani emirates, to the south toward the lamidat of Adamawa, and to the west and northwest, toward Kano, Damagaran, and Zinder.

Rabīh reconquered Damagaran. For a time, the inhabitants feared that he intended to attack the rich Hausa city of Kano. However, this is unlikely because Rabīh felt that in the west he was too far from his bases. Indeed, he was not at all opposed to peaceful trade, since he needed relatively modern weapons that he could obtain only from distant countries via protected caravans. Even though he had his own arsenals, he depended on foreign sources for some raw materials. He and many of his men were also used to having Mediterranean products. He ensured the safety of roads around the capital city, encouraged merchants from Tripoli to come to the city, and protected Shuwa Arabs better than the previous ruler had. Shuwa Arabs had been living in the Chad basin for several centuries and had maintained a certain level of autonomy. In 1895, he gave them approximately 400 camels raided at Kukuwa to facilitate their access to the Fezzan. From the west, Hausa merchants brought large amounts of merchandise to Dikwa by donkey. Rabīh's commercial activities probably extended all the way into Yorubaland. He sought to make contact with the British Niger Company on a number of occasions to procure firearms and cannonballs and, for local ammunition production, sulfur and powder cartridges. He was also looking for many other items, from sewing needles to Groningue swords, as well as paper, writing materials, eyeglasses, fine silk fabric, saddles for horses, and various small manufactured objects.

English and French Prevarications

Obviously, all of this worried the Europeans, who were beginning to move their peons much further ahead. The French were concerned about the ties that the British were thinking of establishing with Rabīh. The French thought that the Belgians, who had set up outposts in Bahr al-Ghazal in 1894, had also negotiated with Rabīh. The French were also suspicious about German movements toward the interior of Cameroon. Rabīh, however, had learned from his experiences in the Sudan to be wary, and wanted to avoid Europeans as much as possible. The combination of circumstances resulted in an utterly surprising British move: they hoped to make contact with Rabīh. They apparently saw him as both a rampart against the French and a potential ally owing to his old ties with Zubair Pasha, who had in his later years became an agent of the intelligence service in Cairo.[24] This is why, when a pilgrim brought Zubair Pasha a letter that Rabīh had sent him two years earlier from Ndam, in the heart of present-day Chad, the British decided to gather information on his movements. Their methods were rather curious: from Cairo, they sent by land two agents carrying a letter from his former master. They were tasked with reaching Rabīh in the heart of Africa. They also sent a third agent by sea. He landed in 1894 at Calabar in the Niger River Delta, and from there traveled upstream to seek Rabīh. The most extraordinary thing was that the enterprise was successful: two of the men (the third died en route) finally met Rabīh, and one reappeared in Nigeria after having crossed the continent uneventfully. However, the attempt to create ties failed: Rabīh refused all contact.

Though it was unsuccessful, the undertaking was nonetheless reported to the French, whose fears increased as a result. It precipitated their intervention in the area from the Congolese basin. Émile Gentil and his men traveled up the Congo and Ubangui, and arrived on the Chari in 1897, on their way to Bagirmi. There, they learned that Rabīh was involved in the death of the explorer Crampel. Gentil signed a protectorate treaty for Bagirmi with King Gaorang. From that time on, despite the bitterness of the battles that followed, Rabīh's days were numbered.

Resistance was fierce, and much blood was spilled. The victims included the expedition of Ferdinand de Béhagle, an explorer leading a commercial mission who tried to meet Rabīh in Bornu. At first, he was well received, but the relationship deteriorated and Rabīh finally threw him into jail. In 1898, a new French mission was set up to counter Rabīh's operations in Bagirmi. Gentil was once again given the command, but Henri Bretonnet first led an advance with a few Congolese and Senagalese tirailleurs. Rabīh interpreted the action as aggression, and prepared to attack him on the Chari. A furious battle followed, in which almost all of the French perished. Rabīh ordered that de Béhagle be executed in revenge at Dikwa on October 15, 1899. Thus it was war. An indecisive battle at Kuno, a fortified city on the river occupied by Rabīh's forces, was one of the most ferocious in the history of colonial conquest. The French shot 50,000 cartridges and lost almost half of their 344 men. Rabīh lost seventy-eight of his best bazinqirs and a large number of irregulars. Gentil was delayed in his progress upstream, and Rabīh was rebuilding his forces as best he could by recruiting 3,000 new soldiers. Eventually, the situation was resolved by the arrival of two other French missions. One had crossed the Sahara from North Africa and was led by Foureau and Lamy; the other had come from Dakar, and was composed of survivors of Voulet and Chanoine's murderous expedition. It was led by Joalland and Meynier, who attacked Rabīh with the Bagirmians' help. The final combat took place at Kusseri, near Lake Chad. Rabīh was crushed. The French lost nineteen men, including Commander Lamy, and fifty-three were wounded. However, probably over 1,000 men were killed on the other side, including Rabīh himself (April 22, 1900). A month later, Gentil decreed the French conquest of the entire right bank of the Chari. The sultanate of Bagirmi fell under France's direct control in 1915.

Rabīh was a cruel leader who did not hesitate to crush and exterminate his enemies in bloody massacres. However, he was also a great strategist, and his wars were not gratuitous, as they constituted the foundations of his wealth. It was not possible to always raid the same area when the zone was semidesert and sparsely populated. He constantly had to go farther afield to find slaves, which required obtaining from the coasts the weapons that ensured his artillery could beat the horsemen of the Sahel. Indeed, at the time, there were two opposing tactics, which may be described respectively as ancient and modern. On one hand, the Muslim kingdoms born out of conversion and jihads continued the aristocratic tradition based on horses. On the other hand, Rabīh, who was better informed owing to his experience with European military techniques, focused on modern weapons. This, linked with the scope of his long-distance trade, was what gave him the advantage. The foundation of his power was his army, which included between 3,000 and 4,000 men, most of whom were infantrymen, and 50 to 200 standard bearers, all of whom were Muslim and among his oldest companions and faithful slaves. The rest of his army, which he gained through conquest, was mixed. Naturally, all the soldiers lived off the land. Rabīh had about 4,000 rifles and twelve cannons seized from the Crampel mission, though he rarely used them. He had great difficulty recruiting good gunners, most of whom came from Tripoli. Since gunpowder was hard to come by, he also began developing a corps of archers, most of whom came from the Lake Chad area. Discipline was strict. Rabīh considered all of his men to be his slaves, and he did not hesitate to use the whip and even order summary executions.

The End of an Era

Rabīh's death did not put an end to the fighting. The torch was picked up by his son, Fadl Allah, then age twenty-seven, who withdrew to the capital city with 3,000 men and 400 guns. The ensuing period was complicated. To the consternation of the British and Germans, whose areas of influence were acknowledged, the French took the initiative to cross the Chari River and to pursue the enemy to the west.

When they arrived at Dikwa, there remained only about 100 Tripolitans and members of the Bornu royal family, including the eldest son of the former Sultan Garbai. The French seized the ammunition reserves and thirty-five old cannons. They pursued Fadl Allah toward the south, but were unsuccessful, though not empty-handed: they seized several hundred heads of livestock, slaves, and an estimated 6,000 prisoners, 5,000 of whom were women. Gentil wanted to appoint a safe sheikh to lead the country: his candidate was Sanda Kura, a descendant of the branch of the former dynasty that had taken refuge in Damagaran and had given its allegiance to Kusseri. From then on, the French imitated their adversary's military tactics, which were based on taking booty. The livestock of Shuwa Arabs, who were guilty of having supported Rabīh, were requisitioned and sent to Kusseri. In order to take the throne, Sheikh Sanda Kura had to agree to pay 30,000 thalers. When he failed to do so, he was dethroned and replaced by Prince Garbai, Rabīh's former favorite. Prince Garbai was in turn required to pay the 21,000 thalers owed by his predecessor, plus 50,000 additional thalers. He was brought back to the capital, escorted by twenty-five tirailleurs.

The French strategy from that time forward was not different from that of its former adversary: thousands of miles from the Congolese base, a small army had to be set up and at the same time the adversary had to be exhausted. The French used the scorched-earth technique, and continued to demand heavy ransom from conquered provinces.

Fadl Allah decided to get closer to the British, who were irritated by the French presence on their land. Indeed, at the same time, in January 1900, the Royal Niger Company was accused of creating obstacles to the free trade on the river guaranteed by the Berlin Conference. The company charter was revoked in favor of the protectorate covering the north of Nigeria and governed by High Commissioner Frederick Lugard. The following year, contact was renewed. For a time, the English seriously considered recognizing the son of Rabīh as the sheikh of Bornu. Lugard was not in favor. Meanwhile, the French finally defeated Fadl Allah, who was killed in August 1901, not far from Maiduguri. They had his head cut off and preserved in salt. It was then brought back to Dikwa and displayed on the city wall, along with the heads of two of his standard bearers, to the triumphant shooting of ten tirailleurs orchestrated by a French officer.

Despite European agreements, the French remained at Dikwa, and required Sultan Garbai to pay the remaining 6,500 thalers he owed. Faced with such rapacity, Garbai had no trouble complaining to the British authorities, who asserted their claim to control the area. The Germans, to whom southern

Bornu had been promised, were also marching on Dikwa. Instead of waiting for them, the French immediately withdrew to the east of the Chari. In 1902, a sort of Solomon's judgment made Garbai the sheikh of the area of Bornu under British influence, with Maiduguri as the capital city. (The project of rebuilding the ancient capital city of Kukawa had finally been abandoned.) Garbai's competitor, Sanda Kura, was enthroned at Dikwa as sheikh of German Bornu. (The area was later incorporated into Cameroon.) Since that time, the sheikhs have been chosen from that dynastic bloodline.

More skillful than the French, Lugard implemented the practice of indirect rule. He refrained from exacting even the least payment, and put an end to French extortions of ransom. British authority, which delivered the people in the area from long years of raids, was willingly accepted. At the beginning of the twentieth century, Bornu began experiencing something that resembled prosperity again. In 1914, memories of Rabīh's years were limited to great bitterness in dynastic circles. They also meant the loss of the privileges of some minority groups that used to be prestigious and had taken Rabīh's side, such as the Shuwa in the interior and the small Fulani principalities to the west. Nonetheless, Rabīh's destruction of earlier structures, and the attraction of the Sokoto Empire and Kano to the north accelerated cultural change. Islam became stricter than that which had predominated at the great epoque of Al-Kanemi's dynasty, and which had so irritated Al Hajj Umar when he passed through. Were there other cultural influences? The impact of the Turks was not new because Bornu had long been a hub for trade with Tripolitania. There was also contact with the north through the huge Sanusi brotherhood, which had been spreading trade from Cyrenaica to Lake Chad since the middle of the century while resisting to British, Italian, and French ambitions all over the Sahelian area. However, Sanusiyya's influence was relatively forgotten, while the Bornu court remained marked by rituals imported by Rabīh, including the guards' ceremonial dress, which still included antique rifles around 1950. Some bazinqirs settled there and established families; the locals called them Turks. The Arabic spoken in Chad has absorbed a number of words belonging to the military vocabulary of Nilotic Arabic. Finally, at the political level, the rapid invasion from the east led the people of the central and western Sudan to have a deep-rooted distrust of *jallaba*, in other words, transhumant Muslim traders of Nilotic origin.

What is even more surprising are the methods adopted by the French in the Chad basin. The phenomenon can be explained by the distance from the colonial bases of operations in the Congo basin. They were so far away that settlers and exploration and conquest "missions" had no choice but to live off the land. French raids certainly did not surprise the locals, who had been living with raids for decades. The French were just another invading force that was simply more efficient than the previous ones had been. This probably explains the ease with which most of Rabīh's former bazinqirs were able to give their allegiance in the new city created by Gentil, called Fort Lamy (now known as N'Djamena, capital city of Chad).

Paradoxically, the French, who had been ferocious in Bornu, welcomed Rabīh's former troops to the east of the Chari, who formed the core of the city's population. Indeed, right after the battle of Kusseri, Gentil encouraged Rabīh's former allies to come to his side with as many soldiers as possible. At least a thousand moved to Fort Lamy immediately with their families, and soon its inhabitants numbered 15,000.

Assimilation was as rapid as the encounter had been brutal; 250 former bazinqirs were enlisted as *goumiers* (irregular soldiers). They wore red tunics and blue-and-white trousers, and each received a horse and a gun. They were "bandits who had become gendarmes."[25] The Chad battalion, which maintained military control of the area until 1920, also included many former bazinqirs. Some ended up among the colony's notables. For example, Na'im, one of the first to join, was employed as a tax collector in Bornu, where he was noted and indeed punished for his rapacity. However, he later served Tibesti and was decorated with the *légion d'honneur* and the *étoile noire du Bénin*. He died at Fort Lamy in 1935, well known in French circles as one of Rabīh's closest companions. Even Rabīh's daughter came to live in Fort Lamy with her mother. Another of Rabīh's wives, Kobra ("the beautiful cobra"), who had accompanied her father in service to Rabīh, moved to the city and prospered there. In the early twentieth century, she was the head of a wealthy household.

Gentil sent five of the sons of Rabīh's primary standard bearers to be educated at the Saint Marie mission in Libreville, Gabon. One of them, Ibrahim Babikir, was the son of the standard bearer who was Rabīh's top general and who was killed with him. Babikir ended up as Chad's counselor to the French Union. In 1950, his brother Djama published a biography of Rabīh.[26] A woman who had traveled with Crampel along with other young girls (Crampel was known to be fond of them), and who had been captured by Rabīh and then rescued by the French, visited them often.

In short, despite the stereotype that was spread by the French colonial imagination of Rabīh as a bloodthirsty tyrant from whom France had delivered Africa, at the end of the nineteenth century there was an extraordinary symbiosis between African and European adventurers. The former, open to the outside world, were quick to integrate into the new system. The latter did not hesitate to adopt and use local raiding and battle techniques for colonial purposes. Shaka's equal, Rabīh, merits the title of "Africa's Napoleon," which Europeans have given to a whole series of despots, more than does Mirambo, who was all in all more modest in his ambitions and exploits.

4

Animism's Resistance— Openness and Introversion

Central-Western Africa

The Reformism of the Coastal Empires

At the dawn of the nineteenth century, the coastal groups and immediate hinterland were in full expansion, no matter what their political organization: centralized state, city-state, kinship-based society, or even British colony (Sierra Leone). States such as that of the Asante based their power on their location between the savanna and the rain forest. The kingdoms of Abomey and especially of Porto-Novo; the peoples of the Niger River Delta and backcountry, the Cameroon coast, and the Portuguese-dominated islands of São Tomé; and the Orungu and Mpongwe living at the mouth of the Ogooué were all dependent on the Atlantic economy. While the slave trade had resurged at the end of the eighteenth century, after the downswing resulting from the American War of Independence, in the nineteenth century most of the societies, especially those along the lower Niger, were able to convert to "licit" trade.[1]

Some of them, such as the Abomey Kingdom and the empires in the Niger River Delta, played decisive roles in nineteenth-century politics, military, and economy.

A Small National Autocracy: The Abomey Kingdom

Royal power strengthened in Dahomey at the end of the century owing in part to the combination of remarkable domestic policy and a strong economy until the last third of the century. Like many coastal groups, the kingdom was formed when the Atlantic slave trade began to flourish in the seventeenth century. It was a strong political community of Fon language and general culture, and had a system that combined war and trade. During the dry season, the army, under the leadership of the king and various provincial chiefs, traveled into the surrounding countryside to capture prisoners for the slave trade. During the rainy season, Fon soldiers became peasants again and engaged in subsistence agriculture in a relatively fertile area that was also well populated, especially since each generation of children born to slaves in Dahomey became Dahomean in turn.

Toward the end of the eighteenth century, however, the American War of Independence gave rise to a serious crisis from which King Adandozan came out poorly. We know little about him because his cousin and successor, Ghezo, removed him from the official tradition after he took power by force in 1818. Ghezo ruled until his death in 1858. His long reign was beneficial to the country as it underwent difficult times: beginning in the 1830s, the English constantly sent missions and attempted to convince the king to abandon the slave trade. However, the slave trade was central to Abomey's political organization because it fed the royal coffers, as long as the king returned victorious from his campaigns every year. His expeditions were toward Ewe lands in the west and especially Mahi territory to the north and Yoruba regions to the north-east, all the way to the Egba area of Abeokuta. A large part of his success could be attributed to the use of African muskets that the king received in exchange for slaves.

Ghezo unquestionably centralized power. He played a subtle game in which, as far as possible, he maintained slave trading as one of his kingdom's basic sources of revenue while encouraging palm oil production for export. The production was based on plantations that grew naturally throughout the lower country. Beginning in 1841 and especially through the 1851 agreement, he gave the two Régis brothers from Marseille, until then known mainly for their trade in slaves, a virtual monopoly over exports of palm oil. It was to the disadvantage of English entrepreneurs, who were nearby since the port of Lagos was located at the other end of the lagoon. During a transition period of nearly twenty years, the new business, which had a dozen production centers scattered along the coast, did not replace the slave trade at all, but complemented it. Major producers began using slaves on their plantations. Thus, in the second half of the century, the plantations were precarious but sustainable family businesses that generally remained undivided until the twentieth century. Neither the king nor his ministers (*cabécères*) had any interest in opposing the slave trade that, while not affecting the prior organization, increased their revenue. The port of Whydah, which exported 800 tonnes of oil before 1850, exported more than twice as much in 1876.

The king also took advantage of French-British competition in all areas, including religion: Catholic and Protestant missionaries faced off against each other, not without encouragement from their respective countries. The kingdom of Abomey thus avoided direct Western influence more successfully than its neighbor and competitor, the coastal kingdom of Porto Novo, which became a French protectorate in 1866.

It was probably under Ghezo's rule that Abomey's political structure took its final form: a pyramid system, with the king and his court at the summit, supported by female elite corps that he also helped to systematize: the famous Amazon warriors. They were a complementary link with his people because they were specially recruited in villages to become the "king's wives."[2] History has been reconstituted from a relatively large number of travelers' stories, which emphasize the despotism of the king of Dahomey. This is a Western notion that should not be accepted out of hand. In African terms, the king's authority was more eminent than real. Certainly, he was the master of all slaves, but, at the end of every military campaign, he gave many of them to dignitaries and good officers. As the inheritor of an interior kingdom, he, like many other African chiefs, did not have the right to see the sea. Thus, at Whydah, the country's slave-trading port, he acted only through the intermediary of his major dignitaries. They were the *yovoghan* (literally, the "chief of the Whites"), who were responsible for relations with Europeans, who included the famous "Cha-Cha," Francisco Felix da Souza, who was Brazilian or more likely a Portuguese of mixed blood. Da Souza, who died in 1849, was a major slave trader who funded the plot that enabled King Ghezo to usurp the throne. When he died, he was replaced by a new favorite, the former slave Quenum, who fathered a line of notables, merchants, and intellectuals.

Thus, a complex aristocracy grew in the kingdom, composed of both local dignitaries and African-Brazilian merchants, former African slaves who had returned from Brazil. They were remarkable cultural mediators, conversant in both Western and African cultures, accustomed to the opulence inherited from plantation owners, Christian but polygamous, businessmen and politicians whose power stemmed from their wealth and knowledge. The king's only real link with international trade was through tribute and gifts received from leading dignitaries, and the famous annual "customs" held in the capital city, to which European traders from the coast were imperatively invited.

Ghezo's son Glele succeeded him in 1858. His accession to the throne indicates there was a reaction of the "conservative" party, which was opposed to any form of modernization, particularly with respect to abolition of the slave trade. At that point, Western pressure was becoming more and more direct. The Dahomeans suffered a certain number of setbacks in their annual campaigns (especially in 1851 and again in 1864 against the Egba who were supported by the British). This, combined with inflation caused by massive imports of cowries by German steamships, led the king to increase taxes. The English had taken control of Lagos, and territorial claims were becoming louder. To the great dismay of traders, in 1851, 1865, and especially 1876, Dahomey was subject to blockades by the British navy. It gradually lost control of its outlet to the sea, Cotonou, which was ceded to the French by Glele's rival, the chief of Porto Novo. It became a protectorate in 1863, and its status was renewed in 1876 and recognized by Glele in 1879.[3] Yet, defeat was still far away. Glele's successor was enthroned under the name of Béhanzin in 1889. Faced with the disintegration of the provinces and French attacks, he had no choice but to be a military leader. Followed by his people, he mounted fierce resistance to conquest from 1890 forward, and took to the bush when the French conquered Abomey in 1893–94.

The Asante Kingdom: A Military and Merchant Monarchy

The Asante Kingdom, born of a confederation of Akan-speaking peoples, followed more or less the same chronological development as Abomey, even though it was not on the coast. It was separated from the ocean by a Fante zone over which it claimed suzerainty, which threw the Fante into the arms of the British a number of times. This occurred following the 1806, 1826, 1852, and 1863 Asante expeditions. In 1844, a British governor was appointed under the Foreign Jurisdiction Act.[4] He made the Fante chiefs sign a treaty, the Bond, by which they agreed to cease human sacrifice and "other barbarous customs." The Asante, however, showed great resistance.

Like the Abomey Kingdom, the Asante Kingdom operated on the military, political, and commercial levels. It owed its originality more to trade with the backcountry than to contact with the forested south and European arms suppliers. Trade with the backcountry was based on large-scale kola nut production for markets that were essentially Muslim and located more to the north, in the Sudan-Sahel area of West Africa. Finally, overall prosperity was guaranteed by gold deposits: gold dust was the monetary base, and gold exports made up for the decline of the slave trade. Kumasi, the capital city, was the center of a network of caravan routes linking it with the provinces. The provinces were governed, or rather held ransom, by powerful families in the city, which controlled most of the wealth. It was only near the end of the eighteenth century, under the reigns of Osei Kwadwo and then of Osei Kwame (1777–1803) that the *Asantehene,* owner of the "golden stool," symbol of his power, prevailed over the land-based and military oligarchies of the traditional chiefs. He forced them to accept imperial public servants, who depended on him for their authority and fortune. In a farming society, where subsistence was generally achieved because of a relatively wide range of crops (manioc, yams, plantains, and corn, though the latter declined in the nineteenth century), the capital city's power gradually grew. At the beginning of the nineteenth century, Kumasi had a population of between 25,000 and 30,000 people, most of whom were engaged in activities related to government and skilled work. Indeed, during the eighteenth century, once the territory had been expanded considerably (more or less to the present-day borders of Ghana), the idea came to be accepted, as it had been in Dahomey, that power was based on trade rather than war and military exploits, though one entailed the other. Appointment of senior public officials by the *Asantehene* depended increasingly on their ability to accumulate wealth in jars of gold dust, slaves, and weapons, and thus in terms of dependents and soldiers. It became commonplace for a high chief to lend money to a subordinate so that the latter could demonstrate his worth by making a fortune and paying the loan back with interest. Thence came a hierarchy of dignitaries (*Hiahene*, *Kyidomhene*, and *Ankaasehene*) whose promotion depended on their success. Osei Kwame also tried to manage the state with the help of educated Muslims, which was a policy favorable to Islam that ended up rendering him destitute. However, the innovations were strengthened by the great law-making king, Osei Bonsu (around 1803–24).

Despite the increasingly finicky development of a slow and costly court ritual, the kingdom began to decline under the long reign of *Asantehene* Kwaku Dua Panin (1834–67), a contemporary of kings Ghezo and Glele of Abomey. This was for two reasons: on one hand there was increased pressure from the Whites who sent support from the coast for the Fante courtiers (the British governor of the Gold Coast visited Kumasi in 1848), and on the other hand the king became more autocratic, and began to force his subjects to pay increasingly large sums in the form of taxes and other contributions since he wanted trade to be reserved for Muslim Hausa. The Hausa foreigners were confined to a reserved quarter and were easier to control. The conditions of trade and balance of power changed. In 1862, one of Kwaku Dua Panin's wealthy protégés, Kwasi Gyani, finally placed himself under British protection in order to preserve his property. The *Asantehene* Kofi Kakari (1867–74) and Mensa Bonsu (1874–83) left behind solid reputations for incompetence and corruption. The former squandered his fortune, and the latter was greedy; Mensa Bonsu's avidity, which was felt all the more strongly owing to the economic crisis at the end of the century, led to his destitution.[5] The civil war that followed (1883–88) finally shook the foundations of the country and prepared the ground for British annexation in 1898.

Ewe Cultural Eclecticism

Compared with the solidity of the Akan and Fon empires, it is striking to see how, on the rest of the coast, economic growth adapted to a political situation long marked by extreme dispersion of power. This was the case of the societies of Ewe culture that occupied the backcountry of the Slave Coast. Slave traders had long been visiting some fifteen trading posts, such as Keta and Aneho, the Europeans' "Little Popo." The posts had been more or less colonized by Fante from Elmina, which explains why they were called the Mina. In the eighteenth century, the wealth of such businessmen made the small towns prosperous: two-story homes were not unusual. At the same time, in the upper country, the Asante were being pushed back from Dahomey by the Fon and moving into the Atakpame Basin. Dismemberment and rivalry for power, combined with courtiers' attraction to the coast, resulted in the area being populated by disparate refugees who were united mainly through commercial activities, which predisposed them to urban life.

This was the case for the various peoples living on the shores of Lake Togo (which means "on the hill") and Be Lagoon. This dispersed population is what European documents from 1884 call the "Togo Kingdom," which had no king. The people nonetheless recognized that they all worshipped the god Nyigblin. This explains the role of one of the country's most famous priests, Be-Togo, who, while living as a recluse (surrounded by some thirty young ritual wives) in the Iveto forest, incarnated the country's religious, and thus political, unity. Selected in the greatest secrecy from among the oldest men, condemned to permanent seclusion, subject to a whole series of prohibitions, including rejection of any sign of modernity, and moreover condemned to a relatively rapid death followed by a long interval before a successor was named, the Be-Togo's federating role was due more to his sacred absence than to an effective presence.[6]

In contrast, the neighboring city of Aneho was growing, moving from slave trading to commerce in palm oil under the influence of an enterprising man, Akouete Zankli. He was the son of a local sailor who had been employed by a man named Law at the end of the eighteenth century. Under the name of George Lawson ("Law's son"), Akouete came back from England, where his father had sent him to be educated. He soon became the richest man in the country, and remained so until his death in 1857. During that time, there was a long and confusing crisis followed by a new division of interests. Lawson remained England's man as the French and especially the Germans began to arrive.

The problem was that the Gold Coast protectorate was beginning to seriously conflict with local interests. The British administration was sustained only by customs duties applying not to exports, for English industry needed cheap raw materials, but to imports, particularly those with the worst reputation under the Victorian government: alcohol and tobacco. Customs duties soon tripled, providing 80 percent of the protectorate's revenues in 1880. Moreover, again to increase revenues, in 1874 the governor of Accra suddenly decided to annex the posts under Keta's control: to the west of the border, customs duties were heavy, but there were none to the east. It is easy to understand the reaction of local traders, particularly that of George Williams from Sierra Leone and Christian Rotman, agent of the Bremen factory, who moved to the free zone. A whole series of African entrepreneurs followed them. This was the origin of Lome in 1880. In a way, it was a cosmopolitan African free town based on trade. It remained so until 1897, when it fell under German control.

The Nigerian Palm Oil Kingdoms

Around the Niger Delta, owing to the extent of the palm tree plantations in the backcountry, there were even more commercial groups organized into small competing, neighboring communities. Their relative isolation on islands and at the many turns in the delta ensured their independence. From 1830 to 1920, the area was the world's top exporter of palm oil and nuts. A good example of such a community is the Igbo group on the western bank of the Niger, namely, the Anioma. They had a relatively hierarchical slaving society based on lineage and reflecting their many interactions with neighboring groups. The Anioma area, on the edge of the Niger, a commercial crossroads not far from the Benin Kingdom and at the extremity of Igboland, had long been a hub of navigation on the river and a place where different peoples mixed. The inhabitants demonstrated a great ability to adapt. In the eighteenth century, their economy was based on yam farming and slave trading. With the developments in the Atlantic market, their agriculture and lifestyle changed. They gradually replaced yams (which were used to feed slaves) with palm oil as the labor force slowly dropped. They began growing rice and manioc toward the end of the century, and had finally become the primary producers in the area at the beginning of the twentieth century. European intervention, which began in 1857, was a disruptive intrusion, and, in the last third of the century, led to very difficult relations with the first missionaries and to a tenacious resistance movement, the *Ekumeku,* from 1883 to 1914.[7]

Farther south, the city-states of the Niger Bend (Brass, Bonny, Calabar, etc.) were remarkably active, both socially and politically, in the nineteenth century. Focal points of intense slave trading, for several centuries they had been bringing together different peoples that had large-scale trade as their common ground. However, beginning in the 1920s to 1930s, the slave traders had to comply with the anti-slave-trading mission of the British navy. The inhabitants quickly converted to exporting palm oil. Since the palm tree plantations were located in the backcountry, the ports had an increasingly commercial role that took the shape of a kind of informal empire enforced by producers' indebtedness. Producers came to the ports for imported manufactured goods, Indian cotton cloth, weapons, alcohol, and various small items. Since palm tree plantations require a much larger labor force than slave trading, more slaves were used locally. For example, in Duke Town (which was part of Old Calabar) the population had grown from 2,000 to 6,000 by 1850, with around 60,000 slaves in the surrounding plantations.[8] Wealth became the most important sign of success, and the society became stratified into "households" led by rich entrepreneurs, some of whom had been educated in England. They were well aware of the methods of Western commercial capitalism. Despite the inflexibility of the social hierarchy, some capable slaves became rich in service to their masters. The most famous of those was Jaja of Bonny who, tired of being rejected by the aristocratic families, finally left the city to found a new, well-located town, Opobo, in 1869. It attracted many Igbo, merchants, warriors, and "fetishers."[9]

The turmoil was no less intense in the interior, where Yorubaland was profoundly shaken throughout the century. This was probably the most visible evidence that the states were deteriorating. Yet, we should not exaggerate the coherence of previous empires, the tradition of which was actually developed in the nineteenth century by people sharing a culture but whose denomination as a single "ethnic group" (the Yoruba) was created by the British. (Formerly, "the Yoruba" designated only the inhabitants of the Oyo area.) Indeed, at least one researcher has cast serious doubt on the unitary idea of prior centralized groupings, even though the existence of the state of Benin to the south around Benin City, and the more controversial existence of the Oyo state to the north are relatively well established.[10] A.G. Hopkins[11] has shown how, in the nineteenth century, the growth of the slave trade favored the formation of a category of warriors who helped undermine the Yoruba political structure. At the beginning of the century, Uthman dan Fodio's Fulani Empire to the north also began exerting pressure. It forced most Yoruba "cities" (*ilu*) to move southward, beginning with the city of Oyo, which in 1837 moved from Oyo-Ile to New Oyo, some eighty miles away. Ibadan, for example, was deserted by its Egba inhabitants, and by the early 1840s resembled a large military camp full of armed people from more or less everywhere.

The switch to palm oil did not have much of an effect on the situation. The issue of security became more complicated with the appearance of many small producers in the second half of the century. This was different from the slave trade, which required a relatively large amount of capital. This capital allowed a small group of large producers to control many dependents, slaves, and serfs, who ensured the subsistence of a large number of captives, even though capturing slaves was often subcontracted to minor bandits.

In contrast, any ordinary African peasant could engage in the oil trade as a cottage industry because palm trees grew naturally. It has been estimated that, in 1892, there were 15 million palm trees producing in Yorubaland. The leading chiefs imposed their authority less through direct production than through stronger control over trade routes via considerable taxes and fees. Control of the routes became vital. The great economic depression in 1873–93 also played a role. Yorubaland, doubly shaken in its international economic balance since the beginning of the century, first by abolition of the slave trade and then by the catastrophic drop in oil prices, had to engage in intense competition while weathering an economic crisis, and profits dropped brutally.

It all translated into the so-called Yoruba wars, which began in 1827 with Oyo's destruction of the city of Owo (30,000 inhabitants), and culminated in the last third of the century when British penetration was confirmed. The last Yoruba war, which was also the most severe, broke out in 1877. It helped to devastate the country, and, at the end of a long and indecisive struggle, no chief managed to prevail over the others. The troubles were less the cause than the result of the military regimes' crises. The economic depression intensified domestic discord, revealing internal conflicts in Yoruba chiefdoms, between chiefs and other chiefs and chiefs and workers, and among competing ministates. It translated both their last attempt and their incapacity to adapt to a new socioeconomic order dictated by the demands of industrial Europe.

The Yoruba nonetheless had behind them a solid cultural tradition, attached as they were to the ancestral and sacred city, the only one that had not been moved: Ife. They also occupied (and this is something shared with the Asante, though the historical heritage is very different) a remarkable strategic and commercial position. They were neither coastal, which protected them from direct control by Whites, nor Sahelian. They acted as intermediaries between the Hausa and Fulani world of the interior, and the Christian world of the coast. This probably gave them the power to resist both the former and the latter. At the end of the century, the Yoruba, like the Asante, remained attached to their ancient beliefs, which were remarkably and durably impermeable to monotheist religions, no matter what they were.

The Equatorial Coast and Late Reign of Slave Trading

The south of the Gulf of Benin was a world apart since it was under the influence of the Portuguese in the archipelago of São Tomé and Principe, and the Spanish on Fernando-Po. Those islands were dominated until the end of the century by the slave trade, which was officially tolerated by the English until 1826–31. It was then replaced by the fiction of "contract workers," whose exploitation was still ongoing in 1930, when the International Labour Organization raised a scandal.

At the beginning of the nineteenth century, members of the Mpongwe and Orungu peoples from Gabon had been settled on the coast for over a century.

The Mpongwe, who lived on both banks of the Ogooué, were, like the traders of the Niger Delta, organized into small chiefdoms, each of which included at most a few hundred subjects. The Orungu, who lived around Cape Lopez, were more centralized. They supplied ivory, dye wood, wax, ebony, and, of course, slaves. Toward the end of the eighteenth century, they exported perhaps 500 slaves per year. The British slave trade prohibition made them more dependent on the Portuguese of São Tomé, where they sent some 4,000 slaves between 1809 and 1815.[12] The chiefs were mostly commercial entrepreneurs who had been influenced by the West early on. For example, King George on the left bank of the Ogooué (his real name was Rassondji) sent two of his sons to be educated in Europe between 1809 and 1818. The first American missionaries arrived in King Glass's court on the left bank in 1842. A missionary who visited King Denis (more precisely, Antchouwe Kowe Rapontchombo) at the tip of the left bank said that "he was one of the most remarkable men [who I have] ever met in Africa."[13] Having succeeded to the throne in 1810, Denis granted the French a piece of land and the right to settle there in 1839. He reigned until his death in 1876.

Unlike the people living on the west coast, the Mpongwe and Orungu did not innovate and adopt a new replacement product such as palm oil. The decline in their trade made them all the more dependent on and permeable to European economic and cultural influence. This did not prevent the area from vegetating to such a point that the French were tempted to withdraw from it—until Brazza believed he had found a new Eldorado there in 1875.

The Peoples of the Interior

A Hybrid Attempt: The Bamum Kingdom

A completely different case was the quite extraordinary attempt by a local ruler to take advantage of the various cultural influences to which he found himself subjected at the end of the century. Njoya was the chief of a small mountain state tucked away in the Cameroon backcountry at an altitude of 3,200 feet. Protected by his relative isolation, he was subject to two influences: the Muslim Fulani from the northwest, and the Christian Whites from the coast. The state began to take form at the beginning of the nineteenth century. At that time, fearing the advances of Uthman dan Fodio's Fulanis, the Bamum dug a wide trench around their capital city, Foumbam, to protect themselves from the Muslim horsemen. At the end of the century, the advancing raids of both Rabīh and the British Niger Company from Benue and Njola led the king to strengthen his authority over an area of about 3,000 square miles, home to 60,000 people. Njoya, who rose to the throne in 1890 and reigned until 1924, in other words, under French domination, developed his power at the same time that the Germans were beginning to settle in the country. The modest size and isolation of his kingdom made it possible for him to continue asserting, exceptionally late in history, the intangibility of ancient values, based on technology and symbols that were related to kinship, military, and slave-trading traditions. His capital city, which was built in the image of both his palace and power, also seemed to come out of the most ancient past. Nevertheless, this "traditional" ruler was open to modernity. While he did not convert, Njoya accepted the presence of Christian missionaries and a school, and the introduction of improved artisanal techniques. He even went so far as to have his scribes create an original form of writing.[14]

Construction of an Ethnic Identity: The Kikuyu

In cases where social groups were not structured as nation-states (the kingdoms of Abomey and Asante, the city-states of the Niger River Delta, the small Great Lakes states and Ethiopia) or as colonial edifices (the jihad empires, Zanzibar, Egypt, Sudan, and South Africa), they continued to combine kinship traditions and transversal networks maintained by shared religious beliefs. There are examples of this everywhere in Africa. Such groups dominated all of central and eastern Africa beyond the coastal zone occupied by the Swahili. High savanna plateaus and forested basins were most likely to shelter such groupings. Toward the northeast, one of the many examples was the Kikuyu. Their population was the densest and most flourishing in the interior Kenyan plateau in the nineteenth century.

The Kikuyu, who were given this generic name by the British, included half a million people at the end of the nineteenth century. It was the largest Bantu group in the northeast, in central Kenya to the north of Nairobi. Their territory, as was later recognized by colonizers, included some 800,000 acres on a plateau about 100 miles long and 35 miles wide, and was bordered on the north by Mount Kenya and to the west by the great Rift escarpment. To the west and south, their neighbors were the Masai, from whom they were separated by a thin band of forest, which was useful in case of conflict. However, their relations with the Masai were far from dominated by wars, which increased only at the end of the nineteenth century. They also engaged in many forms of exchange with them, from trade to intermarriage.

Other important neighbors were the Athi, who found refuge in the forested borders. They were distant relatives of both the Kikuyu and the Masai, which explains their importance in the history of land acquisition, the ivory trade, and Kikuyu migrations. Since the plateau dropped toward the north, the south (near the future city of Nairobi) received more rain and was more fertile.

Moreover, thanks to its altitude, it was relatively protected from malaria and sleeping sickness, which caused great suffering in surrounding areas. For the Kikuyu, the plateau was a refuge. Estimating dates of events in Kikuyu history is now particularly difficult because the solar year did not exist for them. The Kikuyu made a rough distinction between the alternation of two long and two short rainy and dry seasons, and estimated time in accordance with age groups, which were identified by initiation ceremonies. While there was an initiation ceremony for girls every year, initiation for boys took place only every nine seasons (more or less every 4.5 years), which makes calculating dates difficult.

At the end of the nineteenth century, Kikuyu society was patriarchal, decentralized, and based on extended families. Every community (*mbari*) was linked with one of the ten clans that were supposed to date back to the mythical founder, Gikuyu. Identity was recognized in a transversal manner between clans in case of serious danger, and through a precise system of age groups (*mariika*). Age groups distinguished children, young initiates, junior adult warriors (adults who had been initiated fourteen or fewer years previously), senior warriors (who were responsible for defense), and, finally, elders.

The Kikuyu were primarily farmers, but also had livestock; they raised cattle, as well as sheep and goats. Land ownership was related to lineage (*mbari*) and controlled by the head of the clan (*mulamari*), which ensured the survival of all. A man without land was received into the clan as a dependent with the relative guarantee that he would till the land: he was an *ahoi* (voluntary tenant). Indeed, *ahois* were sought after along the borders owing to the many tasks that were necessary. It was their dispersion around Mount Kenya that expanded Kikuyu lands at the dawn of the nineteenth century. The Kikuyu can be seen as colonizing pioneers who, throughout history (before the groups that gradually came together carried the name), incorporated and submerged neighboring peoples, including the Athi. This explains the coexistence of many cultural features, owing to the process of mutual absorption as the farmers advanced and cleared the forest in the early seventeenth century.

Control of the Land

Given these different factors, control of the land was essential to the Kikuyu, unlike the people of the forest, who were not threatened by lack of land. However, their gradual settlement on the highlands of the plateau increased only in the final decades of the nineteenth century. The people had not traveled far; they had migrated from the northern and eastern parts of the country, which had probably been ravaged repeatedly by famine since the seventeenth century. Power relations were based on the land that the Kikuyu acquired through war, of course, but above all through complex agreements, intermarriage and counter-gifts or payment, or long transfer procedures involving mutual adoption.

This notion of land appropriation raises questions. Was their strong awareness of control of the land a recently acquired cultural feature owing to dispossession by Whites? Or did it exist prior to that? Since the Kikuyu were land clearers, it is logical to think that both played a role. Since land was owned according to the principle of the first occupant, land clearers claimed ownership. The phenomenon was relatively new in the seventeenth century until which time the Kikuyu had migrated as hunters and pastors. Once they arrived in an area more amenable to agriculture, their progress as peasants began, and continued throughout all of the nineteenth century. It was at that time that the group began to take form. A powerful element of integration, notably with the Athi, was alliance through vows of mutual adoption: both parties promised to treat each other as brothers and to help each other in time of need. *Mbari* genealogies reveal such mixing.[15]

This led to neither private nor communal property, but collective ownership for all *mbari*. Thus, before the Europeans arrived, land was not passed from one *mbari* to the next. It was the European intrusion at a time when pressure was growing on the Kikuyu that caused the lack of land that changed the situation. In 1910, the Kikuyu began to demand recognition of private property. Some argued that they had known it before, and that land use could be transferred by (patrilineal) inheritance, by marriage, or as compensation.

The Kikuyu and the Masai: A Myth

The idea that Masai herders terrorized their neighbors is a myth fabricated by the first white settlers. Certainly, there were conflicts and rivalries, but also much exchange. First, their lifestyles were relatively complementary. Though Thomas Spear has shown with respect to the Masai Arusha in the north of Tanzania that the Masai also grew grain and fished,[16] they were primarily herders, and so the Masai were very vulnerable to the climate and to livestock diseases. Peace entailed specific rituals in which the two parties swore mutual support in a solemn rite. In case of epidemic, smallpox, or civil war, large numbers of Masai could take refuge with their neighbors. They also left their women and children as security, as was done between the Asante and Dahomeans. Many young Masai were adopted by Kikuyu families, which increased mixing. Trade was profitable to the Kikuyu, for the Masai offered them everything they needed: livestock, milk, leather, skins, beads, and cowries, which came from the coast.

Contact began in the eighteenth century. Peaceful exchanges were more common than wars since families on each side were related to each other. Between about 1800 and 1830, the Kikuyu and Masai collaborated to expel a third group, the Barabiu, who planned to invade the highlands. The agreement continued until the major attack of epizootic plague in 1889–90. In the 1880s, the two groups began raiding each other regularly, and the legend of permanent war between them came about in the 1890s. Groups of bandits began to form and, led by fearless chiefs, pillaged the Kikuyu and Masai in turn by allying themselves first with one and then with the other. Thus, Wang'ombe was the son of a Kikuyu who apparently made many trading trips into Masai country and was killed on one of them. His young son first found refuge with Masai relatives, and then took side first against one group and then against the other. It seems that in 1891 he organized a raid that involved more than 500 Kikuyu and Masai warriors. He used Masai mercenaries many times, particularly between 1892 and 1894, and was still engaging in battle in early 1902. His was not an isolated case. Insecurity grew with demographic pressure, and natural and colonial calamities, particularly following the great famine of 1898–99.

The same type of event happened between the Kikuyu and their neighbors on Mount Kenya. In particular, the Kamba to the northeast maintained strong trade relations with the Kikuyu. In the 1840s, trade with the coast north of Pangani was still in Kamba hands, to the detriment of the Swahili. They were excellent hunters, and acquired a great deal of ivory. However, they were most of all intermediaries, who only occasionally had direct contact with the Arabs and Swahili. Their caravans could include as many as 500 men. They ranged widely, from Mount Kenya to Mount Kilimanjaro, and from there to Mombasa. Around 1870–80, the Arabs and Swahili began competing directly with them, and the Kamba were forced to withdraw toward the interior, where they acted as intermediaries for the people of Mount Kenya. Toward the end of the century, the Kikuyu knew them as nothing more than bandits who kidnapped women and children for slave traders on the coast. Once again, as in the case of the Masai, relations deteriorated at the end of the century.

Until then, trade had been mainly in the hands of, strong, mature women who were no longer prey to Masai or Kamba warriors. Trade expeditions were long and complicated, and normally conducted by an experienced man who knew where the Masai would probably be found. Lodgings were organized with friendly families. There were also temporary markets on the borders, especially in times of famine. The Kikuyu offered corn, millet flour, dried bananas, green bananas, and cane sugar. The Masai also bought honey, pots and calabashes, swords, and red ochre. The Kamba were looking for ivory and tobacco, and sold beads, copper wire, salt, and cowries. Internal trade was the most prevalent, and involved exchanges in kind, though at the end of the nineteenth century small iron bars, goats, and cowries were increasingly used as monetary equivalents. As among the Masai, cowries and beads were highly prized for their ornamental value.

Harsh Reality: The Arrival of the Europeans

The encounter with the Europeans was by no means positive. Since the 1840s, the Kikuyu had been aware of their existence because some Kikuyu had traveled to the coast with the Kamba. Then their greatest soothsayer, Cege wa Kibiru, announced that strangers would arrive from the east, out of the sea, looking like frogs because of their white color and carrying sticks that spit fire.

The area was first penetrated by the Imperial British East Africa Company (IBEAC), a charter company created in 1888. In a brutal manner, it prepared the way for the true British occupation in 1895. The Kikuyu attitude to the new arrivals (Swahili, Arabs, and Europeans) was not immediately negative, but they were wary. They appreciated trade, but tried to prevent the foreigners from settling. Contact soon transformed into atrocities on both sides. The Kikuyu acquired a horrifying reputation among the Europeans.

The IBEAC's goal was Buganda, and the company intended only to set up transit stations on the borders of Kikuyu country: Machakos and Dagoretti (as well as Fort Kiawariura) were established in 1889 and 1890, and were soon self-sufficient. For the Kikuyu, seeing caravans travel through was one thing, but having settlers on their land was another. Kikuyu porters were mistreated, and soldiers from the coast (*askaris*) pillaged, stole food and livestock, and raped women. It was all exacerbated by alcoholism, to the point that twelve Somali soldiers were brought in specifically because their religion protected them from *tembo*, the local beer.

Relations were so bad that Kiawariua was abandoned by the company, but the land was too useful to be deserted. A new fort was built, Fort Smith, near the village of Chief Waiyaki, who, rightly or wrongly, was considered to be the head chief. Agents and their auxiliaries pillaged the country for personal gain. In 1892, the whole thing ended with a punitive expedition that burnt thirty villages and arrested the chief, who died in chains on the road to Mombasa. This led to increasingly savage skirmishes until 1896.

This activity also caused refugees to gather around Fort Smith. There were a thousand in 1894, most of whom were Masai, which again intensified conflict between the pastor-gatherers and the Kikuyu farmers. Finally, the situation was poisoned by a series of ecological disasters: locusts in 1894, 1895, and 1896, famine in 1897–98, cattle plague in 1898, and finally famine and a smallpox epidemic in 1898–99.

Mortality was very high, estimated at 50 to 90 percent of the population. This explains why, in 1902–3, the land that the British took possession of was considered empty. Most of the survivors had taken refuge to the north. This also led to an increase in banditry, which the Europeans tried to counteract by creating the post of Mbiri in 1900. In other words, the Europeans were giving signs of setting down local roots; the area was no longer considered simply a means of getting to Uganda. In 1904, Pax Britannica was a fact. However, the Masai, who had lived farther to the south in areas closer to lands coveted by both the Zanzibarites and the Europeans, lost the most.

Independent Reactions: Central Africa and the Great Lakes Kingdoms

In the Congolese basin, from southern Cameroon to the Congo and from central Africa to the Great Lakes kingdoms, the rainy forest dominates, covering nearly 35 million acres and stretching more than 2,000 miles, except on the edges of the northern and southwest savannas.

Social and Political Organization Based on Households

Jan Vansina suggests that the social and political history of the whole region was dominated by "households," which is a concept also used for the city-states of the Niger Delta, though the households were smaller. A household was a residential unit under a "big man," and also a unit of production involving ten to forty people, of which a small minority were free men. The others were dependents, pawn laborers (to pay back a crime or someone's death), servants, prisoners of war, and slaves. The household system also contained the embryos of castes: fishers, hunters (who were often groups of pygmies enfoeffed to Bantu farmers), and palm wine tappers. Households were always in competition with one another to increase their members. Methods included both war and matrimonial alliances. Marriages were concluded in various ways by the big man, who was generally polygamous and could offer women as spouses to young clients to attract them into the house. In such cases, women could be given as gifts (tokens of peace), in trade, as surety, for payment, or in exchange for a dowry. The household was a spatial unit that generally belonged to a village of rarely more than around 100 inhabitants, which it could abandon to move to another one. This happened frequently because villages needed new land at least once a decade. Therefore, flexibility was a feature of the system. Cohesion was guaranteed through witchcraft, implying that evil was always of human origin. It was important to detect sorcerers. Big men, because they were superior to others, were also magicians, in a way, with supernatural power. Competing chiefs often used accusations of witchcraft against one another, which affected both ends of the social spectrum: both the unfortunate and those who were (too) successful.[17] The beliefs encouraged the establishment of separate secret associations for men and women, which regulated the social and political structure.

The village was placed under the control of the strongest head of household, who most often had conquered rather than inherited his land. He was assisted by the other big men in the neighborhood. Boys' initiation into adulthood, which was often a long process, could lead to the establishment of inter-household age-sets, which were useful for collective farm work and hunting, as well as in time of war. Villages were often scattered in small clumps in the forest, thereby constituting kinds of districts that could subsist longer than a village on its own. When a household was combined with a lineage-based hereditary system, chieftainships and sometimes monarchies emerged. Thus, on Bioko Island (Fernando Po), facing Duala country, the twenty-seven Bubi chieftainships did not unite until 1835–45 under the authority of Chief Moka, who died in 1899 at the presumed age of 105.

The very foundation of society, a household was both ephemeral and determining, The expansion of one household tended to have a domino effect and spread political imbalance throughout an area. A chain reaction would be set off, which would not end until it had reached the borders of the system, either in an area where there were too few people, or near another set of districts of greater or equal strength. This happened every time ecological or commercial conditions favored the growth of a house-hold. However, the process began accelerating in the eighteenth century thanks to new factors: an increase in the slave trade and elephant hunting, along with the arrival of missionaries in the nineteenth century, and direct intervention by Westerners. On the coast of Cameroon in 1827, the British founded the naval base of Port Clarence (Malabo), which caused consider-able immigration of Africans from the interior. Around the 1840s, trade had become intense there, and missionaries were beginning to preach the Gospel. The same thing happened in 1843 on the coast of Gabon, when the French founded Libreville.

The clearest result could be seen to the north, in the constant southwest movement of a series of peoples, including the Fang from Gabon, who were still descending toward Ogooué and the coast at the end of the nineteenth century. From the south, the Ba Congo came to the central transit trade area on the Congo River by Malabo Pool (the future Stanley Pool). In the nine-teenth century, the kingdom of Congo was not much more than a memory, as was that of Loango. In contrast, the highly decentralized Tio kingdom of the Bateke owed its fortune to its protected location, for it was farther from the coast, though still open to the Atlantic slave trade, since slaves were brought there over land and by the river.

The Eastern Highlands

The eastern highlands, between the rivers Uele and Lualaba (Upper Congo), had always been a crossroads between the savanna to the north and the forest to the south, serving farmers, hunters, fishers, and herders, as well as Bantu, Ubangi, and Sudanese peoples. In the eighteenth century, the households grew and changed into more efficient chiefdoms, and the first monarchies saw the light of day at the turn of the nineteenth century. This was the case for Namiembila, son of a "self-made man" who had begun as a client but was later adopted in the1750s. Namiembila undertook new conquests in 1800 and especially 1815, occupying the whole southern expanse of the Uele and giving birth to the Mangbetu Kingdom. However, political relations continued to be expressed in terms of kinship among close relatives, faithful clients, and slaves. The Mangbetu Kingdom did not survive the competition from Namiembila's sons, one of whom dethroned him in 1853. From then on, despite the legitimacy guaranteed by the oracle Mapingo, a series of civil wars shook the kingdom and the last king, Mbunza, fell in 1873. Owing to the slave raids by the Azande princes to the north, the situation became so critical that an ancient war charm, the *nebeli,* mutated into a secret association, which was, however, unable to resist the Belgian advance.[18]

The Maniema

Farther south and to the Upper Congo, the relatively rich lands of Maniema, a trading area with centers of high population density, resulted in an unstable combination of chieftainships. The chiefs' powers were limited by interlocking associations (*mbwami*) with hierarchical titles that could be acquired through institutionalized initiation rites. The criteria were circumcision, male gender, wealth, and, for senior titles, the status of married man with many relatives. The *mbwami* took the place of a government. To the east, such privileges gave rise to a dominant class that, beginning in the eighteenth century, turned toward a more or less hereditary aristocratic monarchy presided over by the *mwami* (sacred king).

In Maniema, in the east of present-day Congo, the *mbwami* and *mwami* institutions were interwoven, and so it is impossible to say which came first or how local variations can be explained. In contrast with the extreme decentralization shown by the multiplicity of brotherhoods in the north, the southern part of Maniema was dominated by a single brotherhood with centralizing tendencies. The number of people incorporated into the association and territory grew. They had the same interallied set of patrilineal kinship groups and at the same time gave rise to a large number of mini-states. In the northern part of Maniema, in contrast, societies tended more than anywhere else to be fragmented into minuscule autonomous households, probably because they were based strictly in the forest, in areas that were the least populated of the whole region. Their hunting grounds covered huge areas of the forest. The only uniting features, which played crucial integrating roles for the myriad of small communities, were brotherhoods founded on *esomba* healing rituals. They gave a specific cultural cachet to the area. The only thing we know about them is that they evolved quickly in the nineteenth century. Those who could perform the circumcision and divination rituals gained great prestige since they often replaced ineffective ancient religions after Zanzibar's domination had imposed radical changes in social structure and chiefs' roles.[19]

At two locations in central Africa, the system lent itself to veritable monarchies, which flourished in the nineteenth century. In one case in the Great Lakes area, the evolution was widespread: in the eighteenth century a whole series of small states arose there, and in the nineteenth century they reached their height. Though they were small, their government and military structures were remarkably centralized. They included the kingdoms of Ganda, Ankole, Rwanda, and Burundi. Even more surprising was the Kuba Kingdom's emergence between the Kasai and Sankuru rivers in central-western Africa. The Kuba Kingdom was exceptional for its centralization, and political and artistic achievement, despite the fact that it was located in the middle of an area where there was, generally, a political vacuum.[20]

The Great Lakes States: The Genesis of Ethnic Groups

Like other areas, the Great Lakes region was covered by a myriad of small chiefdoms with cultures that may not have been shared but at least had similarities, such as the sacred king ritual, supported by religious dances and oracles.[21] It was on that substrate that relatively centralized monarchies emerged around Lake Victoria in the seventeenth and eighteenth centuries. The political structures incorporated ancient beliefs, myths, rituals, and customs (including human sacrifice). They added control over all livestock, banana growing (which was dominant in Buganda to the east), and cereal (corn and millet) production in Burundi to the west. The new kings confiscated the ancient gods, myths, and rituals of royal genealogies, and used them to the advantage of the reigning dynasty. Their power became autocratic and militarized. In the nineteenth century, the centralization of power was similar to that of the slave-trading kingdoms on the west coast, with one major difference: the interior kingdoms were not in direct contact with the world market at the time. Political structures were established internally, based on the articulation between war and trade. Like the Asante kings, the kings of Buganda, Burundi, and Ankole tied the old system of lineage-based chiefs to a hierarchy of administrative chiefs who did not have to answer in any way to the people they governed. As in Dahomey, they used the people both in the fields, for subsistence farming and to tend the herds, and in war, in raids. In the dry season, raids provided the booty and women that were necessary for survival and to expand the group.[22]

Was it at this time that, for economic and political aristocratic reasons, the competition/segregation that later came to distinguish the "Hutu" and "Tutsi" of Rwanda and Burundi began to emerge? The two groups had different genetic origins in an extremely distant past, but had shared the same language and culture for centuries. (The second group to arrive, which was probably the Tutsi, adopted the local language rapidly.) Their political differences emerged much later.[23] Social status had much to do with it. Tutsi lords monopolized livestock ownership, and thus benefited from a high-protein diet based on meat and milk, which was reserved for them. This may also explain their tall stature, which in fact is seen only among a small proportion of privileged individuals. Indeed, one was not necessarily born Tutsi; one could become Tutsi through wealth or marriage. The colonial and postcolonial histories of these small monarchies has been rewritten to such an extent, from both inside and out, that it has been overlooked how clans that are identified in oral sources are interlocked. Close kinship relations existed between Hutus and Tutsis which, against all verisimilitude, is often denied in historical studies.

Paradoxically, a general explanation for the growth of these structures can be found in the relative protection provided by distance from the areas most ravaged by slave raids. This was in contrast to coastal kingdoms that were enriched by both the Atlantic and Indian Ocean slave trades. The population density in areas where people took refuge in the mountains, such as Rwanda and Burundi, was high, and conducive to more stable political organization. However, the area remained open to new currents, which generally entered through intermediaries. In the mid-nineteenth century daring traders, such as Arabs from the east, entered the bastion of Rwanda; Portuguese *pombeiros* ventured inland from the Angolan and Mozambique coasts. At the end of the century, foreign pressure became threatening, and local kings were soon involved in international slave-trading affairs. One of the most involved was also the most accessible: the *kabaka* of Buganda, who created a veritable commercial flotilla of pirogues on Lake Victoria.[24] Active intervention by missionaries increased internal differences; the diplomatic skills of the local chiefs were no match for the economic and cultural weight of the invaders.

What can be inferred from this complex situation is that the ancestral system was well adapted to low population densities and trade, even long-distance trade, provided it passed through intermediaries. However, centralized societies emerged in areas that were relatively rich in resources and had flourishing populations. These societies were often in contact with Europeans and open to new influences, such as growth in the slave trade and interregional commerce.

Last-Ditch Solutions of Another Time:
From Angola to Mozambique

Throughout the century, dismantling of earlier political structures was widespread across the area for many different reasons. The west was ravaged mainly by Portuguese *pombeiros* and, on the Namibian coast, by the initial competition between German merchants and Boer slave traders.[25] To the east, societies were violently shaken by the combined impact of the Zanzibarites and Indians from the north coast and the ocean, the Nguni from the south, and former Portuguese *prazeiros*, along with, in the last third of the century, British, Portuguese, and Boer adventurers. In the interior, people were subject to the rising power of one or another of these groups, depending on the time, as trade in ivory, slaves, and especially arms penetrated deeper and deeper into the heart of the continent. Missionaries began to venture farther inland as new concepts of law and commerce reached these areas.[26] To this was added the unprecedented spread of major epidemics, including sleeping sickness, and cattle diseases that ravaged much of the area from north to south.[27]

From the Lunda Empire to the Kazembe Kingdom

At the beginning of the century in Angola and Kasai (in present-day Congo), there were still remnants of the Lunda Empire. Originally, it had been a centralized structure headed by a king, the *Mwata Yamvo*. Since the end of the sixteenth century, he had imposed his suzerainty over a series of peripheral groups based on power derived from corn and copper production. The overall principle was that every subordinate group paid tribute to the group above it, but each group remained free to choose its own means. The network of central African kingdoms, both large and small, stretched almost from the Atlantic coast to the Tanzanian plateau. There is a 1796 narrative by a mixed-blood trader from Goa named Pereira, who went from Tete on the middle Zambezi to the kingdom of Kazembe to the north. He left a fabulous description, struck as he was by the ceremonial protocol surrounding the king. Clothed in silk and wearing a feathered cap decorated with beads and gold, the king was hidden behind a hanging and could be seen by only a small number of the elect. This was a frequent tradition in Africa. At that time, Kazembe was still a distant dependent of the Lunda Empire. However, the Lunda capital was not visited by a European until the 1840s, and the Portuguese adventurer who came back left a rather disappointing description of it. At the time, the network of interdependence still made it possible for foreigners to travel with little risk from one coast to the other. In 1852, the Portuguese at Benguela on the Atlantic coast recorded the arrival of three "Zanzibari" traders from the interior. David Livingstone made it to Luanda in 1854, and then the Portuguese sent one of their own to the Zambezi Valley.

In the second half of the century, increased arms acquisition and intensification of ivory hunting and slave raids in the interior shook up political legacies. Banditry and war undermined the ancient territorial chiefdoms rooted in kinship structures and reinforced by religions based on rain worship and the role of spirit mediums ("fetishers"). Msiri, the slave-trading Nyamwezi chief whose caravans went toward the Indian Ocean, took over the Katanga area, which was linked to the north by Tippu-Tip on the Upper Congo. The result was the disintegration of the former chiefdoms that, in both the north and south, retained barely any memory of the past grandeur of the Congo and Lunda empires.

The Ivory and Slaves of the Angolan Coast

Throughout the previous period, the demand on the west coast for skins, beeswax, dye wood, and even ivory had remained reasonable: elephant hunting involved only a few thousand part-time hunters operating in areas that were still largely protected from the Western market. Everything changed at the end of the eighteenth century. The demand for ivory skyrocketed, and the market for slaves supplanted all the rest. The Portuguese were incited to continue penetrating ever farther into the interior. The autonomous states had economies based on interdependent internal relations organized around exchanges of tribute for protection. They were replaced by predatory powers that would send raids ever farther to acquire male slaves for export and women to be used locally to reconstitute or increase the predatory population. From then on, tens of thousands of individuals, accounting for perhaps a third or even half of the total population, found themselves uprooted every year. The expansion of the raids maintained savage civil wars. On the fringes of the slave-trading empires built by the "merchant princes," who were then in direct contact with European buyers, colonies of fugitive slaves (known as "marrons") took refuge. They were reduced to banditry, especially during droughts, as in the last third of the century. Some marron groups became strong enough to pillage their former masters in return, as did the Kisama who had taken refuge on the lower Kwanza River. Others were simply highway robbers. The more the group was involved in commercial exchanges, such as in the case of the Bobangi, the more women, who were taken in excessively high numbers, were the major losers. Women were used to pay war debts and to people the harems of chiefs, where they were employed mainly to renew slave stocks.[28] All of this generated a virtually permanent atmosphere of violence in which an increasing number of Luso-Africans participated.[29] The geographical dislocations were conducive to the expansion of slavery. Forced labor, applying to young males for whom there was no longer a market on the Atlantic after the 1850s, was introduced and exploited to a maximum by African entrepreneurs involved in "licit" trade in wax, ivory, and rubber.

The Aberrant Case of the Kuba Kingdom

These events make the growth of the Kuba Kingdom all the more surprising. In the nineteenth century it had the advantage of being located far from the coasts. The first Europeans who visited it in 1885 saw it as the last example of the royal courts that had once flourished in equatorial Africa, in the heart of an area that was then characterized by political disintegration. In 1880, like the Great Lakes states, it was a small kingdom with between 120,000 and 160,000 inhabitants. It was smaller than Belgium, but had access to three complementary natural environments: forest, savanna, and rivers, and was located between the Sankuru River to the north, the Kasai River to the west, and the Lulua River to the south. The land provided a wide range of resources, including meat, fish, plantains, corn, manioc, tobacco, and peanuts. Salt could also be extracted. Cooperative production helped the population grow. In the nineteenth century, visitors were fascinated by the elaborate royal protocol and sophisticated social and political organization. The kingdom brought together a number of chiefdoms, the largest of which was the Bushong, which accounted for almost half of the total population. Bakuba originality is clear: aside from the king, who had an impressive harem, monogamy was the rule. Moreover, ancestor worship did not exist and sacrifices were rare, though diviners played an essential role in detecting witchcraft. Most rituals revolved around the king, and religious symbolism was expressed through a truly exceptional tradition of court art.

In 1892, the capital was still a remarkable site, encircled by a high wall and enclosing an aristocracy of nobles, merchants, and artisans, who were prohibited from engaging in agriculture. Farming was reserved for a large labor force of female slaves. Society was stratified among city and village dwellers, free men, and slaves. The city was sustained by the villages subject to it, some of which were free but paid tribute mainly in the form of game meat. Slaves in villages belonging to the king's family were also required to perform public works of all kinds. The leading military chiefs were required to live in the capital, but raised soldiers in the provinces in time of war. Military operations targeted recalcitrant chiefs, rebel villages, where repression was brutal, and, more rarely, external powers, such as the Luba.

Political life in the capital was organized around five councils, at least two of which seemed relatively recent at the end of the nineteenth century. Members served for life and were co-opted from aristocratic clans. We know that the royal council met to elect the king in 1892. There was also a legal council that could criticize the king and even had a veto, and a court of justice that served as an appeals court in case of conflict among chiefdoms. Finally, as in the coastal kingdoms, there was an annual celebration that lasted several weeks and took place toward the end of the dry season. All the local chiefs converged on the capital bringing tribute and the village censuses. Jan Vansina[30] highlights the group's internal prosperity and the interregional trade in raffia cloth, basketry, pottery, and prestige goods. However, the slave trade certainly brought in much wealth. It is hard to explain the late survival of an apparently exceptional political structure in the area. Its size may have been exaggerated by twentieth-century traditionalists, but its flourishing art is nonetheless testimony to its extraordinary development.[31]

The Patchwork of Powers in Mozambique

In Mozambique, Portuguese penetration had been both more adventurous and more indigenized than in Angola. On the Atlantic, the Portuguese had a direct presence only on the coast. They relied mainly on allied chiefs in the interior, as the British and French did in West Africa. However, in the Zambezi Valley, the Portuguese introduced the *prazos* system, which involved more or less hereditary lands belonging to mixed-blood warlords. A kind of Afro-Portuguese aristocracy raided the country through institutionalized banditry. The cultural mixing and Portuguese fiction were facilitated by inheritance rules by which the eldest daughter inherited the *prazo*, and was more or less required to wed a warlord. The *prazeiros'* clients were soldiers (*chicunda*) organized into a complex system of slaves and officers placed under the command of a *capitão*. The soldiers ended up feeling more attached to the *prazo* than to the *prazeiro*, and established homes in stable settlements with separate political and social organizations. In the nineteenth century, they finally formed a veritable caste that the Portuguese administrators turned into an ethnic group in the Zambezi Valley: the Achicunda. The rest of the population was composed of slaves and free peasants responsible for feeding the soldier population. They were regularly raided by the various bands fighting for control of the country.

Everything was upset in the first decades of the nineteenth century by a conjunction of disasters: the dramatic ecological crisis of thirty years of drought and famine, the arrival from the south of Nguni invaders from Natal, and, to the north, the Zanzibarites' short-circuiting of trade. All of this destroyed the old societies in which a delicate balance had been maintained between subsistence farming, panning for gold, and the ivory trade.

The first change was a massive increase in the slave trade, which began in the eighteenth century with the demand from French sugar cane plantations on Ile de France and Ile Bourbon. Demand also began growing in Madagascar in 1800. In the nineteenth century, the trade burgeoned with the embargo on Atlantic trade, since slave trading from Mozambique to Cuba, the United States, and Brazil remained legal until 1832. Illegal slave trading then took over as the demand in Zanzibar increased, despite English hostility. The raids were occurring in a disastrous ecological context.[32]

Between 1794 and 1802, southern Africa as a whole suffered from severe droughts. The series of arid years led to an ecological disaster beginning in 1817 that continued into the 1830s. In Mozambique, from north to south, it was the worst drought ever recorded, and was made worse, beginning in 1827, by plagues of locusts. The earlier predatory system no longer functioned because peasants were no longer able to ensure the subsistence of armed bands. The periodic fairs disappeared, the *chicunda* deserted, and banditry increased.

This was also the time when, more or less forced off their land for the same reasons,[33] armed Nguni bands arrived from the south and invaded the country. They began infiltrating the area bordering Delagoa Bay between 1819 and 1821, and compensated for the crisis by expanding their conquests. Their leading chiefdom was initially that of Nxaba, and then, beginning in the mid-1830s, the state of Gaza, between the Limpopo and Zambezi rivers. Gaza was founded by Soshangane (d. 1856), who had broken away from his companion Zwangendaba of Zimbabwe. Zwangendaba destroyed the pastoral economy of the ancient Rovzi chiefdoms by advancing all the way to the shores of Lake Tanganyika (where he died in 1845). The Nguni introduced into Mozambique the centralized military system that was invented by Shaka and that ensured the power of the elites through large numbers of soldiers and huge herds of livestock.

These events shook earlier structures. Despite a few attempts by the Portuguese government on the coast to establish some supply lines from the interior (notably at the Island of Mozambique to the north, and at Quelimane and Sena on the lower Zambezi), Afro-Portuguese families were abandoned by their slaves and forced to leave. Many emigrated to Brazil and India before the 1840s. Their places were taken by a new generation of warlords, who were often of Indian origin, and whose strength was based more than ever on firearms and strongholds. Toward the middle of the century, Nguni military activity resulted in the Zambezi being shared by five slave trading principalities, of which the leading one was headed by Da Cruz. Wealth was increasingly based on elephant hunting and slave trading, this time with the Muslim world. The armed bands continued to gain territory throughout the second half of the century, at the price of incessant war.

In the north of the country, the threat of Nguni invasions cast a shadow over the people. Pressure from Zanzibar and increased trade across the Indian Ocean enabled the Yao, a people from the interior, to play a dominant role, much as the Nyamwezi had: in both cases, a number of them did not become part of the proletariat when it came in contact with the Swahili ports. Since the eighteenth century, the Makonde (from the areas now covered by Mozambique and Tanzania) and the Yao, who were organized into relatively independent chiefdoms, had served as brokers, bringing slaves and ivory to the coast. In the first half of the nineteenth century, the Yao from south of Lake Nyasa in Malawi had to face both drought and Nguni invasions. As elsewhere, wars and famine restructured the country. Next to deserted areas, uprooted Yao gathered around solid chiefdoms tending toward becoming states and centered on defensive strongholds, such as Mwembe, capital of the Mataka chiefdom visited by Livingstone in 1866. Beginning in the 1850s, conversion to Islam gave the chiefs the opportunity to throw off old beliefs and sacred cults that had guaranteed kinship structures. The chiefs kept power until the beginning of the twentieth century. As among the Nyamwezi, their villages began to adopt the coastal Swahili style. Increasingly organized in a warlike fashion for slave raids and armed with muskets by their Swahili partners, they colonized the interior highlands. Local peoples, such as the Manganja, were reduced to paying them tribute. In the north they were the Islamized counterpart of the more or less Christianized Afro-Portuguese warlords in the south.

5

The Meeting of Cultures

Southern Africa

As in West Africa, the first decades of the nineteenth century were extremely violent in southern Africa. Was this, as has been argued until recently,[1] a consequence of the explosion of the Zulu population on the coast of the Indian Ocean? Given Shaka's expansion and brutality, was the violence caused by destructive expeditions as Shaka's leading generals advanced toward the high plateaus of the interior (the Highveld), into the backcountry, and to the north (in a movement known as *mfecane*)? Or was it more a corollary of European activities, particularly slave-trading operations that diffused far into the interior from the Cape and from Delagoa Bay on the Indian Ocean? The classical view of Zulu history has been challenged by three arguments:[2]

1. The troubled times in southern Africa were not a result of the rise of the Zulu Kingdom; the emergence of the Zulu Kingdom was more a corollary than a cause.
2. The classical interpretation is of White settler origin, cobbled together out of a form of South African historiography interested in portraying Shaka as an atrocious enemy. The English liberal (anticolonial) school was eager to adopt the cliché to prove the indigenous independence of African history. Today, the conservative regionalists of *Inkatha* would be only too happy to strengthen Shaka's myth in Kwazulu-Natal.
3. In reality, the major reason for the troubles was the increase in slave raids on the borders of the Cape Colony and by the Portuguese of Mozambique, and the spread of such raids into the interior by culturally mixed raiding peoples (the Griqua).

While researchers have been arguing the pros and cons of these two theses for a decade, the factors in question were probably not exclusive.[3] They belong to complex relations of dominance, subordination, and resistance within the various African societies in the area and between those societies and Whites, including missionaries.[4]

Map 5.1   **South Africa in the Last Third of the Nineteenth Century**

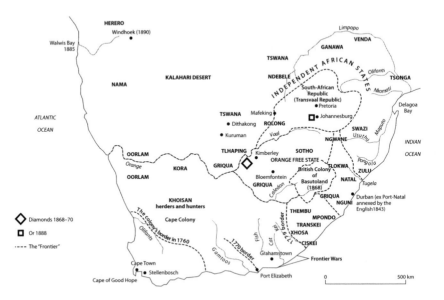

Upheaval at the Beginning of the Nineteenth Century

The argument that the *mfecane* (Zulu expansion) was the cause of *all* the problems must be rejected. It was supposed that, given the implicit but challenge-
able thesis that the area used to be peaceful, conflicts began in the northeast
after Shaka took power in the 1810s. Zulu depredations would have created
waves of migration that in turn spread violence from neighbor to neighbor
across the whole area. Thus, the Zulu would have devastated the Natal to the
south of Thukela River, thereby causing hordes of refugees, known as the
Fingo, to flee southward and put pressure on the border of the Eastern Cape
Province. The Zulu would have also forced their neighbors to the west, the
Ngwame, to cross the Drakensberg Mountains (toward the area where they
later became known as the Swazi). This succession of movements throughout
the 1820s and 1830s was known as the *Difaqane*, which apparently devastated
the Highveld. The area was thus conveniently left unoccupied when the Boers
arrived after the Great Trek of 1836.

   In the 1820s, all of southern Africa was affected by population movements
and unprecedented social and political changes. The period was marked by
massive migrations, sporadic raids and battles, and frequent famines. Why
should everything be blamed on Shaka? The conventional chronology of

battles supposedly conducted by the Zulu in the 1820s has not been proven correct: the troubles on the Thukela River seem to have been caused by local groups seeking an opening onto Delagoa Bay, and Shaka's action would have been initially defensive, not offensive. Finally, we now know that most of the Fingo from the south (now known as the Mfengu) were not of Zulu but of local origin. The whole thing was a myth made up by a few missionaries and adopted by people with vested interests as a means of gaining legitimacy. In fact, the Fingo were the remnants of various peoples who were turned into contract laborers by the British after settlers had taken their land following a violent English repression in 1835 called the "Sixth Xhosa War."

A partisan White tradition has long been reworking the history of southern Africa. What we now take for granted often springs from insufficiently documented sources that were manipulated long ago by unscrupulous observers, English merchants, Boer settlers, confused missionaries, and Shaka's vanquished indigenous adversaries.

Archeology and oral sources provide consistent evidence that insecurity had long reigned on the plateau. For example, there are the remains of cave refuges, and Tswana "towns" of several thousand refugees. Conflicts among peoples were not something new on the Highveld in the nineteenth century, even though they may have increased strongly at that time owing to greater pressure from both endogenous (drought) and exogenous (White advances) factors. Splits and mergers had been occurring among peoples for a long time.

The veld was the theater where two long-lasting concomitant dramas were played out. First, Nguni-speaking peoples, in particular the Ndebele (in Nguni), and Matabele (in Sotho and Tswana), were constantly moving westward beyond the Drakensberg Mountains. Since the seventeenth century, they had been using the great valleys of the Limpopo and its tributary the Olifant as trade routes. They advanced all the way to the heart of the Highveld, where Pretoria is located today. It is not hard to imagine that the small, mobile groups, armed with short assegais, had settled along a line of forts above the upper Limpopo well before the advance of Mzilikazi. From there they had been able to engage in trade and minor banditry at the expense of the herders and many iron workers in the area. The diaspora that took several centuries has been reduced by tradition to the *Difaqane* of the period after Shaka. Second, there were the preexisting Tswana "towns" of 10,000 to 25,000 inhabitants, which have been dated to at least as far back as the mid-eighteenth century. In 1801, the town of Dithakong had between 10,000 and 15,000 inhabitants, and remained large even after the chief took some of his people to settle at Kuruman, eighty miles to the south. The agglomerations were a sign not only of the formation of a state, but also of the increasing insecurity in the area owing to demographic expansion. They were strategic points of control of production and trade, and were expanding, though they were threatened. They ensured the circulation of ivory, horn, livestock, skins, and furs from the edges of the Kalahari, across the Highveld, and all the way to Delagoa Bay.

The demographic growth can be explained by the gradual spread of corn owing to the relatively good rainfall in the second half of the eighteenth century. We also have to take into account a long-term cycle linking demographics, land clearing, spread of the tsetse fly, and flight of populations to higher, healthier land. The process would explain both the earlier flourishing of the Tswana as described in many traditions, and the crowding of people into the highlands of the north. It began at the turn of the nineteenth century. The Tswana expansion was as much a cause of the violence in the nineteenth century as the Zulu spread, particularly since the people in the interior were also subject to depredations by Whites' agents. Indeed, the first official Dutch envoy to explore the area north of the Orange River arrived in 1779, and found European bandits were already there.[5]

Therefore the troubles cannot be reduced to the *Difaqane* produced by the *mfecane* alone. The *Mfecane* theory was based on the questionable assumption that, outside the Cape area, European expansion was barely felt by the Africans of the interior until the Great Trek in the 1830s. Yet, to take only one example, missionaries had been in Twsana country since the beginning of the nineteenth century. In 1820, they settled in Kuruman, the new capital city, which had between 8,000 and 10,000 inhabitants only three years later. The historian Julian Cobbing seems to exaggerate the size of the slave trade at Delagoa Bay, which probably only began developing in the 1820s after the troubles had erupted, and it is likely that he wrongly criticizes the actions of the missionaries, who probably did not really play a big role in slavery. Nonetheless, the Dutch had a trading post at Delagoa Bay in 1721–29. Their commercial presence was felt in the eighteenth century, as were the raids for slaves to supply the settlers on the Cape, which ravaged the whole country. Serfdom similar to the Brazilian "peon" system (requiring Cape "Hottentots" to carry certificates of residence and passes provided by their masters) was legalized in 1809 but officially prohibited in 1828, and slavery was abolished in 1834. However, passes were maintained for "native foreigners." The pass law was later strengthened for miners, and slavery was replaced by compulsory seven-year contracts. The Masters and Servants Act of 1856 was not abolished until 1974.

While British capitalism was beginning to prevail in Cape Town, the same was not true in the small settlements along the far border. They were in league with the Griqua, bands of thieves operating in the Highveld. Griqua were traders of various origins, such as from earlier mixing between Khoisans and

Europeans (who had been colonizing the land with virtually no White women for nearly two centuries). The Griqua and other bandits called themselves *bastaards*, a derogatory term used by Boers. Settlers continued to supply them with weapons so they could increase their raids and deliver *mantatees*, Tswana and Sotho slaves, to work on the settlers' farms. In 1795, there were approximately 1,000 slaves on the frontier, then 4,500 in 1823 and 5,500 at the time of emancipation ten years later. Even though the first missionaries in Tswana country cannot reasonably be accused of consciously promoting the raids,[6] nearly everyone acknowledged the impact of the operations. They were also linked with the even less well-known slave trade in Namibia, the veld, and the Kalahari.

Was it only the Mozambique slave trade in Delagoa Bay and the expansion of raids in the interior that exposed the societies to such ferocious pressure that they found no way out but through violence? Were there not other factors? The series of droughts was catastrophic at the beginning of the century: between 1800 and 1803, in 1812, and again in 1816–18, when rust and cattle plague destroyed harvests and livestock. The effects were even worse on the Highveld where the ecosystem was more vulnerable. Moreover, the population had increased in the preceding century. Traditions gathered by the first travelers describe an environment that had been damaged over many years. Strategies for resisting famine were undermined by the ongoing social and political changes. Famine forced people to move en masse to sources of water. Classical historiography has interpreted the major battle at Dithakong in 1823 as resulting from the simultaneous arrival of peoples fleeing the *mfecane*. It was only the result of ordinary people converging from disaster zones and looking for livestock and food in the only nearby center that was still functioning. Informants from that time said that 40,000 to 50,000 people from three "nations" were involved.[7]

The same interpretation obviously applies to Zulu country: a parallel can be seen between the chronology of droughts and the periods of demographic and political unrest under the reigns of Dingiswayo and his successor Shaka. The proximity of Delagoa Bay played a role, probably less owing to the slave trade, which increased only after 1820, than to the fact that the ivory trade had been growing since the mid-eighteenth century. The ivory trade was controlled by chiefs and gave them great power over their subjects; as elephants became rarer, the misery of the chiefs' dependents increased. This created a context favorable to a political change such that the strongest would dominate their weaker neighbors. The Zulus' role cannot be denied in this respect.

However, it is no longer possible to talk generally of "Zuluified" hordes, such as has even been done in the case of the Kololo of southern Zambia and Namibia. Like the rest of southern Africa, central and southern Namibia were affected by the nearby Cape. The first livestock raids took place in the seventeenth century. Between 1800 and 1835, there was interaction among slave traders from the Cape, Mozambique, and Angola, whose routes followed the Zambezi and Orange rivers. Along the Namibian coast, which was difficult to reach from Angola owing to foul tides, slave-trading ships from the Indian Ocean and American whaling ships crossed one another. Beginning in 1843, there was also a rush to harvest the guano piles on the coast, which could be up to 150 inches high. In 1845, a missionary claimed to have seen thirty-five boats sailed by some 6,000 sailors around Ichaboe Island, where there were major guano deposits. This generated strong demand for labor, but even stronger demand for beef. At the beginning of the century, an American captain boasted of having exported more than 50,000 head of livestock from the Namibian coast. Exports also included oil, ivory, skins, dried fish, and, of course, slaves.

For many centuries Khoi herdsmen (whom the Boers called Hottentots) had been pushed toward the arid lands of the interior. By the end of the eighteenth century, they had been largely decimated and reduced to slavery on settlers' land. In 1820, there were fewer than 12,000 in eastern areas, 6,000 of whom lived on the border. At the beginning of the century, most had re-formed clans led by chiefs or "captains" whose authority came from links with settlers, for example, the fact of having served as recruiting agents or armed guards. A revolt between 1799 and 1803 enabled the Cape government to eliminate the captains' last privileges. Some escapees entered into the service of Whites and adopted the Afrikaans language. The 1828 ordinance exempted them, but not other Africans, from the pass laws and gave them the right to acquire plots of land inside the colony. The British government ensured that the clause could not be rescinded without the Crown's consent. Despite the reticence of the Boer settlers, this promoted mixing and gave birth to the category of "Colored." Some Khoikhoi managed to keep their land rights throughout the century: the land was recognized as forming reserves, which were located around missionary stations and given the generic name of "Namaqualand." Many Hottentots retained an adventurous nomadic lifestyle based on slave trading and banditry. They were known as the Korana in the west and the Griqua elsewhere. Others integrated into the colony, even though communes' rights to elect their own municipal councils had been applied to the virtually exclusive benefit of Whites since 1836. The 1853 Constitution provided for property-based voting, which meant the Khoikhoi could be represented minimally in parliament. The rest fled to Xhosa country, where they merged into the population.

The San (the so-called bushmen) lived in small bands of hunter-gatherers, and fared little better. Since they had to raid livestock to survive, settlers saw their eradication as justified: San men were executed, and women and children were put into slavery. Those who remained fled into the desert. The Namaqua of central Namibia subsisted by engaging in slave raids to supply the southern colonial market. In the second half of the eighteenth century, they were pushed ever northward by increased firearms imports. Between 1800 and 1840, they were trapped and decimated by new arrivals: the Oorlam, or local Griqua, who had formed groups on the northwest frontier of the Cape. ("Oorlam" comes from *"oor landers,"* which means "people from other lands" in Afrikaans.[8]) The Oorlam were a mixture of Khoi survivors, fugitive slaves, *bastaards,* outlaw settlers, and other bandits. They were more or less Christian, and controlled trade between the coast and the interior highlands. They lived along Fish River (not to be confused with the river of the same name on the Eastern Cape) because the rest of the land was too dry. They increased their attacks on the Namaqua and Korana, who used to live there but had been reduced to slavery or weakened and pushed to the north. Clearly, this process was not Shaka's fault, but rather had Western origins.[9]

Therefore, the troubles in southern Africa was not caused by the *mfecane* alone, but by the explosive combination of demographic growth, the resulting lack of land, and the livestock shortage. All was exacerbated by drought right when slave raids and growing demand for ivory on the coast were upsetting the balance of power. This is, in any case, the present state of our knowledge.

Shaka and the Zulu Revolution: Revision of an Analysis

What certainly marks the period that began in the 1820s was the increase in violence involving an impressive number of chiefdoms and small, mobile, predatory states. Methods were expeditious: most of the vanquished men were executed while the women and children were incorporated into the group. It was a period when, instead of the lineage system based on semitranshumant herding that had dominated until then, conquering states developed autocratic military techniques. They were formidably efficient and based on systematic use of age classes and initiation training. The hypothesis that has been advanced so far is that there was Sotho influence on the northern Nguni.[10] However, there is no reason not to look to the Thembe states or others in southern Mozambique in the eighteenth century, which had been influenced by mixed Portuguese occupation for many years. It is even possible to consider the Rozvi state in the Zimbabwe area as a relevant factor at the end of the seventeenth century.

What was Shaka's real role? At the beginning of the 1820s, he was the leading political player south of the Thukela River, but he far from dominated the whole region. He had recently, and under controversial circumstances, taken leadership of the Zulu chiefdom following Chief Dingiswayo. He was beginning to regroup his forces to repel attacks by his neighbors. When the first Europeans landed in Port Natal in 1824, it was still a new state. Shaka, as usurper, had a difficult time dealing with his adversaries in the royal family. As his power increased, he gave rise to strong resistance from the leading chiefdoms, especially in the north. This is why he moved his capital, KwaBulawayo, and several of his regiments to the lower Thukela. Because Shaka's supremacy was far from secure, he was careful in his lifetime to maintain a reputation for invincibility through possibly embellished narratives, which the first travelers willingly recorded.

The south bank of the river was of obvious strategic interest, which explains some of Shaka's campaigns and especially his concern to have his lands border on the sea, not far from Port Natal. From there, he could launch raids to capture livestock. However, none of his expeditions took the dramatic turn they are traditionally given, namely, the ravaging of almost all of Natal and expulsion of the inhabitants toward the Cape "frontier."

Shaka welcomed the arrival of English merchants. In his view, they provided three advantages: they were sources of manufactured goods, could be used as intermediaries with the British authorities of the Cape, and could be employed as potential allies against his enemies. Some of the merchants who bought ivory directly from him were used in this way. In 1827, they played an important role in his regime, and this is one of the possible reasons for his assassination the following year. Indeed, beginning in 1829, merchants and missionaries, who had not managed to establish good relations with Shaka's murderer and successor, Dingane, began to ask the British government to take action in the backcountry of Port Natal. It was only after his death that Shaka's detestable reputation became established among Europeans. Until then he had been seen in a rather positive light by visitors, aside from some exceptions.[11]

Many points should be examined with regard to the reconstruction of Shaka's career. While it is certain that young male recruits did not have the right to marry without Shaka's authorization, there is no evidence that the same applied to young women (aside from a document from 1873, which was written too late to be credible). On the contrary, a contemporary claimed that they could be married as soon as they were fourteen and were subject to extensive polygamy with older husbands. This could not have had the supposed negative effect on the birth rate.

Were the chiefs who fled from Shaka actually former generals irritated by his autocracy? This is far from certain. In the 1820s, there were at least four large groups in the area: Sekwati's Pedi to the north, Sobhuza's Diamini in the eastern Transvaal, Moshoeshoe's Mokoteli (Sotho) near the Caledon River, and Shaka's Zulu to the south. The Zulu gradually conquered many of their neighbors, and others certainly wanted to avoid that danger. However, there is no evidence that, for example, Mzilikazi, chief of the Ndebele, was one of Shaka's friends. On the contrary, Mzilikazi and his people, like many other Ndebele before them, crossed the Drakensberg Mountains to escape Zulu pressure. Like Shaka, Mzilikazi wanted to establish his authority while conducting the usual livestock raids on the Highveld. He also found himself in conflict with the movement of Boers toward the interior and with the Griqua and other bands of White origin that had been moving north from the Orange River since the beginning of the century. In 1829, a kind of military confederation finally expelled the Ndebele. In 1831, the Griqua stole 6,000 head of livestock. Two years later, the Ndebele retaliated. The raids upset the area's economy, cities were deserted, and people found refuge in scattered communities based on hunting and gathering. The Difaqane did take place, but it was the people of the veld themselves who were the cause, not Shaka.

Since history has not yet been sufficiently "revisited," we will not say anything more about Shaka. It is certain that his legend was constructed very quickly, mainly around the middle of the century by both White historiography and Black identity claims after the British took over Natal in 1844. Shaka became a mythical Manichean figure: on one hand he was a monster, and on the other, a hero. He has been used in this way by the generations that have followed.

Lesotho: Colonized Bastion

The area that was to become Lesotho is relatively well known owing to, among other things, the presence of French missionaries from the 1830s on. It provides another example of how an indigenous group evolved in the nineteenth century in response to successive waves of pressure from modernity. In the early 1820s, following a terrible drought, the Sotho, who had until then practiced very loosely structured transhumant pastoralism, were united behind an energetic chief, Moshoeshoe. This was in reaction to growing pressure from the Boers, who were beginning their Great Trek into the interior. The Sotho gradually took refuge in the most mountainous part of their lands, which was relatively sheltered from European incursions.

Their history can be broken down into three major periods. The first was the merging of formerly disparate groups into a single nation. The Sotho nation was based on recognition of a shared chief by different peoples both from Tswana country and from Sotho, as well as the fringes of Zulu country to the east and Xhosa lands to the south. During that relatively prosperous period of demographic growth, despite the loss of some of their land owing to introduction of the plow and draft animals by missionaries, the Sotho were able to combine increased farming, larger herds, and their commercial skills. They acted as the breadbasket for their Boer neighbors.

The second period was the colonial era, when the land was annexed by the Cape Colony between 1868 and 1884. Overall, the country managed to stand up to the oppression and maintain some economic prosperity, at the same time giving rise to a revolt that put an end to direct South African control. The chiefs took advantage of their alliance with the colonizer, which returned to them a portion of the taxes that they were responsible for collecting. Yet, they were not rejected by their subjects, who considered them indispensable for their protection. Finally, return to the British Crown's direct control, which was considered inevitable by the governing elite to avoid incorporation into the Boer state of Orange, could not prevent the Sotho from descending into poverty. Little by little the Sotho were forced to enter the dominant economy. Men were systematically employed in migrant labor, which had become indispensable in the Rand mines.

As elsewhere, the formation of Lesotho came out of a long period of troubles at the turn of the nineteenth century. People found themselves caught between the Zulu to the east and pressure from various refugee groups: the San and the Tswana were pushed ahead of the first Europeans as they moved northward. Besides armed groups of Khoi, Kora, and mixed marauders fleeing slavery, all were attracted by the more fertile banks of the Orange River. The flames of widespread banditry were fanned by weapons purchased in the Cape. The series of ecological disasters at the end of the eighteenth century were worsened by the major drought in the 1820s. Finally, around 1824, young Chief Moshoeshoe took the initiative to lead his people some sixty miles away, into the impregnable mountains that were to become the center of his kingdom. He and his people were found there in 1833 by the first missionaries to live with them. Sotho national unity increased not only against the Griqua bandits from the west, who raided livestock and slaves, but also against the Boers, who undertook their Great Trek in 1836.

The Sotho had long lived like the Tswana, in compact groups of at least a hundred compounds. Their towns had several thousand inhabitants. When Wesleyan missionaries settled in Griqua country to the west in 1840, they were still neighbors with the Sotho. However, pressure from Boers, who desired more pastureland as the demand for wool grew, increased conflicts in Orange. In 1856, some 13,000 White settlers (including 3,000 men in their prime) owned 1.2 million sheep distributed over nearly 1,300 farms. About 100 of the farms belonged to Englishmen (who were generally not residents), and some of them covered 40,000 acres. In the 1850s, speculation became intense and lucrative. In principle, Whites had to ask Moshoeshoe for permission to use his land; in practice, expropriation skyrocketed. While the British had tried to delimit his land, it was constantly shrinking. In 1843, an initial treaty was meant to set the borders, but in 1849 Sotho lands were again reduced by forty miles to the east. The government first tried to have the Crown annex the whole area between the Vaal and Orange Rivers but in 1854, for financial reasons, the English withdrew to the south. They left the indigenous people in the north to deal with the Boers on their own.

Leading 10,000 men, Moshoeshoe was victorious against the Boers in 1858. However, with consolidation of the Orange Free State, war broke out again. The Boers gradually occupied most of the easily accessible land, thereby cutting into Sotho territory. In 1865–66, Moshoeshoe was forced to abandon the fertile lowlands on the north bank of the Caledon River. He was nearly eighty years old. His sons were fighting over what remained of their inheritance. Finally, Great Britain, which Moshoeshoe had been petitioning for help since the 1860s, annexed the rest of the country in 1868 and imposed a new treaty. It was only in 1872, two years after Moshoeshoe's death, that the borders of Lesotho (then called Basutoland) were finally set, squeezed between the Caledon and Orange rivers.[12]

As they gradually withdrew into the southern mountains, the Sotho were able to adjust to the new landscape. They reduced the size of their villages and adapted to a diversified complementary economy based on farming, raising livestock, and trading. Increasingly in the nineteenth century, beads, along with copper bracelets from Zulu country, were used as currency. European money also began to be accepted in the 1830s.

The Sotho developed real solidarity among their chiefs, who used their wealth to bring in more and more dependents. The basic system was the *mafisa*: rich livestock owners shared risk by distributing animals among those who had none. In exchange, the recipients had use of the animals' milk and the right to a few calves. Their farming methods were quite sophisticated, and involved the rotation of crops such as sorghum, corn, and tobacco. This increased productivity even before plows and beasts of burden (oxen) were adopted in the 1850s. By the 1880s, there was a plow for every twenty inhabitants. This was all complemented by remarkable ironwork, leatherwork, and woodwork. Under the influence of missionaries, the Sotho adopted European technology. By the 1860s, their blacksmiths knew how to make bullets, guns, and even cannons. Around 1880, the chiefs began replacing their round mud homes with stone buildings, and stonecutters replaced women as construction workers. Since women were not permitted to touch livestock, use of oxen to draw plows radically changed the sexual division of labor. Yet, women did not have less work, for they were responsible for everything that had not benefited from technological improvement.

The chiefs also encouraged trade, which made it possible for them to acquire more cattle. Trade in foodstuffs with the Boers, who concentrated exclusively on livestock raising, began in the 1840s with the opening of a few European stores. There were about twenty in 1872 and more than 100 in 1900. Sotho carriers were required to pay taxes from which Whites were exempt. The Sotho desired knives and farming implements. They also adopted the horse, which enabled Moshoeshoe to create a cavalry unit of several hundred. The solid Sotho community was attracting refugees from all surrounding areas, even from Zululand and the Cape Colony. They were welcomed on the condition that they recognized Moshoeshoe's authority.

However, the Sotho also demonstrated their resistance to imported ideologies. Missionaries were considered a necessary evil to maintain contact with the world but initially Christianity had little impact. Those attracted to the missions were social pariahs, and wearing European clothes became more or less synonymous with misery. If all sects, including Seventh Day Adventists, are taken into account, the number of adult Christians was barely 14,000 in 1894, and there were still fewer than 20,000 in 1904.

Rainfall was erratic, temperatures were extreme, and arable land was relatively rare since a little less than a third of the country was located lower than 6,500 feet. The population density grew in part because of the kingdom's relative prosperity and acceptance of many refugees. The population increased sevenfold over fifty years. There were approximately 50,000 Sotho in 1847, 70,000 in 1852, and 80,000 in 1855. The flow of refugees, including those from Zulu country and the Cape Colony, accelerated as troubles increased in the second half of the century. The Sotho were estimated at 180,000 in 1865 and at perhaps 200,000 ten years later. In 1895 there were 250,000, and nearly 350,000 at the time of the first census in 1904. Sotho villages and high mountain pastures were located at altitudes of over 6,000 feet. It seems there were 600 villages above the sources of the Orange, each of which had a population of 300 to 400. The result was erosion accelerated by rapid deforestation. In the final third of the century, the country was no longer self-sufficient, and land disputes were becoming common.

Basutoland had been temporarily attached to the Cape Colony. However, faced with colonial demands, the Sotho began to acquire as many guns as possible. They used them in the 1881–82 revolt known as the Gun War. Despite the fact that the chiefs, who were then protected by the British, may have abused their power, the majority of the people nonetheless obeyed the elite. They chose the lesser of two evils and, in 1884, returned under British protection to shelter themselves from the South African settlers. This spelled the end of balance in the country. While the Sotho had begun supplying the Kimberley diamond mines with grain in the 1870–80s, the construction of the railroad in 1886 made them uncompetitive. The ecological disasters of the 1890s accentuated the crisis. Land hunger gave young men no choice but to become migrant workers. Migrations had occurred before, but in 1875, owing to the relative labor shortage, a miner needed to work for only one or two months to earn enough to buy a gun. After 1890 young people had no choice: 20,000 passes were distributed in 1893, and twice that in 1899, including 25,000 for contracted farm and domestic workers. At the same time, the increase in migrants led to a drop in pay. Colonization reinforced the gap that was growing between the people and their leaders by creating the Basutoland National Council in 1903. Almost all of those who served on the council were chiefs. In less than a century, the country had gone through a complex, and exemplary, process. The territory was redefined just as a nation of multicultural origins was being formed. The nation was able to ensure its security through use of a single language and recognition of a single power. It established open relations with colonial modernity while preserving its core values. However, over time, the imbalance among the powers caused it to lose both its political autonomy and its economic system.

The English, the Africans, and the Boers: The Genesis of Segregation

What happened in Basutoland was happening more or less everywhere in South Africa throughout the nineteenth century. In 1795, during the French Revolution wars, the British reacted to the French takeover of Holland by occupying the Cape. They gave the post back for a short time in 1802, but took it again in 1806, at the beginning of the Napoleonic wars. It was a strategic location until the Suez Canal opened in 1869.

In the nineteenth century in South Africa, a new social order slowly but surely emerged. It was based on violence and reciprocity, and generated a special system of representation. Unlike in Algeria, where Islam was a rampart against Christianity, South Africa's strong point was the development of a resolutely Christian civilization on its frontiers. Frontiers were interactive places of colonization and cultural exchange, and were also part of the Cape economy.

The country had only 15,000 Whites in 1790, but the British doubled that number and began sending merchants, hunters, and missionaries into the interior in the 1820s. Until 1825, Cape wines were highly prized in London and merino sheep were introduced to produce wool for the British textile industry, which was in full expansion at the time. The west of the province, which was poorer owing to the nearby desert, was dominated by Bastaards and mixed settlers, who were often Christianized. They had pushed the Khoi and San (bushmen) into the dry lands. In fact, the Khoi and San had become mixed very early on, and all the groups would finally come to be placed in the category of "colored." On the eastern border, which was more hospitable, the first dissidents of Boer descent, of whom there were close to 100 at the turn of the century, began to spread. In both the east and west, the people on the borders, who were mostly impoverished hunters, were quickly integrated into the Cape economy. They supplied the Cape Colony with products of hunting, and livestock resulting from their trading or raiding. They were most often financed by the colonial elite to whom they were in debt.

On the vast expanses of the veld, landowners allowed their "serfs" to live more or less as they wished. They organized their own subsistence, as long as they took care of the herds and fulfilled their masters' periodic demands. This was the beginning of a shared culture, based on exchanges of food and women. Notwithstanding, there were also misunderstandings that made conflict possible at any time. Within the structure, an intermediary society gradually emerged based on slavery and patriarchal relations. The area became infested with bandits, but it was also a place of intense social and cultural exchange. The first missions, established between 1803 and 1814, were used as refuges by all parties.[13]

This pioneering phase was not yet the beginning of the establishment in South Africa of "races" as rigid castes. That social construction resulted as much from the British concern to set clear boundaries between the "native people" and the dominant class of the triumphant imperial economy, as from the rigid primitive Calvinism of retrograde Boers. In the first half of the nineteenth century, segregation began to be established systematically.[14]

Indigenous people had the choice between leaving or submitting, in other words accepting, along with their wives and children, to become serfs on the farms of Whites. Given the situation, the country entered a crisis toward the end of the eighteenth century, following a series of drought years. The frontier was seething with unrest between 1799 and 1803. It began with the first "Kaffir War" now known as the first Xhosa War, which was a desperate attempt to halt the settlers. It was the largest popular uprising until the 1856 revolt, and was led by Bantu-speaking farmers from the south whose ancestors had mixed with herders. (Their language contained clicks like the Khoi languages, and in Khoi, *xhosa* means angry man.). At the beginning of the nineteenth century, they numbered between 70,000 and 100,000. Over the previous two centuries, they had moved westward all the way to Transkei, where they were the dominant group known as the Gcaleka. Their land there was protected from malaria and the tsetse fly, and had been described in 1680 as extremely fertile, incredibly peopled, and full of livestock.[15]

The British occupation of the Cape translated into vexatious measures against the Boer settlers. English replaced Dutch as the official language, the florin was replaced by the pound sterling, and newspapers began to be published in English. In 1825, a council was created to advise the governor. It was transformed into a legislative council in 1834 and included a few settlers' representatives, but only unofficially.

In the early 1820s, 5,000 new British settlers arrived, which gave rise to the beginnings of land hunger. To remedy it, the eastern frontier began to be pushed back. As early as 1809, the British had prohibited Africans from crossing the border; it was not until 1840 that they considered admitting local Blacks into a colony conceived of as completely White, or at the most colored. Colored was a category composed mainly, aside from the Bastaards, of people of mixed Indonesian descent. The Xhosa were forced eastward across Great Fish River. The retreat became increasingly painful as small independent Christianized Black communities developed in the interstices left by poor White people. The communities were "creolized" and centered on their church or school. Between 1780 and 1870 (before the diamond rush), the number of White settlers grew from 20,000 to 300,000, while the African population was between 2 and 4 million. The frontier wars continued for a century. A sign of the advance was the massacre of British soldiers in 1811–12, followed by retaliation and construction of Grahamstown Fort as a pivotal point in the line of defense. In the end, 20,000 Xhosa were expelled across Great Fish River.

Following new troubles in 1818, the British became well skilled at dividing and conquering. They had allies settle on the lands of hostile peoples, particularly on those of the Gcaleka. In 1819 and 1820, the frontier was pushed back again. In 1825, faced with a labor shortage, recruitment of Black workers was authorized in the Cape Colony. This is when race-based legislation really began. It was a means of separating the "civilized" from the "barbarians." One of the signs was that, in 1833, for the first time, a very formal ceremony was held for the public hanging of an African who had been found guilty of murdering a young Englishwoman. It was the invention of a culture and discourse based on the settler's superiority and negative stereotypes of Black people. Africans became unworthy of being considered independent. Rejecting the prior patriarchal culture, memories were eliminated to produce legal racial dependency. Between 1834 and 1879, a whole series of vagrancy laws were passed that ensured that Africans were tolerated only as workers in service to Whites.

A group of Bastaards and Christianized Khoi, who were protected by missionaries, had settled on the Kat River in 1828–29. Their land was being nibbled away, a process that was supported by an ideology that made "Kaffir farming" intolerable to Whites. In 1835, the British began invading again, and crossed the Great Kei River. Strong support from the government in

London was required to restrain local colonial appetites. It did not help that thousands of Africans were killed in the battle, and about as many Gcaleka were requisitioned as workers; they became the famous Fingo who were scattered across the colony's farms.

From south to north, the already well-established advance of Boer farmers north of Orange River became an organized movement after 1834. The Great Trek was provoked by the British emancipation law suppressing slavery in 1833. Nevertheless, it was not just the flight of small conservative farmers forced out by modernization of the Cape. It was also the final result of decades of gradual advancement of the frontier by determined bands of adventurers, who had become increasingly well armed and equipped. It was similar to the American pioneers' conquest of the West. Approximately 4,000 Boers migrated between 1836 and 1840 with their families, slaves, livestock, wagons, and guns to an area that had already been largely destabilized by slave raids. In 1837, they allied with the Griqua, and managed to push the Ndebele into what is now Zimbabwe. A number of small independent states formed around the strongest White leaders. Their economy was based on elephant hunting and slave trading with the Portuguese. Andries Pretorius rapidly became their leader. Farms were gradually established, and they employed forced labor. Some of the Voortrekkers also moved toward the east, where they entered into agreements with the first British settlers.

Confrontation became inevitable between the new arrivals and Dingane's Zulu, who were defeated in battles in 1838 (at Blood River) and in 1840. Taking advantage of the Zulu's internal problems, the Boers aided the rise to power of Mpande, who ruled over a reduced Zululand. The Boers also established farms in Natal. However, the concomitant arrival of thousands of English settlers finally led to British annexation of the province in 1843. An iron-fisted regime was set up by Theophilus Shepstone (who later became secretary for native affairs): the so-called hut tax was introduced in 1849, Black reserves were drawn up in 1852, and forced labor was widely practiced. Zulu Chief Mpande (1840–72) proved in fact to be a formidable ruler who rebuilt the military power of his little kingdom. His son Cetshwayo, who was brought to office in 1856 following a civil war, began by seeking Natal's support in reestablishing his power against Boer infringement. Then, in 1879, he finally turned his army of 30,000 against the British invaders.

In the interval, internal social and ideological changes were coming about through the influence of missions and Griqua banditry. Depending on the situation, chiefs made alliances of convenience, but they constantly lost ground. In the north, Mswati's Swazi Dlamini and Manukosi's (Soshangane's) Gaza provided slaves for both the Portuguese and the Boers of Transvaal. They spread over the veld and incorporated neighboring groups. At Manukosi's death (1858), civil war broke out among the Gaza. The Swazi, Boers, and Portuguese got involved. Mswati took advantage of the situation to assert his authority almost all the way to Lourenço Marques, and the Gaza decided to emigrate toward the north, into eastern Zimbabwe. However, Mswati died in 1865, followed by Ndebele chief Mzilikazi in 1868. With the invasion of the Gaza and Ndebele kingdoms in 1893–96 and the crushing of the Venda resistance in 1898, by 1900 there were no longer any independent African societies in southern Africa.

To the south, the Zulu found themselves competing with the Swazi and Boers. By the 1880s, they were forced to submit, and were divided into a number of competing provinces with much reduced power. The Boers annexed huge amounts of land—at least on paper. In 1887, what remained of Zululand (aside from slightly less than a third, which was turned into a reserve in 1902–4) was finally integrated into Natal with a view to providing labor force. The Zulu nonetheless balked. The farmers and plantation owners had to set up a flow of indentured labor from southern Mozambique, which took a few decades to systematize. In the meantime, beginning in the 1860s, Indian coolies were used on the sugar plantations. Many Indian merchants immigrated so that at the end of the nineteenth century there were more Indians in Natal than Whites. In 1893 a young Indian lawyer named Gandhi who had been educated in England began to hone his nonviolent resistance tactics against the first segregation laws in South Africa.

Toward the interior, in contrast, the British gave free rein to the Boers and also to the Sotho under Moshoeshoe. Moshoeshoe, having beaten his Tlokwa rivals in 1853–54, was temporarily able to benefit from the Whites' division to consolidate his power in his mountainous southern bastion.

By the accords of 1852 and 1854, the British acknowledged the independence of the Boers' Orange Free State and Transvaal (then called the South African Republic), where Africans were prohibited from using firearms and gunpowder. Despite a number of civil wars that continued into the middle of the century, the Boers adopted constitutions and established parliaments in Orange Free State and Transvaal, though they were not able to unite the two states into one. Sheep farming developed in Orange, which was a major exporter of wool via the Cape in the 1860s.

In the Cape Colony, banks, insurance companies, and other enterprises had set down roots before the 1850s. A wealthy class of businessmen, bankers, and farmers developed. Cape Town had 50,000 inhabitants, as did Port Elizabeth, which was created in 1820. Through the 1853 constitution, a representative government was inaugurated with a legislative assembly that was elected by property owners. (Voting was not secret until 1887.) There were initially a few Black voters, but their numbers decreased, and then disappeared entirely in 1936. Cape Colony's executive branch did not become independent from London until 1872.

The wars of 1811, 1819, 1835, and 1846 had already dispossessed the Xhosa on the frontier of much of their land. The British annexed another piece of the frontier between the Great Fish and Great Kei rivers in 1847–48. As in Natal, the hut tax was applied in the area, known as British Kaffraria, which was one of the contributing factors to a new Xhosa war in 1851–53. In 1853, the war led to a local messianic rebellion that united chiefs, the workers of White farmers, squatters, and poor peasants against the antivagrant laws. Repression was especially violent because, given the insufficient labor force, it was intended to make the western Xhosa lands an official British possession. Moreover, an epidemic of bovine pleuropneumonia killed much of the Xhosas' livestock in 1854–55. Influenced as they had been by Christianity since the end of the eighteenth century, they reacted with a messianic popular revolt similar to others that had occurred in the previous twenty years, with prophets more or less announcing the end of the Whites. In 1856, the prophet Mhlakaza and his niece Ngonqanse, who conveyed to him messages from their ancestors, led desperate peasants to purify themselves of their ancestors' anger by destroying what remained of their harvests and herds. Did the British voluntarily turn a blind eye? In any case, the resulting famine led the survivors to come to the colony by the thousands in search of work: between February and September 1857, 24,000 refugees poured across the border.

The disaster was made complete by the great drought of 1862. The people who later became the Ciskei lost half their numbers. Some of the uprooted people, the Fingo, finally resettled in 1865 to the east of the Great Kei, in what became known as Fingoland. Kaffraria was placed under the control of British magistrates and incorporated into the Eastern Cape ten years later. During those ten years, 6,000 settlers of German origin moved there. The Xhosa were forced out into the "royal reserve" along the river. In an effort to re-create an indigenous local peasantry, they organized into "villages" of about twenty huts, each under the control of a headman. This system was to become standard: whether they were peasants on reserves, squatters on private Crown lands, or tenants on land owned by Whites, men became migrant workers (such as domestics, cleaners, and guards) in cities and mines (over 10,000 Zulus left for the diamond mines in Kimberley between 1868 and 1870), while women remained in the fields. Around 1874, some 2 million hectares belonging to private settlers and companies were cultivated by Africans. Very few were able to benefit from the 1858 law authorizing "natives of approved character" to buy more than the ordinarily approved four acres. Yet some chiefs managed to form a wealthy new minor peasantry that was linked by the grain market and work in the mines (there were about 2,000 mines in the Eastern Cape at the end of the century). This was the group from which black political consciousness first emerged in the subsequent century.[16]

The South African economy, which was based on Cape wines and wool, was not very prosperous, despite guano harvesting on the coast, a little copper in the Western Cape, and ivory in the interior. Only a little more than 5,000 tons of wool were exported in 1855, which was much less than in Australia. At the beginning of the 1870s, only a few miles of railroads had been built. The 240,000 White settlers accounted for only a third of the inhabitants of South Africa, and two-thirds of them spoke Dutch or Afrikaans. Everything changed in 1866–67, with the discovery of diamonds in the Vaal River Valley. In only a few years, the diamond rush attracted 50,000 multilingual pioneers, including 20,000 Whites and 30,000 Africans, to the city that would be named Kimberley in 1873. It was located 550 miles from the Cape and 340 miles from East London, the closest South African port. The first prospectors worked on a small scale; in Kimberley itself there were up to 1,700 mining concessions. However, production was quickly centralized and mechanized until, in 1889, De Beers Consolidated Mines became the only producer. The company was controlled by Cecil Rhodes, a young British man who had been raised in South Africa and began his fortune in diamonds. Work was segregated, and Black miners found themselves relegated to compounds. Both functional and residential segregation began to take form. It was strengthened when gold was discovered. In 1895, the pass law prohibited Africans who had been unemployed for more than three consecutive days from entering the Witwatersrand. Competition increased the racism of poor Whites. Africans were prohibited from engaging in any union activity, yet they carved out a place for themselves in the new circumstances. They worked as miners and as unskilled railway workers (the railroad reached the Cape ports in 1892, Delagoa Bay in 1894, and Durban in 1895). They also found jobs in the many interstices of "informal" activities necessary to the lives of both Whites and Blacks. For example, they worked as cleaners, drivers, and masons. (Prostitution was still dominated by poor White women.[17])

The discovery of diamonds and precious metals hastened political restructuring. It put an end to the independence of the last indigenous peoples by bringing the Cape and Natal together. In 1890, Cecil Rhodes became the prime minister of the Cape Colony. The diamond mines were located in an area that was claimed by Orange, the Transvaal, the western Griqua under the leadership of Nicolaas Waterboer, and the Tswana chiefs from the south. Defending English rights, the lieutenant governor of Natal arbitrated in Waterboer's favor, and the latter requested British protection against the Boers.

The territory was annexed under the name of Griqualand West, and finally incorporated into the Cape Colony in 1880.

Part of Transkei, the hilly region between the Cape and Natal, was initially called Griqualand East and was acknowledged as belonging to a Griqua chief, Adam Kok, who was a rival of Waterboer. Griqualand East was rapidly taken over by White settlers. The rest of Transkei remained occupied by small subjected Xhosa and Thembu farmers. (The latter is the group from which Nelson Mandela is descended.) A century of struggles over the border came to an end with the Xhosa War of 1877–78. The Transkei became a vast reservoir of workers, and its last remote locations were annexed in the 1880s and 1890s. Finally, in Natal in 1894, the Cape Colony took advantage of the Mpondo's internal divisions, which were similar to those between "old" and "modern" Zulu, and appropriated their territory without a fight.

The British Crown in the person of Lord Carnarvon, secretary of state for the colonies under Disraeli's Tory government, desired above all the establishment of a confederation. Faced with little enthusiasm in the Orange Free State to the south, the confederation was begun clumsily in the north by the secretary for native affairs in Natal, Theophilus Shepstone. He wanted to take advantage of the bankruptcy of the South African Boer state (the future Transvaal), invaded it in 1877, and proclaimed it a British colony. The armed defense of the alliance of three strong Boer men, Paul Kruger, Piet Joubert, and Martinus Pretorius led to the English defeat. The republic was reinstated, though under imprecise British suzerainty with respect to external affairs.

The governor of the Cape Colony then decided that Cetshwayo's Zulu Kingdom was the last obstacle to the confederation. The colonial army penetrated into his territory in January 1879. The elimination of some of the English troops at Isandhlwana slowed the invasion, but British technological and diplomatic superiority increased internal problems, and Zululand was annexed in 1887.

In the eyes of the English, when gold was discovered in 1886 in the Northern Province, thirty miles from Pretoria, the capital, there was no longer anything to hinder confederation. At the end of the century, gold production in the Northern Province was between a quarter and a third of the world's total. In the heart of mining country, Johannesburg mushroomed, attracting huge numbers of British settlers and massive amounts of British capital. The 124 companies that had until then been independent began to be brought under the umbrella of the powerful Chamber of Mines in 1890. In 1899, they formed nine groups controlled by European capital.

Obviously, the Boers were not pleased. After two years of cattle plague (1896–97), which reduced both White and Black livestock breeders to poverty, the bloody Anglo-Boer War (1899–1902) broke out, and the Zulu launched their last assault, which was crushed by Natal (1905–6). The Anglo-Boer War lasted three years. It consolidated the distinction between the Boers and the British, though neither group was in any way homogeneous. The Boers included, in addition to old-stock settlers who were mostly grain, cattle, and sheep farmers, a growing number of Whites with no land. Linked by language, they began to call themselves Afrikaners. Whites of British ancestry were mainly city-dwellers, and included an aristocracy descended from people who had initially settled on the Cape. They were joined in the ports and mining towns by waves of migrants that included merchants, farmers, and businessmen, as well as a large number of young male workers, who formed the majority in Natal and the interior provinces. The flow made the group labeled "colored" all the more complex, since it included people of mixed blood from all times and circumstances: Khoi, Indonesians, Madagascans, and Africans, who had been brought there as slaves in the past.

The British came out the winners from the political and cultural unrest. Pragmatically, they left their adversaries a great deal of autonomy, which culminated in 1910 with the political independence of the White Union of South Africa. The treaty that brought an end to the Boer War specified that Blacks could not participate in the future parliamentary government.[18]

6

Colonial Intervention

In some parts of Africa, colonization began well before the nineteenth century. Ever since the Age of Exploration, all European maritime nations had been acquiring footholds abroad. Luanda and St. George of the Mine on the Gold Coast were among the earliest to be occupied by Europeans. They both became Portuguese possessions in the sixteenth century, and the latter was known as Elmina by the time it came under British control. By the mid-seventeenth century, the French were in Saint-Louis du Senegal, and the Dutch in Cape Town. By the end of the eighteenth century, the British had solid footing in Cape Town, which was taken from the Dutch East India Company between 1795 and 1803, then from the Batavian Republic in 1806. The British occupied holdings along the coast to Freetown, which became the center for "liberated" slaves in the 1790s.

When the Europeans decided to penetrate into the backcountry, it was, however, a turning point. In 1788, this became the goal of the African Association, a learned society in London that brought together scientists, politicians, and wealthy patrons. It was created for the development of British trade and political prestige inside the continent. This led to another key event in 1795, when the Scottish explorer Mungo Park reached the banks of the Niger River.[1] Until then, Europeans had known of the river by hearsay only, if it was, and this is more than doubtful, the same river referred to in antiquity by the geographer Ptolemy and historian Herodotus. The Niger River and the wealth of Timbuktu city, a myth that had been conveyed by Arabs since the city had been closed to Christians, were two geographical mysteries that intellectuals at the end of the Enlightenment hoped to solve.

In the first decades of the nineteenth century, the Western exploratory push into Africa was virtually monopolized by the British. There were only two exceptions: Bonaparte's adventures in Egypt and two memorable French expeditions: that of Mollien in Senegal in 1819 (the young explorer had survived the sinking of the *Méduse* off the shore of the Cape Verde peninsula), and especially that of René Caillié in Timbuktu in 1828, though the English cast doubt on the authenticity of his success, since they had not yet been able to

Map 6.1 European Penetration on the Eve of the Berlin Conference (1884)

Areas of Penetration :
- French
- British
- Portuguese
- Boer
- German
- Spanish
- King of Belgium

0   1 000 km

visit the city. Overall, the new curiosity had a disinterested appearance until the mid-nineteenth century. It was an expression of the dynamic energy of a nation in the midst of the Industrial Revolution: scientific and ethical motives corresponded to economic innovations, and combined with the actions of philanthropist adversaries of the slave trade.

The Beginnings of Colonial Imperialism in Sub-Saharan Africa

Industrial England's search for new markets paid off: trade between Europe and Africa increased tenfold between 1820 and 1850. The increase was especially strong and rapid in West Africa via both the Atlantic Ocean along the coast, and across the Sahara through the Maghreb. Morocco, Tunisia, and especially Tripoli served as major storehouses for English textiles sent to the interior. Trade was growing constantly in the Sudan, and the area was punctuated with British consular posts, which worried the French who were already concerned about linking Algeria to the areas south of the Sahara.[2] This was a direct corollary of the Industrial Revolution, for such trade was becoming increasingly profitable. Owing to mass production, the cost of imported manufactured goods dropped persistently over the century. Prices were often halved initially, such as between 1820 and 1850, when craft production was being replaced by industrial manufacturing. British cotton fabric dropped from a shilling a yard in 1817 to only three and a half pence in 1850. Salt went from six to three and a half pence over the same period, and by 1825 gunpowder of the quality traded with "natives" had slipped from eight and a half pence per pound to five pence. Western demand for tropical raw materials (such as oils, seeds, and dye wood) increased at the same rate as the textile, lighting, and soap industries. This resulted in a noticeable, though less extreme, rise in their value on the world market. The materials for which there was the greatest demand, such as palm oil, peanuts, and wood, were at their highest price in 1820. The price of copal gum increased one hundredfold, and that of ivory fourfold between the end of the eighteenth century and 1830. After that, prices tended to stabilize or even drop slightly, except for that of peanuts, which increased again by 350 to 450 francs per ton between 1847 and 1865. The double profit margin benefited expatriate companies involved in imports and exports, and encouraged trade in raw materials, which very naturally replaced trade in slaves because they involved more or less the same partners, networks, and commercial techniques.[3] In the other direction, the drop in prices and growing demand for raw materials led to an impressive expansion in goods imported into Africa. Between 1820 and 1850, imports of British cotton fabric went from 350,000 to 16 million meters, spirits from

450,000 to nearly 700,000 liters, salt from 1.5 to 5.5 million liters, and iron from 600 to 3,700 tons. Imports of hardware, barrels, and casks used to ship oils and cowries also increased. French exports of spirits, wines, fabric, gunpowder, and ammunition flourished.

In appearance, the terms of trade favored Africans because they sold their materials at increasingly higher prices and bought manufactured products at ever cheaper rates. This made it easier for them to give up the Atlantic slave trade, which was becoming more and more risky. First disregarded but then hunted down mainly by the British, slave traders no longer had a role to play in the industrial era, unlike in the heyday of mercantilism centered on the "sugar islands."[4]

The rupture became palpable at about the middle of the century. It was signaled by direct government intervention in the scientifically and politically most significant expeditions: those of Heinrich Barth in the central Sudan (1850–55) and David Livingstone in eastern and southern Africa, from 1842 until his death in 1876. Barth was a German scholar, and like Livingstone was recruited by the British Foreign Office. In 1848, Livingstone was bedecked with the curious but revealing titles of "Consul for the East Coast of Africa to the south of the dominions of Zanzibar and for the independent districts in the interior," and "Commander of an expedition to explore Eastern and Central Africa." This revealed, in addition to the hope to achieve progress in geography, the desire to open the whole continent to new economic activities under the patronage of Great Britain.

Initially, political intervention was not clear. However, commercial and religious penetration increased opportunities for clashes, which in the field inevitably translated into the beginnings of political control. The process was inseparable from the dominant economic process of the second half of the century: growth in firearms trade, which not only facilitated colonial penetration, but also radically changed power relations in the interior of the continent, between those who could get weapons and their opponents.[5]

Sooner or later, explorers and traders ran up against local structures and preexisting networks. They then resorted to their mother country's authority, and portrayed themselves as victims of their devotion to the national cause. At the same time, the few military officers in Africa longed to distinguish themselves by some form of brilliant action. Gradually, governments managed to take over strategic points that were necessary for protecting their national interests. Great Britain had the lead and was followed closely by France, while Portugal argued for its historical rights.

The process occurred more or less everywhere. First, it arose in South Africa, where pressure from the Afrikaners and the Anglo-Boer rivalry made the issue of borders, which was at the origin of the 1779–1878 Xhosa wars, a constant problem. In West Africa, the first sign was the Crown's 1807 recognition of the colony of Sierra Leone. On the Gold Coast, British intervention was more complex because direct action was avoided. The Fante chiefs had decided to modernize, and were moving toward a federation. They were overtaken by the British, who created a veritable protectorate in the land, though it was not official at first. The interweaving of their economic interests and cultural action resulted first in the Foreign Jurisdiction Act of 1843, which authorized them to intervene in Fante lands though they were still independent. This was followed by the 1844 bond, which was signed by eight leading chiefs and prohibited slave trading and human sacrifice. However, in 1850, the Gold Coast was incorporated into Sierra Leone, where it remained until it became an independent colony in 1874. Under the influence of a Creole upper class that had long familiarity with Western technology and whose awareness had been raised by traders and missionaries, political contestation appeared at mid-century. In 1852, the Hill's Gathering of Fante chiefs recommended a domestic federation partly inspired by the Western model. There was also a desire to modernize among the Egba of Abeokuta and the Yoruba of Ibadan, which rapidly became the leading urban center of West Africa (present-day Nigeria). However, in 1851, in retaliation against slave trading, the British occupied the port of Lagos, and then turned it into a protectorate ten years later.

In the French world, the turning point was in 1851, when the report was submitted by the *Commission des comptoirs et du commerce des Côtes d'Afrique*, of which many members were strongly in favor of expansion. For example, there was the navy officer Bouët-Willaumez, whose exploration of the coast in 1838 had made it possible to establish a number of trading posts, and Victor Régis from Marseille, who was initially involved in the slave trade but later entered the palm oil business in Abomey.[6] In 1843, the king of Abomey gave Régis a de facto monopoly over the palm oil market in the port of Whydah. Libreville was founded on the coast of Gabon in the same year. It was not by chance that the period was consistent with the "foothold" policy that Minister Guizot presented to the French representatives.[7]

Beginning in the middle of the century, technological innovation greatly facilitated European initiatives. As use of steamships spread, it became cheaper to export raw materials to Europe. This also created catastrophic devaluation of cowries because German merchants took advantage of the situation to flood the market with large quantities of cheaper shells from the beaches of Zanzibar, whereas in the past cowries had come from the Maldive Islands. In East Africa, the silver currency introduced in the eighteenth century, the Austrian thaler, became indispensable. People from Africa and the Levant accepted as authentic only coins that were identical to those they had first known, which were the thalers of 1750, which had the portrait of Empress Maria Theresa of Austria on them. Reproduction of the coins became the rule in the nineteenth century, and they were always dated 1780, the year of her death. The worth of the thaler, which was veritable commodity money, was based on the fact that it was struck only at the request of those who brought bars of silver, of no set weight, to be turned into cash. Austria was still striking such thalers in 1960.[8] Generally, European currency was in demand. New import-export houses saw this as an opportunity to gain a foothold in Africa. For example, Peyrissac from Bordeaux arrived in Saint-Louis in 1862. The price of palm, peanut, and other vegetable oils remained high until the 1880s because demand was strong, even though the opening of the Suez Canal in 1869 meant there was competition from Indian peanuts and Egyptian sesame seeds.

The years from 1850 to 1880 may be called a time of "colonial incuba-tion" because there were advances everywhere. In South Africa, all of Xhosa country including Natal was incorporated into the Cape Colony by 1865. The diamond-producing area of Kimberley was encompassed in 1880. In Angola, the Portuguese reoccupied São Salvador, the former capital of Congo, in 1860. The British established a protectorate on Fante lands, and sacked Kumasi, the capital city of the Asante, in 1874. Lagos was colonized, and John Goldie created the United African Company on the Niger River in 1879.

In 1863, Cotonou in Dahomey was on its way to becoming a French pro-tectorate, which happened in 1879 following two naval blockades in 1851 and 1878, and as the conquest of the Senegalese backcountry began.

In Senegal, after the Napoleonic Wars, reoccupation of the posts on the coast and on the river had led to a distinction between the colony in the proper sense, which was very small, and its "dependencies." Attempts at coloniza-tion were modest in the first half of the century. Initially, to make up for the losses suffered owing to the British abolition of the slave trade, an attempt was made to colonize through farming. Two hundred inexperienced settlers failed in the sands of the Cape Verde peninsula in 1817. The experiment was repeated along the river, in the valley of the Middle Senegal. Richard Toll was among those whose attempt ended in failure.[9] Nonetheless, in 1840–50, the Maurel et Prom company from Bordeaux created a strong market for peanuts, which accelerated penetration into the interior.

Louis Faidherbe, who had served in Guadeloupe and Algeria, was appointed governor in 1854. He pushed for control of the Senegal Valley, which he believed extended into the irrigated lands of the Niger basin. He envisioned the establishment of an empire. Émile Pinet-Laprade founded Dakar in 1857 and directed French expansion toward the south of Cape Verde because he wanted to control access to the interior.

Faidherbe reduced the Moors by blocking their access to the river for three years, and his success against Al Hajj Umar in Medina in 1857 strengthened his ambitions with respect to the interior. He turned the stops along the river ("*escales*") into French posts, conquered the Waalo, and contained the Trarza Moors. In short, he gradually conquered a third of what is now Senegal. Beginning in 1859, he obtained protectorate treaties from Senegambian chiefs without consulting the authorities in Paris. He also moved to Kaolack in Sine-Salum. In 1862, he had to reduce the opponents of the chief of Kayoor, Lat Dior, by establishing the post of Thies. This was the beginning of troubles that were to last twenty years. In 1866, the French tried to gain complete control over the peanut trade by negotiating with Great Britain; they hoped to obtain Gambia in exchange for their three Ivory Coast posts and one in Gabon. The proposal was discussed for a long time but never translated into concrete action.

Two ideas guided Faidherbe: first, given the Algerian experience, it was thought that Islam was a force that could be used, and second, there was the prejudice that the Africans of the interior were more reliable that the "corrupted natives" involved in the slave trade on the coast. Al Hajj Umar's threat to French claims also played a role. As governor from 1854 to 1861, and again from 1863 to 1865, Faidherbe was careful to treat local rulers tactfully and to collaborate with the inhabitants of the community of Saint-Louis. There was a precedent for this model; since 1848, the "old" colonies had been represented by deputies elected to the French National Assembly, though no Black African was elected as representative of Senegal until 1900. (During the Second Empire, Senegal's power to elect a deputy was suspended; it was brought back only in 1880.) Faidherbe organized the publication of the *Annuaire du Sénégal* and an official newspaper, the *Moniteur du Sénégal*. He established a school for the sons of chiefs, promoted Koranic schools for Muslims who were hostile to missionaries, set up a few technical schools, and even opened a museum in Saint-Louis. He was also one of the founders of the Banque du Sénégal. However, learning from previous failures, he gave up trying to colonize through European-style farming and chose a trade economy.

From then on, technological superiority gave European ambitions an advantage. It played as much of a role as international economic competition, which was fierce among the various European nations trying to catch up to the British. This hastened the parceling out of Africa during the phase known as colonial imperialism (or the scramble for Africa). The process corresponded to the expansion of European capitalism that was revealed in a change in mentality: imperialist ideology began carrying themes about racial superiority and the "White man's burden," as expressed in the famous poem written in 1898 by Rudyard Kipling.[10] From then on, the West had a duty to spread the benefits of its culture overseas, and at the beginning of the century

English humanitarians started portraying the famous "three Cs," commerce, Christianity, and civilization, as inseparable.

The economic situation was related to the fact that the depression at the end of the century (1873–95) led European powers to depend on markets protected by colonial control. The point of departure was the international Berlin Conference (1884–85). It was an initiative of Otto von Bismarck, the chancellor of the new German state, and invitations were sent to member countries jointly with France. It brought together the political leaders of the European states (including the Ottoman Empire) for two months to resolve differences concerning the African continent. It helped to control appetites by establishing "rules of the game." Almost the entire text (thirty-three articles) concerned free trade (understood as applying to European nations) on the Niger and Congo rivers. Though the conference proceedings do not mention it at all, through a series of bilateral agreements, King Leopold gained recognition for his sovereignty over the independent "state" of the Congo, where he had sent the American explorer Stanley to travel down the Congo River. Finally, two short sections (34 and 35) dealt with parceling out the African continent, a process that was already well under way. From then on, the powers had to "ensure, in the occupied territories [. . .], the existence of sufficient authority to enforce respect for acquired rights," which concerned first and foremost free trade.[11]

The underlying reason was that European competition had led to many political and diplomatic incidents, which revealed the contradiction between widespread expansionism and the resulting increased competition. The crisis reached a breaking point in various places in Africa: in Egypt, with the English-French Condominium Agreement in 1882;[12] at Obok on the Red Sea, where Jules Ferry established an official French post in 1883 in response to the closure of the British post of Aden to French warships; at Fashoda on the Upper Nile, where a violent incident between Marchand's column from the Congo and the British traveling from Egypt almost caused a war between the French and British in 1898; in the Sudan also in 1898, where the British were putting an end to the Mahdist rebellion and imposed a condominium agreement on Egypt that enabled them to occupy Khartoum; in Tunisia, where the French, following tripartite British-French-Italian financial restrictions imposed on the bey in 1869, gained German support and blocked the Italians' railroad ambitions so that they could create a protectorate in 1883; on the west coast, where there were many conflicts between British and French sailors;[13] and in the Congo, where Savorgnan de Brazza for France and Stanley for the Belgian King Leopold battled between 1876 and 1885, with King Leopold arguing that he needed to maintain control over the area to fight against the slave traders from Zanzibar.[14]

The result was a formidable increase in conquests, which ended fifteen years later, at which point the continent was almost entirely colonized. The only exceptions were in North Africa; in Morocco, which resisted German commercial desires as well as it could, and Tripolitania, a shred of the Ottoman Empire that was used as currency to resolve the French-German diplomatic conflict of 1911 in Italy's favor; in sub-Saharan Africa, Liberia, which was under American economic control; and the ancient Ethiopian Empire, which was the only one to have succeeded in repelling the Italians at the Battle of Adwa (1896), though Italy had bought the coastal province of Assab (Eritrea) in 1869.

Everywhere else the conquests were short, from the German East Africa Company's takeover of Tanganyika and Cecil Rhodes's ventures in southern Africa beginning in 1888, to the English-Boer War of 1899–1902 in South Africa. The Portuguese were moving back into Angola and Mozambique. The German company is a good example of the private companies that European governments tried to encourage and protected with a view to resuscitating seventeenth-century-style charter companies. The goal was to promote private enterprise so that it, instead of the government, would undertake the investment required to "develop" territories. The companies had sovereign rights. For example, they could raise taxes and maintain order. This worked well when the stakes were high, though at the price of huge suffering by Africans, who had no state protection. Examples include Rhodesia's gold in Cecil Rhodes's case, and, at the very end of the century, rubber in Leopold's Congo. When profits were small, the companies did not last long. Among the latest but also the most catastrophic undertakings were the French concession companies inaugurated in equatorial Africa in the 1890s.[15] The Germans, who began earlier, failed faster, particularly the East Africa Company, which was launched in Germany by Carl Peters in 1882, and recognized by Bismarck in February 1885. Peters and his two associates, all of whom were under thirty years old, landed in Zanzibar in late 1884 and began signing treaties with a number of chiefs. However, between 1886 and 1890, they had to forgo the zone reserved by the sultan of Zanzibar and the British. In the meantime, the city of Pangani and Chief Abushiri rebelled. After various misadventures, the company ended up with major money problems. Finally, the German Reichstag took it over in 1889.[16]

In West Africa, the colonies took on their definitive configuration. In Senegal in 1889, after the Gallieni interlude (1880), Colonel Archinard, a narrow-minded and expeditious military man, broke with the alliance policy and began violent campaigns against Ahmadu and Samori. Near the coast, Lat Dior, who had spent the end of his reign navigating between resistance and negotiation, was killed in 1886, which enabled the French, with the help of their railroad (built between 1883 and 1885), to establish a direct link between Dakar and Saint-Louis. The formation of the military territory of Upper Senegal and Niger meant the end for the dream of an entente policy with the Muslim empire in the interior, though the British successfully pursued such a policy in northern Nigeria.

Means of administrative control were experimented with, in the form of parcels of land entrusted to local canton chiefs who were responsible for raising the taxes demanded by the French. This approach determined the colonial organization that was to come. In Algeria, which had been under French rule for nearly half a century, there was at the same time a transition from the military phase of conquest, orchestrated by General Bugeaud, to a method of colonization involving "Arab bureaux" and inaugurated by Napoleon III.

German intervention occurred in Togo and Cameroon between 1884 and 1890, the southern part of the protectorate of Nigeria became a colony in 1891 and the northern part in 1901, the French conquered Dahomey in two campaigns between 1892 and 1894, Samori fell in 1898, and the three French columns from Algiers to the north, Dakar to the west, and Brazzaville to the south met in Chad in 1900.[17] Faced with its competitors' ambitions, and despite its linkage of the Maghreb and sub-Saharan Africa, France could not prevent the British presence in Nigeria (which is a huge country and contained half of the population of West Africa). However, England was unable to realize its Cape-to-Cairo dream, which was interrupted for a generation by the German presence in Tanganyika and the maintenance of the Portuguese positions. The whole thing culminated in South Africa, where the Boer War finally broke out at the turn of the century.

Despite much reticence in European parliaments, the conquest had cost little in terms of money, and even less in terms of men, given the disproportion between the adversaries' logistical and technological means. The uneven chronology of penetration also made it possible to use African forces to create new openings. This explains, for example, the use in French Africa of laptots (Africans in the service of France), who were called *Senegalese*. Laptots were often of Soninke origin since Soninke had a long tradition of migrating to coastal labor markets. They were found in equatorial Africa at the time of Savorgan de Brazza's first explorations (1876–85), during the so-called pacification operations in Dahomey in the 1890s, and during the conquest of Timbuktu in 1893. Once demobilized, laptots returned to their usual commercial duties with new expatriate firms, such as the British John Holt and Hatton and Cookson companies, the German Woermann Company, and the French Conquy firm. In about 1883, there were already 600 of these Senegalese in Cameroon, Gabon, and Congo.[18] (Complete information on this topic can be found in various manuals on the history of colonization.[19])

Resistance was sometimes fierce, and conducted by small nations strongly structured around their king. This was the case of the Zulu Kingdom in Natal, the kingdom of Abomey, which forced the French into a relatively tough colonial war,[20] and the Asante Empire, which followed a Queen Mother into its last uprising at the turn of the twentieth century, after a protectorate had been imposed on it in 1897. However, other similar formations, such as the Ganda Kingdom, submitted to protectorate status (1894) and then annexation (1900) without really putting up a fight. The ground had been prepared for conquest: a result of internal divisions and earlier civil wars that had been secretly encouraged by missionaries and merchants. British penetration was obviously facilitated. There too it began with a trade war that pitted not only European against European, but also Europeans against African traders, since European firms sought to compensate for the fall in prices by cutting costs, in particular by supplanting traditional middlemen so as to deal directly with the people in the interior.

The paradox was that the most highly organized resistance in the last quarter of the century came from the most recent political formations. They had sometimes been built barely a generation before by energetic, well-armed warlords with goals that were both conservative and modernizing. For example, there was Ahmadu, son of Al Hajj Umar, and Samori in the west, both of whom were repressed in 1898. Other examples include the slave-trading potentates in central and eastern Africa, such as Rabīh (killed in 1900), Mirambo of Tanzania (who died in 1884), and Msiri of Katanga.[21]

The end of the century corresponded more or less exactly with the takeover of the whole continent. At the same time, colonial governments were being set up. However, it was not until the 1890s that a major means of funding colonial governments became widespread: the hut or head tax, which was then referred to in French as *capitation*. Thus, the beginnings of direct rule were established, in both the French and British colonies, except in the two extremities of the continent, Algeria and South Africa, where there was colonization through settlement, which remained unusual in Africa.

The Genesis of Colonial Government

No matter who the colonizer was, the beginnings of domination were characterized by the small size of the European staff, except in settlement colonies. In Senegal, the so-called protectorate lands were under a form of indirect rule that was similar to the English system. The administrator of an area had at most one assistant and only a small troop of armed men. For information and execution of orders, he depended on good relations with the local chief. Moreover, too few credits were available to encourage initiatives. The only measure that began to be imposed, and only in the last years of the century, was an annual tax meant to fund the colonial budget. Initially, it took the form of a hut tax, but later became a head tax.

One of the crucial problems of such faltering government was slavery. At the time, most African societies had deeply ingrained traditions of slavery, and the colonizers had a desperate need for labor. The conjunction of interest and lack of means incited the colonizers to be prudent. Suppression of internal slavery proceeded slowly.

In Senegal, the 1848 Emancipation Act applied only much later to the protectorate areas. Faidherbe himself, who was an abolitionist, decreed in 1857 that any fugitive slave who tried to hide in Saint-Louis or Gorée should be thrown out as a vagabond. At the Battle of Rip, French officers went so far as to distribute women to deserving African soldiers. In Dakar, emancipation for indigenous slavery was passed only in 1877, and not until two years later in Rufisque. It was Victor Schoelcher's strong plea in the Senate in 1880 that accelerated things (Schoelcher had obtained French abolition of slavery in 1848). The immediate result was the massive departure of slave-owing Fulani into the interior.

In the nineteenth century, the problem barely arose except in the cases of fugitive slaves and slaves in cities governed directly by colonizers. Neither the French nor the British, not to mention the Portuguese, really intervened in the internal affairs of the countries, and domestic slavery was barely affected. This remained the rule in the interior of Futa Jallon, and the British still permitted female slavery until the early 1920s in Zanzibar. Slave trading within Africa continued as long as the empires held—in other words, until the last years of the century.

In contrast, though they were quite slow, there were changes to political structures. One of the most visible effects was the gradual transformation of the customary chief into an administrative chief, in other words, into a very minor colonial civil servant. Not only was the chief charged with performing tasks that had been unknown until then, such as collecting annual taxes from his subjects and recruiting workers for public works, including the construction of posts and railroads, but his position was, as much as possible, stripped of religious meaning. Thus, in Senegambia, the French tried to reduce the entourage of the traditional *buur* by converting traditional warriors or *tyeddo* into peanut farmers. They fought against ancient legal practices such as punishment (through fines and requisition of goods) of the offender's whole family, and by seeking to eliminate ancient local tolls, in particular those on trade. However, it was not until 1898 that the administrative chieftainship officially began to operate in Sine-Salum, with the introduction of administrative circumscriptions (i.e., cantons), though public works generally began only in the first decades of the twentieth century.

The British Crown also established administrative chieftainships. Theoretically, this was inconsistent with British principles, which were based, unlike the French direct assimilation approach, on indirect rule, as had been experimented with by Lugard in Uganda and in the sultanates in northern Nigeria. However, the result was not much different from the French system, at least in the nineteenth century in areas where there had been no previous centralization, which was generally the case around coastal lagoons, particularly in the Nigerian lowlands, Yorubaland, and Igboland. British government was based on a native court, a military regiment, and the intervention of warrant chiefs, in other words, administrative chiefs who were supposed to be recruited from leading families and meant to compensate for the lack of a customary high authority.

Education was rarely out of missionary hands. Faidherbe's attempt to create an *école des otages* (hostages' school) was abandoned in 1871 owing to a lack of funding. The school reappeared in 1892 in the form of the *École des fils de chefs et des Interprètes* (School for the Sons of Chiefs and Interpreters), which was designed to create a corps of auxiliaries for colonization. The latter was the ancestor of the famous École William Ponty in Senegal, which was the only French college there for many years. One such school, funded by businesses, opened in Foundiougne in 1892, and another in Kaolack in 1893. There were also five schools to train girls as housewives in Senegal in 1895. In order to win over the Muslims, a school where the teaching was in Arabic was opened at Nioro in 1896.

The End of Colonial Conquests

We will not linger over the often brutal episodes of this period, which are relatively well known through historiography, and have already been partially discussed in various chapters of this book.

In southern Africa and along the coasts of tropical Africa, European penetration began before the nineteenth century. However, it accelerated in the second half of the century and flourished in the period known as the scramble for Africa, of which the symbolic beginning was the Berlin Conference in 1884–85.

West Africa

The arrival of the French near Gambia in 1887 spurred on the British. The backcountry of Freetown was acquired as protection against the Temne and Mende in the interior, who were rebelling. Penetration on the Gold Coast followed its course. In particular, the British imperial government gave its

Map 6.2 **European Penetration in 1891**

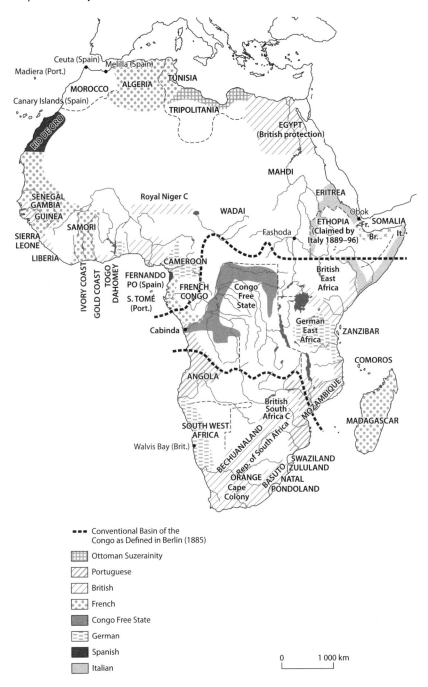

Ceuta (Spain)
Melilla (Spain)
Madiera (Port.)
ALGERIA
TUNISIA
MOROCCO
Canary Islands (Spain)
TRIPOLITANIA
RIO DE ORO
EGYPT
(British protection)
MAHDI
ERITREA
SENEGAL
GAMBIA
GUINEA
Royal Niger C
WADAI
Obok
ETHIOPIA
(Claimed by
Italy 1889–96)
SOMALIA
Fr.
SAMORI
Fashoda
Br.
It.
SIERRA
LEONE
LIBERIA
CAMEROON
British
East
Africa
IVORY COAST
GOLD COAST
TOGO
DAHOMEY
FERNANDO
PO (Spain)
FRENCH
CONGO
Congo
Free
State
S. TOMÉ
(Port.)
German
East
Africa
ZANZIBAR
Cabinda
COMOROS
ANGOLA
British
South
Africa C
MOZAMBIQUE
MADAGASCAR
SOUTH WEST
AFRICA
BECHUANALAND
Walvis Bay (Brit.)
Rep. of South Africa
SWAZILAND
ZULULAND
ORANGE
BASUTO
NATAL
Cape
Colony
PONDOLAND

- - - Conventional Basin of the
Congo as Defined in Berlin (1885)

Ottoman Suzerainity

Portuguese

British

French

Congo Free State

German

Spanish

Italian

0   1 000 km

approval to the conquest of the Niger Delta in 1879. From 1886 to 1898, communities along the banks of the Niger were under the control of the Royal Niger Company, which gradually took over fifty-two cities, from those of the Igbo low country in the south, to Ilorin in Hausaland. In Igboland, which had no centralized political structures, this gave rise to the resistance movement known as the "Ekumeru Wars," after the name of a military and religious Igbo secret society.[22] While the Royal Niger Company succeeded in crushing the movement in 1898, the company charter was revoked by the British government the following year. In 1900, all of the land between Benin City and the river was still in a "very unsatisfactory" state.[23]

Central Africa

The first to colonize the interior of the continent were the Egyptians and Sudanese of the Nile Valley, and the Arabs from Zanzibar. The first Sudanese and Zanzibarite raids, from Khartoum and Zanzibar, in the forests of central Africa were in 1865 and 1869, respectively. Mbunza, the Mangbetu king of Upper Ubangi, died in 1873 in a battle orchestrated by the Sudanese.[24] In about 1880, the Egyptians tried to annex the region to their province of Equatoria, but withdrew when faced by the Mahdists in 1885. However, the respite was brief because the Zanzibar raids from the south soon began. The Arabs allied themselves with the Azande sultans in the upper Ubangi to extend slave trading in the forest. It was not until 1891 that they were in turn defeated by a military column sent by agents of the Congo Free State. A little farther south, on the Lualaba River, Zanzibarite merchants had founded Nyangwe (1869), and then recognized the supremacy of Tippu-Tip in the area. Tippu-Tip accompanied Stanley for a time in 1876 as he traveled down the river, and two years later Stanley signed an agreement that appointed Tippu-Tip as the temporary governor of Kisangani. However, the partners were pursuing conflicting goals: the Belgians wanted to govern through Tippu-Tip and at the same time reduce the slave trade, but Tippu-Tip saw the Belgians as his primary client for ivory. Later, he turned back to the sultan and in 1890, he had to retreat to Zanzibar, where he died in 1905.[25]

The Congo troops were unable to defeat the Zanzibarites until 1892–94, after the creation of a local army, the Congo Free State's *force publique*. It traveled north and eliminated the Sudanese Mahdists in 1901. As soon as the rubber industry began its rocketing growth in 1896, owing to the automobile tire industry, central Africa became the site of bloody exploitation: the so-called rubber wars lasted until 1910, three years after Congo had again been taken over by Belgium.

In French Equatorial Africa, after the first in-principle peaceful and commercial explorations by Savorgnan de Brazza (1876–78, 1882, and 1883–85), a battalion of colonial soldiers was created in 1883. Aside from a series of more or less brutal expeditions that ended with the death of Rabīh in 1900, and exploitation by the major concession companies founded in 1898–99, real occupation did not begin until the turn of the twentieth century.[26] German Cameroon experienced more or less the same series of events: a police force, the *polizeitruppe*, was set up in 1891, and then an army, the *schutztruppe*, was created in 1895. The latter took control of the roads in the Douala backcountry out of the hands of local people. The conquest sped up with the "rubber rush."

On the Atlantic, the coast had been held by the Portuguese of Luanda and Benguela for several centuries. Angola had been an "overseas province" since 1832. The prohibition on slave trading with Brazil was voted in 1836, but enforced only ten years later, and not without resistance. Suppression of slavery over the ensuing twenty years was even more difficult, and the situation was far from clear at the end of the century.

In Mozambique, the slave and ivory trading systems, which were shared by Yao chieftainships, Nguni principalities, and African-Indian and Portuguese warlords, were becoming increasingly predatory. This general configuration was maintained until the Portuguese became caught up in the scramble for Africa. There were many reasons for Portuguese colonization: the financial weight of Indian market capitalism had grown over the century, as had British pressure to eliminate slave trading and promote liberal trade. The conjunction of these two factors, along with missionary ambitions, resulted in an expansion of the search for exportable raw materials into the backcountry. The economic growth of Lisbon also played a role. Above all there was the Boer pressure on Delagoa Bay (recognized as belonging to the Portuguese in the 1869 treaty), since it was a prized outlet for the Limpopo Valley and valuable to the rapidly industrializing mining of the South African Highveld. Starting in 1875, the Portuguese organized a series of exploratory expeditions into the interior, which enabled them to regain control of the countryside. In 1887, six months before Cecil Rhodes's British Africa Company, they launched a Mozambique charter company to engage in mining exploration and logging. Initially, the company (the charter of which was signed in 1891) simply reproduced, in a semifeudal form and in the same area, the military-tribute system that was begun by the Nguni kingdom of Gaza. The Nyasa Company was also launched in 1891 and its charter was signed in 1894. Two of the warlords were reduced through the granting of concessions, while the hitherto impregnable stronghold, Massangano, of a third warlord, Da Cruz, was reduced in 1889.[27] However, banditry remained endemic until the beginning of the twentieth century.

Resistance

Throughout Africa, conquests were particularly brutal. As soon as there was the slightest resistance, villages were burned and villagers were forced to flee into the bush or forest, where they were reduced to hunting and gathering. Yet there were few outright rebellions at the time. Of course, there was the effect of surprise and especially the huge disproportion between the technology available to the colonizers and the local people. Traditional weapons and even slave-trade guns were of little use against colonial armies. However, another explanation comes from what has been shown throughout this book: more often than not, the local peasants had long experience with being crushed by the expansion of new military and political powers that were sometimes colonial but in any case always subjugated those who were conquered. Earlier structures had been ravaged by Al Hajj Umar, Uthman dan Fodio, great merchants such as Samori, and slave-trading despots such as Rabīh, Mirambo, Tippu-Tip, and Msiri. The Nguni conquests that extended all the way to the shores of Lake Nyasa, and, on the Highveld, the Ngwame (Swazi) conquests also swept away existing organization. The new political formations were often the leading adversaries of Westerners, even though what was at stake was generally land that they themselves had conquered little more than a generation before.

Moreover, sleeping sickness, a rise in smallpox, and the expansion of the plague and yellow fever finished off the countryside, which lost, as has been stated earlier, probably 50 percent of its inhabitants in a generation and a half. At the time, strong resistance arose only when nation-states (such as the kingdoms of Abomey, Lesotho, Buganda, the Asante and, at least regionally, Ethiopia) were able to protect their cultural and territorial integrity. Otherwise, "new men" who believed passionately in independence had to take the initiative, as Abushiri did in 1888 in what was to become Tanganyika. Unlike what was to follow in the twentieth century when peasants rebelled against the autocratic power of the Whites, real resistance to conquest was rare and limited to small political formations or lineage-based chieftainships jealous of their autonomy.

Arabs, Swahili, and Nyamwezi: The Pangani Rebellion and Abushiri Revolt

Plantation and caravan slaves made up much of the population of Swahili towns on the coast. In 1888 in the port of Pangani, at the time of the huge cholera outbreak, they were the Swahili aristocracy's workforce. Later they vanquished their masters, and their revolt was more against Zanzibarite authoritarianism than against European intervention. This explains why the Swahili were happy to welcome the Germans.

The time of the rebellion, in mid-August, corresponded with a series of popular festivities that had drawn huge numbers of celebrating people into the city when the seasonal flow of caravans was at its height. Zelewski, the German agent of the East Africa Company, intended to take advantage of the festivities to force the local Omani governor to lower his flag, which he planned to raise over the company's building in the name of the power that he had been given by the sultan of Zanzibar. The crowd witnessed the Arab governor's resistance and his capitulation before the German agent's arrogance. Rebels threatened to set fire to the boutiques of Indian merchants, and the small German troop found itself dangerously surrounded. Zelewski called for help from a gunboat, which landed 100 soldiers, who then desecrated the mosque in the middle of the celebrations. For a time the Shirazi (Swahili) patricians were able to exert some control over the crowd, partly because of the charisma of Bushiri bin Salim, a wealthy planter and caravan entrepreneur who considered himself to be an Arab (even though his mother was probably a black slave). However, respect for the aristocracy was not sufficient to master the crowd during the many public dances used as forms of challenge to the existing power. Bushiri, who was also threatened, left the city in November and turned against the Germans of Bagamoyo. The Shirazi aristocracy and Omani (Arab) elite temporarily abandoned Pangani to the rebels, and Zelewski had to withdraw to Zanzibar.[28] However, the movement finally fizzled out: the Shirazi rebels were abandoned by the poor, who lost interest in the political results, and by the Nyamwezi caravaners, who drew closer to the Germans. It was the beginning of the end of the conquest.

An Unexpected Alliance: The Shona and Ndebele Revolt of 1896

In addition to the rejection that was typical of reactions to settlement colonization at the continent's two extremities (Abd el-Kader's revolt in Algeria and the Xhosa Wars in South Africa), a notable exception to the general picture occurred in 1896–97, when the Shona and Ndebele of southern Africa raised an insurrection against the exactions of Cecil Rhodes's British South Africa Company.

The center of resistance was Matabele country, where in 1885 the chief, Lobengula, was the leading warlord south of the Zambezi. The area was desired by the British of Bechuanaland, the Portuguese of Mozambique, the Boers of Transvaal, and the businessmen of the Cape. Indeed, the appetite of the premier Cape businessman, Cecil Rhodes, had been whetted by the discovery of gold in the Rand, and he intended to mine the deposits that had been found in Shonaland and were suspected in Ndebele country.

Contacted by emissaries from the various parties, in 1888 Lobengula finally ceded the mining concession of a huge area to Cecil Rhodes, who was acting under the cover of his collaborator, Charles Rudd, with the financial guarantee of the De Beers Company. This enabled Cecil Rhodes to negotiate in London and obtain a charter for a company with special rights, the British South Africa Company (1889). A confusing period followed in which Great Britain, Portugal (through the Mozambique Company), and Transvaal challenged, through the intermediary of local chieftainships, the limits of their areas of influence. It all resulted in the Anglo-Portuguese Treaty of June 1891, which gave the British South Africa Company most of King Mutasa's Manica, returned the Gaza Kingdom to the Portuguese, and opened the port of Beira to international trade.

This enabled Cecil Rhodes to organize, from the Cape, the eastward movement in Shonaland of a pioneering column of 200 settlers and 200 company policemen, accompanied by the same number of Ngwato workers, responsible for leading the caravan's 117 wagons. The 400 miles were covered in less than three months. Along the way, they created Fort Victoria and Salisbury (the future Harare, capital of present-day Zimbabwe). In 1892, Rhodes, who was then prime minister of the Cape colony, began extending the railroads from Kimberley in the south and Beira in the east.

As soon as they arrived, the settlers began clearing their farms; each of them received 3,000 acres and the local people had no say. Lobengula thought he would be able to block the British South Africa Company by giving a huge concession on his land to a German financier, but the latter quickly sold it to Cecil Rhodes. Since there was no question of the Ndebele putting an end to the system of raids on which most of their economy was based, conflict was unavoidable. In 1893, the British South Africa Company took the initiative to seize the capital city, Bulawayo. The battles were bloody, but the forces were too uneven: Lobengula died tragically, probably by suicide. The Ndebele were forced to submit. Bulawayo was soon home to 2,000 Europeans. The company modeled the country after Shonaland, and in 1895 the whole area was renamed Rhodesia.

However, the Ndebele had great difficulty enduring work in the mines and control by a police force made up mainly of Shona, whom they despised. A series of calamities struck the country: a drought in 1895, clouds of locusts the following year, and then a cattle plague epidemic. This created favorable conditions for the emergence of a messianic religious movement modeled after a well-established sect that was rooted in ancient Rowzi beliefs. People followed priests who were mediums and had trances in which they called on people to reject Whites. The revolt was also encouraged by the pitiful failure of the expedition (October 1895) that the governor of Shonaland, Jameson, had meanwhile undertaken against the Boers of Johannesburg to try to impose the authority of the *Uitlanders*, namely, the British strangers dominating mining interests. The revolt broke out in Ndebele country in March 1896. In two weeks, 143 settlers were killed. Later that year, to the Europeans' surprise the insurrection began spreading into Shonaland, where 119 Whites were killed in a week in June. Despite the antagonism between the two peoples, they shared the same religious fervor and same prophets, who had appeared first among the Ndebele but whose teachings were consistent with the deepest Shona beliefs. They agreed on the need to work together to reject the hated settlers for their exactions and disdain. The guerrilla war lasted several months. The Ndebele were the first to negotiate with Rhodes, and in August their chiefs were given some advantages provided they entered the new system. However, the Shona groups, which were still holding out hope in December 1896 of restoring the former Rowzi power, were reduced one after the next and finally completely disarmed, despite the late resistance (1900–1904) of a Rowzi chief, Mapondera, in the Mazoe district.[29] In 1897, the southern railroad reached Bulawayo, and the following year the Beira line was completed. Bulawayo became the industrial capital of Rhodesia, and a kind of Ndebele bourgeoisie began to emerge. The opening of the country changed the living conditions, while the defeat destroyed the religious influence of ancient beliefs and put an end to unitary aspirations. A change in direction had occurred: the demoralized peoples had no choice but to accept the new lifestyle, while the company, which had lost esteem in the eyes of the British government owing to its irresponsible actions, gradually had to transfer its power to the Crown.

Overall, once their adversaries had been reduced, Westerners had the fleeting illusion of an easy conquest, in comparison with what they later called "pacification." Pacification was in fact a long guerrilla war of resistance that in some cases ended only with independence almost a century later. For many people, the new occupiers did not initially seem much more dangerous than the previous ones. It was only over time, which passed quickly, that the newly colonized people (they first had to discover what that meant) understood the extent of their misunderstanding and subjection. At that point constant rebellions erupted against colonizers everywhere. This lasted for at least half a century. The process could already be seen in the nineteenth century in Algeria and South Africa, where the conquest had begun fifty years earlier than elsewhere. In the rest of Africa, the rebellions belong mainly to the history of the twentieth century.

Algeria, from Revolt to Colonization

Conquest and Colonization by Settlement

In 1830, Algeria was a well-defined country with no vacant land, where contemporaries were surprised to find no "fanaticism." However, the Algerian government had been weakened by increasingly focused intrusions by European interests. In addition, King Charles X needed to turn French attention away from domestic affairs: the "insult" to France in 1827, which was inflicted when the dey hit the French consul Pierre Deval with a fan, was only a pretext. The origin of the conflict dated back to the time of the *Directoire* (the executive body in France from 1795 to 1799) and a financial dispute concerning the dey's demand for reimbursement for a delivery of grain on which interest was running. Pushed by traders in Marseille, the French nationalist extremists who were in power took advantage of the situation to demand exorbitant advantages, which amounted to denying the dey's sovereignty. Action was swift: the French expeditionary force left Toulon on May 16, 1830, landed 35,000 men from 500 ships on June 14, and the dey capitulated on July 5. At the time, this concerned only the handing over of Algiers, its forts, and the Kasbah, and did not refer to transfer of sovereignty, which would have required the agreement of the Porte.[30]

Officially, the July Monarchy, which came to power at this juncture, did not change Algeria's status. Supposedly, it implicitly acknowledged Turkish power and, for a time, sought a means of controlling the country without annexing it directly. It theoretically recognized various Muslim authorities: first the Turkish aristocracy, and then, when he asserted his power, Amir Abd el-Kader. What was really happening was quite different. In 1830, nearly 52 million gold francs were confiscated from the Algerian treasury. In August, a special jurisdiction was created in the form of *cours prévôtales*, in other words, military courts under the responsibility of a provost. In September the property of expelled Turkish Algerians and of Islamic religious organizations (*habbous* property) was redefined as belonging to the Crown. In 1832, the Algiers Mosque was turned into a cathedral. French troops occupied Mers el-Kebir and the forts of Oran and Mostaganem. In other words, the military penetration was designed from the beginning to clear the way for the first settlers. The *Commission d'Afrique,* created in 1833 following a parliamentary commission on the future of the conquest, wrote a report describing the operation's horrors,[31] but regardless of this it was decided that colonization would be expanded.

At first, the merchant class was not necessarily hostile to the French, but the harshness of the French intervention was such that even those who initially thought they could hold onto their privileges or develop their businesses finally had to resist. In Algiers, trade dropped by two-thirds in two years. Muslims saw Christian appropriation of religious property as a sacrilege. The French army found almost no support, except from a few Turks hoping to be appointed governors of provinces, and from some Jewish intermediaries, who sold them everything they could at top prices. The situation quickly became untenable. Organized revolt began in 1832, and lasted over fifteen years.

Map 6.3 Colonized Africa on the Eve of World War I

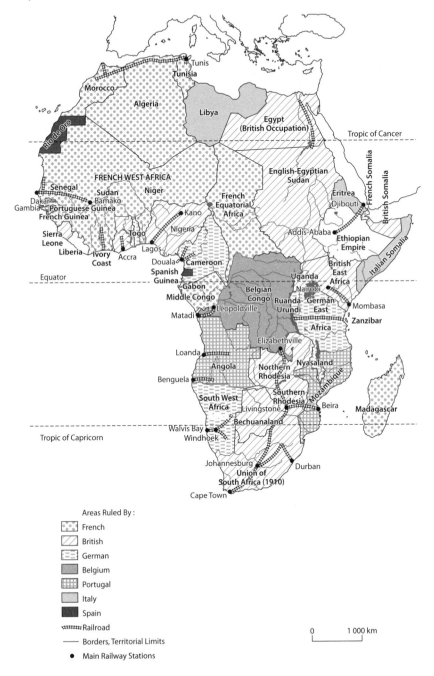

Areas Ruled By :

- French
- British
- German
- Belgium
- Portugal
- Italy
- Spain
- Railroad
- Borders, Territorial Limits
- Main Railway Stations

0   1 000 km

Map 6.4   **Algeria in the Nineteenth Century**

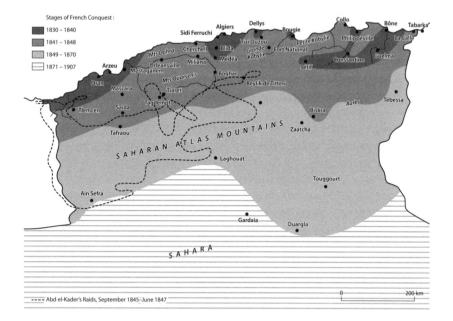

National Resistance? From Abd el-Kader to Kabylia

Faced with the political vacuum created by the dey's fall, resistance groups, which were initially dispersed, merged into a single group that acknowledged only one authority: Abd el-Kader. His father, Mahi Eddin, *moqqadem* of the Qadiriyya brotherhood for all of Algeria, had him recognized by a congress of tribes as amir or "Commander of the Believers" in 1832, when he was barely twenty-four years old. Abd el-Kader managed to unify all of the peoples who were hostile to the French, no matter what their language or social status. He immediately began the holy war proclaimed by his father and, the same year, came up against the French before Oran.[32] However, conscious of the imbalance in power, he used a tactic that was comparable to that of Samori two decades later in West Africa: to gain time, he signed the Desmichels Treaty in 1834. Through it, he agreed to pay homage to the king of the French, who invested him as bey of Oran, through which all external indigenous trade was to pass. However, in exchange, he was promised that Arabs would be able to purchase weapons and that the port of Arzew would be reserved for their trade. The French army still wanted to seize Mascara, the seat of his government, and an ambush by Abd el-Kader's troops at the Macta Pass in 1835 resulted in 500 French casualties. The event drew much attention. Bertrand Clauzel was appointed to lead the army, and recommenced open war.

Despite having taken Mascara, Tlemcen, and Medea, the French failed to gain Constantine in 1836. At that point General Thomas Robert Bugeaud was sent in to negotiate a new treaty with the amir to the west, so as to continue the offensive toward the east. However, the Tafna Treaty (May 1837) was so favorable to the amir that the French broke it and began attacking him again. At the end of 1840, Bugeaud was named governor general of Algeria, and decided to harass the adversary through constant operations that brought the French troops to over 100,000 men in 1847 (one soldier for every thirty inhabitants). In the meantime, the *smala*, as the amir's moving city was called, which was both the capital and seat of his government, was taken in 1843. Nonetheless, Abd el-Kader did not give up, but took refuge in Morocco, from where he controlled his guerillas until he finally surrendered on December 23, 1847.

The war was one of unbelievable violence and cruelty. On the French side, the order was to create terror through a scorched-earth policy and the massacre of local people. Notably, this resulted in the infamous smothering by smoke of whole groups of civilians whom had taken refuge in caves. Soldiers were rewarded for the number of indigenous people's ears they brought back: a pair was still worth ten francs during the occupation of Kabylia in 1857. "We surpassed in barbarism the barbarians whom we were coming to civilize," declared a member of the Commission of Inquiry in 1933.[33] On the Algerian side, the resistance promoted a feeling of communal belonging that had been unknown at the time of the Turks.

Abd el-Kader was an intellectual and marabout from the city. During his pilgrimage to Mecca and stay in Egypt, he was influenced by the "modernist" projects of Mehemet Ali. His goal became to "establish an Arab nationality in Algeria."[34] Breaking with the feudal tradition of favoring personal ties, he appointed as heads of the eight administrative conscriptions (*khalifalik*), including, in the parts of the Sahara close to the areas of Algiers and Orleansville, chiefs who were recognized by the people they were to govern. The chiefs were transformed into salaried public servants. He also unified taxes in accordance with Muslim law, and did not hesitate to innovate when required. For example, in 1839, when he instituted a special war tax, he set an example by selling some of his family jewelry and depositing the money in the public treasury. Centralized financial organization went hand in hand with the need to maintain a standing army of approximately 5,000 soldiers, most of whom were infantrymen (and not the traditional horsemen). When necessary, contingents were raised to increase the forces to 50,000.

Naturally, he encouraged the production of equipment, livestock, and food for his troops, and took the initiative in a number of economic areas, including agriculture, salt and mineral extraction, foreign trade, and export of manufactured goods. He did not hesitate to recruit French and Spanish contract and salaried workers. Colonial penetration pushed him farther and farther toward the south, where he established a series of towns on the edges of the Tell Atlas mountain range and high plains to make up for the loss of Medea, Mascara, and Tlemcen.

For this, he depended on the traditional chiefs and, in the cities, non-Muslim intermediaries, such as Jews and Christians. The best known are Léon Roche, his private secretary, and a Jewish financier, Ben Duran. They both helped him to get around the prohibition on Muslims interacting with pagans. His vision of government was more territorial than tribal, as it was based on the integrity of Algerian land, and he showed himself to be open to economic changes. In an 1839 letter to King Louis-Philippe, in which he offered Christians free trade and the right to travel unhindered in his states, he conducted himself like a head of state comparable to Mehemet Ali as opposed to a jihad leader such as the marabout chiefs of sub-Saharan Africa.[35] Education was an important part of his program, and he went to great lengths to set up a library at Tagemt (Taqdamt).

Abd el-Kader hoped to delay direct confrontation with France as long as possible to give himself time to build the necessary economic and political systems. Indeed, there was considerable disparity between his forces and those of the French, owing to the resistance of the great feudal lords, the reluctance of patriarchal communities to abandon isolation, and the Kabylian cities' distrust of his plans for centralization. However, the French incursions left him no choice, and he resumed open war in 1839. From then on, the loss of the ports and the absorption of resources into the military effort broke all development efforts (much as had happened in Samori's case). The state was so poor that it is surprising that resistance lasted eight more years. The French forced him out of his cities between 1840 and 1842, and Bugeaud compelled the countryside to submit in 1843–44. The 1845 Franco-Moroccan Treaty caused Abd el-Kader to lose the support of the sharif. His only remaining defense was desperate guerrilla measures, which continued long after his surrender: the Algerian budget contained a revenue line labeled "booty from the enemy" until 1872.

The French conquest of Kabylia began in 1851, and that of Djurdjura in 1857. Eastern Constantine rebelled in 1852, and again the insurrection spread from the Tell Mountains in Oran to Constantine in 1864–65. Once more, over 90,000 French soldiers were involved. Finally, 1866–70 was a calm period, though that was unfortunately the result of a famine.

At the same time the Sahara was being conquered. In the Sahara, the caravan city of Ouargla and the Mzab confederation had long been paying tribute to Algiers (which 4,000 Mzabites had helped to defend in 1830). In the first half of the century, the British had tried to control the Saharan routes by establishing consular representatives in the main oases.[36] Tuaregs from the north had resisted at the same time as Abd el-Kader, so Bugeaud naturally included the Saharan trade routes in his conquest. The result was that Algerian caravans were hindered in their travels, and faced competition from those supplied by the English in Egypt and Morocco, by the Italians in Tunis until 1881 and then through Tripoli, and by the Germans in Morocco after 1884.

The last major revolt in Kabylia broke out in 1871, under the leadership of El-Mokrani. It resulted from the fact that the country was left in the hands of settlers when the empire fell. While French power had been military since then, a civilian regime was approved by vote in spring 1870, and came into effect in October–December (the Crémieux Decrees). This gave settlers control over the land. Their excesses provoked the tribes, and discontented people began to assemble in marketplaces, which led to acts of rebellion. In February 1871, the Kabyles attacked the fort of El-Milia. Muhammad El-Hadj el-Moqrani, a leader who was wealthy, powerful, and until then protected by Napoleon III, took control. Indeed, in 1868 he had helped to deal with the food crisis by borrowing, in accordance with Governor General MacMahon's suggestions, money and grain from banks and brokers. The financial crisis and civilian government forced him to pay his debts rapidly. In March 1871, he took over the leadership of a movement that, supported by the Rahmanyia brotherhood and despite his death two months later, spread for a year from Constantine, through Kabylia, and to the gates of Algiers.

Repression was brutal once again. Summary executions and village burnings escalated. Above all, confiscation of leaders' property and, especially, of collective property of rebelling tribes placed the most fertile lands in the hands of settlers in record time.

Concurrently, the civilian government confirmed the difference in status between Algerians and settlers by creating a system whereby indigenous people could be summarily judged and sentenced by administrators without any other form of trial or appeal. This was established by decree in August–September 1874 in "full exercise" communes and was extended to "mixed" communes in 1881. In the early twentieth century, such absolute power was established in sub-Saharan Africa as well. In 1924 a decree made its application general, just when it was about to be abandoned in Algeria (in 1927). The Indigenous Code contained a list of crimes concerning a sufficiently broad range of hostile actions (including disrespectful behavior and statements offensive to a representative or agent of authority) to give public servants free rein with respect to repression, and sentences ranged from fifteen francs to five days in prison. Note that the Indigenous Code concerned only Arabs since, by adopting a divide-and-rule strategy, the civilian government gave French nationality to Algeria's 37,000 Jews in 1870. (A generation later, in 1897–98, the year of the election of Edouard Drumond, the anti-Semitic representative of Algiers, this resulted in a brutal explosion of anti-Semitism by settlers in urban areas.) The 1889 act gave French nationality to (European) foreigners born in Algeria, thereby completing the civil segregation of Algerians, who were definitively transformed into "natives."

Therefore, the conditions were set to connect Algeria with France (1881–90), or rather Algerian settlers with the metropolis, which favored the settlers but eroded the governor's authority with respect to government ministers in Paris. From that day on, Algeria became part of France . . . for French settlers.

Algerian Misery

The result was deep destruction of the Algerian economy and society. Poverty became widespread.

It was not until the very end of the century that the Muslim population in the cities returned to the level of 1830 (in Algiers it was not until 1906, and in Constantine 1911). The loss of livestock due to repression alone was estimated at 18 million sheep and goats, 3.5 million cattle, and 1 million camels, three to five times the herds counted a century later. As terrorized peasants abandoned the land, grain fields shrank, which made confiscation easier. However, until the 1880s, colonization progressed slowly, so the second half of the century corresponded to a general impoverishment of the Algerian people. Their society also regressed as the great "feudal" chiefs of major tents and owners of vast hereditary fiefs regained power under the colonial administration. The French government sought to use them as a base, in particular by making them responsible for collecting taxes. France thus simply continued and accentuated the Turkish regime, at least in the areas where indigenous people took refuge. In contrast, on the wide coastal plains such as Mitidja and Sétif, the lands of the former Turkish aristocracy were transferred to European concession holders in 1847. After the 1871 uprisings, special punitive taxes were collected by the chiefs. They were eight times higher than in a normal year, and that was just the beginning. The land ownership law of 1873 eliminated traditional undivided property, and recognized only duly registered private property. (This law was adopted in French West Africa in 1904.) It enabled settlers to acquire large expanses of land at low prices in the departments of Oran and Algiers. In only ten years,

Figure 6.1   **Algeria: Convictions Under the Indigenous Code, 1882–1919**

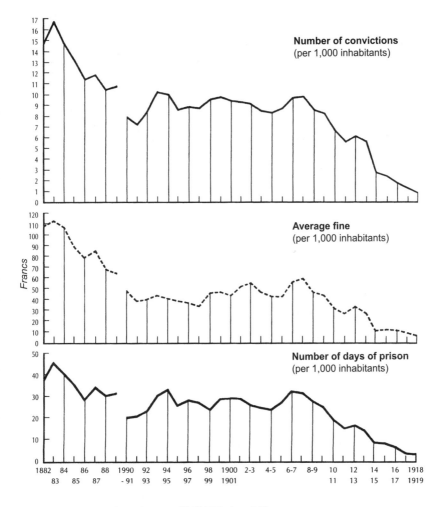

Source: Adapted from Ageron, 1968, Vol. 1, p. 240.

the settlers were able to acquire as much as they had received from 1830 to 1870 (1 million acres). The plundering was topped off by the confiscation of Constantine forests that had survived the 1881 fires, and the 1885 law that ruined the lives of people living in the forests. The legislation pertaining to forests had such harsh effects that it was finally softened in 1903.

Figure 6.2   **Muslim Harvests of Wheat and Barley, 1872–92**

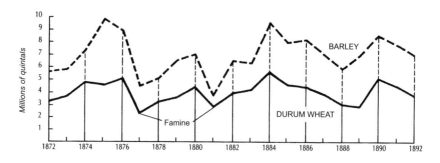

Source: Ageron, 1968, Vol. 1, p. 381.

In retrospect, it is easier to understand why Napoleon III tried for a time to make things a little more fair by promoting an "Arab kingdom policy."[37] However, the episode was too short (1863–69) and the policy's foundations were too unstable (since they consisted in keeping the people under military control) to protect Algerians from a civilian regime run by settlers. The fall of Napoleon's empire, which occurred at the same time as a terrible famine in Algeria resulting from four years of crisis and the Paris Commune drama that sent boatloads of banished communards to Algeria, finally placed full power back in civilian hands. Major colonization was achieved at the expense of the "natives" from 1880 to 1900. Between 1881 and 1898, Algerians had to give up more than 1.2 million more acres of land to Europeans. However, thanks to the end of the armed rebellions and the introduction of the first public health measures promoted by the presence of settlers, the population began to grow. The Muslim population was estimated at 3 million in 1830, but had fallen to 2.7 million by 1860. It then climbed to 3.5 million by 1891, reaching 4 million by 1901 (and nearly 5 million by 1921).

Yet, poverty was such that tax revenues actually dropped after 1880, despite an increase in the number of Arab taxpayers and the beginnings of welfare measures, such as the creation of the *Sociétés indigènes de Prévoyance* (SIP Act of 1893), an experiment that was also transferred to sub-Saharan Africa a generation later. At the dawn of the twentieth century, the Algerian peasantry had lost all hope.

7

The Century's Innovations

Slavery: A Mode of Production That Had Become Dominant

Africa's trade in slaves with the rest of the world declined in the nineteenth century, at least with respect to the West, yet at the same time owning slaves became a sign of social status in Africa south of the Sahara. Ironically, one was the corollary of the other. As outside markets closed, beginning with the Atlantic market, it was advantageous to dump unsold slave "stock" on the domestic market. Domestic economies had to reorient toward production of raw materials that were in demand in Africa (cotton, sugar cane, grain, etc.) and in industrialized countries (vegetable oils, dye wood, gum, etc.), or adopt a predatory economy that was maintained and accentuated by the sale of European-made guns. Both production and predation created great demand for slaves, who were used as laborers, servants, and soldiers.

The century began with the Europeans' official prohibition of slave trading. This had been advocated since the end of the eighteenth century, when a small group of English humanitarians settled in the peninsula of Sierra Leone. Though it took some time before the measures were adopted by all countries and states, this was the beginning of a deep social change in Africa. At the same time, on the Indian Ocean, Zanzibar's domination was becoming more dependent on slave-based production, and this was a social weight until the start of the twentieth century. In that area especially, the slave trade's growth was largely a perverse corollary of the European Industrial Revolution, which began flooding the Arab world with African rifles that had been manufactured or retooled in industrial centers such as Liège in Belgium.

The Risks of the Slave Trade

In the Mediterranean, privateering against Christians, which formerly had been very profitable for the Ottomans, was declining.[1] Peace treaties were signed between Algeria and Spain in 1792, and also by Algeria, Tunisia, and France in 1800–1801. From then on, privateering expeditions became rare. In

1801, privateers brought only four captured ships back to Algiers, only one in 1803, and none in 1811. The year 1812 brought more than 2 million gold francs in plunder, but 1813 produced only one-tenth of that amount.[2] Abolition of the slave trade came into effect in Algeria and Tunisia in the 1840s, and was made official in Tripolitania in 1856. Former Christian captives were emancipated. The only remaining sources of slaves became the south, the Sahel, and its surroundings, where constant jihads largely supplied caravans in the nineteenth century.

The Decline of the Atlantic Slave Trade

In Africa south of the Sahara, the effects of European abolition were felt first on the Senegalese coast, with the English occupation of Goree and Saint-Louis, where the slave trade was outlawed in 1802. When the French came back in 1817, the Vienna Treaty forced them to also abolish the "shameful business." The cannon that the British had installed at the new naval base of Bathurst at the mouth of the Gambia River was there to persuade them not to engage in illegal trade. Yet the slave trade continued in the safety of markets in the backcountry.

In the nineteenth century, Africa exported about 5.4 million slaves to the Americas. Yet, this was 2 million fewer than in the eighteenth century. The reduction was due to the gradual disappearance, in the second half of the eighteenth century, of the illegal Atlantic slave trade. However, in the interior, this was probably the time of the slave trade's greatest expansion. Men, women, and children were raided every day and deported. At least half of them were taken off the continent. The problem was that, despite British insistence on compelling local leaders to give up the slave trade, there was no meeting of interests between the Atlantic market and Africans. The relatively brutal disappearance of the Atlantic market did not put an end to the well-rooted networks of the interior slave trade, which the Europeans studiously ignored.

By the end of the eighteenth century, the switch to an industrial capitalist economy combined with humanitarian movements led a number of Western states to prohibit the Atlantic slave trade: first, in 1802, Denmark (which no longer had much vested in the coast of Africa), then Great Britain in 1807, and the United States in 1808. The other powers had to comply with the Vienna Treaty of 1815, even though Portugal still enjoyed tolerance south of the equator, which enabled it to prolong the slave trade between its colonies of Angola and Mozambique, and the Brazilian market.

The Atlantic slave trade peaked in the eighteenth century with approximately 6 million departures. The rate remained the same in the first half of the nineteenth century, with the export of almost all of the approximately 3.3

Map 7.1   **Internal and International Slave Trading in the Nineteenth Century**

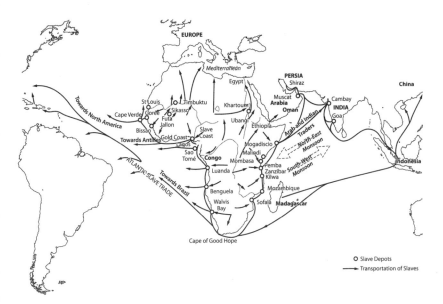

million slaves traded on the Atlantic coast in that century. Later, Great Britain (in 1836) and France (in 1848) proclaimed the emancipation of slaves in their colonies, and then the English occupied the major slave-trading port of Lagos in 1851. This left room only for illegal Portuguese slave trading south of the equator. It is probable that men accounted for at least half of those exported, in comparison with children and women, who accounted for only about a quarter each. Indeed, the percentage of women, who were a promise of fertility, was lower than in the preceding period owing to the predictable end of slavery in America.

Until the 1840s, the most active centers were, first, the Bight of Benin, and second, the center-west coast, from Gabon to Angola. In the early 1830s in the Bight of Benin, the British anti-slave-trading squadron freed nearly 20,000 slaves, who were mainly Yoruba and Igbo, originally from the Bay of Biafra. The other major supplier, namely the coast between Gabon and Angola, shipped as many slaves as in the last decades of the eighteenth century, which was around half the total. Between 1800 and 1835, 275,000 slaves were loaded onto boats from the Loango coast alone by Portuguese, Spanish, and American traders.

Owing to the clandestine nature of the trade, it is difficult to obtain precise figures for the years after 1830. According to one source, only 4,600 slaves were exported from the equatorial coast between 1841 and 1843, but another source reports that 30,000 slaves were exported from the Congo estuary alone in 1859–60.[3] We know that slaves were being exported from the mouth of the river until the end of the 1870s and from the Ogooué Delta until 1900. Illegal traders hid their operations in barracks dissimulated behind fences in deserted spots on the Gabonese coast and in the coves of the estuary of the Lower Congo.[4] Brokers, such as the Bobangi of the Congo River, the Chokwe of the forest, and, on the other side of the continent, Yao suppliers of the coast of Mozambique, traveled farther and farther into the interior to acquire slaves. They even made it to Lunda and Luba lands, and the Upper Zambezi. The unfortunates raided from the heart of the continent were taken to the east coast in Swahili or Yao caravans, or to the west in Kuba or Chokwe caravans. One female slave called Bwanika was abducted and resold several times, and ended up traveling across the continent.

The end of the Western slave trade was not immediate, but was prolonged by various subterfuges, such as the creation of "apprentices" in South Africa (1836) and Nigeria (1903), and the traffic in indentured labor, which was common in both the west and east. French, Portuguese, and Dutch traders and businessmen engaged in such illicit activities everywhere. The French recruited workers at low prices on the Senegalese and Gabonese coasts. They were theoretically under contract and were used on French plantations on islands in the Indian Ocean. The Dutch did likewise between 1836 and 1842 along the Gold Coast to supply their possessions in the East Indies. Eventually, the Portuguese made the islands of São Tomé and Principe, at the bottom of the Bight of Benin, lairs for illegal operations to supply their cocoa and coffee plantations with slave labor. Nonetheless, the scale was no longer the same. Slaves were counted only in tens of thousands of individuals, though some scandals still broke out in the first decades of the twentieth century, especially on the Portuguese coast and also in Liberia.

In the second half of the twentieth century, demand for slaves on the Atlantic market plunged, though the supply remained strong. Prices collapsed. In the Bight of Benin, a young male cost twenty-two pounds in 1790, but fifteen at the beginning of the nineteenth century and only eleven in the 1860s.[5] The change was similar in the Sokoto Sultanate in the interior owing to inflation (of Maria Theresa thalers), and around Zanzibar in 1840–80.[6] As slaves became cheaper, they became easier for Africans to buy, especially since at the end of the century there were almost no purchasers elsewhere.

Maintenance of the Mediterranean Slave Trade

Toward the north and in the Mediterranean world, the wars of conquest and formidable population movements caused by a century of one jihad after the next, from those of Uthman dan Fodio to those of Samori, increased the slave trade in the area to at least 1.2 million people. The slave trade toward the Red Sea and Indian Ocean, which peaked between 1830 and 1880, had been flourishing since the eighteenth century.

Two million slaves were probably exported to the Mediterranean, Middle East, and Arabia. Half of them came from the basin of the Upper Nile and Ethiopian mountains, and about a quarter had crossed the central and western Sahara. Jihads provided a regular, and considerable, supply: Bornu and the Sokoto caliphate exported between 3,000 and 6,000 each year, and perhaps 1,000 to 2,000 left from Timbuktu annually. In Egypt, Mehemet Ali always needed more soldiers for his conquests in Syria and Arabia. The Ethiopian Empire mainly "consumed" women and children, mostly raided by Galla Christians on the borders of Muslim lands. The Egyptian slave trade was at its height at about the middle of the century, when between 10,000 and 12,000 slaves probably passed through the country. In 1867, about 30,000 slaves per year left the Sudan. Though the Ottoman sultan and Emperor Theodoros of Ethiopia were forced by the British to prohibit the slave trade in the middle of the century, it did not decline until Egypt was taken over by the English and the Sudan was isolated owing to the Mahdist rebellion in the 1880s.

The Upswing in the Zanzibar Slave Trade

The slave trade toward the Indian Ocean peaked at the end of the century. Indians had been coming to the Mozambique coasts for ivory since the eighteenth century, at the same time that the Portuguese were withdrawing. In order to acquire Indian cotton cloth, Yao hunters expanded their activities into the interior, all the way to the Luangwa Valley (in present-day Zambia). Zanzibar became the crossroads of the slave trade to Iran, Arabia, and India, in the latter case until 1843, when the British abolished slavery.

Thus, the Island of Zanzibar, which was held by the Arabs of Oman, became the principal center of the international slave trade in the mid-nineteenth century. Here again, ironically, the slave trade intensified on the Indian Ocean at the very time when it was decreasing on the Atlantic Ocean. This was not a coincidence. It was a perverse effect of the Western Industrial Revolution: the arms trade, which was increasingly controlled in Europe, became very difficult in the West. Yet there was a steady flow of "African" weapons. The first stocks to be dumped were those that had been retired at the end of the Napoleonic wars, and the flow continued throughout the century. It began increasing in 1869, with the opening of the Suez Canal, which enabled Western industrialists to use Arabs to hide their trade.[7]

At the end of the century, the slave trade was replaced by the "indentured trade" in the areas around Natal. Coolies received a three-year contract that covered the cost of their travel to the workplace, and they had to do a fourth year if they wanted to settle as free men. If they signed up for another five years on a sugar plantation, they had the choice between free passage home or a plot of Crown land in the area. For a few short years, India and China became rich reservoirs of indentured laborers. They worked on sugarcane and tea plantations, as masons and carpenters, and in various other occupations, including of course as coolies. Between 1897 and 1902, a specialized agency in Karachi recruited workers for the British East African Territories railroad. Of the 32,000 laborers imported, 6,400 remained in East Africa. Between 1899 and 1912, a new Bombay recruiting agency covered all of southern Africa. Indian immigration, which became partly voluntary in the twentieth century, then reached 120,000 in Natal, 20,000 on the Cape, and 10,000 in Transvaal. (It was and remained prohibited in Orange.)

On the Indian Ocean, about half of the slave supply was exported. Slaves were raided and brought along the three main routes from the interior: from Masai country to the north, Nyamwezi country in the center, and, increasingly toward the end of the century, out of the southeast of Africa through the port of Kilwa. Kilwa alone received three-quarters of the slaves destined for Zanzibar, 95 percent of them in 1866. The effects of the abolition imposed by the British in 1873 were felt only very slowly.

General Insecurity

Slave raids were a major cause of death. In 1872, German explorer Gustav Nachtigal reported how in battles in Bagirmi, most adversaries were executed and only women and children were spared for the slave trade. Rabīh became famous for the massacres he ordered. Skulls and skeletons, numbering in the hundreds, of those who were not useful to the raiders were left at the sites of defeated cities. David Livingstone described the appalling mortality in slave caravans along the route from Lake Malawi to the coast. The raids were the leading cause of insecurity in the nineteenth century. The Swahili, Nyamwezi, Yao, South African Griqua, and Portuguese, and their slaves, who were Achikunda, Chokwe, Swahili, and Fulani, along with other soldiers and all the intermediary trading peoples, formed innumerable armed bands that penetrated ever farther into the interior as the slave trade became less predictable on the coasts and on the world market.

Europeans justified their fight against the slave trade by arguing that their African partners would be led to replace the "shameful" trade with "legitimate"

Table 7.1

Slave Exports in the Nineteenth Century

Area	Number of Slaves (millions)	Percent
Atlantic	3.3	61.4
Trans-Saharan	1.2	22.1
Red Sea and Indian Ocean	0.9	16.5
TOTAL	5.4	100.0

Source: Lovejoy, 1983, p. 137.

commerce in raw materials sought by the Western world, such as ivory, skins, ostrich feathers, gold, gum arabic, wax, dye wood, vegetable oils, and cloves. This did not happen. In both West and East Africa, from the king of Dahomey to the sultan of Zanzibar, African leaders quickly seized new opportunities and enthusiastically opened their realms to new markets, but they did not give up their old sources of revenue. On the contrary, growth in exports was gained through slaves, who were used in armies, as porters in caravans, as laborers on plantations, and as workers in the textile industry. Ironically, a condition and corollary of the reduction in the Atlantic slave trade was an increase in slave-based production in Africa.

In the first part of the century, the slave trade was a dual source of income: it was profitable on both the international and domestic levels. In this sense, in Africa, the nineteenth century was the major period of slavery.[8]

Slavery's Greatest Century

Techniques for capturing slaves had been refined, and their use within Africa was at its peak. However, the Western dynamic of abolitionism forced slavery to be restructured at the domestic level.

On the eve of colonization, nearly one in two Africans was a slave, a proportion that was probably much higher than it had been at the beginning of the century. This was because there were two sources of slaves. Some were born into slavery, for example, in areas where slave status was passed down from generation to generation with no possibility of assimilation, such as in the hierarchical societies of the Sudan-Sahel region. However, female slaves generally had very few children. This is supported by studies in the Sahel and among the Bamum,[9] as well as in the Congolese forest.[10] This means that a very large number of individuals who had been born free were later captured and turned into slaves.

Organized Banditry

Slaves could be captured in two ways. Among the coastal peoples who were organized for the Atlantic market, prisoners were taken from annual wars along the borders during the dry season to supply both the internal and external markets. This was the method in the Abomey Kingdom, the Asante Empire, and the slave-trading chiefdoms of equatorial Africa: European traders paid customs duties that authorized them to deal with the local political leader or his representative on the coast. Except in special cases, only outsiders and undesirables were sold.

In the nineteenth century, religious wars that were organized as jihads or more prosaically launched by warlords (Tippu-Tip, Rabīh, etc.) provided the hundreds of thousands, or even millions of slaves that were stocked in the various military and slave-trading emirates and kingdoms of Africa (nobody will ever know the precise number of them). However, the slave trade did not necessarily require a big investment. The operation was so profitable that anyone could give it a try, as long as one's little troop had the necessary weapons and courage. Thus stories of ambushes and kidnappings proliferated. They poisoned the everyday lives of many African peasant men, women, and children throughout the century, even more than in the preceding centuries, since in the nineteenth century slavery became the dominant mode of production. Narratives describe raids as surprise attacks. Villagers were watched by their assailants and, as soon as their guard was down, the warriors descended upon the fields or at the well where the women and children were gathered. Ambushes were also organized to attack isolated defenseless groups,[11] generally of young girls who were highly prized for their reproductive potential and labor.

As a rule, except in special circumstances (such as in case of a major crime), slaves always came from elsewhere. Thus, among the raiding peoples of the Sahara, such as the Tuaregs and Berbers, *Djanawen* meant "Black slave." This is the source of the English term "Guinean." For the Soninke, "Bambara" was long synonymous with "slave," and the same applied, reciprocally, for the Yoruba and Hausa.

On the Atlantic Coast

Despite British efforts, in the first part of the nineteenth century nearly 1.3 million slaves were still shipped from West Africa to the Americas. Three-quarters of them came from the bights of Benin and Biafra, but some were also from the Senegambian coast and the Volta rivers. Yet the only place where there were serious problems adapting was the Gold Coast, where the slave trade had until then been the primary activity of the coastal Fante. The crisis was felt among the Asante in the backcountry, who needed to sell their slaves to the south in order to acquire weapons, of which they were major consumers.

With the exceptions of the Fante coast and Freetown, the slave trade and slavery remained highly interwoven. The increasing difficulties with the Atlantic slave trade nonetheless led local leaders to promote exports of "legitimate" products, such as gum, palm oil, and peanuts, to increase the production of other goods, such as gold, and to develop other markets, as did the Asante, who sold kola nuts to the Sudan area, where massive conversions to Islam generated increasing consumption. In addition to the traditional internal use of slaves (as soldiers, advisors to chiefs, spouses, etc.), the change in mode of production and increased need for porters caused the demand for slaves to skyrocket. Slaves' growing numbers in turn required a reorganization of the economy and society.

In Senegambia and Futa Jallon, slave labor had already existed, but it became the predominant means of production. The colonizers did not eliminate the system at the end of the century; in fact, they employed it. During the conquest, French settlers made major use of captured slaves (especially women), who were distributed as prizes to Senegalese riflemen (*tirailleurs*).[12] In the last years of the century, the French even created *villages de liberté* where they kept "unfree captives" who had supposedly been freed from slavery but were used for labor.[13] In Nigeria, it was not until 1903 that the Master and Servant Proclamation officially turned slaves into "apprentices." However, as in South Africa nearly half a century earlier, apprentices did not have the right to leave their masters without authorization, and vagabonds could be imprisoned. Prohibition of domestic slavery came into effect only in 1916.[14] Internal slavery was not prohibited until 1928, even where antislavery pressure was the strongest, such as in Sierra Leone where the British unloaded thousands of "liberated" people over the century. The reason was that, owing to the impetus of the European presence, trade of salt, rice, and imported manufactured goods for vegetable oils and food from the backcountry was increasing. Toward the end of the century, it was estimated that half of the Mende were slaves.[15]

Areas that produced cash crops were the first to adopt a slavery-based mode of production, especially when the political structure and land ownership system lent themselves to large-scale organization. This was the case in Abomey and the city-states on the Nigerian coast that produced palm oil. It was also the case of the Asante Empire, which produced gold and kola nuts. The adjustment was not always easy. First, between 1807 and 1820, the drop in the price of slaves was brutal and briefly affected the lifestyles of the merchant elites on the coast. However, prices later went back up (owing to the risks involved in the illegal slave trade), and the slave trade increased in the Bay of Biafra. The areas also adapted easily to trading in "legitimate" substitute products (especially vegetable oils). King Ghezo of Dahomey skillfully took advantage of the situation by also playing on the interests of Régis, a French slave trader from Marseilles who was equally eager to deal in slaves and oil. After a short economic crisis, the Asante Kingdom found new resources thanks to the polyvalence of its position, midway between the coast and the Sokoto caliphate, which was a major consumer of kola nuts.[16]

Naturally, on the Gold Coast, forts such as Cape Coast, Elmina, and Accra entered a difficult economic period at the beginning of the century, and the Fante living on the coast were the first victims. However, the change did not affect everyone. Until the 1840s, in the southeast of the Gold Coast, the Danish continued as they had in the past, running slave plantations and producing more goods for local consumption than for export.[17] Indeed, both the Fante and the Asante had plenty of substitute resources, in particular gold, and also kola nuts in the Asante's case. Since they were accustomed to obtaining guns and gunpowder in exchange for slaves captured in their annual campaigns, the Asante of the interior had to adopt a new system. At first, many slaves were kept in the capital city, Kumasi, and the surrounding area, but then, since no one knew what to do with them, many were executed. As in the Abomey Kingdom, human sacrifices were celebrated ritually each year and to a much greater extent at royal funerals, and they increased during this period. However, the king and provincial chiefs soon employed slaves in nut harvesting and gold mining. It is estimated that in the 1870s, slaves accounted for half of the Asante population. The kings of Abomey and Porto Novo did likewise, and encouraged tapping of the natural palm tree forests that created the wealth of their regimes. The Afro-Brazilians on the coast, who were former slaves who had come back from Brazil and had become slave traders themselves, imitated them, as did the leading local dignitaries. In about 1860, Quenum, the son of a leading merchant of Abomey, owned thousands of slaves, as did the "Brazilian," Domingo Martinez. On vast jointly held plantations, groups of slaves produced palm nuts and worked as porters carrying the products of "legitimate" trade. In the capital cities (Porto Novo, Kumasi, and Abomey, where a third of the 30,000 inhabitants were slaves in 1851) and major kola centers, such as Salaga, Bonduku, and Bouna, slaves also performed all the work related to water, wood, and food supply for merchants and caravans. They brought the supplies from large plantations on the outskirts of urban areas. Each plantation had several hundred slaves, who were often grouped into villages of farmers or craftsmen.

Even in stateless societies, where power did not exceed that of a village chief, such as in the lagoon region of Ivory Coast,[18] slavery was widespread and becoming more so. There were hardly any free peasants who did not have at least one or two slaves, not including young people[19] who were frequently left as pledges for a debt or to pay for an offence.[20] It was in the most raided areas that slavery was least common, such as in Mosi and Gurunsi country (present-day Burkina-Faso), which were used mainly as other people's reservoirs of slaves.

In Igboland, where palm oil was produced on the village scale, a class of notables established its wealth on control of inherited land, extensive commercial dealings, and the number of its clients and slaves. The firms that did business on the river employed hundreds of slaves organized in a paramilitary fashion. There is a record of one master who, already in 1841, owned 200 slaves employed in oil and yam production.[21] The process only grew: merchant cities such as Onitsha and ports in the Niger River Delta, such as Bonny and Opobo, ended up as homes of thousands of slaves used as porters and pirogue paddlers. Around 1880, a Calabar merchant possessed 3,000 slaves, most of whom worked on his three plantations.

The same phenomenon appeared in the great Yoruba city-states (Ibadan, Ijebu, Abeokuta, Lagos) owing to incessant wars in the nineteenth century. The majority of the population was no longer free, and warlords and major traders, including a few women, accumulated hundreds or even thousands of slaves whom they used as laborers and soldiers. This was true regardless of whether the notable was animist, Muslim, or Christian. In 1859, Chief Kurumi of Ijaye owned 300 women and an army of 1,000 slaves, not counting those who worked on his plantations. The insecurity of the time required that the largely slave armies had to be fed by other hordes of slaves. Other than Lagos before English occupation (1851), the most slaves were found in Ibadan. Every year several thousand slaves passed through the city. Most were Muslim Hausa: those in the worst condition were sold, women were placed in harems, the most agile were used as soldiers, others were employed as artisans and porters, but most were sent to the fields, where they labored under the orders of team leaders who were themselves slaves. There they were at risk of being raided again whenever there was the slightest trouble. From 1860 to 1870, 100 families owned over 50,000 slaves in the area. Efunsetan Aniwura had 2,000 on her lands, and others in the city.[22] However, unlike in Asante country, where the matrilineal system ensured that the children of a slave woman remained slaves, the more patrilineal system in Dahomey and Yoruba country made assimilation of the second generation easier since the children of a slave wife received their father's status.

Slave Status and Rebellions

Slave status varied. In the forest, slavery often became the lot of the majority, and all forms could coexist, from cohorts of soldiers and porters with whom the chief could do as he pleased to domestic slaves who were relatively integrated into the family. In the 1880s, Bishop Crowther (who was himself Yoruba) described domestic slavery as a relatively protected status, hoping to thereby allay criticism of it. However, large numbers of slaves made such domestic paternalism impossible. Some slaves had a degree of autonomy, and, in exchange for compensation, were authorized by their masters to engage in business and even buy slaves for themselves. Some took advantage of this leniency and became powerful. For example, Jaja, who had been kidnapped as a child in Igboland, became the head of a major trading house in the port of Bonny and eventually created his own city-state at Opobo before the British deported him to the West Indies in 1887.[23]

However, most slaves remained very vulnerable. They were considered to be barely human, which meant they did not undergo initiation rites. For girls, initiation was limited to the sexual use made of them by their masters when they reached puberty or before. Since there were also no burial rites, they could not establish a lineage in a society where ancestor worship was very important. At the sign of the slightest economic downswing, they could be sold. They were also the first to be sacrificed to the gods at chiefs' funerals, at which it was the custom to have several hundred or even a few thousand slaves accompany their master to his new home. These customs have been described in the cases of the Dahomey and Asante kingdoms, but were also common in Igboland and at the enthroning of chiefs in central Africa (such as for Bacongo and Bakuba). In central Africa slaves were also the first to be sacrificed in case of witchcraft, crime, or debt. Several slaves were sacrificed at the burial of the Orunga chief in 1847;[24] his people were major slave traders and accounted for half the population in Gabon. These rituals aimed at exerting social control over a growing slave population. For example, in 1881, the 400 titleholders in Asaba (Igboland) each sacrificed a slave when they were invested with their title. There was also an Igbo custom such that, in case of need, a family could offer the god a slave (*osu*), who then became the property of the priest in charge of the god's altar. *Osus* as a group were both despised and feared.

In some societies where wealth was based on the slave trade, however, very little slave labor was used. For example, among the Bakuba in the Congo, only 10 percent of the population were slaves. They were located mainly around the capital city and used essentially for human sacrifices at royal funerals.[25] In that society, almost all of the fieldwork was done by women, and the difference between the conditions in which free women and slaves lived was very small. Thus the Bakuba saw little point in using mainly male slaves for this work, and they put them instead on the Atlantic market.

Social constraints were so strong that rebellions were infrequent, except perhaps on the Atlantic coast in the most open maritime areas. This point has not really been studied. At the end of the seventeenth century, Nasir al-Din, the leader of the "marabout war," launched the Toubenan movement against the slave-trading chiefs of Senegambia. *Toubenan* means refusal in Wolof, specifically refusal of alcohol.[26] The movement was a call to convert to Islam and reject the drink that was inseparable from the slave trade. The rebel proclaimed that "God does not allow kings to pillage, kill or turn their people into captives [. . .] people are not made for kings; kings are made for people."[27] Lloyds of London's books show the fairly high rate (17 percent) of claims filed concerning slave ships both at sea and on the African coast owing to insurrections, revolts, and pillage. In the nineteenth century in the Niger River Delta, more and more slaves were used in palm oil production and trade. Their awareness was probably raised through contact with Sierra Leonians, the British, and perhaps missionaries, and they rebelled. At Old Calabar, which encompassed four cities, rebellion against human sacrifices began in the 1840s. Slaves made a blood pact and formed an association to oppose the rigidity of the Egbo brotherhood, which was a secret society of merchants linking notables in various cities. The forest of Qua River became a major center for fugitive slaves. Through a series of riots between 1850 and 1870, the associates managed to put an end to the human sacrifices.[28] Martin Klein[29] has also identified two revolts in Senegambia, one in Gambia in 1894, and another near Bakel in Soninke country the following year. At that late date, slaves were becoming aware that the colonial authorities could free them. Other refuge areas became centers for banditry that may have been related to groups of fugitive slaves, but this has been studied very little.

Moreover, rebelling did not make much sense in a place where there were hardly any ways out and the slave was far from his or her place of birth and home. Only a few particularly ill-treated women found refuge in the first missionary centers and some administrative outposts. However, this was unusual since, while the fight against the international slave trade was effective, colonization did not initially put an end to internal slavery. Governors preferred to turn a blind eye, and use "traditional" chiefs as intermediaries. They failed to open a real labor market. Missionaries, from Livingstone to Father Lavigerie, "bought" their first converts; in West Africa the French invented "freedom villages" peopled by slaves whose freedom had been bought but who were placed in a position of dependency that was almost as dire.[30] The tolerance facilitated by British indirect rule was made official by recognition of a transition phase that lasted quite some time in northern Nigeria, on the Swahili coast, and even in Sierra Leone. The phase lasted until the 1920s in Futa Jallon under the French.

Jihad Slavery

Slavery developed on an even greater scale in the Sahel and Sudan, from the Atlantic to the Red Sea. Probably over 1.6 million slaves crossed the Sahara in the nineteenth century, and the jihads also created millions of slaves who were not displaced but enrolled in armies and put to work on farms. The Tuaregs had long been a slaving society on the edges of the desert. In the west, where they harvested gum and salt (especially around Tichit), as well as in the center, where they farmed dates and grain in oases and looked after herds, all heavy labor (well construction, water and wood carrying, loading of caravans, etc.) was reserved for slaves. Tuareg society was very hierarchical. Aristocrats (*imajeren*) accounted for no more than 10 percent of the population, and were virtually absolute masters. Below them were different levels of dependents, the poorest of whom were slaves. However, slaves did have great freedom of movement (for example, they could travel from one spring to the next when they were herding animals), which was necessary for the ecosystem. In the north of the savanna, such as around Hausa cities, there were colonies of former slaves (*irewelen*), who maintained links with their former masters. Many of them had been expelled during droughts, for slaves were the first to be abandoned in times of crisis.

In West Africa, slavery expanded from three main centers. First, there were the Futas and Senegambia, where the Atlantic slave trade had long encouraged intensive use of slaves, and where old wars between traditional warriors (*tyeddo*) and reform Muslims (such as Ma-Ba and the damel of Cayor) had resurged under the influence of major jihads. A British report from 1894 states that along the Gambia River there was only one free man for every two slaves.

Second, there was the heart of the Omarian state, built on the former kingdoms of Segu and Masina. Around 1894 in the Segu area there were some 70,000 slaves, probably over 50 percent of the population. The Fulani had many slaves, as did the Soninke. As in Wolof country, there were several slave ranks, some of which were close to serfdom. Thus, it was common for slaves to be attached to their master's land, and to have to farm it at least five or six mornings a week. This amounted to paying rent in the form of labor. The rest of the time was spent in subsistence farming for themselves on land allocated by the master. A similar arrangement entailed payment of rent in kind, for example, 150 measures (*mudd*) of sorghum (about 700 tons of the grain), per year. It was not uncommon for a Soninke to own more than one hundred slaves.

We might wonder why so few slaves tried to return to their birth countries. Slavery was indeed hard and poor treatment was common. Masters nonetheless gave some autonomy to slaves, and many, since they felt they could not have a better life, stayed in the area to which they had been brought. This permitted them to renegotiate their work relationships. Since what was important to the masters was to dominate people rather than land, a slave might not be able to change status, but could obtain land to farm or join a network of migrant labor. In the eighteenth century, the Soninke migrant worker movement toward the Gambia and Senegal rivers was begun by slaves, who were rented to French and British settlers for two- to three-year work terms in ports and even on boats. This form of emigration, which often led to emancipation, became a confirmed trend in the nineteenth century. This is why, inside Soninke country, most slaves were women. A French report from 1894 reveals that in the Nioro area, men accounted for barely 25 percent of slaves, but women and children made up 50 and 25 percent, respectively.[31] Female slaves were sent out into the fields like men. In other cases, they spun cotton while men wove it. The ratio was eight hours of spinning to one hour of weaving.[32]

The Soninke, who were probably the first Jola in history, were great merchants. Their migrations date back to the Middle Ages, and the slave trade seems like a primitive form of labor migration. Whenever the transportation costs for selling a product were too high, the most economical means was to export workers to the area where production was profitable. Thus, in 1850, the first *navetanes*, or seasonal peanut farm workers in Senegal, were slaves before becoming voluntary migrants after the abolition of slavery. The same process occurred among the Soninke, who were major producers of laptot slaves (pirogue paddlers) for Saint-Louis before they themselves emigrated.

The third region in which slavery expanded after 1860 was an area where slavery had been less intense until that time: the upper basin of the Niger River, bounded to the south by Futa Jallon and to the north by Masina. This was the area controlled by Samori, who took tens of thousands of new slaves, sold many to the north, and enrolled even more in his army. To the south, he swallowed up a few ancient Jola kingdoms, such as Kankan, a well-located commercial center not far from the Bure gold deposits to the north and kola-producing areas to the south. According to explorer René Caillié, there was already slavery there in the 1820s, but on a much smaller scale. For example, a head of family was considered well-off if he had a dozen slaves. Toward the end of the nineteenth century, the number of slaves surpassed that of free people in the area. The situation was the same in the last kingdoms to resist Samori, namely those of Sikaso and Kong, where two-thirds of the inhabitants were reduced to slavery. According to French government censuses in 1894 and especially 1902 to 1904, 30 to 50 percent of the total population lived in slavery, and in some areas the rate was as high as to 80 percent.[33]

Slaves were so numerous that some of them, though only a very small minority, eventually gained important status. Some were given military responsibilities, and others had political positions of trust, which nonetheless confirmed their status since such positions could not be held by free men. Others became true business associates with their masters. For example, in the 1880s at Abeche, capital city of the Wadai Kingdom, there was a merchant of Hausa origin named Hasan Babalay. He dealt in slaves, ivory, livestock, ostrich feathers, cloth, and kola nuts, in short, in everything that was profitable in the area. He had twenty trusted collaborators, all of whom were slaves, and one of them even led a caravan across the Sahara. Hasan Babalay also had approximately thirty wives and concubines who were responsible for taking care of visitors. The system was so well established that even when one of his clerk-slaves ran off with money, he continued working with the others in the same way.[34]

The situation was similar in the Sokoto Sultanate. The more active and populous the city, such as the great market towns of Kano and Zaria, the more slaves it used. According to H. Barth, in the 1850s, slaves accounted for at least half of the urban population in such centers. They were used as laborers by Fulani lords and by Hausa merchants and artisans. The aristocracy employed huge numbers of slaves as domestic servants, messengers, cooks, and so on. Merchants used them as agents, caravaners, and porters.

However, in the Sahel, in cities such as Kano, Bouna,[35] and Bundu,[36] the textile industry employed the most slaves. At Kano around 1880, there were 50,000 dyers and 15,000 indigo dye baths, which employed thousands of slaves. Women spun cotton while men wove. Even though cotton production was more or less a cottage industry, slaves of both sexes were used everywhere in the countryside on the plantations required to supply towns, of which many had hundreds, thousands, and in some cases tens of thousands of inhabitants. From one end of the Sudan to the other, plantations were structured in more or less the same way, though different market crops were grown, including sorghum, millet, pepper, cotton, indigo, and tobacco. Slaves were often organized into villages. They worked for their master five or six days a week, from sunup until the 2:00 P.M. prayers. They could spend the rest of their time securing their own subsistence.[37] They were often placed in teams led by a foreman, who was himself a slave. While it was not impossible for them to purchase their freedom (in cowries or Maria Theresa thalers), it made little sense in a world where servitude was so widespread.

The plantation system spread with the jihads, especially under the government of Muhammad Bello, who, more than his father or his uncle Abdullah, was interested in establishing the empire's stability on economic bases. This explains the large land holdings and huge numbers of former prisoners of war settled around the confluence of the Niger and Benue rivers in the provinces of Ilorin and Nupe. Nupe began exporting vegetable oils, shea butter, and peanuts to the "legitimate" Atlantic market, which once again profited from the domestic slavery system. The Yoruba came to Ilorin to procure slaves from the north. The country was opened by slaves along the Benue to the Yola Emirate, which had been very sparsely populated until then, and then to the north up to the lands under the control of Rabīh, who had enslaved most of the people of Bornu.

In the 1850s in the north of the central Sudan, slavery expanded. In the Nilotic Sudan at the beginning of the century, slaves were at first concentrated in Wadai, Darfur, and the Funj sultanate of Sennar. The arrival of the Turkish-Egyptian army of Mehemet Ali and the conquest of Sennar in 1820 accelerated the slave trade. Approximately 15,000 slaves from Bagirmi were brought to Abeche, the capital of Wadai. Between 1820 and 1840, the flow of slaves saturated the domestic market in Egypt. Many slaves were enrolled by the warlords of the Upper Nile, who were raiding the plantations of others but at the same time also striving to develop their own slave plantations. One of the most famous land-owing merchants was Zubair Pasha, Rabīh's former master. After 1880, the Mahdist state that served as an intermediary for the Egyptians in the area had just as many slaves, and perhaps even more on the domestic level, since under its domination exports of slaves to Egypt were virtually paralyzed.

Slavery among the Warlords

From there the system spread southward into the sultanates of the Upper Ubangi and Upper Congo, which were always ready to raid the animist peoples in the surrounding areas. One of the leading centers was the Dar-Kuti Sultanate in the north of present-day Central African Republic, which had been occupied by Arabs since the 1820s and was surrounded by southern animist lands peopled by the Sara and Banda. The nineteenth-century history of these peoples, who were scattered in a myriad of small groups, was one of a long flight before Muslim raids, which pushed them all the way to the banks of the Ubangi in the Congo Basin. Especially after 1880, Rabīh and then other marauders from Khartoum protected Muhammad al-Sanusi (not to be confused with the sheikh of the Sanusiyya), and the region became one of the major centers of the slave trade, particularly around the capital city of Ndele, until the French conquest in 1911.[38] Indeed, Rabīh was not the only slave raider but simply the leading Khartoumian adventurer who got rich through the slave trade at the end of the century. Three sultans of relatively recent origin, Bangasu, Rafai, and Zemio, had capital cities along the Upper Ubangi, and even gained the approval of European powers.[39] Zemio was protected by the Belgians at the end of the century. In 1926, André Gide met the son of Rafai, who, like Rabīh, had served under Zubair Pasha, and described him as "eager to imitate Whites [. . .]; he wears proper clothes. He lives in the European style and puts on a fine welcome for guests."[40] The French tolerated him until 1940.

To the east there were the areas raided by Zanzibar and subject to the warlords thriving in East and central Africa in the last third of the century, such as Tippu-Tip, whose real name was Hamed b. Muhammad al-Murjelei, and who was born into a family of merchants around 1840. He was one of the symbols of the ties between the areas.[41] Slave-based production methods also became dominant in Ethiopia, especially in Galla cities in the Abyssinian mountains owing to constant wars among rival groups. However, slavery was just as common in the central province of Shoa, where, around 1840, every free family unit, whether that of a farmer or leader, had a number of slaves of both sexes that was proportional to its social status.

In the Sahel, men accounted for about 30 percent of slaves while women accounted for 40 percent or more (and sometimes there were two women for every man), and children for the remaining percentage, which was nonetheless high. Child slaves were generally acquired through abduction or were sold to repay debts because the fertility rate of female slaves was very low.[42] Children born to slaves could be assimilated easily if their father was free and recognized them, but, unlike in forest societies, most Sahelian societies involved castes that protected themselves by forbidding marriage between the free and nonfree. (This was the case among the Soninke, for example.) Thus, slave status was passed from mother to daughter and followed the line, from generation to generation. (Serere society is an example of it.)

Central Africa

On the coasts of Africa and in the coastal backcountry, whether on the Atlantic, the Cape, or the Indian Ocean, both the internal and the international slave trades were always widespread, though the volumes traded varied. The plantation system was first used by foreign colonial masters, such as the Portuguese in Luanda and the Zambezi Valley, the French and Creoles in Saint-Louis, the Danish at Accra (Christiansburg), the Boer descendants of Dutch settlers in South Africa, and the Omani, East Indians, Swahili, Dutch, and Portuguese in East Africa. Forms of slavery similar in principle to that prevailing at the same period in the cotton-growing south of the United States could be found alongside indigenous forms of slavery in Akan, Yoruba, Igbo, Chokwe, Bubangi, Tio (Bateke), Nyamwezi, and Yao countries. For example, the Teke village of Mswata on the Congo had only eight or nine free men, but was home to Chief Ngobila's eighty-six wives and about 125 slaves. The leading merchant princes of Ntamo on the Pool each had at least twenty wives and several hundred slaves. Like the Bobangi and most of the peoples in the Congo Basin and along the Zambezi, these were societies in which slavery was deeply rooted and where a large number of the women who produced basic foodstuffs and ensured the continuation of lineages were slaves. It was the same in Buganda.[43]

As in the Sahel, but for different reasons, female slaves were in demand. In lineage-based societies that are not very hierarchical, a female slave's only hope for social promotion was through marriage with a free man, even though her purchase could not be compared with the matrimonial compensation paid to a free woman's family. In kinship systems based on lineage, the abundance of women and children was prevalent. Therefore it was useful for men to buy at least some of their wives, especially in areas where matrilineal systems were dominant. A man's children by slave wives were integrated into the paternal family in the second generation, and thus belonged entirely and incontestably to him, thereby increasing his status. This practice spread, especially since the rate of reproduction remained extremely low among peoples such as the Alladian of the Lagoon, the Abron, the Ani of southwestern Ivory Coast,[44] and the Chokwe of the forest.[45]

The Economics of Slave Plantations

What is striking is that plantation slavery acquired the same features more or less everywhere, whether the plantation owner was White or Black, Catholic, Muslim, or animist. In every case, the plantation economy was related to exports and industry, but slaves were also used for a wide range of functions in the army, administration, trade, and as concubines and domestic servants.

British intervention prohibited the use of slaves on plantations in West Africa, except for domestic labor. Thus, slaves were found only in places where African power remained strong, such as on the palm plantations of the king of Dahomey and in the backcountry of the city-states in the Niger Delta. However, in the nineteenth century the plantation economy was at its most widespread south of the equator and on the east coast.

From the time when the Atlantic slave trade became impossible, even for the Portuguese, money was invested in sugar cane, then in coffee, and eventually, in the 1880s, in cocoa plantations. From the 1850s forward, the primary centers were the islands of São Tomé and Principe at the bottom of the Bight of Benin where, in principle, slavery in the strictest sense was replaced by "indentured labor," though an international scandal broke out at the turn of the twentieth century concerning that clandestine form of slavery. There were similar attempts in the Angolan backcountry along the Kwanza River behind Luanda (in the Kasenje district). The first plantation was attempted there in the early 1830s by a Brazilian immigrant. In the 1870s, White planters took over the business, and produced coffee, food, and palmnuts. In 1890, there were still 3,800 slaves on twenty-eight coffee plantations. More to the south, behind Moçamedes, sugar cane plantations appeared around 1840. Later, from about 1860 to 1870, cotton benefited from the American crisis, and employed 2,000 to 4,000 slaves. The fishermen who set up businesses on the coast in the 1890s also bought slaves: men worked as sailors while women dried and salted fish.[46]

The slave plantation economy truly boomed on the coast of the Indian Ocean. Zanzibar and Pemba islands became major producers of grain (rice, millet, and sorghum) and, beginning in the 1820s, cloves. Zanzibar Island's slave population grew from 12,000 in 1819 to over 100,000 in the 1830s. The sultan had about 4,000 slaves on his plantations, while the leading dignitaries had to make do with 1,000 to 2,000 each. Still, in 1895, a major planter, Abdalla bin Salim, owned six plantations and 3,000 slaves. His wife managed seven more modest plantations that were farmed by 1,600 slaves. On Pemba Island, many planters had 500 slaves each. In about 1860, the East Indians of Zanzibar had a total of 8,000 slaves, of whom two-thirds were on plantations.[47] The East Indian Jairam Sewji owned 460 slaves, but most had much fewer. The death rate was very high and entailed that 15 to 20 percent of Zanzibar's slaves (9,000–12,000 people) had to be replaced each year. Most of them came from around Lake Malawi, and the rest from the backcountry across from Zanzibar.

On the coast, for about sixty miles to the south up to Mozambique, grain, coconut, and copra plantations developed between 1830 and 1860. The slave economy peaked between 1875 and 1884. On the Kenyan coast to the north, from Mombasa to Lamu, there were nearly 50,000 slaves, accounting for 44 percent of the population. There were almost 10,000 in 1897 on the coast facing the Lamu and Pate archipelago. Eventually, sugar cane was developed on a grand scale behind Malindi after 1860. In the area, six owners had plantations totaling more than 6,000 acres, and the thirteen leading planters, who each farmed more than 3,000 acres, controlled more than half the arable land. The slave population of Malindi included more than 5,000 people, which was about the same number as in Mombasa in 1897.[48]

Slaves lived in villages of between 300 and 400 individuals. On the largest plantations, they worked in teams of fifteen to twenty under the management of a fellow slave. They were fed by the master and also had the right to farm a plot for themselves in their free time. The Arabs expanded the system into the interior, and slave plantations could be found all the way to Tabora and

Ujiji in the 1870s. For example, Tippu-Tip invested in about twenty plantations in Zanzibar and the Upper Congo on the Lualaba River to the west of Lake Tanganyika, where slaves labored to the sound of a gong that marked the beginning of the work day.

More to the south, behind the Island of Mozambique, the Portuguese developed the same system. On the island itself, more than half of the total population (5,800) were slaves in 1875, the official year of emancipation. Some 9,000 others were registered at Quelimane at the time, and the reason only 276 were recorded to the south, at Lourenço-Marques, was that most of them were not declared.

At the time, the Portuguese population was a mixture of a few Europeans, Creoles from Goa, and mixed-blood people who had been involved in the slave trade. Most of them were slave owners, and each had about 100. Inland, the *prazos*, which were ancient fiefs given to the first merchant-explorers, were occupied by Achikunda armies of slave soldiers (some 20,000 in 1806) who terrorized peasants. In the first half of the century, they were responsible for raiding to acquire slaves for trade. Increasingly, they were used as elephant hunters and porters in caravans. Their mobility and dispersion enabled them to become free of their masters and in turn form bands of pillagers.[49] Beginning in the 1830s, they found themselves facing invasions of Nguni warriors who were traveling toward the Zambezi Valley from Zululand. Many Achikunda then left the area and moved into the backcountry, where they spread the food-producing plantation system necessary for their survival. There, they came into conflict with the former Kololo porters, who had been brought there by Livingstone. In the 1880s, the former porters dislodged some of the Achikunda, and in their place put slaves to work, especially in fields of sesame intended for export.

Around Lake Malawi at the very end of the century, there was an extraordinary mosaic of merchant warlords and slave-owning planters (Achikunda, Yao, Nguni, Kololo, etc.). Only the distance from the coast and transportation costs limited the expansion of the slave-based mode of production. Female slaves were especially in demand because they provided both fieldwork and the reproduction of competing groups. They were the first to be seized in retaliatory raids and to be yielded in case of dispute or debt. Their fate, which had little to recommend itself, led many of them to take refuge in the area's first Protestant missions.

The End of Slavery in South Africa

In South Africa, slavery was initiated by planters of Dutch origin, the Boers. In 1807, there were 30,000 slaves but only 25,000 Whites in the Cape Colony where the slave population was maintained until 1828. In that year, there were 32,000 slaves because very few had been freed (only 1,134 were freed in 1807 when the slave trade was banned), and slave status was passed down to the children of slave mothers. The effects of termination of the slave trade were feared, because in the vineyards, in the wheat fields, on the docks of the port, and in workshops, slave labor was fundamental.

Though they initially settled around the Cape, Boer settlers began to scatter into the Highveld. There, as elsewhere, the prohibition on slave imports increased domestic use of slave labor. It was also no simple coincidence that the Great Trek (the Boers' decision to systematize their departure for the backcountry to open new lands away from British control) corresponded in 1836 to the emancipation of slaves decreed by the English in their Cape Colony and other colonial territories. It is chilling to see how, even today, in the museums of the former independent states of Orange and Transvaal (particularly at Pretoria), the great exodus is exalted as that of White people courageously crowded into their famous ox-driven wagons. The Boers left, certainly, but they took 4,000 slaves and apprentices with them, and kept them in slavery. Every family had at least two or three slaves. Indeed, between 1834 and 1838, the British had turned slaves into "apprentices," thereby making general a system that was already used in the Western Cape for the some 17,000 Khoi-Khoi known as "colored" and born of earlier mixing. The children of the "colored" were theoretically free, but required to work without pay until they were twenty-five years old. Men could not change jobs without a pass. Despite the gradual spread of free labor, the Trekkers continued to seize or purchase "apprentices" until the end of the century. The Nguni of the Zulu backcountry in Delagoa Bay became one of the primary sources of "apprentices" for Orange and Transvaal.

Along the Mozambique coast, the slave trade with Brazil was still in full swing. In the 1820s, the fear, which was in fact unfounded, that it would be prohibited increased the trade at the borders of Natal. Delagoa Bay (now Maputo) exported several thousand slaves each year in that direction. The trade continued to grow until about 1850.

Among South African peoples, slave status took many different forms. For example, the Tswana, who lived on the fringes of the Kalahari Desert and who remained sheltered from most of the conquests and wars in the nineteenth century, practiced slavery to a moderate degree.[50] However, among the Nguni, despite the dominant ideology that based social and political cohesion on strong kinship ties, the conquest policy consisted in assimilating by force peoples who were put into slavery in the first generation. The farther north the conquering hordes traveled, the more resources they took from the land, requisitioning food, livestock, and men. Captives were integrated into the army. Young men went to war, and young women were given to soldiers. Few male slaves were allowed to marry, but slave women gave birth to free children. Thus, a troop of a few hundred men could in a few years turn into several thousand through rapid emancipation, which played on the imposition of a new social order based on mobility and uprooting.

Among the Nguni who did not migrate, such as in Zululand, Swaziland, and the Gaza Kingdom, slavery developed as elsewhere for day-to-day labor. It even increased in the 1870s, when more and more free men left for salaried work in the mines and city. Thus, ironically, it was once again the modern economy that had the perverse effect of increasing local slavery.

Shortage of labor was a chronic problem for the British. The prohibition of the slave trade (1807), then that of slavery (1833–38) spread the use of "apprentices." Most often, the system was only disguised slavery owing to the 1841 Masters and Servants Ordinance that prohibited employees from breaking work contracts. This accentuated the scope of raids in the interior by the Griqua and other fringe groups, especially since, beginning in 1828, Black workers, whose passes were controlled by the army and missionaries, were authorized to come to the Cape Colony to work under contract. (Until then, the Cape Colony had been in theory forbidden to Africans.)

However, neither South African societies nor the Natal planters under British control adopted modes of production based on slave labor in the same manner as in the Sahel because a capitalist labor market originating in mining and port operations had already become dominant in southern Africa.

Christianity: The Missionary Factor in Changing Mentalities

Like Islam, Christianity was not new in Africa. Ethiopia had been a bastion of Christianity from the earliest times. The Portuguese had experienced some success with Christianity in the Congo Kingdom in the sixteenth century, and there were still memories of it in northern Angola. The European trading forts scattered along the coast had acted as centers for conversion and education, but at the dawn of the nineteenth century, there were still very few Christians in Africa.

It would be a mistake, which has often been committed until now, to study the influence of the missionaries from only a European viewpoint. That history, which has already been described in excellent works, is not the most important here. Instead, we need to look at African attitudes. During the nineteenth century, the necessity became clear, especially for Africans in direct contact with Whites, to meet and even combat the latter on their own ground and using their own weapons, namely, European education and technology. The trend was not new, especially in West Africa and South Africa. Already in

1769, a chief from Sierra Leone had sent one of his sons to Lancaster to study Christianity, and another to Futa Jallon to study Islam.[51] An even shrewder approach was adopted by a Temne chief who, after selling a piece of land to the French in 1785, sent one of his sons to France, a second to Islamic lands, and the third (John Frederick, later known as Henry Granville) to England. Henry Granville would have returned to convert his brothers if he had not died as he arrived in port. Chiefs from the interior also brought their children to Freetown and put them under the guardianship of white settlers and missionaries. When Governor Macaulay returned to England in 1799, he brought with him twenty boys and four girls, most of whom returned to Africa to ply new trades. (They included a pharmacist, ship owner, printer, and government clerk.) By mid-century, schooling bore fruit in Freetown, and teachers began to be recruited from the families of "liberated" people.

These examples are not unique. On the Gold Coast, the thirst for knowledge went hand in hand with political developments. Among the first demands of the Fante confederation of 1871 was the creation of schools open to all its children. High schools were created at Cape Coast and Accra, and a high school for girls even opened in 1884. The desire for education took root very quickly in Yoruba and Igbo lands in Nigeria under pressure from so-called Saros who had returned from Sierra Leone. Members of the new elite became important players in the political and business worlds of their country. Their influence was disproportionate to their number.

Nevertheless, there were very few Christians at the end of the century. Missionary societies existed, but missionaries were few; they died quickly, and few of them traveled across the country. The most efficient promoters of Christianity were early African believers, who spread the gospel message to their neighbors. Their influence flowed from their roles as interpreters, translation assistants, catechists, and teachers. However, they became active only at the very end of the century, and in most cases not until the beginning of the twentieth century. African Christianity did not really come alive until the formation of independent African churches well on in the colonial period: South Africa is the only place where this occurred before the end of the nineteenth century. Beforehand, the trend had started to catch on but only really took hold when missionaries learned to listen to Africans' needs. On one hand, they had to temper their desire to convert and focus on teaching. Except in Sierra Leone, this did not happen until the very end of the century. On the other hand, religion and development had to coexist, but on the condition that profitable crops continued to be promoted, which was the case with palm oil and, especially, coffee and cocoa at the turn of the twentieth century. In southern Africa, introduction of the plow was also associated with missionaries.

Map 7.2   **Islam and Christianity around 1885**

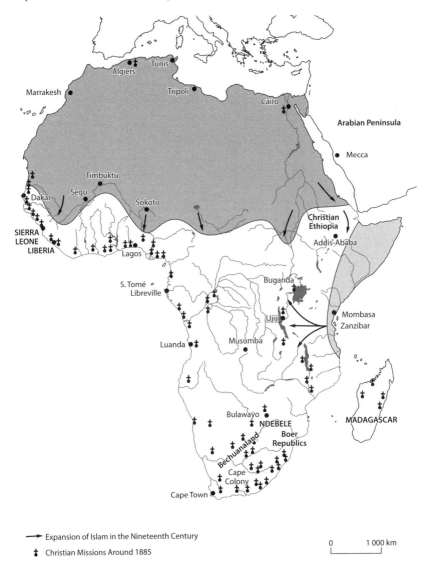

→ Expansion of Islam in the Nineteenth Century

✝ Christian Missions Around 1885

0   1 000 km

In East Africa, Muslim control, which was strengthened by the Zanzibar Sultanate, was too strong for Christianity to take hold. The same was true of the Sahelian-Saharan backcountry, which was shaken by the great Muslim jihads. In contrast, on the west coast, the old Creole centers diversified to a remarkable extent.

Missionary Actions in West Africa

Protestant Advances

The First Settlements: Freetown, Liberia, and the Gold Coast. The first center from which Christianity spread was created by British Protestant missionaries who, at the end of the eighteenth century, had been won over to the "humanitarian" cause of abolishing the slave trade. Missionary zeal, revived by the fight against slavery, coincided with a movement born not in Africa but in England. In 1772, the new case law established through the Somerset decision made slavery illegal on British soil and therefore led to the emancipation of many slaves. (In the Somerset case, the master lost because slavery was not provided for in British law, and it was therefore ruled that it was not authorized.) At the same time, the poverty of the slave population became an issue. The same team of abolitionists, William Wilberforce, George Clarkson, and Granville Sharp, who had promoted rehabilitation of slaves through work, launched the idea of a return to Africa. In 1748, there were already plans to establish an evangelical center on the Sierra Leone promontory for the use of former slaves. In 1807, the settlement became a Crown colony.

Later, beginning in 1816 with the foundation of the American Society for the Colonization of Free People of Color of the United States, American missionaries launched a similar idea for the coast of what was to become Liberia. The need to find a place to disembark emancipated slaves from the United States and the desire to take them off the hands of the New World combined to create the goal of profitable "legitimate" trade between the continents. After two unsuccessful attempts by Methodists, a small group of Black American settlers moved there in 1822. Further efforts were made in the 1830s; later, the little interest shown by the American government made it possible for the colony's leaders to proclaim it an independent republic in 1847. The immigrants belonged to various Protestant churches, and differences were further deepened by the establishment of several missions. The first was an evangelical mission of Basel, Switzerland, which opened in Monrovia in 1827. The American Episcopalian Methodist Church followed, and by 1840 there were at least sixteen churches and chapels for only 5,000 settlers. There were approximately 1,000 Methodists, but that included only 150 from the original local population. Their schools had 600 pupils. There were also American Baptists and Presbyterians, and even an Anglican branch. Around 1890, there were still only 332 Presbyterians, of whom barely half were originally from the area. Indeed, the settlers behaved like conquerors and were initially very poorly received by the Africans of the interior.

From the beginning, missionary undertakings were inseparable from politics. In 1787, the Sierra Leone Company, which was initially responsible for administering the settlement, encouraged a chaplain to come with the first immigrants, most of whom were already Christian. The settlers from Nova Scotia, Black Americans who had enrolled with the British in the U.S. War of Independence, and who arrived in Sierra Leone in 1792, belonged to various sects. Some were Baptist, others Methodist, and some belonged to other churches. Five years later, an Anglican pastor, Melville Horne, arrived. There were attempts by many different groups, particularly by the Wesleyan Methodists after 1811, but the Church Missionary Society (CMS) prevailed in 1804, assisted by Governor Charles Macarthy (1814–24), whose policy was to promote a Christian colony funded by the Crown.

Missionary success was helped by the fact that the liberated slaves, who were landing in growing numbers, were uprooted, and their only means of communication was the English language. Thus English culture predominated. Settlement and education of the inhabitants were conducted jointly by the colonial government and the mission. The latter's primary objective was to train an African clergy. The first schools opened in 1804. Fourah Bay College, created in 1817, obtained the status of university in 1876, and went on to train many young English speakers. Catholic missionaries also moved to the settlement in 1843. Around 1840, there were some 1,500 affiliated members of the CMS, which managed fifty schools with a total of approximately 6,000 students. There were about 2,000 Methodists, of whom 1,500 were students. Conversion rates were nothing like that of the Muslim expansion in the backcountry. Christian missionary work was arduous, and penetration into the interior was negligible. More than 100 missionaries died over twenty-five years, and the undertaking remained resolutely elitist. Only the Africans who were directly affected were quick to grasp the social and technological advantages of Western Christian education.

Another major vector for the promotion of Christianity, concurrent with European economic penetration, was the Creole community that had been living in the coastal regions since the sixteenth century and especially during the eighteenth century. The Creoles were Catholics who lived in Saint-Louis in Senegal, Whydah, Loango, Mozambique, and even Mombasa. On the coast of Benin, there were also many who had come back from Brazil and were known as Afro-Brazilians. In contrast, Protestantism dominated in Bathurst, on the Gold Coast, and in the Niger River Delta. The differences were related to whether the dominant cultural influence was English or French. Earlier generations had been involved in the slave trade. They were the first to understand the interest in participating in the new economy imported from Europe, and they became active in the "legitimate" trade related to vegetable oil production. They played an important social role and also proselytized their religion in accordance with their interests and ambitions. For example, the Yoruba from Sierra Leone decided in 1830 to return to their land to create the city of Abeokuta, and in 1846 they convinced the CMS to send Pastor Townsend and the African Pastor Samuel Crowther to the city. Townsend, helped by Crowther who produced many translations, played a major role as cultural mediator. In 1856 he established the first industrial tile manufacturing, carpentry, and dye enterprise in Abeokuta, launched a cotton plantation, and set up a printing press that, in 1859, published a newspaper in the Yoruba language. Of course, he also established a catechism school.

However, as might be suspected, prior to the CMS advances, one of the first strongholds of Christianity was the Gold Coast, where the Basel mission began working in 1828. Until the 1840s when quinine was first used, the missionaries' short life expectancy meant little came of their efforts. This was exacerbated by the fact that each nationality monopolized the missions of its country. For example, the Danish of Christiansburg (Accra) required that the chaplain work only for Danish citizens. Missionary action became a little more effective with the arrival of the Wesleyan Methodist mission in 1835. Missionary Thomas Birch Freeman, assisted by former students from the Cape Coast Castle School, established missionary posts in the backcountry and even traveled to the Asante capital, Kumasi, in 1839. However, despite the good relations he was able to establish with some chiefs, very few converted. Most remained skeptical about the first schools.

In the eyes of Africans, the actions of missionaries were little different from those of other Europeans, whether they were merchants or soldiers. They sought at most to use them in their internal conflicts, such as between the Fante and the Asante. As the years passed, the more missionaries got involved in the imperialist advance, the more Africans withdrew into their own beliefs. The great missionary design therefore remained far out of reach: missionaries were not establishing Christianity and "civilization" in Africa. Except in the cases of a tiny minority of cultural mediators, it was only little by little, at the end of the century, that Christianity came to be seen as a symbol of social promotion. Around 1840, almost all of the some 10,000 Christians in West Africa were either settlers or freed slaves. Only a few hundred other individuals had been converted. The latter did nothing to promote the cause. Much to the contrary, they acted like privileged superiors, and looked down their noses at the "barbarism" of ancestral customs, which only turned the great majority of the population away from Christianity.

The strictness of some missions was also not conducive to conversion. For example, the Lutheran Church that established a mission in Liberia in 1860 may have decided to begin by immersing itself in the "native" world, but it required that Africans be educated and "civilized" before converting. The first baptism of an inhabitant who was neither a schoolchild nor a mission employee did not take place until 1927. This could not compare with the massive conversions to Islam. Missionaries were not mistaken when they identified Islam as a major obstacle to Christianization in Senegambia, where it was already well established, except perhaps on the Petite Côte on the southern Cape Verde peninsula, which had been Christianized by the Portuguese (at Joal and Portudal).

From Africanization to Colonization: Samuel Crowther and the Royal Niger Company. Many missionaries began to think that the only efficient mission tool was the Africans themselves. In 1856, the Methodist Episcopal Mission in Liberia appointed its first local bishop, which meant ministers could be ordained in Liberia instead of having to be sent to Europe. While by 1880 the mission had only doubled the number of its faithful (then 2,500), it had nonetheless established some twenty-seven missions in the backcountry.

The most important role was played by Samuel Ajayi Crowther, a young ex-slave from Sierra Leone. He was of Yoruba origin, and ordained as a minister in 1843 after having been trained in London and consecrated in Canterbury Cathedral. In 1864 he became the CMS's first African Anglican Bishop for the countries under British jurisdiction in West Africa. He was to be one of the major instruments of British penetration in Nigeria, where the first mission (Wesleyan) had been established in 1842, soon followed by the CMS in 1845. The great hope of the CMS resided in the new city of Abeokuta, where many Saros (ex-Sierra Leonians) had settled. However, opposition from customary circles remained strong. It was only in 1848, two years after the mission was founded, that the first three converts were baptized. (All three were women, and one was Crowther's own mother.) Progress was slow but consistent in Yorubaland.

However, missionaries were increasingly involved in politics. In 1851, they pushed the British to turn the great port of Lagos, which had been a major slave trading post until then, into a protectorate. Crowther, who, because he was African, had no religious authority over urban centers such as Lagos, was appointed to head the Niger mission responsible for advancing into the interior. He was accompanied in Lagos, and then at Abeokuta, by another remarkable African, the future Bishop James Johnson. The beginnings were difficult. Despite a first settlement at Onitsha in 1857, at the entrance to the Delta, it took the CMS twenty years (1873) to establish their second mission at Asaba among the Igbo, who were also known as the Anioma. Initially, the reception in the interior was warm, but that did not last long. In 1888, at the time of the British conquest, there was still only a handful of converts, most of whom were foreigners, slaves, or employees of the Royal Niger Company.

For this reason, the mission was nicknamed *uka-ugwule*, which means "the slaves' church."[52] The incitement to contravene customary rules was a source of much local conflict, which was not unrelated to the conquest.

Despite the provisional Africanization of religious staff, the direct takeover by the British of Lagos, which became a Crown colony in 1861, made missionaries look like tools of a domination policy. This only fanned the flames of internal quarrels. The mission's work in the interior became extremely difficult. In 1887, Crowther complained that he had succeeded in sending only a dozen young people to the schools in Freetown and Lagos.

Eventually, the colonizers became more and more domineering. Young missionaries from Europe, who came from higher social classes than previous ones, could not stand being supervised by blacks, whom the scientific theories of the end of the nineteenth century portrayed as biologically inferior. They managed to sideline Crowther and especially his African assistants, who were accused of being bad Christians and even of engaging in the slave trade. The old bishop, who was then eighty, was forced to step down in 1890. For a generation at least, this was the end of a local corps of ministers. The scandal caused major tensions, and for a time missionary work was paralyzed. On the river, the first movements in favor of an independent Black church began to appear.[53]

The Breme Missionaries on the Togo and Cameroon Coasts. At about the same time, the missions most active on the coast were those working in Ewe lands on the Togo coast and in Duala country in Cameroon. The fathers of the Breme mission had established a post to the east of the Volta River in 1847. After many inconclusive attempts, the final location of the mission was established in 1875. The area was favorable owing to the return of Sierra Leonian Creoles to the region. Above all, the missionary in charge, Franz Michael Zahn, had the cleverness not to apply an expansionist ideology, but rather to denounce colonialism as against the spirit of Christianity. Though he had to rework his theory in 1885, his attitude remained resolutely apolitical, and this won him some converts, especially since his mission focused from the beginning on education. However, it did not really take off until the authorities forced it to move to Lome, a city full of active African businessmen who were won over to European influence.

The race to colonize also led the Germans to prohibit use of English in schools on the Cameroon coast. This resulted in a virtual monopoly of the Basel mission, though its hopes were dashed in the backcountry. It failed completely at Bamum, where Sultan Njoya had given the missionaries a warm welcome for merely political reasons; he was playing Muslim and Christian influences against each other to protect his independence. In contrast, the

expansion on the coast was real because the first Cameroonian coffee planters quickly understood the interest in school. On the eve of World War I, in
Edea country, to the southeast of Duala, there were at least ninety posts with
6,000 schoolchildren and 1,150 people who had been baptized. This was still
a minuscule minority.

The Beginnings of Catholic Action

Except in a few unusual cases, Catholic attempts were even more disappointing, especially since the idea of training an African clergy had not yet even
emerged. This was because the religion was based on administration of sacra-
ments, which was considered to be a business too serious to be entrusted to
Africans. Catholic missionaries were slow to act,except along the Senegalese
coast. In fact, Senegal had never been a missionary target. Portuguese efforts
had left few traces on the Petite Côte, and there had been French priests only in
Saint-Louis and Goree. The British were the first, and around 1820 a number
of Protestant missionary stations opened around Bathurst.

In 1820 at Saint-Louis, a French priest is said to have baptized about 100
people without even leaving his ship. The missionary return was marked in
1819–23 by the arrival of the Sisters of St. Joseph of Cluny in Goree and then
on the mainland; the sisters were to have a very conservative influence on
the education of girls. Indeed, the nuns themselves worked more as domestic
servants for than collaborators with male missionaries. No priest returned
to Saint-Louis until 1840; when brother Gallais arrived at Joal on the Petite
Côte, he complained that he found polygamous converts, who were different
from Muslims only in that they had permission to get drunk.

The starting signal was given by American Catholic missionaries of Irish
origin, who arrived in Liberia in 1842. The French Christian humanitarian
movement began to take off in Paris in the 1840s with the work of Father
Libermann. The founder of the French Sacred Heart of Mary Mission, Libermann was persuaded to assist the mission in Monrovia. That became possible
when, in 1848, the congregation merged with the Holy Ghost fathers. In 1843,
seven missionaries funded by the French Ministry of the Marine and Colonies
were sent to West Africa. However, after a few years, there remained only one
father, who was made Vicar Apostolic of Senegambia and Guinea in 1846, but
died a few months later. He was tolerant of and curious about local customs,
much more so than his successor, Monsignor Kobes, who replaced him in
1848 and proved to be a faithful agent of Faidherbe's colonial expansion.
The first missions began to be established and in 1872, the vicar of Dakar
converted, or rather, recuperated 8,000 Catholics, and created a seminary, a
trade school, and several schools for boys and girls.

Catholic attempts in Protestant lands failed at first, and there was no Catholic missionary foothold in Freetown until 1864 or in Monrovia until 1884. The initiatives of the Société des Missions Africains de Lyon (SMA), which focused more on schools than on direct proselytism, were more successful on the Ghanaian coast: in 1890, after only a few years in operation, their schools had several hundred pupils.

In contrast, the Holy Ghost fathers were relatively successful in 1844 when they established a mission in the new post of Libreville in Gabon. Though American Presbyterians had preceded them by two years, the Catholic missionary activities were energetic, and, given French colonization, the Protestant mission was placed in the hands of the Paris Société Évangélique in 1892. The chiefs and people were more receptive than elsewhere. This was perhaps because they had been engaged in slave trading for several centuries, but also because the area was in a deep crisis since the Atlantic slave trade had been abolished but not replaced, as in other places, by "legitimate" trade.

Nonetheless, solid coastal political formations, such as the Abomey Kingdom, steadfastly resisted. Religious action was also thwarted by strong colonial competition. The first Wesleyan missionary arrived in 1843, just as Régis was entering into business with King Ghezo of Abomey to export palm oil. Ghezo had his work cut out for him as he juggled Catholic and Protestant missionaries, who were not just French and British, but also Spanish and Portuguese. The latter were encouraged by Afro-Brazilians, at least by those who had not returned to Islam. Until the French conquest began in 1890, the kings of Abomey periodically expelled missionaries accused of favoring one European nation or another. However, Abomey also played on competition between the French and British to protect those who seemed the least dangerous and most profitable, namely the French. Christians sought refuge in the little coastal kingdom of Porto Novo, Abomey's traditional enemy.

The Genesis of an Elite

Initially, in the nineteenth century, missionary action accentuated the cultural and social gap between acculturated Creoles and other people, who made up the immense majority of African people. This was largely because of the cultural impermeability of the Western missionaries. Their faith and often their low level of culture, especially in the first half of the century, prevented them from grasping the nuances of the animist beliefs that they sought to combat. Religious misunderstanding was already a negative factor in first contact. The comments of many missionaries on the most natural social actions tell us much about the cultural blockage: for example, they were shocked by women's "lack of modesty," they were horrified and repulsed by nudity, they misunderstood family relations, and they completely rejected polygamy, which was understandable but contradicted the customary organization of rural work. As Western ideology became more favorable to conquest, misunderstanding only got worse. Europeans had to "civilize" Africans, in other words, fight against all "barbarous customs." Among these customs were slavery, which was indeed common in Africa, as well as human sacrifice, which was practiced in some religious circumstances. The moral justification for conquest began to develop, and, at the same time, so did direct intervention in the field by agents of expansion. In the final third of the nineteenth century, missionaries and colonizers worked together hand in hand; for example, this was the case of Father Augouard, a future bishop and a firm nationalist imperialist, who arrived on the banks of Stanley Pool on the Congo River in 1885 at the same time as Brazza's third mission.

At first, Africans had been able to look with interest at the new arrivals who, unlike soldiers, were not dangerous and offered many material promises of goods as well as new talismans. However, indulgence was soon replaced by suspicion, and then by rejection. This does not mean that the ground was not prepared for others, in particular among excluded and poor people from earlier societies, who were often but not always women and slaves. In contrast, for chiefs and free men, the process flourished only when colonialization became a major threat and the impossibility of political resistance clear. Some chiefs saw Christianization as a means of retaining power, and some people agreed that the new religion might favor social promotion and at least provided a means of protection against the worst colonial exactions.

A few examples are especially revealing, such as the massive conversions that occurred on the eve of colonization in various places in Africa, among the Basuto in the south, the Ganda in the center, and the Igbo in the west. By chance (but was it really by chance?), in all three cases, the conversions were to Catholicism in countries that were under British, thus Protestant, domination. Similarly, Protestant missions of various types were received favorably in Angola, which was under Catholic colonial domination. However, we should not exaggerate this reaction, which might be due simply to the fact that people in area tended to gather around the nearest church, and, especially, school. The missions in the imperial era had to deal with an intensely competitive atmosphere in which political nationalism often mixed with religious proselytism. Local chiefs had a difficult time competing to attract the greatest possible number of people to their land, not only because they initially confused missionaries with merchants, but also because they quickly saw that their only political chances lay in playing one partner against the other.

Competition to Convert at the End of the Century: Igboland

On the Calabar coast, to the southeast of present-day Nigeria, Presbyterians set up missions but had little success. The Catholic Mission Africaine de Lyon was attracted to the area twenty years later by a little group of Catholics led by Afro-Brazilians who had first brought in a priest from Porto Novo. The Mission Africaine de Lyon set up a mission in Lagos in 1868. In 1890, they had eight schools and over 600 students in the city. The Holy Ghost fathers (pères du Saint Esprit) followed in 1886, but only in western Igboland at Onitsha and then Asaba (where the first convert was baptized in 1893). The Holy Ghost fathers also set up Christian villages along the coast. They were peopled by slaves whom the fathers bought systematically from traders (around sixty a month, and most were from Nupe). They spread to the area via the method experimented with by the French in the western Sudan under the name of "freedom villages" (*villages de liberté*). Their goal was to solve both the problem of thousands of slaves left by Al Hajj Umar and Samori, and the colonizers' labor shortage. Thanks to the initiative of Cardinal Lavigerie, archbishop of Algiers, this costly undertaking was encouraged in 1888 by a papal encyclical that organized a worldwide collection every January 6 to fund the evangelization of Africa. The system was effective; but the Anioma of Calabar saw little difference between that and their own method, which consisted in buying slaves to work the fields and take care of the dead, since the fathers were apparently doing the same thing for their mission.

Then, the fathers changed their tactics, and focused on funding schools. The first school was opened in Igboland in 1899. They gave up their condescending attitude of paternalistic do-gooders, and took on the more dynamic role of educators. Like the Muslims, they realized that they were more effective if they addressed the leadership rather than only the disenfranchised. However, unlike those of the CMS, their schools were free of charge. By adopting this approach, they more or less reproduced, with a century of distance, what had ensured the success of the experiment in Sierra Leone: they focused on training a local elite. Their greatest feat was to convert several slave-owning chiefs: Idigo, chief of the Aguleri, who brought with him sixty-five families; and, most famously, the chief of Onitsha in 1900. They also converted many other local chiefs who were told not to free their slaves, but to teach them the catechism. In 1901, Obi Ajufo of Igbuzo, a wealthy man with twelve wives and many children, also converted. The campaign bore fruit: in 1902, there were thirteen Catholic schools and 800 students in eastern Nigeria. Clearly, despite intense competition from Protestant missions, conflict with the Royal Niger Company, and the fact that the White Fathers did not really offer their catechists many other advantages, Catholicism also spread due to the sidelining of Bishop Crowther. Those on the coast resented the British authorities who did not promote them in accordance with their qualifications as acculturated people. They were quick to take advantage of other means of social promotion, as well as to oppose colonial authority through their religious choice.

Missionaries in Central Africa

Livingstone, a Pioneer

The real pioneer was Robert Moffat who, in the 1820s, set up the Kuruman mission in what is today Botswana. His son-in-law, the explorer David Livingstone, went into the service of the London Missionary Society (LMS). His passion for geography (he died in 1873 as he was stubbornly trying to discover the sources of the Nile) combined with his conviction that the slave trade, which was then at its apex in the heart of the continent, would disappear from Africa only if it were replaced by "legitimate" trade that was just as profitable. This explains his efforts to establish farming settlements, the inhabitants of which came from the same source as that used by the White Fathers: purchase of slaves. They were evangelized, and also taught about the "benefits" of working for the mission, often in a rather rough manner. From 1853 to 1856, Livingstone crossed the heart of the continent twice, first traversing the Kalahari Desert and, from there, across to the Zambezi River. He discovered the falls, which he named Victoria, and then, crossing through Lunda lands, ended up in Luanda on the Atlantic. From there, he turned around and traveled back toward Mozambique. When he came back to Africa for his 1859–63 journey, he had greater means at his disposal, which resulted from the reputation he had acquired in England. At that point, he concentrated on Nyasaland, where he tried to establish a University Mission, visited Zanzibar again in 1866, and was met by the explorer Stanley in 1871 at Ujiji, in Nyamwezi country.

In fact, it was only after his death that the mission work really began, with the establishment of "Livingstonia" missions in his memory. The first was in Yao country in 1875, on the shores of Lake Nyasa. The following year it moved to the site of what would become the capital city (Blantyre), before being re-founded in 1883. The second Livingstonia mission was established ten years later (in 1894) to the south, on the location of the future first capital of what was to become Northern Rhodesia. The mission at Ujiji, which was first used by Mirambo against competition from Zanzibar, was abandoned in 1884 owing to opposition from the Swahili and Arabs, despite the fact that the two primary slave traders, Tippu-Tip and Rumaliza, were double-dealing with the Europeans and the Arabs.

Protestants in Zimbabwe

In about 1882–84, Frederick S. Arnot decided to travel to the Upper Zambezi to prevent a predicted advance by the Jesuits (which was how the Protestants referred to the White Fathers). His goal was to spread in Barotse country, which was under Chief Lozi Lewanika's control, the teachings of a sect that had recently been born in England and Ireland: the Plymouth Brethren. It preached a fundamentalist Puritanism that rejected all form of hierarchy among clergy. Arnot failed when the Protestant Société des Missions de Paris arrived, which led him to settle instead on the Angolan coast, from where he later spread Brethren missions.

After difficult beginnings, missions of all types converged toward the heart of central Africa starting in the 1880s. Until the borders were drawn, every mission, no matter what its allegiance, spent most of its time watching the others and trying to block them. Thus, they undeniably played a role in the imperial colonial expansion of the time. This was the opinion of the British Consul to Mozambique, Harry Johnston, who also invented the "Cape to Cairo dream," and suggested to Cecil Rhodes:

> [Missions] strengthen our hold over the country, they spread the use of the English language, they induct the natives into the best kind of civilization and in fact each mission station is an essay in colonization.[54]

In Barotse country, Pastor François Coillard (whose wife was Scottish) soon dominated. While conducting a skillful policy of friendship with the Lozi, he worked hard to control their chief. Aware of how difficult it was to convert the local people, he focused mainly on changing their lifestyle and beliefs, fighting against witchcraft by acting more or less as a doctor, and introducing European clothing, which Chief Lewanika adopted, as can be seen in a photograph from 1890. Another picture, taken in 1902 on the eve of Chief Lewanika's departure for London for the coronation of Edward VII, shows him dressed as a perfect gentleman with a very British appearance; but he had not converted. Coillard's influence was greatest through his encouragement of innovation in agriculture, such as banana production and marsh draining. Since he focused on educating the chief and the aristocracy's children, he was eventually in a special position with respect to Chief Lewanika. However, convinced, as were all Europeans of the time, that the Barotse were unable to govern themselves and that they had to be colonized in order to be "civilized," Arnot had no qualms about using his influence to facilitate the intervention of Cecil Rhodes's British South Africa Company by persuading the chief that he was dealing directly with Queen

Victoria. After long hesitation, the chief decided to sign, only to learn soon after that he had been sold to a business undertaking. The missions suffered, but the harm had been done.

Monsignor Lavigerie's Catholics

Catholics were not to be outdone. The Vatican had been interested in the area since the 1840s, but concentrated its efforts on the Upper Nile Valley, under the influence of Monsignor Comboni and the Verona fathers. East Africa remained dominated by the Indian Ocean missions: the Holy Spirit fathers in Zanzibar had founded a small mission at Bagamoyo in 1868. Five years later, there were five missionaries, who had bought the freedom of 324 slaves, including 251 children.[55]

The Catholics' penetration occurred mainly under the impetus of Monsignor Lavigerie, bishop of Algiers from 1867. It was in Algeria that he perfected his tactic of setting up orphanages, charitable undertakings that the French government could not refuse out of respect for Islam. In 1868, Lavigerie had Pope Pius IX recognize the order of the White Fathers (the Society of Our Lady of Africa). The following year, he acquired a huge piece of land in the Chelif Valley, imported muscat vines from Spain, and put the orphans to work under the supervision of lay brothers until they reached adulthood, when they were settled in Christian villages. Ten years later, he needed a new challenge. He used his position in the Church to promote French interests in Tunisia, and then turned his attention to sub-Saharan Africa. In 1877, in order to match the Protestant undertakings, he began trying to interest the Pope in the project so as to take advantage of the route into central Africa that had been opened by Belgian King Leopold II's International Congo Society. Again, the plan was based on the creation of self-sufficient orphanages peopled by buying child slaves from surrounding slave traders. In 1878, accompanied by former papal Zouaves who were responsible for their security, ten White Fathers left on foot from Bagamoyo, where priests from Reunion Island led a small Catholic community. They were active in what was to become German East Africa, where they gained a foothold in the interior, at the post of Tabora. From there they diverged: some went north toward Lake Victoria, and others went south, toward lakes Tanganyika and Nyasa. In 1884, they succeeded in setting up a mission in Mirambo's capital city in Nyamwezi country, despite the CMS's hostility.

Before that, in 1879, they gained a foothold in Ganda country. At the end of the century, after a difficult time between 1886 and 1890 during which many Christians were martyred, they eventually succeeded in the massive conversion of those in power in reaction to the advancing British protectorate.

Religious War in Buganda

In that part of central Africa, there were true religious wars between Protestants, Catholics, and Muslims. The flames were fanned by the Europeans' expansionist ambitions. In the area, Mutesa was the jealous king of a realm with a little over 1 million subjects. He did not allow any missions to be set up until 1875. Arabs had arrived in his kingdom only one generation before. While he was interested in emulating their commercial and technological success, his political goal was to protect himself from Egyptian (therefore Arab-Muslim) plans that had been directed toward the sources of the Nile since the 1860s. (Gordon did not evacuate the forts in southern Egypt until 1879.) He was intrigued when Stanley described the advantages of a Christian presence. However, he permitted missionaries only in his capital city, Rubaga, or near his army. The unexpected result was that Catholic and Protestant missionaries had to live near each other and compete, including in the king's court. Both groups complained at the same time about the human sacrifices that were performed in 1880 to cure the king's illness.

The conflict became serious only when the king died in 1884. His young successor, Mwanga, reacted to news of Carl Peters's German military-commercial expedition's advance southward by turning toward the Arabs. He began by executing two CMS disciples, then exasperated the missionaries with his homosexual practices with his pages. Eventually, he eliminated all the pages who had been won over to Christianity: they were burned alive in May 1886 during an *auto-da-fé* that turned them into martyrs. The flight of the converted into the bush helped to spread conversion, and Catholic and Protestant groups were each soon able to count on 1,000 soldiers against only 300 Muslim soldiers. The king played on the rivalries, until eventually the three monotheist groups joined together and deposed him in 1888 so that his younger brother Kiwewa could take the throne. However, less than a month later, a Muslim coup deposed Kiwewa. The European missionaries were arrested, their missions were pillaged by the Arabs' slaves, and the Arabs in turn imposed their religion, in particular through forced circumcision. Mwanga apologized to the White Fathers and asked the Europeans to help him take back the throne. The CMS missionary refused, but the White Fathers supported him.

The episode determined what was to follow, even though the Catholics and Protestants allied for a time to repulse the Muslim assault and shared high positions in the government after Mwanga's return. The 1890 Anglo-German agreement, which recognized the flag of the British East Africa Company to the south and west of Lake Victoria, made Protestant missionaries the objective allies of British imperialism. Conversion to Catholicism became the symbol of political revolution and loyalty to King Mwanga, based on the rediscovered principle of *"cujus regio ejus religio"* (whose rule, his religion). For a time, the White Fathers even argued in favor of dividing the kingdom in two, in accordance with the inhabitants' choice between Protestantism and Catholicism. The later English intervention led by Lugard, the intrusion of the British East Africa Company, and the imposition of the British protectorate confirmed the movement.[56]

Missionary Brutality

By 1898, the White Fathers showed that they had also decided to make Bemba country to the south a Roman Catholic enclave. Bishop Dupont took advantage of the situation. After having helped Chief Mwamba in his last years, he declared himself the heir and successor, and had the chiefs ratify a document to this effect, which was supposed to be Mwamba's last will and testament. The British South Africa Company put a complete stop to his claims. However, the purpose of the initiative was essentially to legalize the establishment of Catholic missions, and it facilitated peaceful control over the country.[57]

In only a few years, missionaries had greatly contributed to preparing the groundwork for the colonial expansionists, especially the White Fathers of Monsignor Lavigerie, who had originally intended to compete with the Belgians (though they were also Catholic) over the Upper Congo. Moreover, unlike in West Africa, where military leaders distanced themselves from missionaries, in central Africa missionaries' status as the first settlers quickly led them to fill the governmental vacuum and render decisions as if they were the rulers of the country. The White Fathers dominated to the west of Lake Tanganyika, but the LMS was just as strong there, and Scottish missions were among the most brutal. In the last two decades of the century, in the name of Western morals and the supposedly childish and perverse nature of the Blacks (a viewpoint well-documented in reports from the time), the missionaries around Lake Tanganyika acted like rulers, promulgated laws, and rendered their own justice. Among other things, they required that the Africans who worked at missions submit completely to their authority. Soon workers had no choice; if they wanted to be hired they had to comply with the missionaries' rules on hygiene, adopt a Western lifestyle, attend church, and send their children to school. Failure to comply was punished brutally, in particular through abuse of the chicotte (a whip made out of strips of leather that was commonly used in corporal punishment during the colonial era). In 1898, the leaders in London, who had studied the extent of the disaster into which their evangelical works had descended, put an end to the practices that had come to be usual for their missionaries. However, it was not until 1902 that the company took control of the country and missionaries were able to devote themselves to what they had greatly neglected until then: teaching.

Advances in Southern Africa

Missionary influence appeared first in southern Africa. This is not surprising since the first settlers' hold on the interior began earlier there than elsewhere. Among the very first to try their luck, following the Huguenots who had fled France and, in some cases, found refuge on the Cape at the end of the seventeenth century, there was the London Missionary Society, which sent Reverend John Campbell to explore the area in 1812. It was during that trip that he traveled to Tswanaland. Local chiefs had authorized the settlement of a missionary in order to procure weapons, which did not go without causing some misunderstandings and difficulties. Robert Moffat managed to set up a mission in Kuruman only after the Tswana had been forced to move by peoples who had themselves been pushed off their lands by the Nguni. He began translating the Bible into Setswana, an endeavor he completed in 1850, after thirty years of labor. However, he never had more than 100 Christians around him. The real conversion work did not begin before the 1870s, when missions began mushrooming throughout the area, especially around the Bamangwato Chief, Kgama (also known as Khama), a hero in missionary literature, whose capital city, Shoshong, had around 30,000 inhabitants in 1860.

The (Protestant) Société des Missions de Paris was founded in 1828, and sent a team of missionaries to the mountains of Basutoland in 1833. The personality of Pastor François Coillard (1834–1904) did much to change the small group of Basuto mountain dwellers. He shared their difficulties in resisting the Boers, who were in an early Western enclave. However, he was soon facing competition from a Catholic mission that arrived in 1862. Moshoeshoe, who was in conflict with the Boers of Orange Free State, probably considered that he had an interest in surrounding himself with as many missionaries as possible. His political shrewdness is confirmed by the fact that he refused to take sides among them, and accepted baptism only on his deathbed. While few Basuto had converted at the beginning of the twentieth century, conversions to Catholicism increased rapidly, perhaps because it was less strict about the customs that shocked missionaries the most: boys' initiation, women's purchase, and polygamy. Failure to comply did not necessarily lead to excommunication, as in the case of Protestantism, but only to penitence.[58]

At the beginning of the nineteenth century, no other part of Africa had as many scattered missionary stations as the Cape Colony and its backcountry. The Dutch Reform Church won its first Khoikhoi converts in the early eighteenth century. However, in the first half of the nineteenth century, the Tswana,

Xhosa, and Soto were the most receptive to the Christian message. In fact, they may have been the only peoples ready to listen to it.[59] Missionaries settled stations there before 1820. Yet, in the backcountry of Cape Town, the Boers did not make the task easier. Their church refused to address Africans and, to the great dismay of the British, endorsed a strong-armed approach and slavery. Nonetheless, the Xhosa, who lived closest to the border, and the Khoikhoi, who had been living more or less in symbiosis with them for two centuries, were conquered peoples who were relatively open to missions. In 1823, the first Methodist mission was established in Xhosa lands. By 1830, the various missions each had several hundred people living around them, often because they felt the mission provided a form of protection. Missionaries were quick to attack the problem of education, since they were responsible for providing settlers with the clerks and staff they needed. In the early 1820s, the Glasgow missionaries suggested creating a boarding school where young people would be isolated from their society of origin. This was not done until 1841, when the Lovedale Missionary Institute was created. For a century, it was the most prestigious school for Africans; it was unique because it welcomed both White students (primarily missionaries' children) and Black students. It maintained the privilege to do so until it was suppressed by apartheid in 1954. Other boarding schools for Africans were created in the nineteenth century, including the Healdtown Methodist School, and the first school for girls, which was opened by Presbyterians in 1861 at Emgwali. However, it was not until 1916 that the first university college for Blacks was created: Fort Hare University College.

Other areas of South Africa were converted later. For example, conversion was relatively late in Natal, where Zulu chiefs put up strong resistance. The British had originally occupied the province in the early 1840s in order to prevent the Boers from applying their policy of systematic exclusion of Blacks. However, despite their initial intention to eliminate slavery and protect Nguni lands, they quickly came under the influence of Theophilus Shepstone, a Methodist missionary's son residing on the border of the Cape. He became the secretary of native affairs, and advocated direct rule of the vast lands, where colonial authorities would be responsible for eradicating polygamy, witchcraft, and women's purchase, the marriage compensation known as *lobola*. Since they had little means, the British initially depended on customary authorities, though they were disrupted, and "natives" were submitted to the discretionary power of the colony. Missionary success paid the price of this, even though no other area was covered so early with so many missions. The first to establish missions among the Nguni were Americans in 1835. British Methodists followed in 1841, and then the Norwegian Missionary Society in 1844 and the Berlin Mission Society in 1847. Catholics, represented by the

Oblates of the Immaculate Conception, arrived in 1852 and made their first attempts to set up missions in 1856.

This was not the first time the Zulu had been in contact with Europeans. The first Western merchants visited Port Natal (Durban) in 1824, and Dingane had warmly welcomed his first European visitor, the Anglican Allen Gordiner, in 1835. Nonetheless, they expelled an American station in 1842 because they considered an arrogant missionary to be a challenge to royal authority. They allowed others onto their lands only about a dozen years later: King Mpande appreciated them as doctors, technicians, and advisors, but he still rejected all attempts at evangelization. In the 1860s, Mpande's successor, Cetshwayo, continued to require his authorization for any baptism to be performed, and he gave permission with great parsimony.

Eventually, in 1880, there were over fifty missions in Natal and nearly twenty-five in Zululand. They were generally small and run by only two people: the missionary and his wife. Their work consisted mainly in operating a self-sufficient farm where workers were called to prayer daily and where the workers' children went to Sunday school. The result was that, as elsewhere, the number of people converted was barely a tenth of the Black population of Natal (some 10,000 souls). In Zululand, only a few hundred were converted. The missionaries' interpretation was that Africans rebelled against all "civilization," and so they came to give full support to the idea of the Whites' superior authority. They refused to give the few Black ministers any responsibility. Anglican missionaries were the first to adopt a more open policy, beginning with respect to the Nguni. They refused to attack local customs directly, and one of them, namely Henry Callaway, even considered that they were "endowed with intellectual, moral and spiritual capacities equal to our own,"[60] which was an exceptional attitude for the time. Not unreasonably, he attributed the failure of evangelization to social constraints (such as polygamy and *lobola*) that could not be isolated from customary economic structures. He had some success with the introduction of use of draft animals in plowing, but he encountered difficulties that eventually led him to recommend what he had begun by rejecting: domination and the White model.

Other people of Zulu origin were no less distrustful. For example, among the Ndebele in Zimbabwe, Mzilikazi, who had settled there as conqueror in 1828, received the first missionary, Robert Moffat, warmly. Moffat even became one of his personal friends, and succeeded in setting up a mission in 1857. However, in Zimbabwe as elsewhere, White missionaries were convinced that they spoke on behalf of the only true religion, and from the beginning committed a series of mistakes that were to prove costly. A priori, polytheist religions were not unfavorable to Christianity, especially if in their pantheon there was a god who was superior to all other spirits and ancestors. After all, an additional supernatural power was not something to neglect, especially if it could bring to the local people a share of the Whites' obvious wealth. However, aside from a few exceptions, White missionaries behaved very badly without even realizing it. They were impolite, which was difficult for the local people to accept because for them social codes were in themselves signs of belief and religion. They also committed a series of sacrilegious actions that were nearly intolerable. For example, in 1861, in Manganja lands south of Lake Nyasa, Livingstone and the Universities' Mission to Central Africa (UMCA) missionaries chose with astonishing clumsiness to set up their mission on the hill that was the site of the most venerated tomb of the local M'Bona sect. It was natural that the inhabitants vehemently rejected the missionaries.[61]

Indeed, most missionaries were blind to the complexity of what they persisted in seeing only as reprehensible superstitions. For example, they condemned in the same manner all rites that involved recourse to the supernatural, whether they involved truly evil powers employed by a sorcerer, or propitiatory techniques used by the local priest, who was always labeled a "fetisher."

The Nguni's suspicions were not wholly unfounded, though they had initially shown legitimate curiosity by coming to church services in great numbers, which also led missionaries to overestimate their success.

A Fundamental Misunderstanding

What Africans expected from their visitors was real assistance with respect to technology, health care, diplomacy in relation to White powers, and possibly political support in domestic affairs. Many chiefs thought that by permitting a missionary station they could protect themselves from outside intrusions. They were soon disappointed by the missionaries' refusal or inability to intervene in such situations. They had to resolve to use them only as a last resort in order to smooth over some of the many problems that they had with the authorities. However, missionaries' obvious collusion with colonial authorities (e.g., the ease with which colonial officers gave them the land they needed for their settlements) could only inspire distrust. Distrust also came from the fear of new religious techniques that were thought to be evil, or simply the horrified incomprehension of some Europeans, particularly with respect to relationships between men and women. This also explains why most Africans tried to keep children away from missions, by making them believe that they might be eaten, for example, since children could be influenced easily. Another trick, which made it possible to nonetheless receive some of the benefits of missions, such as clothing and a small salary, was to send only one child per family to the mission, and to do so in turns. Resistance to direct missionary action was even more efficient in lands that were not yet under colonial control, such as in Zululand until the war of 1879, and in Pondoland, where the first missionaries were invited in the 1840s.

Underground, but Deep Work

Nonetheless, beginning in the 1860s, a positive mixing of the cultures began to emerge, such as between traditional curative rituals and modern health care. The demand for schools also began to grow. However, Africans remained indifferent to the missionaries' actual raison d'être: the Christian religion. Biblical theories about creation, sin, and damnation were foreign to their needs. Instead of complaining about their inability to understand them, missionaries might have wondered about the strength of the worldview that they were trying to challenge, as well as the resistance to domination that naturally flowed from the mentalities.

Resistance of the local religions did not mean that there was no intermingling in the nineteenth century. Many groups that had been isolated until then were brought into contact with one another; for example, the Shona came in contact with the Matabele diaspora. In some cases, groups even merged. Especially in the last part of the century, many people moved toward more densely populated areas and to cities. The incorporation of more and more slaves into local societies also gave rise to new trends. The changes were accompanied by insecurity and fear, and therefore a will for protection that led to phenomena such as witchcraft and possession rituals. Baptism was seen as an efficient purification rite for eradicating the powerful evil of witchcraft. Various rituals, myths, and prophecies were invented to account for the changes. All of this explains the deep transformations in African mentalities, even though no monotheism was officially adopted. Aside from some exceptions, conversions followed rather than preceded the conquest.

This does not mean that no one converted before the conquest. We have already mentioned Creole communities, which had strong influence on the areas where they were located. They sprung up, sometimes as early as the sixteenth century, in ports occupied by the first slave-trading settlers, such as in Luanda and on the Island of Mozambique, a little later at Saint-Louis du Senegal, and on the Gold Coast, as well as in the settlement at Sierra Leone. However, in the nineteenth century, the people attracted to the first missions in the interior were of many different origins. The origin of conversions was not really religious, except in the case of a few individuals who saw the promise of eternal life as reassuring, and others who were suffering from remorse and found absolution comforting. Most of the converted first had visions or suffered emotional phenomena similar to possession by spirits. Such cases were rare enough to be reported by missionaries. There are records of a conversion at a Methodist mission at Verulam in Natal after several days and nights of constant celebration.[62]

Conversion was accepted by congregations more or less quickly. The dazzling mass conversions to Islam in West Africa had not yet occurred. Massive numbers of Christian conversions occurred only at the end of the century, when subjects had little choice but to follow their leaders. Some missionaries, such as American Presbyterians and Lutherans, were very demanding. They permitted baptism only after several years of probation, and did not hesitate to excommunicate if there was the slightest failing, particularly with respect to polygamy. Others, such as Methodists and Catholics, were more tolerant. However, they did not accept the compromises that became necessary at the end of the century with the emergence of independent Black churches.

Nonetheless, the process was beginning, particularly in South Africa, where a Methodist community of some twenty people developed not far from the little station of Verulam, north of Port Natal (Durban). There was also an energetic Methodist-educated woman who began converting people in her circle in 1873. Even more remarkably, there was a couple preaching the "good word" in Nguni country in the 1880s.

However, a Black clergy was slow to emerge in southern Africa as elsewhere. In 1867, the Methodists were the first to ordain a Black clergyman: Clemens Johns. In 1871, the American Presbyterians followed with two Africans, and then the Anglican Henry Callaway had two more ordained. However, for a long time five was the maximum.

Africans' greatest material concerns at the time were security, land, and work. In this sense, Livingstone's ideas bore fruit. The fact that every mission behaved as a self-sufficient module and often introduced the use of draft animals facilitated the recruitment of workers. They were the first to hear the conversion message, especially since missionaries gave Christians priority with respect to advancement. Missionaries took it to heart to settle in accordance with the law, and they had the protection of both the local chief and, in case of emergency, their home country. Their farms became havens of peace in a very turbulent environment. Not all of their workers converted, far from it; however, many of their children became carpenters and masons, as did other children who learned new techniques in the mission schools.

Many members of the first generation of converts were people who had been left out in the cold by the surrounding system, which was often falling apart. In Africa, they were mainly farmers because, except in Tswanaland, nomads were barely affected by Christianity: in the north they were already converted to Islam, and their mobility made contact rarer. Land was needed in order to survive, but the upheavals had resulted in hordes of landless people. In southern Africa this was soon exacerbated by a growing number of migrant workers who had to find places to live during their travels and whose salaried work cut them off from ancestral customs. For example, many used the services of missionaries to send messages and a little money to their homes in the backcountry. This was how they were introduced to churches. Many of the first guests who sought shelter in the missions were strangers to the area.

For some of them, the missions were not just temporary homes, but offered a solution to their problems. This was the case for those who had been excluded from or marginalized by the system, particularly young people, and especially young women who wished to escape kinship obligations, to flee elderly polygamous husbands, or simply to marry the man of their choice. There were also young girls traumatized by terrifying initiation ceremonies. Girls in this state came to a mission in Natal in 1859.[63] Other young people became Christian without being asked. Some were children entrusted to missions by parents in distress or by chiefs wishing to win the approval of their new neighbors. Indeed, even Zulu Chief Cetshwayo, who had a reputation as an opponent of Christianity, gave his children to a mission as guarantees, as was often the custom in African societies. In Nguni country, the birth of twins was considered unlucky and a source of evil. In such cases, one of the babies would be given to missionaries so that infanticide could be avoided. Extra mouths, sick people, people with handicaps, sterile women, old people with no children, and even lepers were the first to seek refuge in the missions. While missionaries boasted to their European backers of caring for the needy, the nature of their clientele greatly decreased their local popularity since their settlements became synonymous with undesirable and marginalized people.

However, many missionaries made themselves indispensable for other reasons with respect to politics, economy, society, and health care. Local chiefs saw interest in collaborating, and willingly offered missionaries land to live on and even political rights. In Nguni country, some received the title of *nkosi* (chief) in addition to that of *mfundisi* (teacher). Many stations were only tolerated at first, but continued their work, and by the end of the century, the foundations were laid. Chiefs, such as the *kabaka* of the Buganda, ordered their subjects to convert en masse. Especially in conquered lands, people quickly grasped the many advantages that flowed from conversion. For example, before 1882, Christians in Natal were exempt from the Native Law. In Igboland, converting also got one out of forced labor. This does not mean that Africans converted only out of self-interest, but they were quick to accept that particular aspect of modernity. In Cameroon, the first to convert were small-scale coffee planters whom the Germans had settled on the mountainsides. In Nguni country, the number of faithful was great enough at the end of the century for them to be seen as a new community: the *kholva*, or Black Christians. They were halfway between the world of their ancestors and that of their White masters with respect to their lifestyle, often their work, and rapidly their way of thinking.

Some of the first Christians, such as the Nguni in Natal, planters in Cameroon, and Igbo converts, were well-established landowners, but private landownership was not encouraged by Christianization. Christian communities preferred to be based on associations of trustees, whereby land-ownership was reserved for the founders and their families. This made it possible to ward off intrusions by nonbelievers and maintain the collective habits of the past. Trade schools, such as that in Natal, were rarely attended by Christians, but not because, as settlers argued, they were resistant to all forms of modernity, rather because salaried trades were poorly compensated. While an ignorant pagan could accept a shilling a day, no informed Christian would be content with that. Christians were thus distrusted by employers and, especially, could not compete with their European equivalents. Therefore, like the Afro-Brazilians of West Africa, the first converts entered other sectors of the economy. In the 1860s, some invested in sugar cane plantations in Natal, and many began speculating on land or went into business.

After the 1865 depression in Natal, interest in schools increased rapidly. In 1870–80, about 3,000 students, most of whom were boys, attended missionary schools each year. Depending on the sect, the teaching was delivered in English, German, Dutch, and even Zulu, especially among the Americans. Four secondary schools then opened, and in 1880, 149 boys and 83 girls were attending them. However, the demand for schools soon outstripped the offer. By 1876, the first four graduates from Natal entered Howard University, which was the first Black university in the United States, created just after the Civil War. It became common for wealthy families to send their children to continue their education in private missionary schools in the Cape Colony. Afterward they scattered across the country and taught others, which accelerated the spread of the European culture in the hinterland.

Black emancipation soon worried the settlers. After 1880, the advantages related to exemption from the native law began to be eradicated. The right to freely purchase land was gradually eliminated, even for Christians, between 1887 and 1903. Head taxes were reestablished for Black Christians the same year. Assistance for education withered away: in 1908, only 1 percent of the population of Natal was formally educated.[64] Yet, despite the obstacles to education, in the early 1920s, young intellectual Christians and city dwellers began to look back to the myth of past Zulu glory to establish a modern political party: Inkatha.

Independent Black Churches

At the very end of the nineteenth century, independent Black churches were just beginning to appear. In southern Africa, where they first sprang up, they can be classified into two main categories: Ethiopian churches, which were the first and included the Ethiopian Church properly speaking and the African Methodist Episcopal Church; and the others, which were numerous and included the Bantu Methodist Church, the Zulu Congregational Church, and the Africa Church. The word *Ethiopia* referred to a noble idea of free Africa delivered from Whites. In the twentieth century, many more churches sprang up across the continent: the Harrist Church was founded in Ivory Coast at the time of World War I, and Kimbangism began in Congo (Zaire) between the two world wars. The churches were strongly inspired by the liturgy, hymns, and catechism of European churches, but emphasized their Black specificity. In South Africa, the government began to recognize them officially only in 1925.

The Zionist church movement, inspired by the apocalyptic Zionist movement created in the United States (which is unrelated to contemporary Zionism), really began in 1900 in Zululand in the eastern Transvaal, when the Boer War erupted.[65] Ironically, its founder, Petrus Louis Le Roux, was an inspired missionary of the Dutch Reformed Society who was rejected by his White brothers and broke off from the mother association. The movement was successful, especially in southern Africa where it certainly met the expectations of people who were desperate but also avid believers in the supernatural. Today, there are more than 2,000 sects that came out of charismatic groups that focused on miracle cures and the role of prophesy. Almost all of these emerged in the twentieth century.

Economic and Social Changes: Systems of Production and Lifestyles

The nineteenth century was a time of major upheaval in all areas of the continent. The change that was most evident to outsiders was the addition of Africans to the international market economy as something other than as marginal suppliers of slave labor.

Work and production changes were structured. There was growth in slave-based production in both East and West Africa, but for different reasons. Free labor also changed.

The Production Economy

The pastoral and warrior economy gave way to a colonial plantation economy. This occurred earlier in Algeria and, in slightly different forms, in South Africa.[66]

Another brutal change in coastal West Africa was the replacement of the slave trade economy by agricultural production based on palm oil and peanuts. Tropical oilseeds were in high demand in England at the beginning of the century owing to the Industrial Revolution, as these oils were used to grease train components and factory machinery. The candle and soap industries were also expanding. The soap industry began in England and then developed in France from the 1840s on, as white soap was perfected. The adoption of the whitening technique by the Régis brothers in 1852 increased production of Marseilles soap. In the 1870s, margarine also began to be produced. In 1851, a ton of palm oil purchased in Lagos for between £10 and £20 could be sold in Liverpool for £40, which was a very decent profit margin. It was only during the Long Depression of 1873–93 that trade decreased, which proved to be all the more disastrous because at that point palm products and oil accounted for over 80 percent of Lagos's exports. By 1881, a ton went for £30, and in 1891 for only £22. It was the worst commercial crisis that West Africa had experienced since the abolition of the slave trade.[67]

Initially, local chiefs made broad use of slave labor, especially on palm oil plantations, owing to the gradual closing of the Atlantic slave market and the resulting drop in the price of slaves. Peasant production became essential everywhere. Yams could be grown by everyone, and from about mid-century, palm oil exports to western Europe were no longer counted in hundreds of tons but in tens of thousands of tons. Men took part in farming as soon as it paid to do so. Women were also used greatly, not only in subsistence agriculture and in their husbands' fields, but also in local commercialization and transportation of food products, peanuts, palm oil, and kola nuts, the consumption of which increased with the Islamization of the hinterland.[68]

From 1830 to 1920, southeastern Nigeria was the world's leading producer of palm oil and kernels. However, thanks to the Porto Novo palm plantations, the coast of Dahomey also played an important role in supplying France. At the middle of the century, peanuts played the same role in Senegal. All of the coastal countries thus moved relatively easily from slave trading to trade in products that were part of the same import-export system, with a transitional phase in 1815–60, when the two forms of trade were complementary. These countries experienced real prosperity before and until the colonial conquest. However, the regional society and economy were greatly altered.

One of the groups most affected was the Igbo Anioma on the right bank of the Niger River. Their history has been studied in detail.[69] Their strength was based on a remarkable geographical and political position, as they were located just upstream of the delta. This helped to preserve their cultural heritage and identity without requiring them to resort to centralized political structures. The need to protect themselves against Yoruba incursions from Benin City, which was located less than 100 miles from Asaba, one of the primary ports on the river, led them to form large compact villages that were independent of one another. In the nineteenth century, the agglomerations sometimes had several thousand inhabitants. Since the area was virtually inaccessible to Europeans owing to malaria (until quinine was introduced in the 1840s), they controlled traffic on the lower river. The Anioma were in contact with all the people traveling up and down the Niger. When the Europeans began using steamboats on the river (in 1841), they had to gain the support of those living along the banks. The slave trade and also, from the beginning of the century, palm oil production and trade, generated complex economic relations. As more plantations were established, the internal demand for slaves grew. Slaves were used not only in activities related to oil palms, but also in supplying local and regional people with fresh food. Traders, workers, slaves, producers, porters, and piroguiers all consumed yams, corn, and oil, as did the rest of the mixed population swelling the stopover stations such as Onitsha and Opobo on the river. More than a million yams came out of the Bay of Biafra at the end of the eighteenth century. They were traded for salt and manufactured goods. The Igbo's commercial role was well established.[70]

Women's work diversified, and they played a major role in farming and in cottage palm oil production and sale.[71] The complex economy was conducive to the emergence of social classes. The richest families acquired economic and political powers that enabled them to negotiate with the first Europeans, traders, and missionaries. Despite the slow pace of Christian penetration (after an initial failure in 1857, the first Church Missionary Society mission was not established until 1873, and the Catholic mission not until 1888), agricultural and commercial changes led to an alteration in ideologies and rituals that regulated social relations.

Dahomey, the Asante Kingdom, Yoruba and Igbo lands, the Slave Coast, and the Gold Coast thus shifted in less than half a century from the international slave trade, which had completely dominated for 150 years, to trade in commodities. At first the two forms of trade were complementary; then the latter replaced the former. In the first half of the century, there were real social changes, but the economic process was more an evolution than a revolution. Even in Lagos in the middle of the century, where the relatively brutal switch from the slave trade to trade in oil was imposed by the direct domination of the British (of whom Lagos became a protectorate in 1851), the impact was balanced by the opportunity offered to many small entrepreneurs, who were sometimes former slaves, to go into business. However, overall, emancipation had no major immediate effects. Masters and slaves negotiated transitional relationships of dependency, and kept the economy running smoothly.

Elsewhere, all the established powers that had remained independent benefited. The winners were states, aristocracies of planters, and merchant corporations monopolizing trade, such as the Hausa studied later in this chapter.

The transition occurred at different times and in different societies, some of which had centralized power structures (for example, the Asante and the Fon of Dahomey), but others that did not (for example, the Igbo and, to a certain extent, the Yoruba). It was only at the end of the century, following the Long Depression in Europe, that a change in scale occurred and the balance was lost. The Depression led to a drop in vegetable oil prices and a reversal of the terms of trade that had until then been favorable to African leaders (since oil prices had tended to increase while the price of imported manufactured goods constantly decreased throughout the century). It was not until this happened that the crisis caused by adaptation to new British economic criteria was felt in Yoruba and Igbo lands.[72] The era also, and for the same reasons, corresponded to the colonial push into Asante lands and, in the case of the French, into Dahomey.

Eventually, it was on the division of labor between men and women that the impact was greatest. Women had controlled oil production and transportation. As more slaves came to be used in the industry, women lost some of their responsibilities, and also some of their prerogatives. However, they were still very much involved in palm oil production at the beginning of the twentieth century, which seems to indicate that they were able to carve out and keep control of some activities.

The Hausa Diaspora

The new phenomenon in the nineteenth century was the growth in power of the Hausa merchant corporation. Hausa cities had been acting as merchant crossroads since the sixteenth century; however, the Hausa diaspora took form in the nineteenth century. Among other things, the Hausa controlled trade in kola nuts, which were produced in Asante country but consumed across the Sahelian-Sudanese Muslim world, from the Sokoto Sultanate to Bornu and beyond.

The Hausa were not the first to play such a role. Since the sixteenth century, the Jola in the Jenne area had dominated the gold trade on the Volta rivers. Farther west, the Wangara had monopolized the salt supply between the Niger and the coast. Yarse traders, who were of Soninke origin but had adopted the More language (of the Mosi), supplied the Volta river areas with livestock, cloth, slaves, and kola. Odile Goerg[73] has provided detailed descriptions of the caravans operating in Guinea in the second half of the century.

The Hausa diaspora was encouraged by the Fulani jihad. The troubles led groups of immigrants (of a few hundred individuals at the most) to settle in

Hausaland at the very beginning of the century. They were refugees from groups dependent on the Tuaregs of Bornu, who established slave colonies farther south, in Hausaland. Thus, former slaves and low-class nomads abandoned their lean livestock to engage in trade in the savanna. Some moved to Kano and Katsina, where they were rapidly assimilated. From there they dispersed into the sultanate's other cities. By 1850, they occupied whole quarters in urban areas.

Their trade expanded to the north and south. It began with dates and desert salt, and then the diaspora created an opportunity through the huge Fulani demand for kola nuts. The Hausa used the constant flow of new migrants from the north to develop caravan routes from the Sokoto Sultanate to the Asante center of Salaga.

The Hausa corporation was favored by endogamy, the fact that the Hausa language had become the language of trade throughout the savanna, and, of course, Muslim solidarity. Colonies of landlords and brokers sprang up just about everywhere, as the caravans brought together considerable numbers of travelers because of the surrounding insecurity, especially along the northern route. Two key individuals in these groups were the caravan entrepreneur and caravan leader. An expedition could easily include 3,000 or more people, including slaves, donkey drivers, and many women and children. In 1827, the explorer Clapperton observed a caravan of 4,000 travelers, including kola and salt merchants as well as pilgrims, between Sokoto and Kano.

Caravan leaders were serious professionals, experts in business, and sure of their itinerary. They also had the skills to determine, through supernatural means, astrology, and prayer, which route to follow and when to leave. The most famous failure was the destruction of a caravan of over 1,000 people, which was attacked as it crossed Bornu at the end of the 1880s.[74]

The two hubs of trade were Salaga and Kano. The former city was the supply center, while the latter specialized in distribution. In about 1850, the two cities each had between 40,000 and 50,000 inhabitants, not counting large numbers of people who were only passing through.

Consumption increased constantly throughout the century. The sultanate's imports climbed from 70 to 140 tons after the jihad, and up to 250–350 tons at the turn of the twentieth century. Asante country was the only producer until around 1880, when the Igbo area between Niger and Benue also began supplying kola nuts via steamboats that could travel up the river.

The kola trade was indeed profitable. In about 1835, before the cowry was hit by inflation, 100 nuts bought for approximately 100 cowries in Asante were worth 600 to 1,000 cowries when they arrived on the Sahelian-Sudanese market. The profit margin was even greater in the last decade of the century, when 100 nuts bought for about 1,000 cowries could be sold for 12,000 to

15,000 cowries, which would have been equivalent to 5,000 cowries in 1835![75] The trip was long, but it was worth the effort as goods were carried in both directions: the Hausa provided the Volta areas with skins and natron, a cheap salt substitute imported from Bornu (at a rate of approximately 200 tons a year at the end of the century). They also exported huge quantities of dried onions, which were used as a spice. Interregional trade in onions remained very active in the twentieth century. Eventually, costly Kano-woven cloth for chiefs, glass beads from Nupe, North African silk, and of course slaves and livestock were all traded.

The virtual monopoly over production enabled the Asante king, who enjoyed an exceptional position and controlled trade in the backcountry of the Gold Coast, to benefit directly from the exchanges. The Asante were also major consumers and exporters of slaves, and provided the biggest market for salt in the area. Trade in kola nuts was completely "nationalized" around 1840, when growth in Sokoto's demand for kola was concurrent with the great expansion of the Asante Empire. The Asante economy was based on a dual monetary system: gold dust and cowries. Gold was reserved for the king and for use in the capital city, which explains the symbolism of the Asantehene's famous golden stool. To the south, gold was also used with Europeans. Cowries were reserved for the northern provinces, which were in direct contact with the Sudanese area, the primary kola nut consumer. The Asante Empire's policy was to maintain a strict separation between the two worlds in order to ensure that the government had exclusive control over trade. Therefore, at the end of the eighteenth century, Muslim traders were prohibited from traveling south of Kumasi, while the Fante of the coast did not have the right to travel farther north than the capital city. In short, Asante policy with respect to Muslims from the north was similar to that of the king of Abomey, who allowed European traders to stay only in the port of Whydah.

There were also political frictions. During a war with Kong in 1819, the Jola of Kumasi (among whom there were about 300 adult men) refused to fight against their fellow Muslims. This increased distrust between the groups, and market towns were gradually established on the border, which caravans from the interior no longer had the right to cross. To the east of Salaga, in Gonja country, which was located outside the kola production area, such towns were set up to prevent any interference. By the end of the 1820s, Hausa caravans were required to stop there. Government agents were responsible for gathering kola nuts from peasants (a few trees sufficed to produce 2,000 nuts), shipping the nuts, and collecting taxes and profit. All the profit went into the king's coffers, and was used to buy slaves for plantations, the army, or gold mining. The system also restricted domestic private enterprise. Asante entrepreneurs had the right to trade only after the government's deals were completed, and they were discouraged from doing so by a tax of twenty-five nuts per load.

The system was finally broken down when the British intervened in Kumasi in 1874. At that point, the weakened Asante government stopped preventing the Hausa from gaining access to the whole country and dealing directly with kola producers. This favored the establishment of a formidable integrated Muslim trade network from north to south and from east to west, though it was unable to resist the colonial borders for long. In the twentieth century, east-west trade movements were replaced by north-south flows, and the Hausa became the livestock suppliers for the major colonial ports on the coast.

Diversification of Trade Networks in Central Africa

At the midpoint of the century, many more gateways into the interior were beginning to appear along the coasts, where trading houses had been setting up posts since the beginning of the slave trade. The primary commercial goal was no longer officially the slave trade, but "legitimate" trade, especially in ivory, but also in palm oil, peanuts, dye wood, lumber, and, after 1870, rubber. This increased the slave trade and use of slaves in the backcountry (even though the slave trade had been in principle prohibited in Douala, which was on the coast, since 1840). The volume of exports was low, and trade was profitable only because European imports were very cheap. Demand increased elephant hunting, which was undertaken by specialists such as the Kele of the Ogooué estuary and the Chokwe in the Congo Basin. The establishment of factories on the coast and, beginning in 1840, the first religious missions in Clarence, Douala, Victoria, Corisco, and Gabon changed the commercial landscape of the backcountry, which was transformed into an integrated economic space that transcended earlier structures.

Thus, the creation of Kribi in southern Cameroon in 1828 led to the establishment of a new trade network in the interior of central and eastern Cameroon, which had until then been protected from the Atlantic commercial web. Some groups moved to claim some of the wealth that could be obtained along the main routes and others fled for fear of being decimated. This resulted in spectacular population movements: in the 1840s the Fang and Ntumu started to move eastward to the coast from the Woleu and Ntem rivers. Along the Ogooué estuary, Mpongwe groups turned into veritable firms, and, despite an apparent status quo, began borrowing from French culture.[76]

Near Douala, internal competition became so strong that in 1845 the king could not prevent the establishment of a Baptist mission invited by one of his rivals. Around 1856, there was so much discord that the leading firms agreed to arbitration by the British Consul in Clarence. In 1877, the Duala chiefs, frightened by the growth of slave associations and the collapse of "native" institutions, eventually asked Queen Victoria to extend British control over the city.[77]

In 1880, two-thirds of the Congo Basin was organized around a network of trade routes that went from post to post, until they reached the coast. The routes required a restructuring of supply lines for trade items and food for traders and troops. Manioc, which can be turned into "loaves" that keep for several months, was the ideal food for travelers and slaves in the forest. However, it requires more work than bananas, and it is complicated to prepare for consumption. At first it was grown only along major routes, but in the eighteenth and especially the nineteenth centuries, it began spreading across all the basins of the Lower Congo, the Ogooué, and the Kasai rivers. It was grown intensively along the Alima River and around Stanley Pool (Malebo Pool).

In the "River Country" at the confluence of the Congo, Sangha, and Likouala rivers, small towns were built, half on land and half in the rivers. For example, Bonga was built at water level, and had, according to reports at the time, several tens of thousands of inhabitants, fishermen, traders, and slaves. They ate manioc, taro root, bananas, and yams produced upstream and brought downstream by an uninterrupted fleet of large canoes filled to the gunnels. Monetary exchange spread the use of small bars of copper (*ngele*) in Tio lands, and of small bars of iron (*bikie*) in Fang and Ntumu lands. The trading houses that were the hubs of the networks became firms based on women's and slaves' work. Slaves were used as paddlers, fish and game suppliers, general laborers, and soldiers in time of war, not to mention as capital that could be used in difficult times and to repay debts. Thus, at Iboko, upstream of the Ubangi confluent, Chief Mata Bwike, who had seventy wives, became the undisputed leader. Closer to the Pool, Mswata was held by Chief Ngobila, who, with only eight other free men, controlled 86 wives and nearly 125 dependents, in other words, a house ten times larger than normal. Sometimes a slave with initiative could succeed his master, as Ngaliema did on the Pool. He received Stanley in Kintamo in 1877. On the left bank, in Fwilu Basin, the greatest upheaval was the creation of the Kuba Kingdom, which began controlling long-distance trade in gold and ivory from northern Angola in 1750.

This all resulted in complex trading markets around the Pool. It was the primary meeting place of convoys from the interior by river (from Ubangi) and by land (across the Bateke Plateau), and of caravans that traveled from the coast (Loango and BaCongo). The markets were held in open spaces between the villages, and were organized by village chiefs, who were trusted by all because of the *Lemba* association. This association originated from a royal healing power cult at Loango and was spread by merchants. It flowed toward the interior, in large part because of portable charms called *nkobi* (which gave their name to the boxes in which they were kept). The spread of *nkobi* strengthened commercial autonomy thanks to a spiritual guarantee, and, between 1840 and 1880, it fostered the autonomy of the major Tio, Likouala, and Upper Ogooué chiefs. The Mbede/Obamba took advantage of the many trade routes to create centralized states at the end of the nineteenth century. They were governed jointly by warlords and peace lords.[78] However, this development was hindered when, in the late 1870s, Brazza and Stanley began, independently, to found the first European settlements: Brazzaville and Leopoldville (Kinshasa). The activity on the rivers, which was described at length by the first explorers in the 1880s, disappeared in the first decade of the twentieth century, swept away by the spread of sleeping sickness.[79]

Slave-based Forms of Protection and Proletarianization: The Case of the Swahili

In East Africa, the change was even more obvious because it was part of colonization of the backcountry, first by Zanzibarites and then by the Indians and Europeans. The economy in the area was even more mixed than in West Africa. It was based on slave trading, ivory hunting, and farming of both subsistence and export crops.

In the first third of the century, the Busaidi dynasty of Oman moved to Zanzibar, and then extended its power over the whole coast until the 1870s.[80] The Omani governors (*maliwali*) hoped to be accepted by the old urban Swahili aristocracy by respecting its privileges and client system. The Omani were not very concerned with local politics, except at Mombasa, where the Shirazi, led by the Mazrui, put up stubborn resistance. Instead, their attention focused mainly on trade organized through the alliance of Zanzibar merchants with Indian financiers. At Pangani after 1860, Arab settlers dominated the city as a result of their vast slave-based sugar cane and coconut plantations, but also owing to their alliance with the Indian businessmen who financed caravan expeditions into the interior. The Swahili were on the defensive, and invented a complex genealogy that emphasized their origins, supposedly inherited from distant *Shirazi* (Persian) ancestors. Indeed, the Shirazi believed it was important to distinguish themselves from the invading urban masses, which were composed of caravan workers and slaves, who spread along the coast and became the majority in the last third of the century. In September, when the caravans arrived, Bagamoyo had up to 10,000 Nyamwezi porters camping in the poor quarters. They were indebted at exorbitant rates of interest to Indian merchants, which put them in their employers' power. In the 1880s, a Zanzibar businessman, Sewa Haji, used that means to gain a monopoly over porter recruitment in Zanzibar and Bagamoyo. This explains the parallel "invention," especially in the central area across from the islands of Zanzibar and

Pemba, of an "African" ("ethnic") people called the *Mijikenda*. The Shirazi patricians differentiated themselves from the Mijikenda through their way of thinking, which was based on Islam, political roles, scholarly discussions, and lifestyle, such as the kind of clothes they wore and the two-story stone houses with terraced roofs in which they lived. There were 200 Shirazi houses in Pangani when the Germans arrived, but in at least a third of the coastal ports there were only one or two near the mosque. The other homes were made of cob and had thatched roofs (*makuti*). In order to maintain their privileges, the Shirazi established strict endogamous rules, but this was a vain attempt since Swahili culture penetrated far into the interior.

In the mid-century, Zanzibarites created caravan storehouses in the back-country. They were controlled by the Omani, such as in the city of Tabora in Unyamwezi country, which was located at the crossroads of routes leading to the north in the direction of the Great Lakes kingdoms, and to the west toward the Upper Congo Basin. Muslims also established stations on Lake Tanganyika, the most famous of which was Ujiji in the 1840s. Around 1870, at the time when warlord Tippu-Tip was well established in Zanzibar and building his slave-trading empire, some of the customs that were supposedly exclusively Muslim had spread into the interior, such as the Swahili language, clothing made from imported cotton cloth, stone houses, and even circumcision, traditional Koranic healing rituals, Koranic schools, and prayer. Far into the interior, chiefs worshipped at the altar of the international economy. For example, a Mandara chief met by a missionary on the slopes of Mount Kilimanjaro in 1885 spoke Swahili fluently, had a house built in the Zanzibar style, and had called his son Meli, from the Swahili word meaning "merchandise imported by steamship" (mail boat). In 1887, Chief Semboja of the Mazinde (who lived more than sixty miles from the coast on the way to the Upper Pangani River) had a house decorated with European curiosities, including a painting of a steam engine.[81] These signs reveal the deep changes that were advancing very far into the interior. In the 1840s, King Ganda developed a fleet of canoes on Lake Victoria, which he eventually dominated. He planned to control the trade routes while imposing his military superiority on his neighbors. His military advantage came from the guns he had acquired through long-distance trade. Canoe construction was imposed on the inhabitants of the Sese islands, who were expediently turned into slaves. These were the beginnings of a complete transformation, which was interrupted later by colonial intervention.[82]

Especially toward the end of the century, the wealth of the slave-trading warlords from the interior gave them the means to ally with the old coastal families that had been ruined by competition from Zanzibar. Ironically, the warlords were sometimes men from the lower classes, former slaves who had escaped from Zanzibar and took part in the ivory and slave trades, in a manner similar to that of the African-Brazilians on the Atlantic coast. Since they were "new men," they used modern means of domination based on the accumulation and redistribution of imported goods, especially weapons and manufactured items. One of the most efficient tools of cultural syncretism was the spread of what had always been practiced on the coast: mixed marriages. On the men's side, this involved widespread use of concubines, and on the women's side, remarriage by widowed or divorced patricians who had thereby acquired some independence, but not enough to get by without a husband's protection.

Social ties were strengthened by changes in working conditions. In the second half of the century, the economy combined slave plantations and proletarianization of caravan workers, porters, elephant hunters, and mercenaries. The whole thing was financed in large part by Indian capital.

The slave population was bigger than ever. Despite the reticence of their masters, for Muslims were not supposed to be slaves, many converted. There were also many varied forms of slave status. As in the west, there were plantation and domestic slaves, but a number of entrepreneurial slaves were also authorized to ply their trades and organize caravan expeditions for their masters.

As the coastal entrepreneurs advanced farther inland, the hunters and porters in the interior were less able to do as they pleased. Nyamwezi caravans arrived at the coast only at the beginning of the nineteenth century. ("Nyamwezi" is from a generic noun meaning "people from the west" that began to be used in a broader sense at the beginning of German colonization; likewise, the Yoruba of Nigeria and Kikuyu of Kenya were in fact "named" by the British.) Increasingly financed by Indian and Omani businessmen, Nyamwezi became a "nation of porters" controlled by Arabs.[83] They were paid by the day or task, and they became proletarianized, even though they were able to maintain some of their traditional collective organization. For example, they elected representatives with special privileges owing to ritual responsibilities. The representatives conveyed their claims with respect to rations, walking time, and the number of rest periods per day. The few who resisted did so violently, such as Mirambo, a Nyamwezi chief who set himself up as a rival of the Arab merchants of Tabora.

Monetarization of the economy became the rule. Most inhabitants were linked with the general economic circuit in one way or another. Even though subsistence farming remained dominant until the end of the century, everyone produced at least a little bit for the local, regional, or even international market: food for city dwellers and caravans, cowries gathered on the beaches and sold to German brokers in Zanzibar, copal resin, mangrove reeds, plantation crops, ivory, and slaves. People from the Shambaa highlands and Zigua plains brought tobacco to the coast. Yao tobacco from the backcountry of Mozambique was highly appreciated in Zanzibar. Sesame seeds, which were introduced only around the middle of the century by French and German merchants via the northern archipelago of Lamu, had become one of Pangani's main exports by 1880. Women brewed beer, dyed cotton cloth, and sold mats made from raw materials that they grew in their fields or bought from Indian merchants. Use of imported raw materials spread. Blacksmiths used iron imported from Europe. Rice from India, which was eaten especially during celebrations, became more popular. At the peak of the slave trade, the most humble farmers participated in the production of a surplus. After 1870, payment in legal tender (Maria Theresa thalers) became the norm on the coast and nearby hinterland. Farther inland, only standard imported goods were accepted as payment. While at the beginning of the century cotton cloth was a symbol of immense prestige, in the latter decades, villagers demanded cloth, beads, and copper wire, not to mention guns.

Even though the dominant cultural model was Swahili, by 1870 and long before colonization, no one entertained any illusions: next to Sultan Bargash, the greatest economic power was the West, led by the British. Indeed, two of the sultan's British advisors were known to all: General Lloyd Matthews and General Consul John Kirk. This trend was fostered by the increase in the price of ivory guaranteed by the West's insatiable demand, while the drop in the price of manufactured goods made the terms of trade look all the more favorable to local entrepreneurs.

The changes in the power relations among the Omani, Swahili, and Nyamwezi can be illustrated by the different ways that social relations in three of the main ports evolved:[84]

- In the center, facing Zanzibar, Bagamoyo was dominated by the Omani. It was the terminus of the primary ivory route from the west, which was jealously guarded by the Nyamwezi of the interior. This created instability in the backcountry. The Swahili no longer intervened except to grant right of way, which was less and less recognized by the Zanzibarites, who were allied with Indian financial backers. This is one of the reasons why, at the end of his reign, Bargash considered transferring his capital not far from there, to Dar es Salaam, where, he thought, Zanzibarite supremacy would protect him from growing British intervention against the slave trade.
- To the north, Pangani controlled the route to Masai country and western Kenya, where Kamba ivory hunters from the interior had been the pioneers. They gradually met with more competition from the Swahili

around 1830, who eventually replaced them in the 1860s. Like the Omani, the Swahili had an advantage over the Kamba: they had access to credit. However, this led to financial mistakes at the end of the century with respect to their rivals in Zanzibar. Credit functioned from the island, through six- to eight-month advances on merchandise. Owing to British opposition, by the 1870s the Swahili could no longer use slaves to pay their debts to Indian creditors.

From 1867 to the conquest, Pangani was second only to Bagamoyo in terms of volume of ivory exported. The other ports were far behind. By the end of the 1870s, its exports doubled, and reached 70,000 pounds in 1885.

The interior routes were complex because ivory was traded for livestock or for handmade goods from the slopes of Kilimanjaro, especially at Taveta. However, the handmade goods were obtained from their producers in exchange for copper wire, cloth, and beads from the coast. Intermediaries then traded the goods with the Masai for their ivory. Taveta never fell under the control of people from the coast as Tabora did, but in contrast played an active role in social and cultural diffusion, in both directions. Even though crossing the Rift was difficult, especially in the dry season when herders could engage in raids, there was frequent contact with the Llooikop, who were Masai refugees who had been rejected by their peers following a defeat and whose herds had been confiscated. The Masai in turn followed the caravan route, and some even came to Pangani to live as slaves or transform themselves into Swahili. Less hierarchical than in Bagamoyo, internal relations thus favored multiethnic contact, especially since it was not unusual for there to be intermarriage in which a new wife was brought to the coast. In the other direction, there are a number of examples of Swahili from Pangani who moved to the backcountry; for example, the ivory broker Fundi Hadj moved to Kilimanjaro. This explains why the notable Kimemeta (famed for being a caravan leader, traditional doctor, and Muslim scholar), whose debts placed him at the sultan's mercy, succeeded in convincing local chief Mandara (and his Masai warrior clients) to support the Shirazi part of the city against the Omani in the political crisis of 1888–89.

- Between the two, at Saadani, the Omani had never managed to impose a governor of their choice given the conjunction of interests between the Swahili and the people of the interior. In 1857, when the explorer W.F.P. Burton crossed it, the city was still nothing more than a village of a few hundred inhabitants. However, the route was favored by the Europeans in the 1870s, and in 1889 the port was competing so strongly with Bagamoyo that the Germans tried to destroy it. One of the reasons for this was that Chief Bwana Heri bin Juma, who had been responsible for Nyamwezi caravans since 1860, had skillfully "shirazicized" himself while still maintaining close links to the backcountry. This enabled him to remain independent from both Zanzibar and the Germans until the very end. He so perfectly symbolizes the cultural merger between the "Arab" (coastal) and "African" (interior) worlds that various sources do not agree on his true origins. Nonetheless, his strong ties with Zigua chiefs and with Mirambo show why this destination was preferred for Nyamwezi caravans. In a way, Bwana Heri incarnated the complexity of social and political relations at the end of the century. He was a proselytizing Muslim, but a friend of missions; favorable to European economic penetration, yet the sworn enemy of the Omani and Germans. In the end, he managed to extricate himself, and to return to Saadani without collaborating. He died peacefully in Zanzibar in 1897.

Modernization of Farm Work: Central Africa

Once it eventually began, which was late in central interior Africa, the change sometimes occurred very quickly. This was the case in (present-day) Zimbabwe when the column of the 196 pioneers of the British South Africa Company took possession of Shonaland in 1890. They were soon joined by the first settlers, adventurers, gold seekers, and farmers. (Every pioneer received 3,000 acres.) There were already 1,000 Whites in 1893, accompanied by missionaries: Jesuits in 1890 and Methodists in 1892. However, the Europeans preferred engaging in mining, trade, logging, and transportation. In 1893, there were only six White farmers in Shonaland. In 1903–4, between 300 and 400 European farmers in the country were farming only 5 percent of the arable land, and produced only 10 percent of market crops.[85] The hut tax was introduced in 1893 and standardized in 1894. It consisted first in seizing the livestock and crops of those who refused to pay, which was one of the major causes of the huge revolt that led, between 1896 and 1897, to the union between the occupiers of Shonaland and their hereditary enemies, the Ndebele.

However, at the same time, the African peasantry rapidly went to work near cities (including the capital city, Livingstone). There were still too few European mines and farms to compete. Missionaries had introduced the use of draft animals in farming. As in the past, farmers were mostly women, but young men were relatively quick to come and to earn the ten shillings of tax. Until World War I, they tried to avoid *chibaro*, in other words, migrant contract labor in mines and worksites, which was still very dangerous. Instead, they sought cash crops. All farm products could be sold. According to travelers' reports, by 1891, there were "native" farms of corn, sorghum, pumpkins, rice, beans, tobacco, and even potatoes. Production began rising steeply again in 1899 when the Boer War created problems in supplying the Rand and Rhodesian mines with European products. It was only after World War I that, because of competition, White settlers managed to paralyze local production.

The First Laborers: Natal and Rand

In contrast, the change was early but uneven in South Africa, where a real working class emerged at the turn of the twentieth century. This resulted from a slow process in which missionaries played an essential role because Christian teaching was based on the Western work ethic and intended to modify the new employees' perception of time. As had been the case in the English Industrial Revolution, the "natives" had to be taken from peasant to industrial time.[86] However, the difference lay in a specific colonial logic that maintained the contrast between master and servant, thereby blocking evolution into a real capitalist society.

The Nguni from the north (Zulu) had difficulty adapting as a result of a mutual misunderstanding. After an initial period of collaboration in a context of apparent equality, they became very reticent to be hired. From the beginning there was a misunderstanding about labor contracts. The Zulu calculated according to lunar months (twenty-eight days), which were disdained by the settlers as "Kaffir months," and during moonless nights (which were sacred), no one would work. However, the Zulu term *ynianga* (lunar month) appeared in the dictionaries prepared by missionaries as the translation for "solar month." It was impossible to get a worker to agree that his monthly salary would be paid three or four days late and that those days would not be paid. Even worse, the words *uNyaka* and *umNyaka* were used indifferently to designate the whole year; the former designates the rainy (planting) season, and the latter the dry season. Settlers thought they were hiring their employees for the whole year, while the employee thought he was hired for the rainy season. The same kind of confusion occurred with respect to the workday, which was understood by the employee to be from sunrise to sunset because evil came out at night. This infuriated the settlers, who demanded an average of ten to twelve hours of work each day in winter, when it was time to harvest the sugar cane.

Modernity first appeared in cities. At the end of the century, when dockers were attracted by night work because it was better paid, Whites began to worry about the elimination of the "natural curfew." This led to the establishment of an official curfew of 9:00 P.M. in Pietermaritzburg in 1871, and in Durban three years later. The laws were on the books until the end of apartheid.[87] Use of electricity on the wharfs of Durban from 1880 on did not make things easier. In 1881, workers began demanding weekends off. In the final third of the century, the demands of Black workers took on modern tones in South Africa. White laborers, though they were influenced by socialism, did not wish to see Black workers accorded status similar to their own. Nonetheless, organized labor was gestating in African mines at the turn of the twentieth century. With a clear delay, analogous processes occurred elsewhere, particularly in Christianized West Africa.[88]

New Social Players: Gender Relations, Urbanization

Gender Relations

Very little is yet known about the evolution of women's status before the twentieth century. Despite some independence, they were generally subject to men's authority. In 1891, a Jesuit father asked Shona Chief Chipanga how many subjects he had. "We do not count the women," answered the chief. He took a handful of dust, let it pass through his fingers, and added, "*This* is a woman." They were considered virtually nonexistent. However, this was not true of all societies. Basing her theory on linguistic analysis, Oyeronke Oyewumi[89] argues rather convincingly that the man-woman differentiation among the Yoruba did not imply that the latter bowed before the former, because differentiation by *gender* was much less clear than that based on *seniority*. Yoruba vocabulary places little or no importance on masculine or feminine: words of authority are neutral. The terms that are translated as "man" and "woman" are rigorously symmetrical: *okunrin* and *obinrin. Rin* designates a human being, and *okun* and *obin* refer strictly to the morphological difference. The worldview, and thus gender relations, was therefore not based on the same presuppositions as those of Western societies, which have been based since the pre-Socratics (Parmenides) on binary and complementary oppositions (full versus empty, white versus black, good versus bad) that imply the superiority of one over the other. The theme is made systematic in the Judeo-Christian myth of creation in which woman is a subsidiary of man. This viewpoint reached its peak precisely at the same time as colonial imperialism, with the Freudian theory about the "lack" of a penis.

The argument is interesting, at least concerning gender relations in societies that were not touched by Islam. Yet, even unconverted animist societies were affected by the missionary ideology, which considered the "natural" inferiority of the woman to be unchallengeable. Undoubtedly, the nineteenth century was a time of major change for women. Monotheist religions, namely Islam, which was on an upsurge, and Christianity, played roles in it.

Nonetheless, a point that is important today with respect to the female condition is difficult to assess before the twentieth century: few sources exist and little research has been done on the nature and evolution of sexual initiation and the progression, or not, of genital mutilation.

Islam and Women

To what extent did the jihads influence women's behavior and behavior toward women? Overall, there was a conservative effect. In Hausaland, some women in the royal family had held eminent political positions in the past. Nevertheless, under the influence of Islam their roles dwindled, as did the sacred roles they played in the ancient religion of possession (*bori*) condemned by the reformers' strict Islam. Toward the end of the eighteenth century, the orthodox movement of Uthman dan Fodio strengthened the claustration of women, even though a tradition reconstructed at the time attributes the custom to a sultan of the sixteenth century. Beforehand, going to the market was one of the favorite pastimes of Hausa women. Even among Fulani herders, women performed many kinds of work, which made sexual segregation impossible. However, Uthman objected to what he called "nudity with women" (in other words, their tendency to wear neither a long robe nor a veil), and to public mixing of men and women for pagan practices, such as dancing. He forbade wives to go to market, to work in the fields, to carry wood, and even to visit relatives, which is highly important in African life, unless they had explicit permission from their husbands, were veiled, and went out at twilight when no one would see them. However, he also deplored the ignorance of women, and encouraged the education of at least his own daughter, Asma. He recommended that women be given a rudimentary education so that they could understand the sacred texts and know their rights. Noblewomen were the losers, but women of the common folk were better protected because the sharia gave them a say with respect to matrimonial compensation, recognized that they had rights over their children, and reserved part of the inheritance for them, including land. So far, no biography of Al Hajj Umar has asked about how he spoke about women; but it is likely that it was from a social conservative viewpoint.

The changes were less clear in Senegambia, where the Wolofs converted massively to Islam only at the end of the century. Some Wolof and Serere women continued to play important political roles, especially the *linguère* (king's mother), guardian of sacred objects, and the king's first wife (the *awa*), who possessed her own slaves and fields. There was also Princess Djembet, who, in 1833 and despite the opposition of the people of Waalo, married the Moorish chief of the Trarza in reaction to the French advance. Her sister, N'Datate Yaala, succeeded her in 1846 and refused to ally with the French.[90]

In contrast, Tukuloor society was Islamized from an early date, and had a patriarchal attitude toward women.

Swahili Women

The imported Islam of the Oman Sultanate had similar influence in Swahili country, making veil wearing and confinement of aristocratic wives systematic. These rules did not apply to common folk (and even less to slaves), as they tended to from the end of the twentieth century. However, at the same time, women's independence increased through a very high divorce rate, especially among the Shirazi. This enabled a woman whose first marriage had been arranged by her family to sometimes choose a new husband, as long as he was Muslim and not a slave, without having to go through the serpentine trials of obtaining authorization from her family. She could also draw closer to her maternal kin through her mother, grandmothers, sisters, and daughters.[91]

Women and Christianity

The missionaries of the nineteenth century were also proponents of social conservatism with respect to women. The customary patriarchy was replaced by that of Western society, in which political and family power belonged to men. The missionaries' vision of African women revealed their misunderstanding of active, apparently independent women who worked in the fields more than men, and whose breasts were naked, always ready to suckle children. Missionaries began by prohibiting their female parishioners from engaging in what they saw as provocation and indecency. They also fought against polygamy, which they considered to be the worst vice of lust. This had local effects, but the impact really began to be felt only at the beginning of mass conversions at the very end of the century.

In South Africa, which was Christianized earlier, religious influence over women was strongest. It was a puritan society that was hard on White women, and even harder on Black women. In the customary societies of tropical Africa, the growth of slave-based production made women's condition worse. In West Africa, they were frequently kidnapped to be used as concubines and to people the harems of emirs and their sons. In central Africa, where the slave trade was in full swing in the second half of the nineteenth century, missionaries recorded women's stories about their precarious and difficult fates. They were used as pack animals and for pleasure, frequently given as security and guarantees for debts, and sold as concubines and laborers by Swahili traders in the east and the Congolese in the west. In this respect, the life of Bwanika, who was born in Luba country at the time of the Katanga warlord Msiri, is a tragic but good example. She was sold (sometimes to the east, sometimes to the west) and married ten times between 1886 and 1911.[92]

Zulu Women

However, even if we ignore the most brutal transformation, women's condition changed in noticeable ways, including in societies that remained rather impermeable to the new religions. A recent study tracks the differentiation of female status among the Zulu back to the time of Shaka. Among the Zulu, social stratification was in accordance with at least three categories: noblewomen, especially royal princesses whose marriages were essential political tools; warriors, some of whom played leadership roles in the military; and lost (or low-status) women. Usually, marriage was a primary means of Zulufication. Women's various forms of influence were all the more important since the society was strongly exogamic, and most women came from elsewhere. The study is based on stories told by mothers to their children, which Henry Callaway gathered systematically in 1850–60.[93] They also reveal the original emergence of women's primary role in divination.[94]

Anlo-Ewe Women of Ghana

A complex evolution was brought to light by an in-depth analysis of the Anlo-Ewe, a people of a little more than 100,000 living on the southeast coast of present-day Ghana. The group is patrilineal, but women used to enjoy relative independence: they cultivated their own fields, which they received from their father or mother, and were involved in the choice of their husbands. However, there was a clear distinction between "natives" and foreigners, who did not worship the same gods, did not perform the same funeral rites, and continued to refer to their place of origin. Most foreigners had come from the west, and had been pushed out after 1679 by the expansion of the Akwamu Kingdom. Under pressure from demographics and the slave trade, the local people, who claimed that their ancestors had settled there earlier, began to create groups that were closed to foreigners. In the nineteenth century, creation myths emerged according to which the local people were the special descendants of five original clans, the "first five." This defensive ethnic construction imposed endogamic marriage, at the expense of women's independence. To these myths was added the invention of a common religion, that of the god Nyigbla (introduced by the "foreign" Dzevi clan), who assembled the gods of the other clans around him on a site in the capital city, Anloga. The religion strengthened Anlo unity owing to the obligation that every major clan dedicate one or two of its girls to the god. Recognition of Anlo identity was accompanied by a hierarchy among the clans. The social differentiation created out of the prosperity stemming from the slave trade favored marriages between cross cousins (marriage of the daughter with the son of her father's sister) in order to preserve family wealth. This was codified in the nineteenth century.

The "strangers" reacted. Some demanded endogamy for their own women; others fabricated a "local" past. For example, the Amlade clan came to be included in the Amlo, even though their membership in the "first five" was contradicted by the total absence, unlike in the cases of the others, of land holdings in the original areas. Recognition of the clan as Amlo was achieved owing to the success of businessmen on the coast, first in the slave trade and then in "legitimate" commerce. For example, Tettega was a rich aggray bead broker of Ada origin who married a slave trader's daughter in the city of Woe in Anlo country. His son, Gbodzo, who was related to the African-Brazilian community, received the sought-after title of Right Wing Commander of the army in 1831–33. This was a sign of a change flowing from new power relations. Clan membership and ethnic seniority were becoming less important than the wealth and political or economic roles of the new notables.

Women were the losers, as their opinions were no longer taken into account. For the strongest among them, the way out was to adhere to religious sects, which freed them from customary constraints. They often volunteered to be dedicated to the god Nyigbla. A little later, many became members of the religion launched around 1847 by a stranger who was the son of an Anlo mother and a mixed-blood Danish father, Elias Quist. The religious association that he created around the Yewe sanctuary also masked his slave trade operations. (At the end of the century, he was one of the wealthiest men in the country.) Eventually, palm oil's success accelerated the social distortion by leading to inflation of matrimonial compensation: in order to escape from marriages planned by their families with rich but old men, young women, protected by their brotherhood, began opting for common law marriage at about the turn of the twentieth century. This reintroduced their right to choose their spouse.

This reconstruction, which is based on some of the players' biographies in the nineteenth century, but also on much conjecture, is plausible. The changes to African societies at the time could not help but influence the evolution of society as a whole, in particular with respect to gender relations.

Mixed-Blood and Creole Women

As in the previous centuries, a few women situated at the crossroads of cultures played preeminent roles. However, their power decreased with the decline of the slave trade and growth of the production economy. Overall, there was a drop in the number of women entrepreneurs, such as the famous *signares* of Saint-Louis. The only ones who maintained their social rank were the ladies in Portuguese colonies, where long-standing cohabitation and the late continuation of the slave trade favored alliances between mixed-blood businesswomen and local aristocrats.

In Mozambique even more than in Angola, the *prazo* system emphasized the role of women, who inherited land and whom one therefore had to marry in order to use the property. Many were of Asian origin, from Gao or Macao. These female masters (*donas*) had equivalents among the Afro-Portuguese *nharas* of Guinea, the great property-owning ladies of São Tomé and Principe, and the ladies (senhoras) of Luanda. Since they generally outlived their husbands, some women accumulated *prazos* and slaves through a series of judicious marriages. Thus, Dona Francisca de Moura e Meneses had her slaves mine for gold, and in 1798 became known as one of the pioneers of expeditions to Kazembe. A late example is Dona Luiza Michaela da Cruz, sister of Antonio da Cruz, alias Bonga. She was the descendant of a famous condottiere from Zambezi, Nicolau da Cruz, who was originally from Siam and had entered into the service of the Portuguese at the end of the eighteenth century. She married four Portuguese military officers one after another, and in 1874 was convicted of twenty-four murders: her victims had been thrown to crocodiles.[95]

The rich *prazeiros* were happy to engage in polygamy, though they sometimes maintained a Jesuit or Dominican chaplain. The result was a mixing of aristocracies in which it was not uncommon for a Portuguese man to marry a chief's daughter. For example, Antonio da Cruz married a descendant of Monomotapa's dynasty. The opposite also occurred: in 1884 at Msiri's court in Garanganze, there was Dona Maria Lino da Fonseca, a mixed-blood woman from Zambezi who had been sold to him when she was twelve years old. These women, situated at the intersection of the patriarchal Portuguese tradition and matrilineal African society, were links between the two cultures.

Urban Changes

In Africa, the modern urban revolution began in the nineteenth century, before colonialism. Cities were created and expanded. They were highly effective centers of cultural mediation between earlier societies and the intrusion of Western modernity, and included coastal agglomerations that had previously been affected by colonization, as well as booming, entirely African, centers.[96]

The former were centers of Creolization that had been established from the time of the first contact with foreigners: Muslims in the east, Christians in the west.

On the east coast, the Swahili cities were very old. However, their configuration changed as they came under the colonial control of Zanzibar and as trade in ivory and slaves grew. Two revealing examples are the old Swahili city of Mombasa, where the Mazrui family aristocracy had completely dominated, and Pangani, across from Zanzibar, which became a major outlet for caravans from the interior. In the nineteenth century, these agglomerations evolved from strongholds of Swahili conservatism to large heterogeneous cities where a vigorous bourgeoisie of merchants and planters rubbed shoulders with the former aristocracy. The cities were peopled mainly by slaves, workers, porters, and others from the interior. In 1865 Bargash, the sultan of Zanzibar, created the port that, over twenty years later, in 1887, the Germans would renovate under the name of Dar es Salaam.

On the coast of southern Africa, especially on the Atlantic side, the old merchant cities held by the Portuguese (Luanda), British (Accra), and French (Saint-Louis) likewise became vectors for penetration of the new Western culture born out of the Industrial Revolution. Since it required many laborers with many different skills, the growth in "legitimate" trade in agricultural and forest products (vegetable oils, gum, dye wood, etc.) turned them from relatively sleepy trading posts into industrious commercial ports. Cities such as Cape Town and Freetown became models of colonization in the early twentieth century.

Saint-Louis of Senegal: The Slave Traders' City

French reoccupation in 1817 marked a clear start to the growth of Saint-Louis. Around the end of the eighteenth century, the city included some 1,500 free Blacks and mixed-blood people (compared with 250 in Goree) and 200 Europeans. Being a "habitant" of Saint-Louis had become a privilege, which, until abolition, included the advantage of not being enslaveable. This differentiated the people of Saint-Louis from those of surrounding villages. The Wolof arrived en masse, attracted by the city's commerce, and the population more than doubled between 1817 and 1830, going from 6,000 (including 600 Europeans) to 13,000. In comparison, the islet of Goree plateaued at 2,500.

Goree had trouble getting past the abolition of the slave trade. It eventually succeeded because of the export of peanuts, which began between 1833 (at Bathurst) and 1841 (in Goree). In 1822, the obstinacy of the Goree merchants won them the right to deal in foreign goods without paying taxes. The island became an official free port in 1852. Trade went from less than 2 million francs in 1840 to over 10 million in 1859. In 1856, Goree surpassed Saint-Louis. Peanuts, rather than slaves or gum, provided the French with the arguments they needed to undertake the conquest of the country.

However, at Saint-Louis, the number of dwellings (*habitations bâties*) counted in the census increased from 500 at the beginning of the century to 1,500, and the number of houses built in the "colonial" style, with a second story, balcony, and verandah, to more than 300. The French had a long tradition of arming Senegalese auxiliaries to defend the city. As at Goree, they appointed a notable "habitant" as mayor. The commercial activity of the colony increased sixfold when the French took over again, and increased from 2 to 12 million francs between 1817 and 1830.

The upper class was composed of French *négociants* (traders) who had increased from four or five to thirty by 1837. They were either on-site representatives of French firms or independent operators, and they controlled capital, imports, and exports. Their control over *guinée* imports gave them a clear advantage with respect to trade on the river. During the same period, the number of Creole "habitants" increased from 40 to 150. They belonged to a number of different categories; retail merchants controlled the Saint-Louis market, and licensed dealers had small shops. Their numbers compensated for the fact that they had little capital. The river was mainly in the hands of traders, who were often of mixed blood and whose status was based on the number of canoes they controlled. The profit they made resulted from differences in the price upstream and downstream, once they subtracted the cost of maintaining their canoes and paying taxes and customs to the Moors. Such charges varied depending on the port, the year, the size of the boat, and the amount of gum traded. The largest traders were in direct contact with France. However, most often, they borrowed their stock of guinées from merchants in Saint-Louis, and reimbursed the loan at the end of the season. Many had slaves working for them. Others hired canoe-men and laptots, whose numbers doubled in the 1830s. Such workers were sometimes independent Africans from Waalo, Kajoor, Futa, or Galam, but many were slaves rented by the leading traders. Between 1823 and 1848, an indentured labor system began, which amounted to binding workers with strict contracts. In the off-season, there were also many independent laptots or *marigotiers*, who were farmers or fishermen who continued their small trade in the labyrinth of waterways nearby. Toward the end of the decade, the livelihoods of about 3,000 people were based in some way on the gum trade and the international commerce of Saint-Louis.

Luanda, a Mixed City

Like Saint-Louis, Luanda was the site of a former colonial city, but its population stabilized in the eighteenth century. Until then, given that there were very few White women, the upper crust was composed of a mixed-blood

Creole aristocracy, and the city was peopled with slaves. In the nineteenth century, with the decline of the slave trade, the Portuguese returned to the forefront as representatives of Western capitalism. They imported Portuguese textiles, foodstuffs, and handmade products, as well as goods manufactured in northern Europe. They were wealthy, but there were few of them. There were only a few hundred at most, but they were still major slave owners. (Between them, they owned 86,000 slaves, of whom 40,000 were women.) They lived around the bourgeois merchant quarter of the lower town, not far from the port, where the major trading houses and service providers were located. Gradually, the Afro-Portuguese, who used to be the leading slave traders, became employees of the Portuguese as clerks in the town and retailers in the interior. They were pushed out of the upper town, where there were still a few beautiful family homes known as *sobrados*. These houses generally had two stories and windows with balconies that were supposed to ensure healthy air. Wealthy mixed-blood widows remained powerful. At least one of them, Dona Ana Joaquima dos Santos e Silva, was a veritable commercial power in the backcountry in the nineteenth century.[97]

Freetown and Colonial Creolization

Freetown, which was originally a colony of former slaves from Great Britain and Nova Scotia, was run by Governor Macarthy from 1814 to 1824. The city benefited from his constructive governance and from the first settlers' land speculation. The city quickly became a cosmopolitan place where the social origin of its inhabitants could be seen in the style of their buildings. Europeans, the first settlers from Nova Scotia, and maroons occupied houses that were built out of stone or rough-hewn beams, and had shingled roofs and sometimes a second floor. In contrast, "liberated slaves," who were the most recent immigrants, worked as peddlers and craftsmen, and lived in cabins of mud brick (*banco*) and bamboo. Between the two extremes, there was every possible variation. The city grew rapidly, going from 400 houses (at most a few thousand inhabitants) in 1796 to 30,000 inhabitants in 1869. About half were Krio, and the rest were considered "natives."[98] The urban culture was forged through the creation of a common language: Krio (a Creole based on English, Portuguese, French, and various Bantu languages). This was necessary because the inhabitants were of many different origins. Krio became a written and published language at the end of the century.[99] At the same time, an original form of urban management was established, and put in the hands of headmen who were appointed by the liberated slaves of their quarter and acknowledged by the British. A municipal council was confirmed in 1893, three years before the whole country became part of the protectorate.

Cape Town, a White City

The formerly colonial city that changed the most in the nineteenth century was Cape Town. At the time the slave trade was abolished (1807), it had almost twice as many slaves as White settlers (9,307 slaves compared with 6,435 free people, of whom only 800 were freed slaves). Most of the slaves were of Indonesian origin. There was still only a very small number of local "Hottentots": just 626, or 4 percent of the population. The city was composed almost entirely of international immigrants and their descendants.

In 1836, emancipation had a remarkable result: within a dozen years, the city came to have a White majority. Since the end of the slave trade, there had been fewer and fewer slaves, and in 1831 there were only 5,800 left. In contrast, the number of free people doubled because the city continued to serve as moorage for poor immigrant sailors from Holland, Germany, and Ireland. The 1840 census found 10,784 Whites compared with 9,304 colored people. At the time, the city was declining, and had been overtaken by Port Elizabeth, which was the major exporter of wool in the eastern province.

The mining boom at the end of the century changed everything. Construction of a railway from Cape Town to Kimberley began in 1860. Soon it was extended to Rhodesia, and the port became the primary market for British interests trading in precious metals. Improvements began on the docks in 1870. Between 1875 and 1904, the number of inhabitants doubled, going from 33,000 to 78,000. At that point, the city was no longer predominantly White because African laborers were flocking to it. However, despite a segregation policy that had become a defensive weapon, until the apartheid era, Cape Town remained the least segregated city in South Africa.

Urban Innovations in the Interior of Africa

In the interior of West Africa, the changes were even clearer. Political transformations and the increase in trade resulted in the establishment, movement, growth, and renewal of many transborder, stopover, and production-based cities, such as Kong, Bobo-Dioulasso, Bouna, Salaga, and Kano. The most dramatic change was the shift of Yoruba cities southward, owing to pressure from the Fulani jihad expansion of Uthman dan Fodio and the attraction of outlets to the Atlantic market. This was the start of the wealth of two refuge cities, Ibadan and Abeokuta, which had, respectively, 60,000 and 100,000 inhabitants at the middle of the century. The former began in 1829 as a military camp that received soldiers from all parts who were fleeing the incessant wars. The latter was the site where many small Egba town dwellers took refuge a few years later. Its growth resulted from the initiative of a colony of Saros, who were former slaves from Sierra Leone. Both cities were typical of the great transition markets where various forms of government met and mingled. While the regimes were based on ancient customs, they were remodeled in accordance with modern economic currents.[100]

The Emergence of Colonial Cities

At the end of the century, African urban centers were ripe for modernization. Whether the cities were already centers for international mining and banking interests, such as Cairo, Cape Town, and Johannesburg, or remained small administrative centers or modest market towns, such as Ouagadougou and Libreville, the cities became the hubs for colonial imperialism and the economic interests of Whites who would soon possess the entire continent. These centers of banking and business, which were focal points for the labor market, played an ongoing role as places of colonization.

This was true of cities in general but not all of them. Modern historians have tended to assume that most cities resulted from the colonizers' will; that ports such as Dakar, Bathurst, Abidjan, Conakry, Cotonou, Port Harcourt, Port Gentil, Dar es Salaam, Beira, and Port Natal (Durban), or strategic hubs such as Johannesburg, Lusaka, Nairobi, Leopoldville, Brazzaville, Fort Lamy (Djamena), Yaounde, and Bamako, were founded by the colonizers from scratch, or at best, built on tiny villages in the heart of areas to be conquered and exploited. This is only partly true. For the most part, Europeans were few and sought expedience, so they used existing centers. What they did change, in line with their expansionist interests, were transportation and export networks. When choosing the African towns that would become the centers of their power, they used criteria such as good location, a dynamic and diverse urban society, and leaders with sway or even power over the surrounding region. Europeans sought cities that met these criteria so that they would be able to graft their operations onto existing structures, thereby saving time and resources.

Colonizers had to choose: they could destroy old cities, or at least neglect them and leave them to collapse so as to eliminate powers that were hindering or overshadowing them, or they could turn the cities to their benefit. The former strategy was relatively unusual. It was a costly solution, both militarily and politically. Yet there were a few examples where this happened more or less quickly: Goree, Abomey, Kilwa, Sofala, Omdurman, Jenne, Timbuktu, Musumba, and most of the former Bantu capitals. Despite everything, the sites rarely disappeared from the map. However, most often colonizers were careful to capture cities ready to change at the right time, those that were strong enough to keep or regain power: Addis-Ababa, Mombasa, Khartoum, Saõ Salvador (Mbanza-Congo), Lagos, Ibadan, Ife, Porto Novo, Kumasi,

Bobo-Dioulasso, and Ouagadougou. Reversing the dominant trend, instead of asking which cities the colonizers *created*, we should instead examine which were *imposed* on colonizers, if only by their prior willingness to collaborate in the new order.

While they had always been vectors of "modernization," cities became synonymous with openness to colonization, in other words, dependency on the West.[101]

Culture and the Arts

Sacred Art

It is well known that in Africa sacred art generally involves wood carving and sometimes copper work. Examples include masks and statues, which can be very large. Such art is difficult to date but clearly very ancient, though works rarely last more than 100 years since the materials do not stand up well over time. However, there is evidence of at least two cases of artistic explosion: the Bakuba and the Luba in central Africa.

Kuba art reflects history, and was closely connected with the growth of the monarchy in the nineteenth century. Like the masses of cowries from Angola, masks were among the prestigious goods that belonged to the monarchy. White clay (kaolin) was used in the highest expressions of sacred objects. Kuba sculpture is characterized by dynastic statues (*ndop*), of which there was probably one per king from the end of the eighteenth century to the civil war prior to the death of King Kot a-Mbweeky II in 1896. The masks, royal drums, and many other objects also inspired thousands of pieces in wood, metal, and clay that are now dispersed in the world's major museums. They show an exceptional variety of forms and more than 200 different decorative styles. In the nineteenth century, the dominant tradition was of anthropomorphic inspiration. In the south, there were mainly small figurines (*nnoon*) that were perhaps used as charms. The Teke on the right bank of the Congo river also sculpted small fetishes, most often male, with a remarkable unity of style in which triangular forms predominated, the faces of figures were decorated with long parallel scars and square beards, and the figures' legs were massive and bent. Some had small boxes in their stomachs containing magical medicine.

Researchers explain that in Luba beliefs there was a link between the body and memory: the former was both the seat and model of the latter.[102] Luba art dates back to the seventeenth century, but the techniques used in the ironwork were maintained until the 1930s, as was the ritual accompanying the casting of royal insignia and symbolic objects of power. Study of the nineteenth century is possible because of notes and photographs taken by the explorer

W.F.P. Burton, and also the archives collected by the Royal Museum for Central Africa in Tervuren, Belgium. Body scarification and arrangements of beads in necklaces were related both to rituals and to mnemonic techniques. One group of objects remains especially enigmatic: *lukasa*, rectangular boards with a slightly concave surface considered to be the interior. The interior of *lukasa* were decorated with iron pins, sometimes holes, and also beads of different sizes and colors. The other side, which was considered to be the outside, was covered with geometrical motifs. *Lukasa* were read and interpreted by "memory men" whose function was ritual preservation of the official history of a lineage, chiefdom, or the royal court. Objects used by Luba diviners, such as bowls in the form of characters, gourds with different contents, and stools of authority, could also be interpreted in this way. All these items were meaningful with respect to Luba oral history, which was maintained until colonization.

Oral Literature, Written Literature

Transmission of oral literature, in other words *orisha* (a term adopted at the Lagos Festival of Arts in 1977 based on a Yoruba religion of the same name), follows rules of design, understanding, and publication that are different from those of written literature. So far only a few specialists have investigated this, and not enough is yet known. The genre mixes sculpture and other visual arts with literature in the proper sense. Songs, dances, and poems crisscross and complete one another in a kind of "total theater" or epic narrative involving religious and celebratory references that are difficult to date. We have very little data on it for the nineteenth century, and we know only that it was a time of reconstruction of myths in response to surrounding changes, especially in jihad country where the past was greatly rethought through the lens of Islam.

However, both north and south of the Sahara, the passage from oral to written was in process for a number of African languages, but not all: some peoples resisted the change. Berber literature remained oral while Swahili had been written since the sixteenth century. In the nineteenth century, Fulani poetry was systematically transcribed into Arabic writing.

Since there were no printing presses, writing remained a skill of a small circle of initiates throughout the continent. It had existed in various forms in North Africa for many years. In the nineteenth century, Arab scholars were notable essentially for their talents as copyists of older texts. Only Egypt, under the energetic influence of Mehemet Ali (who himself learned to write), spread the teaching of writing to the lower classes quickly, within only a few decades. However, in Africa south of the Sahara the changes were sometimes spectacular.

The only "native" writings were in Arabic or, to a much more limited extent, Swahili (then transcribed into Arabic characters). The foundation of education was Koran school, where students learned the alphabet and how to recite the Koran. There had been *madaris* (or *medersa*) in a few Sudanese towns and the main urban centers in North Africa since the Middle Ages. *Madaris* were institutions that trained the *ulama* destined to become scribes, theologians, and magistrates. They learned the exegesis of the Koran, the prophetic tradition, and Muslim law. Students were attracted from afar to some *madaris* in the large cities of North Africa, but also in Timbuktu, Jenne, Katsina, Agades, and even Kankan, an isolated Muslim stronghold in Volta country. The ecological and social conditions of the Sahel, where there were many nomads, lent themselves well to an itinerant system of education, especially since *ulamas* combined their religious mission with long-distance trade. The most audacious spent much of their time on the pilgrimage route, which could last several years and was at the time a feat performed by very few individuals. Sometimes they stopped to teach for a year or two, and disciples also progressed by going from one *madari* to the next as they acquired knowledge.

Teaching was done in more or less the same manner everywhere. The master, sheik, or *malam* would be seated cross-legged on a carpet or sheepskin with a few books and manuscripts at hand. On a tray filled with sand or on the ground, he would trace the appropriate signs with his finger. Seated on mats, the students also studied their books, which they annotated with a pen dipped in a locally made ink based on gum arabic. Education included the master's readings of texts in Arabic, and his comments on them in the local tongue. He would also answer questions from students. Upon completion of a cycle, students received *ihaza*, certificates stating that they had received the teaching transmitted to their master from the latter's master, and so on for many generations. This explains why it was interesting for students to then go elsewhere and study with a more famous scholar. In the nineteenth century, the great Fulani invention was not only to study Arabic, but also to use its alphabet to transcribe popular literature in Pular. The system helped not only to spread Islam, but also to create a network among intellectuals that was diffuse but broad, since the best scholars felt at home from Senegambia to Hausaland, Bornu, and beyond.

In this way, the Fulani aristocracy encouraged a period of intense intellectual activity, attracting students from all areas. At Futa Jallon, African methods for teaching Islam were perfected. They were based on reading the Koran, interpreting it, and studying the basic texts. Arabic characters were used to write Pular, which made it possible for local scholars to transcribe Fulani didactic poetry. Teachers recited the texts in schools, mosques, and village squares, where they were made accessible to women and common folk. This made Fulani literature somewhat popular. However, written literature remained minimal, first because paper was rare, but also because of cultural sociology. At the highest level, scholars copied, translated, and composed religious treatises, and politicians engaged in diplomatic correspondence. For most people, the only texts available were those of local scholars associated with Koranic tablets; they were among the charms and amulets produced by clerics. Writing remained associated with magic.[103]

Uthman dan Fodio, who was the son of an imam and had been raised surrounded by books and precious manuscripts, some of which had been brought from North Africa and Arabia, learned to read and write in Arabic when he was very young. The team that he led to power was remarkably erudite, and produced the works of the movement's golden age. Uthman was a prolific writer, who left behind approximately 100 theological works in Arabic, Pular, and even Hausa. His brother Abdullah was also a poet, who wrote mainly in Hausa. It has even been claimed that it was because the scholars of the movement's first days were killed in combat that it lost its original religious aura and the army was gradually taken over by professionals. Nonetheless, the teaching (including the texts of both Uthman dan Fodio and Al Hajj Umar), based on a rhetorical didactic, was not very inventive when compared with the Arabic originals. Yet, it marked Islamic culture in West Africa and was the primary vector for that culture until fairly recently. Even some women, such as Uthman dan Fodio's daughter, were literate.

The Eastern coast, including the Mozambique Channel, was an area of social and cultural diversity rooted in varied interconnected civilizations. Swahili writing, which had been used since the sixteenth century, especially in the nineteenth century when the Arabs of Oman dominated the region, also gave rise to religious literature, which was abundant but rather conventional. In contrast, oral literature was in full expansion, both in terms of poetry, which was highly valued at all ceremonies, and in terms of popular songs. Research shows the extent of the political messages that were delivered in this way, for example, in about 1895 there was a saying concerning the German conquest to the effect that if a child cries to be given a razor, give him one to play with; the Mrima wanted to play with power, and look what has happened to them.[104]

The rest of the written literature in the nineteenth century was limited. An exceptional but somewhat remarkable example was Njoya, king of the Bamum (in what is now Cameroon). He promoted the invention of a writing under the combined influence of Arabic and European languages at the end of the century. Created by attentive scribes, there were at least three consecutive versions of the alphabet. It was used to record the kingdom's annals, which are still employed today as basic sources of its history.[105]

There are virtually no known texts written in French by Africans in the nineteenth century. However, this does not mean that none exist, for there has been little attempt to find them. There are many texts in Portuguese that have been kept by old Creole families in the cities, and repertories of some of them are in progress.[106] In contrast, texts written in English began to become popular thanks to missionaries and the urban press. At the end of the nineteenth century in the countries under British domination in West Africa, there were a dozen Africans with PhDs, including missionaries, several jurists, a doctor, teachers, and journalists. In other words, African social sciences (which have been studied very little to date) could have surfaced if the colonial ethnographic model had not quickly submerged it. Indeed, in 1938, before E.E. Evans-Pritchard's work on the Nuer (1940), which is wrongly considered the first text on African anthropology, there was a dissertation written by an African, Jomo Kenyatta, and directed by Bronislaw Malinowski.[107] The first newspaper appeared in 1860 in what was to become Nigeria. In the cities, people wrote in both local tongues and English. The first Yoruba-language version of the Yoruba people's history was written by Samuel Johnson, an Anglican priest from Oyo. It was only after his death that his brother adapted it into English based on his notes. The sad story of the manuscript of more than 1,000 pages, the fruit of twenty years of work, completed in 1897, and lost two years later by the British publisher, shows how little interest the missionary's European counterparts had in his great work. A similar instance is the history of the Gold Coast and the Asante written (in English) by the Ghanean pastor C.C. Reindorf, which was published at the author's expense in 1895. Yet both works show the importance of acculturation. Johnson's version of Yoruba history is one of redemption through endurance of suffering. Reindorf, trained by the Basel mission, did not cast doubt on the contributions of Western civilization, but remained rooted in the Creolized culture of the coast. Through his father, he descended from a family that had worked at the Danish counter of Christiansburg (which became Accra), and he was also a modernizing cocoa and coffee plantation owner, though he kept slaves as domestic servants.[108] In South Africa, the first scholars, who were also generally missionaries influenced by the Christian message, published in the Sotho and Zulu languages. It was only later that they were limited to English in the name of universality.

Yoruba bishop Samuel Ajayi Crowther left many writings, as did a number of nationalists, especially those from Sierra Leone because missionary schools had been teaching children there since the beginning of the century. In Liberia in 1857, Edward Blyden (who was from the West Indies) recommended assimilation through evangelization. However, in his work *West African Countries and Peoples*, the Sierra Leonian doctor James Africanus Horton (born in 1835 from a liberated slave of Igbo origin) spread the theory of African independence, arguing that around 1865 the country was further advanced than Liberia had been twenty years earlier. He also contributed to the emergence, in 1868, of the Fante Confederation, and published *Letters on the Political Condition of the Gold Coast* in 1870. With Edward Blyden, he called for the creation of a university, which resulted in the transformation of Fourah Bay School, from which he had graduated in 1855, into a university in 1872. Originally founded in 1816, it had been restructured in 1827 by the Church Missionary Society to train teachers and catechists.[109] In the next generation, members of the elite included the lawyers Mensah Sarbah and Caseley Hayford of Gold Coast. These are only the most well-known members of an elite that worried the British at the end of the century. Many members of this group went to England at various times to argue for their demands.

In Sierra Leone, Krio, a language of communication used by ex-slaves all across the continent, was first written at the end of the century. Early political developments can be seen in the English-language Sierra Leonian press (as well as in Fante country in present-day Ghana). Newspapers also echo popular literature (songs, slogans, poems, and fables), and there is still much data to be mined: in April and June 1888, the *Sierra Leone Weekly News* published two poems in Krio.[110]

The development was similar in South Africa, where three famous educational institutions for Africans were opened in the middle of the century: Lovedale, which dates from 1838 and had eleven African students compared with nine White students (mostly missionaries' children) in 1841; Healdtown, which was founded in the Eastern Cape in 1853; and St. Matthews in Ciskei. In South African schools in the nineteenth century, the number of girls was, surprisingly, higher than the number of boys, which has probably left traces that could allow us to learn more about a still-obscured part of society.[111] New ideas spread across the continent. The flow was accelerated by use of steamships: from 1852, there had been a regular sea link between the Cape and the west coast of Africa, which was also visited regularly by Germans from the east coast.

Since there is no consistent literary corpus, it is a matter of some urgency to examine school archives and the press of the time, which was very lively in some English-speaking areas (for example, in present-day Sierra Leone and Ghana) to find echoes of the developing urban culture, especially in the second half of the century. We should also look for "native" writings in Portuguese, in particular by the women who played such a big role in Creole economic and social life in the formerly colonized cities of Luanda in Angola. Some of those women were able to read and write. At this point, there is only conjecture based on twentieth century written and oral sources, which had certainly been developing for generations.

Obstacles to Science

Scientific and technological advances were clearest in Egypt, where universities were established in the 1820s, in particular the medical and polytechnical schools, with programs designed for undergraduate and high school levels, and for teacher training. Certainly, the shock caused by the 160 young scientists who accompanied Napoleon Bonaparte's *Armée d'Orient* to Egypt was decisive.[112] Nonetheless, except during the short time of the French occupation, European advances in Africa did not initiate *transfer* of modern scientific knowledge. Instead, initially at least, knowledge transfer was a means of countering the expansion. What is fascinating in the Egyptian case is the way imported European skills and technology were adapted and appropriated by the Egyptians. In Egypt, there were not only institutions (universities and learned societies), but also scientists and scientific content, through teaching programs and manuals, notably in mathematics, mechanics, and astronomy.[113] The scientific modernization of Egypt was the fruit of Mehemet Ali's goal for the Egyptian people to take charge of the country's scientific destiny as the government took responsibility for scientific education and updating technology. This explains why, in the second half of the century, teachers, students, manuals, and popular scientific publications were almost exclusively Egyptian. The foundation was a scientific language in Arabic that was carefully developed, despite the opposition of French professors from the 1830s on. The French believed that teaching had to be in French so that students would be able to keep abreast of scientific developments. Yet, throughout the century, thanks to considerable investment in translation, this problem was overcome. The result was the creation of a veritable scientific community, especially after 1850 (around the Helwan Observatory, for example). The history of this teaching corps can be traced back five generations. In the appropriation of new knowledge, a primordial role was played by Egypt's ancient scientific heritage and culture, which had survived despite the relatively low quality of texts taught in the eighteenth and nineteenth centuries. During the period, the weakness of teaching resources was happily eliminated through copying of major authors. Egyptian officials were interested in relating modern science to traditional scientific applications and purposes, and in reconstructing a scientific language integrated into the existing linguistic fabric. This is clear in the case of the mathematical vocabulary, which began to flourish at the same time as the literary renaissance in Arabic.

However, by breaking with the attempt to integrate new knowledge into historical continuity, the British occupation established new relations between science and British history, and between science and Egyptian society.[114] This led to the program of the re-Westernization of modern sciences at the turn of the twentieth century, which was favored by the re-adoption, for political purposes, of arguments in favor of Western languages, especially English.

Celebratory Arts

Celebrations and the accompanying songs and dances in honor of gods and kings, or that mark important events in family life, especially funerals, have played a role in Africa for centuries. This was because for the dominant class, kings, and chiefs, authority went hand in hand with generosity. Patricians counted on their clients, who in turn depended on their patrons' munificence. This explains the relative frequency of celebratory rites in the form of theatrical and musical shows, where the wealth of the powerful was displayed, along with the dependency of their subjects. From the nineteenth century, there are many detailed descriptions of animist and Muslim rites. In the second half of the century, before the collapse caused by European intervention, they reached their climax. Indeed, many cultures peaked at that time, before they rapidly disappeared, or at least lost their independence.

This was the case for royal festivities in slave-trading kingdoms, in particular, the famous annual celebrations (which Europeans called "customs") that were especially lavish for royal funerals in the Dahomey Kingdom at Abomey, in the Asante Kingdom in Kumasi, in the small chiefdoms of the Niger Delta, and probably also in most of the monarchies in the interior.

The system reached its peak around 1850, once the slave trade abolition crisis had been overcome. This was also the time when human sacrifices were most abundant, since slaves could no longer be disposed of on the Atlantic market. In Asante, there were executions for the funerals of the king, his mother, and the kingdom's leading dignitaries, and also for the annual yam festival, a high point of forty days of communion between the people as a whole and the king.[115]

In Dahomey, the major celebrations were both fairs and dynastic ceremonies that strengthened political unity while providing the kingdom with the major share of its revenue. This can be seen from the horrified yet admiring descriptions by contemporary Europeans: Royal military power included up to 10,000 soldiers, economic power took the form of payment of tribute and was displayed in a parade of the king's wealth that lasted several days, and religious power was shown in holy ceremonies that lasted five to six weeks and in sacred human sacrifices that revealed the Dahomian view of the world and the hereafter.[116] As in Asante country, the celebrations peaked around the middle of the nineteenth century, with the sacrifice of several dozen slaves a year, though several hundred or even a thousand could be sacrificed when a king died, not counting his wives, who were buried with him at his funeral.

There were similar rituals in Shirazi country in East Africa. The "five chairs" festival was celebrated with pomp and circumstance south of Pangani, where, surprisingly, the people used the same symbol (a stool) as the Asante to represent power. There were fifteen stools near Tanga, and twelve at Baga-moyo. They made mythical reference to the five, twelve, or fifteen original Shirazi conquerors, who were supposed to have established a kind of loose regional confederation. The chiefs (*majumbe*) collected various taxes, and in exchange distributed wealth and had livestock sacrificed during celebrations in their honor. Every community had a specific set of big drums (*ngompa kuu*), and often also a great horn (*isiwa*) carved from an elephant tusk. At festivities, there were elaborate dances in honor of dignitaries dressed in the finest imported cloth. White symbolized Muslim purity, and magnificent turbans symbolized authority. At lower levels, *akida* chiefs composed dance guilds and associations (*chama*), the purpose of which was to use celebrations to keep the rest of the community under control. In order to move up in the hierarchy, applicants had to pass through costly initiation rites in which they had to demonstrate their generosity. The celebrations were thus an intrinsic part of the power hierarchy.[117]

The celebrations all provided opportunities for dances and *ngoma* (which means both dance and drum) accompanied by poetry recitations and songs with political and social significance. In the second half of the century, urban competitions between rival groups became widespread. Each group defended the colors of its protector by provoking the adversary, which could give rise to problems. Indeed, the purpose of the dances was also to incorporate new immigrants and resolve conflicts caused by social tensions. The same kind of thing can be found in a typical Saint-Louis celebration known as *fanals*, which involves a parade of carts, horsemen, and dancers organized by the different quarters of the city, and has its origin in early acculturation in the seventeenth century. Young urban Africans found ways to express their dis-satisfaction through dance and ritual derision.

However, the nobles sometimes lost control of the festivities. This happened in Pangani in 1888. By chance, the phases of the moon placed two ordinarily distinct celebrations on two consecutive days: the great religious festival of Idd al-hajj, which was very important to Muslim patricians, and the carnival for the new year, which was a popular celebration linked to ancestor worship and female fertility. During the carnival, roles were ritually inversed and Nyam-wezi caravaners flooded into the city. This led to a profusion of competitions through song and dance, and much indulgence in food and drink.

However, the cultural context had changed. Many had been drawn to urban life on the coast, where they moved into increasingly far-flung quarters where housing was precarious. They became clients of local aristocratic houses.

The ideal was to appear as a *mwungwana*, in other words, a gentleman or city dweller, instead of as a yokel from the backcountry. Of course, they suffered from the notables' rejection and xenophobia. It is not surprising that the Nyamwezi of Bagamoyo and Pangani, who were hostile to the Shirazi and Omani aristocracies, were sympathetic to the German intervention of 1888. The cultural expansion had led to revolt.

At the end of the century a number of syncretic processes were under way. Not only had European-manufactured products penetrated more or less everywhere, but political and cultural exchanges had increased in both the Muslim and animist worlds. Christianity, new technology (for example, new weapons), and new political ideas changed the situation. At the same time, African societies had been dispossessed of their internal customs through the colonial constraints that began weighing on them in 1895–1900.

Conclusion

In sub-Saharan Africa, the nineteenth century was the major period for internal slavery and slave trading as well as the century of Muslim political revolutions. While adherence to Christianity was rare in 1900, throughout the nineteenth century, from the time of the Egyptian revolution to colonial imperialism, Western capitalism was clearly infiltrating the entire continent. Almost everywhere in Africa in the second part of the century, political regimes emerged that were in some respect "modern," or at least innovative. It was a century full of change and with a weighty heritage that would later mire societies in the twentieth century.

One thing that is clear from the many case studies described in this work is that the relations and ties between the north and south, and the east and west, were much stronger and well-defined than partial regional histories might lead us to think.

Despite a major difference between North Africa and sub-Saharan Africa—namely the longer history of widespread popular Islam in the north—there were many similarities between the regions north and south of the Sahara. There were analogous social structures based on a complex interplay of hierarchy and kinship, and trade in commodities was beginning to predominate over the slave trade. There was also greater contact and more commercial and cultural exchange than ever before. Rabīh was famous in Egypt and known to Tippu-Tip in the Upper Congo. Population movements, religion (pilgrimages), economics, politics, and cultural exchanges created links between Morocco and the Niger, Senegal and Arabia, the Niger River and Cairo, and the Atlantic Coast and Zanzibar. By contrast, between 1880 and 1940, during the early part of colonial imperialism in the twentieth century, and again during the first twenty years of independence marked by military regimes and one-party systems, people withdrew inside colonial-era borders and virtually all societies regressed in ways that should not be idealized. Indeed, the perverse effects of global changes had made Africa the world leader in slavery for several centuries, culminating in the precolonial nineteenth century, which shaped African social organization and condemned it to lag behind in the "modern" capitalist economy.

All of Africa experienced major change in the nineteenth century. It occurred on the Maghrebian borders to the west and on the coast, in Ethiopia, in the Zanzibar Empire, in the slave-trading heart of central Africa, and in the southern Africa of the internal revolutions of Boer colonialism. A number of varied forms of colonialism predated the ravages of European colonial imperialism, both in East Africa under the domination of the Oman and Zanzibar Sultanate, and in West Africa where competing internal empires sought to predominate. The most backward area was the central-western coast, from present-day Cameroon to Namibia, owing to the maintenance of an international economy largely imposed by the Portuguese (who had strong footholds in Luanda, São Tomé, and Principe) and to a lesser extent by Spanish privileges. Their monopoly over the slave trade was still tolerated at the international level, although it was by then of another era. They managed to keep it more or less alive almost until the end of the century. This explains why the area was scattered with aging, decadent structures that made the people more vulnerable to Western exploitation, which was brutal (especially that of the Germans in Namibia), despite two internal experiments that had been promising but were doomed: the Bakuba in the Congo, and the Bamum in Cameroon.

The upheavals were to transform all African societies. The primary vectors were the expansion of the great monotheist religions and the introduction of capitalist modernity. Social strata became more diverse. Traditional status, which was often extremely hierarchical (based on religious aristocracies, chieftainships, dependencies, and slavery), began to interweave with status gained through rapidly expanding new activities. New economic trends generated caravan leaders, porters, hunters, soldiers, and producers of all sorts of raw materials for export. In both sub-Saharan and North Africa, especially but not only in ports, the changes fostered a new kind of urban life, which was still favored only by a minority but had a determining influence on the environment and cultural change.

The century began and ended with ecological calamities caused by dramatically long periods of drought. At first, African societies succeeded in preserving their independence, and they recovered, at the cost of many political, religious, and economic adaptations, by the middle of the century. However, the people were less resilient half a century later owing to the virtually universal loss of social and economic autonomy and political independence. The summit of horror was probably reached in the Congo Basin where Jan Vansina estimates that, under Leopold's reign, at least half the population was annihilated between 1880 and 1920.[1] For Africans, the century began with severe challenges and ended in ecological, demographic, and political disaster.

Notes

Introduction

1. Iliffe, *Africans: The History of a Continent;* Mbokolo, *L'Afrique noire. Histoire et civilisations.*
2. D'Almeida-Topor, *Les Amazones.*
3. Coquery-Vidrovitch, *The History of African Cities* and *African Women.*
4. Amadiume, *Reinventing Africa,* and Oyewumi, *The Invention of Women.*

1. People and Their Environment: Africa's Climate and Demography

1. Webb, *Desert Frontier,* versus Zeleza, *A Modern Economic History of Africa.*
2. Adanson cited by Webb, *Desert Frontier.*
3. Gallais, *Travaux et documents de Géographie tropicale.*
4. Paul Marty, *Les chroniques de Oualata et de Mema* (Paris: Librairie Orientaliste Paul Geuthner, 1927).
5. Iliffe, *Famine in Zimbabwe,* 1890–1960, 19.
6. Prenant in Lacoste, Nouschi, and Prenant, *L'Algérie: passé et présent,* 390.
7. Eldredge, *A South African Kingdom.*
8. Dias, "Famine and Disease in the History of Angola," 349–98.
9. Wood in Dalby and Harrisson Church, *Droughts in Africa.*
10. Zeleza, *A Modern Economic History of Africa,* vol. 1.
11. Ballard, "Drought and Economic Disaster," 359–78.
12. Iliffe, *Famine in Zimbabwe, 1890–1960,* 17–18.
13. Yacono, "Peut-on évaluer la population de l'Algérie vers 1830?"
14. Zeleza, *A Modern Economic History of Africa,* vol. 1.
15. Vansina, *Paths in the Rainforests,* 307.
16. Forde, *The Role of Trypanasomiasis in African Ecology.*
17. Panzac, "The Population of Egypt in the Nineteenth Century," 11–32.
18. Valensi, *Fellahs tunisiens.*
19. Forde, *The Role of Trypanasomiasis in African Ecology.*
20. Kea, *Settlements, Trade and Polities.*
21. Vansina, *The Children of Woot.*
22. Valensi, *Fellahs tunisiens.*

2. Political and Warlike Islam: The Maghreb and West Africa Before the Colonial Conquest

1. Brett, *The Berbers.*
2. Valensi, *Fellahs tunisiens,* 83 [our translation].
3. Valensi, *Le Maghreb avant la prise d'Alger,* 33–35.
4. Y. Lacoste, A. Nouschi, and A. Prenant, *L'Algérie: passé et présent,* 160 [our translation].
5. Triaud, *La Légende noire de la Sanusiyya.*
6. Valensi, *Le Maghreb avant la prise d'Alger* and *Fellahs tunisiens.*
7. Stora, *Histoire de l'Algérie coloniale.*
8. Y. Lacoste, A. Nouschi, and A. Prenant, *L'Algérie: passé et présent,* 191–95.
9. Cited by Monod, "A propos d'un document concernant la conquête du Soudan," 775–76 [our translation].
10. Caillié, *Travels through Central Africa to Timbuctoo,* 311 [our translation].
11. Cited by Abitbol, *Tombouctou et les Arma,* 157 [our translation].
12. Diata, *The Bamana Empire.*
13. Robinson, *The Holy War of Umar Tal.*
14. Anne Raffenel, *Nouveau voyage dans le pays des Nègres,* vol. 1 (Paris, 1856), 436 [our translation].
15. Ly-Tall, *Un Islam militant en Afrique de l'Ouest au XIXe siècle.*
16. Manchuelle, *Willing Migrants,* chapters 2 and 3.
17. David, *Les navétanes,* 1980.
18. Manchuelle, *Willing Migrants,* 59, 82, 91, 261.
19. Robinson, *The Holy War of Umar Tal.*
20. Klein, *Islam and Imperialism in Senegal*; Barry, *Le Royaume du Waalo* and *Senegambia.*
21. Webb, *Desert Frontier.*
22. Manchuelle, *Willing Migrants.*
23. Webb, *Desert Frontier.*
24. Pommegorge, *Description de la Négrétie.*
25. Webb, *Desert Frontier,* 108.
26. See chapter 6.
27. Webb, *Desert Frontier.,*
28. Vikør, *Sufi and Scholar on the Desert Edge.*
29. Triaud, *La Légende noire de la Sanusiyya,* 1.
30. Vikør, *Sufi and Scholar on the Desert Edge.*
31. Robinson, *The Holy War of Umar Tal.*
32. Sanankoua, *Un empire Peul au XIXe siècle.*
33. Robinson, *The Holy War of Umar Tal.*
34. Hanson, *Migration, Jihad, and Muslim Authority in West Africa.*
35. A.H. Ba and J. Daget, *L'Empire Peul du Macina (1818–1853)* (Paris, 1962).
36. The details of this stay are known from the *Sokoto Chronicle,* which was written at Segu in the early 1860s by an elderly eyewitness.
37. Robinson, *The Holy War of Umar Tal.*
38. Myron Echenberg cited by Klein, *Slavery and Colonial Rule in French West Africa,* 57.
39. Klein, *Islam and Imperialism in Senegal.*
40. Person, *Samori.*

3. Political and Merchant Islam: East Africa

1. Laurens, *L'expédition française d'Égypte* (our translation).

2. Couland, "L'Egypte de Muhammad Ali."

3. Ibid.

4. Fargette, *Méhémet Ali.*

5. Cf. chapter 6.

6. Marcus, *A History of Ethiopia.*

7. Baxter, Hultin, and Triulzi, *Being and Becoming Oromo.*

8. McCann, *People of the Plow.*

9. Quoted by Ronald J. Horvath, "Addis Ababa's Eucalyptus Forest," *Journal of Ethiopian Studies* 10, no. 2 (1968): 19.

10. Cited in Bennet, *Mirambo of Tanzania.*

11. Cf. E. Mbokolo, *L'Afrique noire. Histoire et civilisations,* vol. I, 186–94.

12. Sheriff, *Slaves, Spices, and Ivory in Zanzibar.*

13. Cooper, *Plantation Slavery on the East Coast of Africa.*

14. Glassman, *Feasts and Riots.*

15. Until then, cowries, which are conveniently sized small shells that were generally used as currency by Africans in the Sudan area, had come exclusively from the Maldive Islands.

16. Renault, *Tippo-Tip.*

17. N.R. Bennet, *Mirambo of Tanzania, 1840–1884* (London: Oxford University Press, 1971).

18. Hill and Hogg, *A Black Corps d'Elite.*

19. Hallam, *The Life and Times of Rabih Fadl Allah.*

20. Karrar, *The Sufi Brotherhoods in the Sudan.*

21. Ewald, *Soldiers, Traders and Slaves.*

22. Bjørkelo, *Prelude to the Mahdiyya,* 103.

23. Hallam, *The Life and Times of Rabih Fadl Allah,* 107.

24. Zubair Pasha's career did not end there. He played an important role in preparing the British campaign of 1899 against the Mahdi. In reward, he was authorized to return to the Sudan, where he continued to be consulted by the authorities and finished his life as a gentleman farmer on his former land. He died in 1913. Hallam, *The Life and Times of Rabih Fadl Allah,* 223–24.

25. Hallam, *The Life and Times of Rabih Fadl Allah,* 304.

26. D. Babikir, *L'Empire de Rabah* (Paris, 1950).

4. Animism's Resistance: Openness and Introversion: Central-Western Africa

1. Cf. chapter 7.

2. H. D'Almeida-Topor, *Les Amazones. Une armée de femmes dans l'Afrique précoloniale* (Paris: Rochevignes, 1984); Bay, *Wives of the Leopard: Gender, Politics and Culture in the Kingdom of Dahomey.*

3. Coquery-Vidrovitch, "Le blocus de Whydah et la rivalité franco-anglaise au Dahomey," 373–419.

4. Cf. chapter 6.

5. McCaskie, *State and Society in Pre-colonial Asante.*

6. Gayibor, *Histoire des Togolais.*

7. Cf. chapter 6.

8. E. Mbokolo, *L'Afrique noire: Histoire et civilisations*, vol. 2 (Paris: Nathan Aupelf-UREF, 1992), 136.

9. See the excellent synthesis by Dike in ibid., 132–38.

10. Lloyd, *The Yoruba*; concerning the history of Yoruba cities, see Coquery-Vidrovitch, *The History of African Cities South of the Sahara*, 157–69 and 245–56.

11. Hopkins, "Economic Imperialism in West Africa: Lagos," 580–606.

12. Patterson, *The Northern Gabon Coast to 1875*, 42.

13. Ibid., 49.

14. Tardits, *Le Royaume Bamoum*; Coquery-Vidrovitch, *The History of African Cities South of the Sahara*, 263–66.

15. Muriuki, *History of the Kikuyu 1500–1900*.

16. Spear, *Mountain Farmers*.

17. Vansina, *Paths in the Rainforests*, 97.

18. Vansina, *Paths in the Rainforests*, 175–77.

19. Ibid., 186–92.

20. See Vansina, *The Children of Woot*.

21. Wrigley, *Kingship and the State*.

22. For a detailed discussion of how this evolved, see Mbokolo, *L'Afrique noire*, II: 31–43.

23. Froment in M. Delneuf, J.M. Essomba, and A. Froment, eds., *Sur les traces des Ancêtres. Paléo-Anthropologie en Afrique centrale: un bilan de l'archéologie au Cameroun* (Paris: L'Harmattan, 1999).

24. Reid, "The Ganda on Lake Victoria," 349–63.

25. Cf. chapter 5.

26. Cf. chapter 7.

27. Cf. chapter 1.

28. Harms, *River of Wealth, River of Sorrow*.

29. Miller, *Way of Death*.

30. Vansina, *The Children of Woot*.

31. Cf. chapter 7.

32. Newitt, *A History of Mozambique*.

33. Cf. chapter 5.

5. The Meeting of Cultures: Southern Africa

1. J.D. Omer-Cooper, *The Zulu Aftermath: A Nineteenth Century Revolution in Bantu Africa* (London: Longman, 1966).

2. Cobbing, "The Mfecane as Alibi," 487–519.

3. Hamilton, *The Mfecane Aftermath*.

4. Cf. chapter 7.

5. Parsons, *The Mfecane Aftermath*, 332–35.

6. Cobbing, "The Mfecane as Alibi."

7. Eldredge in Hamilton, *The Mfecane Aftermath*, 159–60 and Hamilton, *Terrific Majesty*.

8. Wilmsen, *Land Filled with Flies*, 92.

9. Gewald in Hamilton, *The Mfecane Aftermath*, 417–36.

10. Omer-Cooper, *The Zulu Aftermath*, 27; Bonner, *Kings, Commoners and Concessionaires*, 24–25.

11. C. Hamilton, ed., *Terrific Majesty.*

12. Eldredge, *A South African Kingdom*; and Perrot, *Les Sotho et les missionaires.*

13. Crais, *White Supremacy and Black Resistance.*

14. Keegan, *Colonial South Africa.*

15. Cited in Crais, *White Supremacy and Black Resistance*, 25.

16. Crais, *White Supremacy and Black Resistance.*

17. Van Onselen, *Studies in the Social and Economic History of the Witwatersrand.*

18. Thompson, *A History of South Africa*, 115.

6. Colonial Intervention

1. See the excellent novel inspired by the African adventures of Mungo Park: T.C. Boyle, *Water Music* (New York: Penguin, 1980).

2. Boahen, *Britain, the Sahara and the Western Sudan.*

3. Newbury, "Northern African Trade in the 19th Century," 233–46; C.W. Newbury, *British Policy Towards West Africa: Select Documents 1875–1914* (Oxford: Clarendon Press, 1971); Law, *From Slave Trade to "Legitimate" Commerce.*

4. Williams, *Capitalism and Slavery*; C. Coquery-Vidrovitch, *L'Afrique et la crise de 1930: 1924–1938: actes du colloque* (Paris: Société française d'histoire d'outre-mer, 1976).

5. For further information on the arms trade, see *Journal of African History* 12, nos. 2 and 4 (1971).

6. Schnapper, *La Politique et le commerce français dans le golfe de Guinée de 1838 à 1871.*

7. Brunschwig, *L'avènement de l'Afrique noire du XIXe siècle à nos jours*, 55–62.

8. Flandrin, *Les Thalers d'argent. Histoire d'une monnaie commune.*

9. Barry, *Le Royaume du Walo.*

10. Too often we tend to overlook the fact that the poem was not written about Africa but during the Spanish-American War of 1898, which gave the Philippines and control over Cuba to the United States.

11. H. Brunschwig, *Le partage de l'Afrique noire* (Paris: Flammarion, 1971) [our translation].

12. Robinson and Gallagher, *Africa and the Victorians.*

13. Newbury, *The Western Slave Coast and Its Rulers.*

14. A. Hochschild, *King Leopold's Ghost: A Story of Greed, Terror and Heroism in Colonial Africa.*

15. Coquery-Vidrovitch, *Le Congo [AEF] au temps des grandes Compagnies concessionaires 1899–1930.*

16. W.O. Henderson, *Studies in German Colonial History*, 11–21; Brunschwig, *L'Expansion allemande outre-mer du XVe siècle à nos jours*, 111–18.

17. Cf. synoptic table of conquests.

18. Manchuelle, *Willing Migrants*, 121.

19. Such as Coquery-Vidrovitch and Goerg, *L'Afrique occidental au temps des Français*; Cain and Hopkins, *British Imperialism: Innovation and Expansion.*

20. Garcia, *Le royaume du Dahomey face à la pénétration coloniale.*

21. For details on the conquests, see Mbokolo, *L'Afrique noire*, II: 255–328.

22. D.C. Ohadike, *The Ekumeku Movement.*

23. Quoted by D.C. Ohadike, *Anioma*, 150.

24. Vansina, *Paths in the Rainforests,* 308.

25. Renault, *Tippo-Tip.*

26. M. Michel, *La Mission Marchand*; Brunschwig, *Brazza explorateur*; Coquery-Vidrovitch, *Brazza et la prise de possession du Congo*, and *Le Congo au temps des grandes Compagnies concessionaires.*

27. M. Newitt, *A History of Mozambique* (Bloomington: Indiana University Press, 1995).

28. Glassman, *Feasts and Riots,* 199–238.

29. Ranger, *Revolt in Southern Rhodesia, 1897.*

30. Cf. Lacoste, Nouschi, and Prenant, *L'Algérie: passé et présent.*

31. Text in Lacoste et al., *L'Algérie: passé et présent*, 256, 257.

32. B. Stora, *Histoire de l'Algérie coloniale, 1830–1954* (Paris: La Découverte, 1991), 19.

33. Ibid., 2 [our translation].

34. Emerit, *L'Algérie au temps d'Abd el-Kader*, 148–49 [our translation].

35. P.J. Louis, *L'émir Abd el Kader, 1808–1883* (Paris: Hachette, 1925), 1950–51.

36. Boahen, *Britain, the Sahara and the Western Sudan 1788–1861.*

37. Rey-Goldzeiguer, *Le Royaume arabe: la politique algérienne de Napoléon III.*

7. The Century's Innovations

1. Cf. chapter 2.

2. L. Valensi, *Le Maghreb avant la prise d'Alger (1790–1830)*, 68.

3. Vansina, *Paths in the Rainforests,* 265–71.

4. du Chaillu, *Voyages et aventures dans l'Afrique équatoriale*, 44–50.

5. Manning, *Slavery and African Life.*

6. Lovejoy, *Transformations in Slavery*, 139.

7. *Journal of African History*, Papers on Firearms, 173–254, 517–78.

8. Meillassoux, *The Anthropology of Slavery*; Memel-Foté, *L'Esclavage dans les sociétés lignagères de la forêt ivoirienne (XVIIe–XXe siècle).*

9. Meillassoux, *The Anthropology of Slavery*, 79–85.

10. Harms in Robertson and Klein, *Women and Slavery in Africa.*

11. Meillassoux, *The Anthropology of Slavery*, 71; Curtin, *Africa Remembered.*

12. Klein, *Slavery and Colonial Rule in French West Africa.*

13. Bouche, *Les Villages de liberté en Afrique noire française.*

14. Ohadike, *Anioma*, 195–97.

15. Lovejoy, *Transformations in Slavery*, 163.

16. Lovejoy in R. Law, ed., *From Slave Trade to "Legitimate" Commerce.*

17. Kea in Law, *From Slave Trade to "Legitimate" Commerce.*

18. Memel-Foté, *L'Esclavage dans les sociétés lignagères de la forêt ivoirienne.*

19. Cf. supra.

20. Falola and Lovejoy, *Pawnship in Africa.*

21. Ohadike, *Anioma*, 186.

22. Lovejoy, *Transformations in Slavery*, 173–75.

23. Cf. chapter 4.

24. K.D. Patterson, *The Northern Gabon Coast to 1875* (Oxford: Clarendon Press, 1975), 53.

25. Vansina, *The Children of Woot.*

26. Ibrahima Thioub, *AOF: Réalités et héritages: sociétés ouest-africaines et ordre* (Senegal: Direction des archives du Sénégal, 1997).

27. Quoted by Mbokolo, *Le Monde Diplomatique*, April 1998 [our translation].

28. Lovejoy, *Transformations in Slavery*, 183.

29. Klein, *Slavery and Colonial Rule in French West Africa*, 102.

30. D. Bouche, *Les Villages de liberté en Afrique noire française (1887–1910)* (Paris/The Hague: Mouton, 1968); Klein, *Slavery and Colonial Rule in French West Africa.*

31. Manchuelle, *Willing Migrants*, 32–37.

32. Klein in Robertson and Klein, *Women and Slavery in Africa*, 85.

33. Tables in Klein, *Slavery and Colonial Rule in French West Africa*, 252–56.

34. Works, *Pilgrims in a Strange Land*, cited by Lovejoy, *Caravan of Kola.*

35. Boutillier, *Bouna, royaume de la savane ivoirienne.*

36. Meillassoux, "Le commerce précolonial et le développement de l'esclavage à Gumbu du Sahel," 182–89.

37. Denham, Clapperton, and Oudney, *Narrative of Travels and Discoveries in Northern and Central Africa.*

38. Cordell, *Dar al-Kuti and the Last Years of the Trans-Saharan Trade.*

39. Dampierre, *Un royaume Bandia du Haut-Oubangui.*

40. Gide, *Voyage au Congo* [our translation].

41. Renault, *Tippo-Tip.*

42. Meillassoux, *The Anthropology of Slavery.*

43. Vansina, *Paths in the Rainforests*; and Médard and Doyle, *Slavery in the Great Lakes Region.*

44. Augé, *Le Rivage alladian*; Terray, *Une histoire du royaume Abron*; Perrot, *Les Ani-Ndenye et le pouvoir.*

45. Gray and Birmingham, *Pre-colonial African Trade*, 175–201.

46. Clarence-Smith, *Slaves, Peasants and Capitalists in Southern Angola.*

47. Lovejoy, *Caravan of Kola*, 224.

48. F. Cooper, *Plantation Slavery on the East Coast of Africa* (New Haven: Yale University Press, 1977), 81–97.

49. Isaacman, *The Tradition of Resistance in Mozambique.*

50. Lovejoy, *Caravan of Kola*, 240.

51. Sanneh, *West African Christianity*, 130.

52. Peel, *Religious Encounter and the Making of the Yoruba.*

53. Ohadike, *Anioma*, 106.

54. H.H. Johnston to the BSAC, July 17, 1890, cited by Oliver, *The Missionary Factor in East*, 128.

55. Oliver, *The Missionary Factor in East Africa.*

56. Ibid.

57. Rotberg, *Christian Missionaries and the Creation of Northern Rhodesia.*

58. Perrot, *Les Sotho et les missionnaires européens*; E.A. Eldredge, *A South African Kingdom.*

59. Landau, *The Realm of the World.*

60. Etherington, *Preachers, Peasants and Politics in Southeast Africa*, 43.

61. Schofeleers, *The Interaction of the M'Bona Cult and Christianity, 1859–1963.*

62. Etherington, *Preachers, Peasants and Politics in Southeast Africa.*

63. Ibid., 97.

64. Ibid., 179.

65. Sundkler, *Zulu Zion and Some Swazi Zionists*.

66. See chapters 5 and 6.

67. A. Hopkins, "Economic Imperialism in West Africa: Lagos, 1880–1892," *Economic History Review* 21, no. 3 (1968), 580–606.

68. Martin, *Palm Oil and Protest*.

69. Ohadike, *The Ekumeku Movement* and *Anioma*.

70. Ohadike, *Anioma*, 184.

71. Martin, *Palm Oil and Protest*.

72. Hopkins, "Economic Imperialism in West Africa," 580–606.

73. O. Goerg, *Commerce et colonisation en Guinée 1850–1913* (Paris: L'Harmattan, 1986).

74. Lovejoy, *Caravan of Kola*, 102.

75. Ibid., 118–20.

76. Mbokolo, *Noirs et Blancs en Afrique équatoriale*.

77. Vansina, *Paths in the Rainforests*, 303–4.

78. Ibid., 290–97.

79. Sautter, *De l'Atlantique au fleuve Congo*; Coquery-Vidrovitch, *Brazza et la prise possession du Congo*.

80. See chapter 3.

81. Glassman, *Feasts and Riots*, 50.

82. R. Reid, "The Ganda on Lake Victoria: A Nineteenth Century East Africa Imperialism," *Journal of African History* 39, no. 3 (1998): 349–64.

83. Sheriff, *Slaves, Spices and Ivory*.

84. Glassman, *Feasts and Riots*; Burton, *The Urban Experience in Eastern Africa*.

85. Schmidt, *Peasants, Traders and Wives*, 65.

86. Thompson, "Time, Work-discipline, and Industrial Capitalism," 56–97.

87. Atkins, *The Moon Is Dead!*

88. Coquery-Vidrovitch, *Africa: Endurance and Change South of the Sahara*, chapters 10–12.

89. O. Oyewumi, *The Invention of Women: Making an African Sense of Western Gender Discourse* (Minneapolis: University of Minnesota Press, 1997).

90. B. Barry, *Le Royaume du Walo: le Sénégal avant la conquête* (Paris: Karthala, 1985).

91. John Middleton, *The World of the Swahili: An African Mercantile Civilization* (Cambridge: Yale University Press, 1992).

92. Wright, *Strategies of Slaves and Women*.

93. Callaway, *Nursery Tales, Traditions, and Histories of the Zulus, in Their Own Words*.

94. Hanretta, "Women, Marginality and the Zulu State," 389–415.

95. M. Newitt, *A History of Mozambique* (Bloomington: Indiana University Press, 1995), 230–31.

96. Cf. C. Coquery-Vidrovitch, *The History of African Cities South of the Sahara*, 217–324.

97. Miller, *Way of Death*; Stamm, "La société créole à Saint-Paul de Loanda," 578–610.

98. Kandé, *Terres, urbanisms et architectures "creoles" en Sierra Leone*.

99. Goerg, *Pouvoir colonial, municipalités et espaces urbains*.

100. Coquery-Vidrovitch, *The History of African Cities South of the Sahara,* 252–64.

101. Ibid., 329–30.

102. Roberts and Allen, *Memory: Luba Art.*

103. Goody, *The Interface between the Written and the Oral.*

104. Glassman, 1994.

105. Tardits, *Le Royaume Bamoum.*

106. Madeira, *Les Lumieres en Afrique* (for the sixteenth to the eighteenth centuries).

107. Jewsiewicki, *Cambridge History of Sciences,* forthcoming.

108. Jenkins, *The Recovery of the West African Past.*

109. Nwauwa, "Far Ahead of His Time," 107–22.

110. Goerg, *Pouvoir coloniel, municipalités et espaces urbains.*

111. Coquery-Vidrovitch, *African Women: A Modern History,* 234–39.

112. Laissus, *Il y a 200 ans, les savants en Égypte.*

113. P. Crozet, "A propos de l'enseignement scientifique en Egypte," 69–99; Crozet, "Langue scientifique et fait national," 259–84.

114. Crozet, *op. cit.*

115. Terray, "Le pouvoir, le sang et la mort," 549–62; McCaskie, *State and Society in Pre-colonial Asante.*

116. Coquery-Vidrovitch, "La fête des Coutumes au Dahomey," 696–716.

117. Glassman, *Feasts and Riots,* 153–74.

Conclusion

1. Hochschild, *King Leopold's Ghost.*

Bibliography

This bibliography is not at all exhaustive. It includes only (but not all) works actually used in the book and rather focuses on recent publications (revised edition, given the fact that the French edition was published in 1999). I assume that the reader is already familiar with older classics and basic manuals; they are not included here unless specifically mentioned in the text. I have organized the bibliography by theme and region in an attempt to follow the structure of the book. The reader may thus have to consult more than one category.

Themes

General Works

Ajayi, A. and M. Crowder. 1985. *Historical Atlas of Africa*. Cambridge: Cambridge University Press.

Coquery-Vidrovitch. 1988. *Africa. Endurance and Change South of the Sahara*. Trans. David Maisel. Berkeley and Los Angeles: University of California Press. Originally published in French as *Afrique noire. Permanences et Ruptures*. Paris: Payot, 1985.

Coquery-Vidrovitch, C. and O. Goerg, eds. 1992. *L'Afrique occidentale au temps des Français: Colonisateurs et colonisés c. 1860–1960*. Paris: La Découverte.

Coquery-Vidrovitch, C. and H. Moniot. 1974. *L'Afrique noire de 1800 à nos jours*. 5th revised ed. 2005. Paris: PUF.

Delneuf, M., J.M. Essomba and A. Froment, eds. 1999. *Sur les traces des Ancêtres. Paléo-Anthropologie en Afrique centrale: un bilan de l'archéologie au Cameroun*. Paris: L'Harmattan.

Iliffe, J. 1995. *Africans: The History of a Continent*. Cambridge: Cambridge University Press.

Mbokolo, E. 1992 and 1995. *L'Afrique noire. Histoire et civilisations*. 2 vols. Paris: Nathan Aupelf-UREF.

Parker, J. and R. Rathbone. 2007. *African History: A Very Short Introduction*. London: Oxford University Press.

Shillington, K. 1995. *History of Africa*. Revised ed. New York: St. Martin's Press.

Christianity

Bhebe, N. 1979. *Christianity and Traditional Religion in Western Zimbabwe 1859–1923.* London: Longman.

Chadwick, H.O. 1994. *The Oxford History of the Christian Church. The Church in Africa 1450–1950.* London: Oxford University Press.

Chidester, D. 1992. *Religions of South Africa.* London: Routledge.

Clarke, P.B. 1986. *West Africa and Christianity.* London: Edward Arnold Ltd.

Elphick, R. and R. Davenport, eds. 1998. *Christianity in South Africa. A Political, Social, and Cultural History.* Berkeley: University of California Press.

Etherington, N. 1978. *Preachers, Peasants and Politics in Southeast Africa, 1835–1880, African Christian Communities in Natal, Pondoland and Zululand.* London: Royal Historical Society.

Falola, T. and B. Adediran, eds. 1983. *Islam and Christianity in West Africa.* Ile-Ife: University of Ife Press.

Faure, J. 1978. *Histoire des missions et églises protestantes en Afrique occidentale des origines à 1884.* Yaoundé: Editions Clé.

Kalu, O.U., ed. 1980. *The History of Christianity in West Africa.* London/New York: Longman.

Landau, P.S. 1995. *The Realm of the World: Language, Gender, and Christianity in a Southern African Kingdom.* London: James Currey.

Oliver, R. 1952. *The Missionary Factor in East Africa.* London: Longman.

Peel, J.D. 2000. *Religious encounter and the making of the Yoruba.* Bloomington: Indiana University Press.

Perrot, C.H. 1970. *Les Sotho et les missionnaires européens au XIXe siècle.* Series F. Annales. Abidjan: University of Abidjan.

Picciola, A. 1987. *Missionnaires en Afrique 1840/1940.* Paris: Denoël.

Ranger, T.O. 1975. *Themes in the Christian History of Central Africa.* Berkeley: University of California Press.

Rotberg, R.I. 1965. *Christian Missionaries and the Creation of Northern Rhodesia 1880–1924.* Princeton, NJ: Princeton University Press.

Sales, J.M. 1971. *The Planting of the Churches in South Africa.* Grand Rapids: William B. Eerdmans Publishing Co.

Salvaing, B. 1995. *Les Missionnaires à la rencontre de l'Afrique au XIXe siècle (Côte des Esclaves et pays Yoruba, 1840–1891).* Paris: L'Harmattan.

Sanneh, L. 1983. *West African Christianity. The Religious Impact.* London: Hurst and Co.

Schoffeleers, M. 1975. "The Interaction of the MBona Cult and Christianity, 1859–1963." In T.O. Ranger and J. Weller, eds. *Themes in the Christian History of Central Africa.* Berkeley: University of California Press: 14–29.

Spear, T. and N. Kimambo Isaria. 1999. *Eastern African Expressions of Christianity.* Athens: Ohio University Press.

Sundkler, B. 1976. *Zulu Zion and Some Swazi Zionists.* London: Oxford University Press.

Sundkler, B. and Steed, C. 2000. *A History of the Church in Africa.* Cambridge: Cambridge University Press.

Colonization

Conklin, A.L. 1997. *A Mission to Civilize. The Republican Idea of Empire in France and West Africa, 1895–1939*. Stanford: Stanford University Press.

Crowe, S.E. 1942. *The Berlin West African Conference, 1884–1885*. London: Longman.

Boahen, A.A. 1964. *Britain, the Sahara and the Western Sudan 1788–1861*. London: Oxford University Press.

Brunschwig, H. 1957. *L'Expansion allemande outre-mer du XVe siècle à nos jours*. Paris: PUF.

———. 1963. *L'avènement de l'Afrique noire du XIXe siècle à nos jours*. Paris: Armand Colin.

———. 1966. *Brazza explorateur. L'Ogooué 1875–1879*. Paris/The Hague: Mouton.

———. 1971. *Le partage de l'Afrique noire*. Paris: Flammarion.

Caillié, R. 1830. *Travels through Central Africa to Timbuctoo, and Across the Great Desert, to Morocco, Performed in the Years 1824–1828*. London: Henry Colburn and Richard Bentley (reprint 1992. London: Darf) (translated from 1829. *Journal d'un voyage à Temboctou et à Jenné, dans l'Afrique centrale*).

Cain, P.J. and A.G. Hopkins. 1993. *British Imperialism: Innovation and Expansion 1688–1914*. London: Longman.

Coquery-Vidrovitch, C. 1962. "Le blocus de Whydah et la rivalité franco-anglaise au Dahomey." In *Cahiers d'Etudes Africaines* 2, no. 7: 373–419.

———. 1966. *Brazza et la prise de possession du Congo. La Mission de l'Ouest africain, 1883–1885*. Paris/The Hague: Mouton.

———. 1972. *Le Congo [AEF] au temps des grandes Compagnies concessionaires 1899–1930*. Paris/The Hague: Mouton.

———. 1976. "La mise en dépendance de l'Afrique noire, 1800–1970." In *Cahiers d'Etudes Africaines* XVI, nos. 1–2 (61–62): 7–58.

Crais, C.C. 1992. *White Supremacy and Black Resistance in Precolonial South Africa*. Cambridge: Cambridge University Press.

Garcia, L. 1988. *Le royaume du Dahomey face à la pénétration coloniale. Affrontements et incompréhension (1875–1894)*. Paris: Karthala.

Gide, A. 1927. *Voyage au Congo. Carnets de route*. Paris: Gallimard.

Henderson, W.O. 1962. *Studies in German Colonial History*. London: Frank Cass & Co.

Hochschild, A. 1998. *King Leopold's Ghost: A Story of Greed, Terror and Heroism in Colonial Africa*. Boston: Houghton Mifflin.

Hopkins, A. 1968. "Economic Imperialism in West Africa: Lagos, 1880–1892." In *Economic History Review* 21, no. 3: 580–606.

Isaacman, A. 1976. *The Tradition of Resistance in Mozambique: Anti-Colonial Activity in the Zambezi Valley 1850–1921*. London: Heinemann.

Michel, M. 1972. *La Mission Marchand, 1895–1899*. Paris/The Hague: Mouton.

Miège, J.L. 1968. *L'Impérialisme colonial italien de 1870 à nos jours*. Paris: Société d'Édition de l'Enseignement supérieur.

Monod, T. 1964. "À propos d'un document concernant la conquête du Soudan [Rapport d'un résident français à Rabat, 1798]." In *Bulletin des Séances de l'Académie royale des Sciences d'Outre-mer* X (3–4): 775–6.

Northrop, D. 2002. *Africa's Discovery of Europe 1450–1850.* New York: Oxford University Press.

Ohadike, D.C. 1991. *The Ekumeku Movement. Western Igbo Resistance to the British Conquest of Nigeria, 1883–1914.* Athens: Ohio University Press.

Price, R. 2009. *Making Empire: Colonial Encounters and the Creation of Imperial Rule in Nineteenth-Century Africa.* Cambridge: Cambridge University Press.

Robinson, R. and J. Gallagher. 1967. *Africa and the Victorians.* London: Macmillan.

Schnapper, B. 1961. *La Politique et le commerce français dans le golfe de Guinée de 1838 à 1871.* Paris/The Hague: Mouton.

Stoecker, H., ed. 1986. *German Imperialism in Africa. From the Beginnings until the Second World War.* London: C. Hurst and Co.

Williams, E. 1944. *Capitalism and Slavery.* Chapel Hill: University of North Carolina Press.

Culture and Society

Amadiume, I. 1997. *Reinventing Africa. Matriarchy, Religion and Culture.* London: Zed Books Ltd.

Berger L. & White F. 1999. *Women in Sub-Saharan Africa. Restoring Women to History.* Bloomington: Indiana University Press

Coquery-Vidrovitch, C. 1997. *African Women: A Modern History.* Trans. B.G. Raps. Boulder: Westview Press. Originally published in French as *Les Africaines. Histoire des femmes d'Afrique noire du XIXe au XX siècle.* Paris: Desjonquères, 1994.

———. 2005. *The History of African Cities South of the Sahara.* Trans. M. Baker. Princeton: Marcus Wiener Publishers. Originally published in French as *Histoire des villes d'Afrique noire des origine à la colonisation.* Paris: Albin Michel, 1993.

D'Almeida-Topor, H. 1984. *Les Amazones. Une armée de femmes dans l'Afrique précoloniale.* Paris: Rochevignes.

Feierman S. 1990. *Peasants Intellectuals.* Madison: University of Wisconsin Press.

Goody, J. 1993. *The Interface between the Written and the Oral.* New York: Cambridge University Press.

Hodgson, D.L., ed. 2000. *Rethinking Pastoralism in Africa: Gender, Culture and the Myth of the Patriarchal Pastoralist.* Oxford: James Currey.

Jenkins, P., ed. 1998. *The Recovery of the West African Past. African Pastors and African History in the Nineteenth Century: C.C. Reindorf and Samuel Johnson.* Basel: Basler Afrika Bibliographien.

Madeira, C. Forthcoming. *Les lumieres en Afrique.* Paris: Ed. de l'EHESS.

Nwauwa, A.O. 1999. "Far Ahead of His Time: James Africanus Horton's Initiatives for a West African University and His Frustrations, 1862–1871." In *Cahiers d'Etudes africaines,* 39, no. 1, 153: 107–22.

Oyewumi, O. 1997. *The Invention of Women: Making an African Sense of Western Gender Discourse.* Minneapolis/London: University of Minnesota Press.

Parsons, N. 1998. *King Khama, Emperor Joe, and the Great White Queen. Victorian Britain through African Eyes.* London: University of Chicago Press.

Roberts, M.N. and F. Allen. 1996. *Memory. Luba Art and the Making of History.* New York: Museum for African Art.

Robertson, K. and M.A. Klein. 1983. *Women and Slavery in Africa.* Madison: University of Wisconsin Press.

Schildkrout, E. and K. Curtis, eds. 1998. *The Scramble for Art in Central Africa.* Cambridge: Cambridge University Press.

Schmidt, E. 1992. *Peasants, Traders and Wives: Shona Women in the History of Zimbabwe, 1870–1939.* Portsmouth: Heinemann.

Stamm, A. 1972. "La société créole à Saint-Paul de Loanda dans les années 1836–1848." In *Revue française d'Histoire d'Outre-mer* 59, no. 213: 578–610.

Ecology

Ballard, C. 1986. "Drought and Economic Disaster: South Africa in the 1880s." In *Journal of Interdisciplinary History* 27: 359–78.

Coquery-Vidrovitch, C. 1996. "Ecologie et Histoire en Afrique noire." In *Sociétés Africaines et Diaspora* 1, no. 1: 103–28.

Dalby, D. and R.J. Harrisson Church, eds. 1974. *Droughts in Africa.* London: International African Institute.

Dias, J.R. 1981. "Famine and Disease in the History of Angola, c. 1830–1930." In *Journal of African History* 21, no. 3: 349–98.

Forde, J. 1971. *The Role of Trypanasomiasis in African Ecology.* London: Oxford University Press.

Gado, A.B. 1993. *Une histoire des famines au Sahel. Etude des grandes crises alimentaires (XIXe-XXe siècles).* Paris: L'Harmattan.

Gallais, J., ed. 1977. *Travaux et documents de Géographie tropicale.* No. 30. Bordeaux/Paris: CEGET/CNRS.

Iliffe, J. 1990. *Famine in Zimbabwe, 1890–1960.* Gweru: Mambo Press.

Webb, J.L.A. 1995. *Desert Frontier. Ecological and Economic Change along the Western Sahel 1600–1850.* Madison: University of Wisconsin Press.

Yacono, X. 1954. "Peut-on évaluer la population de l'Algérie vers 1830?" In *Revue Africaine,* 3rd quarter.

Economy

Atkins, K.E. 1993. *The Moon Is Dead! Give Us Our Money! The Cultural Origins of an African Work Ethic, Natal, South Africa, 1843–1900.* London: James Currey.

Curtin, P.D. 1975. *Economic Change in Precolonial Africa. Senegambia in the Era of the Slave Trade.* 2 vols. Madison: University of Wisconsin Press.

Flandrin, P. 1997. *Les Thalers d'argent. Histoire d'une monnaie commune.* Paris: Editions du Félin.

Goerg, O. 1986. *Commerce et colonisation en Guinée 1850–1913.* Paris: L'Harmattan.

Gray, R. and D. Birmingham. 1970. *Pre-colonial African Trade: Essays on Trade in Central and Eastern Africa before 1900.* London: Oxford University Press.

Harries, P. 1994. *Work, Culture and Identity. Migrant Laborers in Mozambique and South Africa, c. 1860–1910.* London: James Currey.

Journal of African History, eds. 1971. "Papers on Firearms in Sub-Saharan Africa, I & II." In *Journal of African History* 12, no. 2: 173–254; no. 4: 517–78.

Kea, R.J.A. 1982. *Settlements, Trade and Polities in the 17th Century Gold Coast.* Baltimore: Johns Hopkins University Press.

Kriger, C. 1998. *Pride of Men: Ironworking in 19th Century West Central Africa.* Westport: Heinemann.

Law, R., ed. 1995. *From Slave Trade to "Legitimate" Commerce: The Commercial Transition in Nineteenth-Century West Africa.* Cambridge: Cambridge University Press.

Lovejoy, P. 1980. *Caravan of Kola: The Hausa Kola Trade, 1700–1900.* Zaria: Ahmadu Bello University Press.

Manchuelle, F. 1997. *Willing Migrants: Soninke Labor Diasporas, 1848–1960.* Athens: Ohio University Press.

Martin, S. 1988. *Palm Oil and Protest: An Economic History of the Ngwa Region, South-eastern Nigeria, 1880–1980.* Cambridge: Cambridge University Press.

Meillassoux, 1969. "Le commerce précolonial et le développement de l'esclavage à Gumbu du Sahel." In *The Development of Indigenous Trade and Markets in West Africa.* London: I.A.I. and Oxford University Press.

Newbury, C.W. 1966. "Northern African Trade in the 19th Century." In *Journal of African History* 7, no. 2: 233–46.

Reid, R. 1998. "The Ganda on Lake Victoria: A Nineteenth Century East Africa Imperialism." In *Journal of African History* 39, no. 3: 349–64.

Thompson, E.P. 1967. "Time, Work-discipline, and Industrial Capitalism." In *Past and Present* 38: 56–97.

Zeleza, P.T. 1993. *A Modern Economic History of Africa.* Vol. 1, *The Nineteenth Century.* Dakar/Oxford: CODESRIA.

Slavery

Bouche, D. 1968. *Les Villages de liberté en Afrique noire française (1887–1910).* Paris/The Hague: Mouton.

Campbell, G., Miers, S., & Miller, J.C. 2007. *Women and Slavery.* Vol. 1, *Africa, the Indian Ocean, and the Medieval North Atlantic.* Athens: Ohio University Press.

Cordell, D.D. 1984. *Dar al-Kuti and the Last Years of the Trans-Saharan Trade.* Madison: University of Wisconsin Press.

Curtin, P. 1968. *Africa Remembered: Narratives by West Africans from the Era of the Slave Trade.* Madison: University of Wisconsin Press.

Ewald, J.J. 1990. *Soldiers, Traders and Slaves: State Formation and Economic Transformation in the Greater Nile Valley, 1700–1885.* Madison: University of Wisconsin Press.

Falola, T. and P. Lovejoy, eds. 1994. *Pawnship in Africa: Debt Bondage in Historical Perspectives.* Boulder: Westview Press.

Klein, M. 1998. *Slavery and Colonial Rule in French West Africa.* Cambridge: Cambridge University Press.

Lovejoy, P. 1983. *Transformations in Slavery: A History of Slavery in Africa.* Cambridge: Cambridge University Press.

Manning, P. 1990. *Slavery and African Life: Occidental, Oriental, and African Slave Trades.* Cambridge: Cambridge University Press.

Médard, H. and S. Doyle, eds. 2007. *Slavery in the Great Lakes Region of East Africa.* Eastern African Studies, James Currey: Oxford, Fountain Publishers: Kampala, EAEP: Nairobi, Athens: Ohio University Press.

Meillassoux, C. 1991. *The Anthropology of Slavery: The Womb of Iron and Gold.* Chicago: University of Chicago Press (translated from French: *Anthropologie de l'esclavage. Le ventre de fer et d'argent,* 1986).

Memel-Foté, H. 2007. *L'Esclavage dans les sociétés lignagères de la forêt ivoirienne (XVIIe–XXe siècle).* Paris/Abidjan: IRD/CERAP.

Miller, J. 1988. *Way of Death: Merchant Capitalism and the Angolan Slave Trade 1730–1830.* Madison: University of Wisconsin Press.

Newbury, C.W. 1961. *The Western Slave Coast and Its Rulers.* London: Oxford University Press.

Renault, F. 1987. *Tippo-Tip. Un potentat arabe en Afrique centrale au XIXe siècle.* Paris: Société française d'Histoire d'Outre-mer.

Robertson, K. and M.A. Klein. 1983. *Women and Slavery in Africa.* Madison: University of Wisconsin Press.

Scully, P. 1998. *Liberating the Family? Gender and British Slave Emancipation in the Rural Western Cape, South Africa, 1823–1853.* Oxford: James Currey.

Shell, R. 1994. *Children of Bondage: A Social History of the Slave Society at the Cape of Good Hope 1652–1838.* Hanover: University Press of New England.

Soundiata, I.K. 1996. *From Slaving to Neo-Slavery: The Bight of Biafra and Fernando-Po in the Era of Abolition, 1827–1930.* Madison: University of Wisconsin Press.

———. 1999. "La Traite esclavagiste, son histoire, sa mémoire, ses effets." In *Cahiers des Anneaux de la mémoire No. 1.* Nantes: UNESCO/Karthala.

Wright, M. 1988. "Autobiographies, histoires de vie et biographies de femmes africaines en tant que textes militants." In *Cahiers d'Études africaines,* XXVIII–1(109): 45–58.

———. 1995. *Strategies of Slaves and Women: Life-Stories from East Central Africa.* London: James Currey.

Geographical Areas

Southern Africa

Bonner, P. 1983. *Kings, Commoners and Concessionnaires: The Evolution and Dissolution of the Nineteenth Century Swazi State.* Cambridge: Cambridge University Press.

Callaway, H. 1868. *Nursery Tales, Traditions, and Histories of the Zulus, in Their Own Words.* London: Trübner.

Cobbing, J. 1988. "The Mfecane as Alibi: Thoughts on Dithakong and Mbolompo." In *Journal of African History* 29, no. 3: 487–519.

Comaroff, Jean. 1985. *Body of Power, Spirit of Resistance: The Culture and History of a South African People.* Chicago: University of Chicago Press.

Crais, C.C. 1992. *White Supremacy and Black Resistance in Precolonial South Africa.* Cambridge: Cambridge University Press.

Davenport T.R.H. and C. Saunders. 2000. *South Africa: A Modern History.* 5th ed. London: Macmillan.

Eldredge, E.A. 1993. *A South African Kingdom: The Pursuit of Security in Nineteenth Century Lesotho.* Cambridge: Cambridge University Press.

Elphick, R. and H. Giliomee. 1979. *The Shaping of South African Society: 1652–1820.* Cape Town: Longman.

Guest, B. and J.M. Sellers, eds. 1985. *Enterprise and Exploitation in a Victorian Colony: Aspects of the Economic and Social History of Colonial Natal.* Pietermaritzburg: University of Natal Press.

Hamilton, C., ed. 1995. *The Mfecane Aftermath. Reconstructive Debates in Southern African History.* Johannesburg: Witwatersrand University Press.

————. 1998. *Terrific Majesty. The Powers of Shaka Zulu and the Limits of Historical Invention.* Harvard: Cambridge University Press.

Hanretta, S. 1998. "Women, Marginality and the Zulu State: Women's Institutions and Power in the Early Nineteenth Century." In *Journal of African Studies* 39, no. 3: 389–415.

Jolly, P. 1996. "Interaction between South-Eastern San and Southern Nguni and Sotho Communities, c. 1400 to c. 1880." In *South African Historical Journal* 35: 30–61.

Keegan, T. 1996. *Colonial South Africa and the Origins of the Social Order.* Charlottesville: University of Virginia Press.

Morton, B. 1997. "The Hunting Trade and the Reconstruction of Northern Tswana Societies after the Difaqane, 1838–1880." In *Journal of South African Historical Studies* 36: 220–39.

Ranger, T.O. 1967. *Revolt in Southern Rhodesia, 1897: A Study in African Resistance.* London: Oxford University Press.

Thompson, L. 1990. *A History of South Africa.* New Haven/London: Yale University Press.

Van Onselen, C. 1982. *Studies in the Social and Economic History of the Witwatersrand, 1886–1914.* 2 vols. Harlow: Longman.

Wilmsen, E.N. 1989. *Land Filled with Flies. A Political Economy of the Kalahari.* Chicago/London: University of Chicago Press.

Central-Equatorial Africa

Austen, R.A. and J. Derrick. 1999. *Middlemen of the Cameroon Rivers: The Duala and Their Hinterland c. 1600 c. 1960.* Chicago: University of Chicago Press.

Clarence-Smith, G.W. 1979. *Slaves, Peasants and Capitalists in Southern Angola 1840–1926.* Cambridge: Cambridge University Press.

Dampierre, E.D. 1967. *Un royaume Bandia du Haut-Oubangui.* Paris: Plon.

du Chaillu. 1861. *Explorations and Adventures in Equatorial Africa; with Accounts of the Manners and Customs of the People,* Reprint 1969. New York: Negro Universities Press.

Hallam, W.K.R. 1977. *The Life and Times of Rabih Fadl Allah.* Ilfracombe: Arthur H. Stockwell Ltd.

Harms, R.W. 1981. *River of Wealth, River of Sorrow: The Central Zaire Basin in the Era of the Slave and Ivory Trade 1500–1874.* New Haven: Yale University Press.

Mbokolo, E. 1981. *Noirs et Blancs en Afrique équatoriale. Les sociétés côtières et la pénétration française (vers 1820–1874).* Paris: EHESS.

Muriuki, G. 1974. *History of the Kikuyu 1500–1900.* London: Oxford University Press.

Patterson, K.D. 1975. *The Northern Gabon Coast to 1875.* Oxford: Clarendon Press.

Reid, R. 1998. "The Ganda on Lake Victoria: A Nineteenth Century East African Imperialism." In *Journal of African History* 39, no. 3: 349–63.

Soundiata, I.K. 1996. *From Slavery to Neo-slavery. The Bight of Biafra and Fernando-Po in the Era of Abolition, 1827–1930.* Madison: University of Wisconsin Press.

Tardits, C. 1980. *Le Royaume Bamoum.* Paris: EDISEM/Colin.

Vansina, J. 1973. *The Tio Kingdom of the Middle Congo 1880–1892.* London: IAI and Oxford University Press.

————. 1978. *The Children of Woot: A History of the Kuba People.* Madison: University of Wisconsin Press.

————. 1990. *Paths in the Rainforests: Toward a History of Political Tradition in Equatorial Africa.* Madison: University of Wisconsin Press.

Works, J.A. 1976. *Pilgrims in a Strange Land. The Hausa Communities in Chad 1890–1970.* New York: Columbia University Press.

Wrigley, C. 1996. *Kingship and the State: The Buganda Dynasty.* New York: Cambridge University Press.

North Africa

The Maghreb

Ageron, C.R. 1968. *Les Algériens musulmans et la France (1871–1919).* Paris: PUF.

————. 1980. *"L'Algérie algérienne" de Napoléon III à De Gaulle.* Paris: Sindbad.

Berramdan, A. 1987. *Le Maroc et l'Occident 1800–1974.* Paris: Karthala.

Bessis, J. 1986. *La Libye contemporaine.* Paris: L'Harmattan.

Boutaleb, A. 1990. *L'Emir Abd el-Kader et la formation de la nation algérienne: de l'émir Abd el-Kader à la guerre de libération.* Algiers: Editions Dalleb.

Brett, M. and E. Fentress. 1996. *The Berbers.* Oxford: Cambridge University Press.

Burke, E.I. 1976. *Prelude to Protectorate in Morocco: Precolonial Protest and Resistance 1860–1912.* Chicago: University of Chicago Press.

Emerit, M. 1951. *L'Algérie au temps d'Abd el-Kader.* Algiers: Editions de l'Empire. Reprint, Paris: Bouchene, 1999.

Julien, C.A. 1961. *Histoire de l'Afrique du Nord.* 2nd ed. Paris: Payot.

Karrar, A.S. 1992. *The Sufi Brotherhoods in the Sudan.* London: Hurst.

Lacoste, Y. A. Nouschi and A. Prenant. 1960. *L'Algérie: passé et présent. Le cadre et les étapes de la constitution de l'Algérie actuelle.* Paris: Editions sociales.

Laroui, A. 1970. *L'histoire du Maghreb. Un essai de synthèse.* Paris: Maspero.

Rey-Goldzeiguer, A. 1977. *Le Royaume arabe: la politique algérienne de Napoléon III, 1861–1870.* Algiers: Société d'Edition et de Diffusion.

Shuval, T. 1998. *La Ville d'Alger vers la fin du XVIIIe siècle. Population et cadre urbain.* Paris: CNRS.

Stora, B. 1991. *Histoire de l'Algérie coloniale. 1830–1954.* Paris: La Découverte.

Triaud, J.L. 1995. *La Légende noire de la Sanusiyya. Une confrérie musulmane saharienne sous le regard français (1840–1930).* 2 vols. Paris: Editions de la Maison des Sciences de l'Homme.

Valensi, L. 1969. *Le Maghreb avant la prise d'Alger (1790–1830).* Paris: Flammarion.

————. 1977. *Fellahs tunisiens. L'Economie rurale et la vie des campagnes au XVIIIe et XIXe siècles.* Paris/The Hague: Mouton.

Vikør, K.S. 1995. *Sufi and Scholar on the Desert Edge. Muhammad b. Ali al-Sanusi and His Brotherhood.* London: Hurst and Co.

Egypt

Beaucour F. and Y. Laissus. 1990. *The Discovery of Egypt.* Trans. Bambi Ballard. Paris: Flammarion.

Couland, J. 1988. "L'Egypte de Muhammad Ali: transition et développement." In Coquery-Vidrovitch et al., eds. *Pour une histoire du développement.* Paris: L'Harmattan.

Crozet, P. 1994. "A propos de l'enseignement scientifique en Egypte. Transfert et modernisation des sciences exactes 1834–1902." In *Egypte/Monde Arabe (Le Caire)* 18–19: 69–99.

———. 1996. "Langue scientifique et fait national: le cas de l'Egypte à partir du XIXe siècle." In Petitjean, P., ed. *Les sciences coloniales: figures et institutions.* Paris: ORSTOM/UNESCO: 259–84.

Fargette, G. 1996. *Méhémet Ali. Le fondateur de l'Egypte moderne.* Paris: L'Harmattan.

Hill, R.L. and P.C. Hogg. 1995. *A Black Corps d'Elite: An Egyptian Sudanese Conscript Battalion with the French Army in Mexico 1863–1867, and Its Survivors in Subsequent African History.* East Lansing: Michigan State University Press.

Karrar, A.S. 1992. *The Sufi Brotherhoods in the Sudan.* London: Hurst.

Laissus, Y. (ed.), 1998. *Il y a 200 ans, les savants en Égypte.* Nathan: Muséum national d'histoire naturelle,

Laurens, H. 1989. *L'expédition française d'Egypte.* Paris: Armand Colin.

Mitchell, T. 1988. *Colonizing Egypt.* Cambridge: Cambridge University Press.

Panzac, D. 1987. "The Population of Egypt in the Nineteenth Century." In *Asian and African Studies* 21: 11–32.

Sinoué, G. 1997. *Le dernier pharaon: Mehemet-Ali, 1770–1849.* Paris: Pygmalion.

Solé, R. 1998. *Les Savants de Bonaparte.* Paris: Le Seuil.

East Africa

Alpers, E.A. 2009. *East Africa and the Indian Ocean.* Princeton: Markus Wiener.

Baxter, P.T.W., J. Hultin, and A. Triulzi, eds. 1996. *Being and Becoming Oromo: Historical and Anthropological Inquiries.* Uppsala: Nordiska Africainstitutet.

Bennet, N.R. 1971. *Mirambo of Tanzania, 1840–1884.* London: Oxford University Press.

———. 1978. *A History of the Arab State of Zanzibar.* London: Methuen and Co.

Bjørkelo, A. 1989. *Prelude to the Mahdiyya: Peasants and Traders in the Shendi Region.* Cambridge: Cambridge University Press.

Burton, A., ed. 2002. *The Urban Experience in Eastern Africa c. 1750–2000.* Nairobi: British Institute in Eastern Africa.

Cooper, F. 1977. *Plantation Slavery on the East Coast of Africa.* New Haven: Yale University Press.

Crummey, D. 2000. *Land and Society in the Christian Kingdom of Ethiopia. From the Thirteenth to the Twentieth Century.* Oxford: James Currey.

Ewald, J.J. 1990. *Soldiers, Traders and Slaves: State Formation and Economic Transformation in the Greater Nile Valley, 1700–1885.* Madison: University of Wisconsin Press.

Glassman, J. 1995. *Feasts and Riots. Revelry, Rebellion, and Popular Consciousness on the Swahili Coast, 1856–1888.* Portsmouth: Heinemann.

Hassen, M. 1990. *The Oromo of Ethiopia: A History 1570–1860.* Cambridge: Cambridge University Press.

Isaacman, A.F. 1972. *The Africanization of a European Institution: The Zambezi Prazos 1750–1902.* Madison: University of Wisconsin Press.

Marcus, H.G. 1994. *A History of Ethiopia.* Berkeley: University of California Press.

McCann, J.C. 1995. *People of the Plow.* Madison: University of Wisconsin Press.
Newitt, M. 1995. *A History of Mozambique.* Bloomington/Indianapolis: Indiana University Press.
Renault, F. 1987. *Tippo Tip. Un potentat arabe en Afrique centrale au XIXe siècle.* Paris: Société française d'Histoire d'Outre-mer.
Sheriff, A. 1991. *Slaves, Spices and Ivory in Zanzibar.* Athens: Ohio University Press.
Spear, T. and R. Waller, eds. 1993. *Being Maasai: Ethnicity and Identity in East Africa.* Athens: Ohio University Press.
Spear, T. 1997. *Mountain Farmers: Moral Economies of Land and Development in Arusha and Meru.* Berkeley: University of California Press.

West Africa

Abitbol, M. 1979. *Tombouctou et les Arma. De la conquête marocaine du Soudan nigérien en 1591 à l'hégémonie de l'Empire peul du Masina en 1833.* Paris: Maisonneuve et Larose.
Barry, B. 1985. *Le Royaume du Waalo: le Sénégal avant la conquête.* Paris: Karthala.
————. 1988. *Senegambia and the Atlantic slave.* Trans. Ayi Kwei Armah. Cambridge/ New York: Cambridge University Press.
Bathily, A. 1989. *Les Portes de l'or. Le royaume de Galam (Sénégal) de l'ère musulmane au temps des négriers (VIIe–XVIIIe siècles).* Paris: L'Harmattan.
Boilley, P. 1999. *Les Tourags Kel Adagh. Dépendances et révoltes, du Soudan français au Mali.* Paris: Karthala.
Boutillier, J.L. 1993. *Bouna, royaume de la savane ivoirienne. Princes, marchands et paysans.* Paris: Karthala-ORSTOM.
Cissoko, S.M. 1988. *Le Khasso face à l'Empire Toucouleur et à la France dans le haut Sénégal 1854–1890.* Paris: L'Harmattan.
Denham, D., H. Clapperton and W. Oudney. 1826. *Narrative of Travels and Discoveries in Northern and Central Africa in the Years 1822, 1823 and 1824.* London: John Murray.
Diata, S.A. 1997. *The Bamana Empire by the Niger: Kingdom, Jihad and Colonization 1712–1920.* Princeton: Markus Weiner Publishers.
Hanson, J.H. *Migration, Jihad, and Muslim Authority in West Africa: The Futanke Colonies in Karta.* Bloomington: Indiana University Press.
Klein, M. 1968. *Islam and Imperialism in Senegal: Sine-Saloum, 1847–1914.* Stanford: Stanford University Press.
Law, R. 1995. *From Slave Trade to "Legitimate" Commerce: The Commercial Transition in Nineteenth-Century West Africa.* Cambridge: Cambridge University Press.
Law, R. 2004. *Ouidah: The Social History of a West African Slaving Port 1727–1892.* Oxford: James Currey.
Ly-Tall, M. 1991. *Un Islam militant en Afrique de l'Ouest au XIXe siècle. La Tijaniyya de Saïku Umar Futiyu contre les pouvoirs traditionnels et la Puissance coloniale.* Paris: L'Harmattan.
Oloruntimehin, B.O. 1972. *The Segu Tukulor Empire.* London: Longman.
Person, Y. 1968/75. *Samori. Une révolution dioula.* 4 vols. Dakar: IFAN.
Pommegorge, P.D. 1789. *Description de la Négrétie.* Amsterdam. Reprint, Paris: Institut national des langues et civilisations orientales, 1974.

Robinson, D. 1985. *The Holy War of Umar Tal; The Western Sudan in the Mid-Nineteenth Century.* Oxford: Clarendon Press.

Salifou, A. 1971. *Le Damagaran ou sultanat de Zinder au XIXe siècle.* Niamey: Centre nigérien de Recherches en Sciences humaines.

Sanankoua, B. 1990. *Un empire Peul au XIXe siècle. La Diina du Masina.* Paris: Karthala.

Zakari, M. 1985. *Contribution à l'histoire des populations du sud-est nigérien. Le cas du Mangari (XVIe–XIXe siècle).* Niamey: IRSH.

The Coast

Augé, M. 1969. *Le Rivage alladian. Organisation et évolution des villages alladian.* Paris: ORSTOM.

Bay, E.G. 1998. *Wives of the Leopard: Gender, Politics and Culture in the Kingdom of Dahomey.* Charlottesville: University of Virginia Press.

Coquery-Vidrovitch, C. 1964. "La fête des Coutumes au Dahomey: historique et essai d'interprétation." *Annales* 4: 696–716.

David, Philippe. 1980. *Les navétanes, histoire des migrations saisonnières de l'arachide en Sénégambie des origines à nos jours.* Paris: Karthala.

Dike, K.O. 1956. *Trade and Politics in the Niger Delta 1830–1885.* Oxford: Clarendon Press.

Gayibor, N.L. 1996. *Histoire des Togolais. I. Des origines à 1884.* Lomé: Presses de l'UB.

Goerg, O. 1997. *Pouvoir colonial, municipalités et espaces urbains. Conakry-Freetown des années 1880 à 1914.* 2 vols. Paris: L'Harmattan.

Jones, Adam and Peter Sebald, eds. 2005. *An African Family Archive: The Lawsons of Little Popo/Aneho (Togo), 1841–1938.* Oxford: Oxford University Press.

Kandé, S. 1999. *Terres, urbanisme et architectures "créoles" en Sierra Leone, XVIIIe–XIXe siècles.* Paris: L'Harmattan.

Lloyd, P.C. 1973. *The Yoruba: An Urban People?* London: Oxford University Press.

McCaskie, T.C. 1995. *State and Society in Pre-colonial Asante.* Cambridge: Cambridge University Press.

Newbury, C.W. 1961. *The Western Slave Coast and Its Rulers.* London: Oxford University Press.

Ohadike, D.C. 1994. *Anioma. A Social History of the Western Igbo People.* Athens: Ohio University Press.

Perrot, C.H. 1982. *Les Ani-Ndenye et le pouvoir au XVIIIe et XIXe siècles en Côte-d'Ivoire.* Paris: Publications de la Sorbonne.

Priestley, M. 1969. *West African Trade and Coast Society. A Family Study.* London: Oxford University Press.

Terray, E. 1994. "Le pouvoir, le sang et la mort dans le royaume asante au XIXe siècle." In *Journal of African History* XXXIV–4, no. 136: 549–62.

———. 1995. *Une histoire du royaume Abron de Gyaman. Des origines à la conquête coloniale.* Paris: Karthala.

Wilson, L.E. 1991. *The Krobo People of Ghana to 1892: A Political and Social History.* Athens: Ohio University Center for International Studies.

Chronology: Europeans in Africa

1. The Advance into the Interior

Decade	African Points of Reference	European Factors
1781–1790		1787: Committee for the Abolition of the Slave Trade 1788: Creation of the African Association 1789: Discovery of sugar from beets
1791–1800		1795: Creation of the London Missionary Society 1799: London Church Society
1801–1810	1805: Uthman dan Fodio rebels at Gobir 1806–56: Said, sultan of Oman 1808: The Asante defeat the Fante at Abora	1807: Abolition of the slave trade in the British Empire 1807: Formation of the Radical Party in England
1811–1820	1800–23: Reign of Osei Bonsu in Asante 1805–47: Reign of Mehemet Ali 1818–58: Reign of Ghezo in Abome 1816–28: Reign of Shaka Zulu 1818–44: Ahmadu of Masina	1815: Treaty of Vienna; end of the Napoleonic Wars
1821–1830	1828–39: Dingane, Zulu King	1823: Stearic acid is extracted from palm oil 1829: Quinine first prepared
1831–1840	1832–47: Abd el-Kader's resistance 1838: Dingane in Natal	1833–38: Abolition of slavery in the British Empire 1837: Construction of the first propeller steamship

European Interventions

In West Africa	In Southern Africa	In East Africa
1787: First shipload of poor Blacks from England arrives in Sierra Leone		
1795: Mungo Park reaches the Niger River	1795: The British capture the Cape	1798–1801: Napoleon Bonaparte's expedition to Egypt
1807: Sierra Leone, Crown colony	1803: Third Xhosa War 1806: The British return to the Cape	1810: The British take Ile de France and Ile Bourbon
1816: The British leave Saint-Louis and Goree 1817–20: Colonel Schmaltz, Governor of Senegal	1817: Immigration of 4,000 English settlers to the Albany district 1818–19: Fifth Xhosa War	
1821–26: Baron Roger, Governor of Senegal 1828: René Caillié at Timbuktu 1830: McLean arrives at the Gold Coast 1830: The Civil Code is introduced in Senegal 1830: The French land in Algiers		
1832: Richard Lander completes the exploration of the Niger 1832–40: Sultan Said transfers his capital from Muscat to Zanzibar 1838–39: Naval prospecting by Bouët-Willaumez to Gabon	1834–35: Sixth Xhosa War 1837–38: The Boers' Great Trek	1837: American consulate in Zanzibar 1840: British consulate in Zanzibar

2. The Clash of Powers

Decade	African Points of Reference	European Factors
1841–1850	1844–86: Amatifu, Sanwi king 1847: Independence of Liberia	1842: Guizot's "points d'appui" speech 1843: Goodyear invents vulcanization of rubber 1844: Morse telegraph in the U.S. 1848: Abolition of slavery in the French Empire
1851–1860	1858–89: Glele, King of Abome 1860: Masaba, King of Nupe	1852: Whitening of palm oil soap 1857: Quinine is introduced in Niger Valley
1861–1870	1868–98: Amadu succeeds Umar Tall 1870: Tippu-Tip at Kasongo 1870: Msiri at Bunkeya	1863–64: Lincoln abolishes slavery in the U.S. 1865: Colonial Laws Validity Act 1866: Transatlantic telegraph cable laid 1869: Suez Canal opens
1871–1880	1871: Al-Mokrani's revolt in Kabylia 1871: Mankesim Constitution (Gold Coast Fante) 1872: Lobenguela succeeds his father, Mzilikazi, as king of the Matabele	

European Interventions

In West Africa	In Southern Africa	In East Africa
1841–42: Niger expedition 1843: France occupies Assinie, Grand Bassam, and the Gabonese coast 1843–44: Gold Coast, British Crown colony (Foreign Jurisdiction act and bond)	1845: The British annex Natal	1848: Livingstone appointed "Her Majesty's consul at Quilimane for the eastern coast and the independent districts in the interior, and commander of an expedition for exploring eastern and central Africa"
1850–55: Heinrich Barth explores around Lake Chad 1852: Lagos becomes a British protectorate 1854: Faidherbe in Senegal 1857: Siege of Medina by Al Hajj Umar Tall	1852–54: Transvaal and Orange republics: Sand River and Bloemfontein conventions 1853: Colony of the Cape Constitution 1853–56: Livingstone explores Luanda on the Zambezi 1856: Last Xhosa uprising	
1863: Porto-Novo becomes a French protectorate	1867: Diamonds discovered at the confluence of the Orange and Vaal rivers	1859–66: Livingstone explores the Shire and the Nyssa
1871: The French abandon Ivory Coast 1874: The Dutch cede their Gold Coast settlements to the British 1874: The British annex the Fante lands 1875–78: Brazza's first mission on the Ogowe 1879: Taubmann Goldie founds the United African Co. on the Niger River 1880: Makoko-Brazza Treaty	1879: Isandlawana, Zulu victory over the British	1873: Sultan Bargash abolishes the African slave trade 1873–76: Gordon is governor of the Egyptian province of Equatoria 1874–77: Stanley explores the Congo basin 1876: Scottish missions in Blantyre 1877–81: Emin Pacha is governor of the Egyptian province of Equatoria

3. Colonial Partition

Decade	African Points of Reference	European Factors
1881–1890	1884: Kabaka Mouanga succeeds Mutesa I in Buganda 1889–94: Behanzin is king of Abomey 1884: Death of Mirambo of Tanzania 1888–89: Abushiri rebellion 1889: Menelik is consecrated emperor of Ethiopia	1884: Imperial Federation League 1884–85: Berlin Conference 1886: Daimler and Benz build the first automobile 1887: First British Imperial conference 1888: Abolition of slavery in Brazil 1889: Dunlop invents tires 1889–90: Colonial conference in Brussels 1890: Foundation of the *Comité de l'Afrique française*
1891–1900	1900–1939: Kabaka Sir Daudi Choua II in Buganda 1891–98: Mahdist insurrection in the Sudan 1894: Asante mission to London 1895: Three Tswana chiefs' mission to London 1896: Shona and Ndebele rebellion 1899–1920: The "Mad Mullah's" insurrection in the Somalias	1891: Pan-German League 1893: Foundation of the *Union coloniale française*

European Interventions

In West Africa	In Southern Africa	In East Africa
1883: Lüderitz settles in the Bay of Anga Pequeña 1884: Nachtigal's mission to Togo and Cameroon 1885: Leopold II is King of Congo Free State 1885: Charter of the Royal Niger Co. 1885: Charter of the German East Africa Company 1890: Anglo-French Declaration (Say-Barroua line)	1885: Gold discovered in Witwatersrand 1889: Cecil Rhodes obtains the charter of the British South Africa Company	1884: Dr. Peters is in East Africa 1890: Anglo-German and Anglo-French border treaties (Zanzibar-Madagascar-Kivu-Uganda-Tanganyika) 1890: Zanzibar is an English protectorate 1890: Kilwa is taken by the Germans 1891: Execution of Msiri of Katanga
1894: The Abomey Kingdom becomes a French protectorate 1896: Asante King Prempeh is made prisoner by Baden-Powell 1897: French-German convention on the borders of Togo and Cameroon 1898: French-English convention on the borders of Nigeria 1898: Samori beaten by the French 1900: Rabīh killed in the Kusseri Battle	1899–1900: Anglo-Boer War	1894: Uganda becomes a British protectorate 1895: Kenya becomes a British protectorate 1896: Gallieni in Madagascar 1898: The British discover the Highlands of Kenya 1898: Fashoda

Index

About the Author

Catherine Coquery-Vidrovitch is professor emeritus of modern African history at University Denis-Diderot Paris-7, and was adjunct professor at Binghamton University, State University of New York, Department of Sociology (1981–2005). She has published eight books, among which three have been translated into English: *Africa South of the Sahara: Endurance and Change*, University of California Press (1987); *African Women: A Modern History*, Westview Press (1998); and *The History of African Cities South of the Sahara: From the Origins to Colonization*, Princeton University Press (2006). The latter was selected by *Choice* as one of their best books of the year. Her latest book published in French is *Des victimes oubliées du nazisme. Les Noirs et l'Allemagne dans la première moitié du XXe siècle* (Paris, le Cherche-Midi, 2007).

She has edited about twenty books on African studies and the third world, and has published more than 200 articles and chapters on African history. She was given the 1999 ASA (African Studies Association) Distinguished Africanist Award in Philadelphia. From 2000 to 2005, she was a member of the ICHS (International Conference of Historical Sciences) international bureau.